CW00677228

Colour Identification Guide to

Moths of the British Isles

To my wife
Jacky

Colour Identification Guide to
Moths of the British Isles

(Macrolepidoptera)

Bernard Skinner

Colour photography and text figures by
David Wilson

VIKING

VIKING

Published by the Penguin Group
Penguin Books Ltd, 80 Strand, London WC2R ORL, England
Penguin Putnam Inc., 375 Hudson Street, New York, New York 10014, USA
Penguin Books Australia Ltd, 250 Camberwell Road,
Camberwell, Victoria 3124, Australia
Penguin Books Canada Ltd, 10 Alcorn Avenue, Toronto, Ontario, Canada M4V 3B2
Penguin Books India (P) Ltd, 11 Community Centre,
Panchsheel Park, New Delhi - 110 017, India
Penguin Books (NZ) Ltd, Cnr Rosedale and Airborne Roads,
Albany, Auckland, New Zealand
Penguin Books (South Africa) (Pty) Ltd, 24 Sturdee Avenue,
Rosebank 2196, South Africa

Penguin Books Ltd, Registered Offices: 80 Strand, London WC2R ORL, England

www.penguin.com

First published 1984
Second edition 1998
5   7   9   11   12   10   8   6

Text copyright © Bernard Skinner, 1984, 1998
Illustrations copyright © Bernard Skinner and David Wilson, 1984, 1998

The moral right of the author has been asserted

Printed and bound in Hong Kong

A CIP catalogue record for this book is available from the British Library

ISBN 0-670-87978-9

Contents

Preface to the second edition

Since the first edition in 1984 the past twelve years have witnessed a marked growth in the light-trapping and recording of moths. One trusts that the original volume can take some of the credit for this increased interest in the macro-lepidoptera. The first work also solicited a wealth of constructive comment and new information and this is hereby gratefully acknowledged. Eight species are now known to reside in the British Isles since 1984 and these include long-established species which have been overlooked and others which have, perhaps as the result of climatic changes, extended their range from the nearby Continent. Other species still accepted as primary migrants are appearing in small, but increasing, numbers and these may well be ones in the process of colonization. Some immigrant species have appeared recently after a lapse of a hundred years or more and have gone some way to confirm or at least make viable some of the poorly documented and therefore doubted records of the previous two centuries. All this information together with an updated account of the scarcer migrants are included in the new edition. On the debit side the frequency of a couple of formerly rare migrant species has so increased that details of every record is not warranted. In keeping with most of the works on British lepidoptera published in 1997, including the companion volume on caterpillars by Jim Porter, some very recent changes in nomenclature have not been included in order to avoid confusion. These new names will appear shortly in the new edition of 'Bradley and Fletcher' and readers may amend the names in this book as they choose.

B. S. & D. W. 1997

Preface to the first edition

The prime object of this work is to provide colour illustrations of the group of larger moths known collectively as the macrolepidoptera, and so enable all those interested in this subject to identify by wing pattern almost all the species likely to be found in the British Isles. With this aim in mind we decided to figure in colour all the species (including their races and well-known forms) which, during the last hundred years, were either resident in this country or were suspected immigrants reported more than once. Additional guides to identification are given in the text, and include the cross-referencing of similar species and, where necessary, a description of distinguishing characters, illustrated in some cases by black and white line drawings. With one exception, genitalia figures of the small number of very similar species have not been included; this method of identification, which involves the use of specialized techniques and equipment, was considered to be beyond the scope of this book. Students wishing to pursue this subject will find the relevant references in the bibliography.

The second aim, for reasons of economy and easy handling, was to contain this material within a single, moderate-sized volume, while at the same time incorporating as much additional information as this limit would allow. More than twenty years have passed since the last comprehensive work covering all the macrolepidoptera was published, namely the revised (1961) edition of South's *Moths of the British Isles*, and during this time much has been added to our knowledge of the British lepidoptera. This has included the discovery of new resident species, the reporting of new and additional records of migrant species, the finding and describing of subspecies and forms, and a better, but far from complete, understanding of their habits, life-histories, and distribution. It is, perhaps, in distribution that the most dramatic changes have occurred; although a handful of species, mostly colonizers from abroad, have successfully extended their range, a far greater number, formerly well established and sometimes widespread, have seriously declined or become extinct, usually as the result of habitat destruction. There have also been a few important changes in the nomenclature. In view of all these developments we have decided that the text should include all past and present resident species, and all confirmed and possibly genuine immigrant species; and should cover their status, times of appearance of both adult and larva, type of habitat, distribution, and larval foodplants. It was also considered useful to detail the records of most of the rarer migrants, especially because much of this information is scattered throughout the entomological literature and not readily available in a single volume. For reasons of economy the scientific names of well-known and frequently quoted plants are not included in the main text, but covered by a separate index. Details of Continental distribution have been given only for the immigrant species. Finally, descriptions of larvae, unless very detailed, are of little use in identifying any but the most characteristic species, and are best reserved for a separate illustrated volume. Several authors are at present working on such a project.

The preparation of this work has made us increasingly aware of the large gaps in our knowledge of the many aspects of the British lepidoptera. We have also realized what a great amount of important information is possessed by individuals, but never put into print; fortunately, some of this unpublished knowledge has come our way in the form of personal communications and has been incorporated in this book.

While we have made every effort to eliminate errors, these inevitably occur, and therefore readers are asked to report any mistakes and omissions to me so that future editions may be rectified.

Bernard Skinner
David Wilson
1984

Acknowledgements

This book could not have been written without the help and co-operation of a great many people, who have generously and unhesitatingly lent specimens (many of which were the 'cream' of their collections) for figuring or examination, lent rare books and journals, translated foreign literature, supplied specialized photographic equipment, and provided a wealth of valuable information. We would like, therefore, to thank the following:

Dr D. J. L. Agassiz
B. R. Baker
J. Beeching
Dr J. D. Bradley
R. F. Bretherton, CB
J. Briggs
British Entomological & Natural History Society
C. G. Bruce
R. Burrow
G. N. Burton
M. Cade
D. J. Carter
R. G. Chatelain
H. E. Chipperfield
I. C. Christie
L. Christie
J. Culpin
P. Davey
A. J. Dewick
T. J. Dillon
R. Eden
B. Elliott
D. S. Fletcher
B. Goater
M. Hadley
A. H. Hayes

G. M. Haggett
T. W. Harman
J. Heath
G. E. Higgs
T. G. Howarth, BEM
D. Johnson
Dr R. P. Knill-Jones
Dr J. R. Langmaid
M. Marix Evans
R. H. Mays
H. N. Michaelis
Natural History Museum (London)
W. Parker
Dr T. N. D. Peet
E. C. Pelham-Clinton
C. G. Penney
A. J. Pickles
J. Porter
C. R. Pratt
G. A. Pyman
J. Reid
I. Rippey
Rothamsted Experimental Station
B. Statham
A. E. Stubbs
S. Torstenius
W. G. Tremewan
B. K. West

We also thank R. T. Peterson for permission to use his method of pointers which emphasize the diagnostic features of the text illustrations. Finally, we are particularly indebted to both Lieut.-Colonel A. M. Emmet, MBE, and J. M. Chalmers-Hunt for checking the typescript and for much constructive criticism; and to the author's wife, Jacky, for her valuable help.

Bernard Skinner
David Wilson

Introduction

The scientific names, English names, and classification used follow Bradley, J. D., & Fletcher, D. S. (1986) An indexed list of British Butterflies and Moths, modified where necessary with additional and revised nomenclature.

The English names of plants are those given in Dony, J. G., Rob, C. M., and Perring, F. H. (1974) *English Names of Wild Flowers*, Butterworths. Scientific plant names follow Tutin, T. G. and others (1964–80) *Flora Europaea*, Cambridge University Press, 5 vols.

The expanse of the wings is given in millimetres and measured as twice the distance from the centre of the thorax to the apex of the forewing.

Unless otherwise stated, the foodplants listed are those on which the larva has been found in the wild.

The Watsonian Vice-county system of Great Britain and the Praeger Vice-county system of Ireland are standardized lists of geographical regions used extensively in floristic and faunistic recording as they are not affected by boundary or name changes. In the text the initial letter of a vice-county is capitalized (eg, North Devon, East Sussex and Mid-west Yorkshire); whereas other geographical regions are not so defined (eg, north Sussex, mid-Devon and south Yorkshire).

For the purpose of this work Eire and Northern Ireland are referred to collectively as Ireland.

Glossary and Abbreviations

♂ = male   ♀ = female.

* = the information which follows refers to the larval habits and foodplants quoted in the Continental literature.

ab. = aberration.

aestivation = summer diapause (qv).

ciliate (or biciliate) = having a single (or double) row of fine short hairs.

cline = a character-gradient, in which the appearance of a species changes gradually and continuously over a given area.

dentate = notched like a row of teeth.

diapause = state of inactivity.

dimorphic = of two forms.

f. = form (although synonymous with aberration, this term has been used to denote a variety which predominates in part or throughout the range of the species).

frass = larval droppings.

glabrous = without hairs.

instar = the stage between each larval moult.

lunate = crescent-shaped.

ocellate = eye-like.

palpi = labial palps; a pair of short sensory appendages belonging to the mouth parts and attached below the head.

pectinate (or bipectinate) = having a single (or double) row of hair-scales (ie, comb-like).

prolegs = the legs belonging to the abdominal segments of a larva.

serrate = notched like a saw.

sp. = species (singular)   spp. = species (plural).

ssp. = subspecies.

subspiracular = below the row of breathing holes which are present along each side of the larva's body.

tarsus (plural tarsi) = the foot-part of the adult's leg, normally comprising five segments.

tibia (plural tibiae) = the part of the adult's leg immediately above the tarsus.

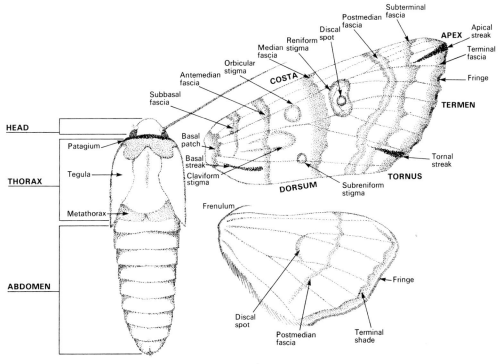

xi

Description of Species

Family: Hepialidae

This family is a member of the Exoporia, a primitive suborder of Lepidoptera, comprising many medium- to large-sized species, of which five are found in the British Isles.

The adults are characterized by their elongate wings and very short antennae. The main flight is from a short time before dusk until dark, although some individuals continue to fly intermittently throughout the night. Both sexes are attracted to light.

The eggs are broadcast by the female as she flies just above the vegetation.

The long, cylindrical and whitish larvae feed on the roots of various plants and pupate in the ground.

Ghost Moth

Hepialus humuli humuli Linnaeus
Plate **1** : *9–10*

Imago. 44–48 mm. Resident. Both sexes come regularly to light. The males are often seen in groups from dusk onwards hovering and pendulating a few feet above the grass; it is stated that the purpose of this curious display, 'leking' as it is sometimes called, is to attract the attention of a passing female. The males are also said to emit a goatish scent. Single-brooded, flying in June and July, inhabiting hillsides, waste ground and other grassy places. Widespread and generally common throughout the British Isles including Orkney and the Hebrides.

H. humuli thulensis Newman, pl. **1** : *11–12*. Ground colour of male forewing ranging from white to ochreous-buff, with the brownish markings, normally found in the female, varying in extent and intensity. The female is darker and less ochreous than the typical form. Widespread and not uncommon in Shetland.

Larva. August to May on the roots of grasses and a wide variety of wild and cultivated plants such as dock, burdock, nettle, hop and strawberry.

Overwinters, probably twice, as a larva.

Orange Swift

Hepialus sylvina Linnaeus
Plate **1** : *20–22*

Imago. 32–48 mm. Resident. Both sexes come freely to light. Single-brooded, flying from late June to early September, inhabiting moorland, gardens, waste ground, etc. Generally distributed and common in England and Wales. Less frequent, but widespread in Scotland as far north as Sutherland.

Larva. September to May of the third year on the roots of bracken, dock, dandelion, viper's-bugloss and other herbaceous plants.

Overwinters twice as a larva.

Gold Swift

Hepialus hecta Linnaeus
Plate **1** : *13–15*

Imago. 26–32 mm. Resident. Both sexes come sparingly to light. The males appear commonly at dusk and emit a scent likened to that of ripe pineapple. In favourable conditions there is a strong dawn flight with the females predominating. Single-brooded, flying from mid-June to mid-July, frequenting a variety of habitats such as woodland rides, parkland, commons and heathland. Local, but not uncommon over much of the British Isles; occurring in Scotland as far north as Caithness and Sutherland, and as far west as the Inner Hebrides.

Larva. July to June of the third year on the stems and roots of bracken and other plants; feeding internally until the final instar.

Overwinters twice as a larva.

Common Swift

Hepialus lupulinus Linnaeus
Plate **1** : *16–19*

Variation. Unicolorous forms with the colour of the forewing ranging from whitish-buff to greyish-brown occur frequently in both sexes.

Imago. 25–40 mm. Resident. Flies mainly at dusk when it is attracted to light. Single-brooded, flying from mid-May to mid-July and sometimes later. Widespread throughout the British Isles; common in much of England and Wales, less frequent in Ireland and rather local in Scotland.

Larva. July to April, on the roots of grasses and a wide range of wild and cultivated plants; frequently an agricultural and horticultural pest.

Overwinters as a larva.

Map-winged Swift

Hepialus fusconebulosa De Geer
Plate **1** : *23–25*

Variation. Ab. *gallicus* Lederer (figs 24–25) is a uniformly brown form occurring with varying frequency over much of its range. Some specimens from Shetland are brighter and more variegated than the typical form and refer to ab. *shetlandicus* Viette.

Imago. 32–50 mm. Resident. Flies from dusk onwards and is attracted to light. Single-brooded, flying from late May to early July; a little later in northern Britain. Widespread, but local, throughout the British Isles, inhabiting open woodland and moorland.

Larva. July to May of the third year on the stems and roots of bracken and probably other plants.

Overwinters twice as a larva.

Family: Cossidae

Three resident species of this family occur in the British Isles. The adults fly at night and are rarely encountered except at light. The maggot-like larvae are equipped with strong jaws and feed internally on the wood or pith of trees and plants. Both the species of Zeuzerinae pupate within the host plant.

SUBFAMILY: ZEUZERINAE

Reed Leopard
Phragmataecia castaneae Hübner
(*arundinis* Hübner)
Plate **1** : *7–8*

Imago. 30–56 mm. Resident. The males come freely to light soon after dark. The female is occasionally seen on the wing, but rarely at light and most frequently found at rest or ovipositing on the stems of reed. Single-brooded, flying in June and July, inhabiting reed beds. Very local in England and confined to Wicken Fen and Chippenham Fen, Cambridgeshire, the Norfolk Broads and a single locality in southeast Dorset.
Larva. August to May of the third year in the stems of common reed.
Overwinters twice as a larva.

Leopard Moth
Zeuzera pyrina Linnaeus
Plate **1** : *6*

Imago. 45–78 mm. Resident. Both sexes are attracted to light and during the day are sometimes found at rest on tree-trunks and fences. Single-brooded, flying from late June to early August, inhabiting woods, gardens, parkland and orchards. Widespread in England as far north as Yorkshire, and in the eastern half of Wales. A specimen from Co. Mayo on 12.vii.1978 appears to be the only confirmed record from Ireland.
Larva. August to May of the third year in the stems and branches of a wide variety of trees and shrubs. Sometimes a pest on fruit trees. Among the recorded foodplants are lilac, sallow, apple, ash, pear, cherry, elm, sycamore, honeysuckle and black currant.
Overwinters twice or three times as a larva.

SUBFAMILY: COSSINAE

Goat Moth
Cossus cossus Linnaeus
Plate **1** : *5*

Imago. 68–96 mm. Resident. Occasionally attracted to light. Single-brooded, flying in June and July. This species has become much scarcer in recent years, although it is still locally widespread in southern England, Wales, and the southern half of Ireland. Less frequent and very local in the Midlands, northern England and central Scotland.

Larva. August to May of the fourth or fifth year, feeding internally on the solid wood of various trees such as willow, birch, ash, elm, poplar, oak and many fruit trees. In captivity it will eat uncooked beetroot and when full grown should be provided with rotten wood or sawdust in which to pupate. The larva must be kept in a metal or plastic container, preferably with an air-tight lid as it emits a strong and rather unpleasant goatish smell.
Overwinters three to four times as a larva, passing the final winter in a cocoon in which it will eventually pupate. The fully grown larva frequently leaves the host tree in the autumn to find a more suitable pupating site in the ground.

Family: Zygaenidae

Ten species represent this family in the British Isles and these are assigned to two subfamilies: Procridinae (Foresters) and Zygaeninae (Burnets).
The adults of all the species fly during the day, preferring hot sunshine, and are attracted to the flowers of their foodplants and other plants.
The three species of Procridinae are similar in appearance and have metallic green forewings, blackish-grey hindwings and smooth bronzy-green bodies. The larvae are very specific in their choice of foodplant, mining into the leaves when young, but later grazing down to the lower membrane, which is left intact. The thin semi-transparent cocoons are usually concealed low down amongst the foodplant.
The seven species of Zygaeninae are also similar in appearance and have black forewings with red spots or streaks, red hindwings, and black, frequently hairy, bodies. The larvae are mostly green with black and sometimes yellow markings, and all but two species feed specifically on plants of the Leguminosae family. The larvae of all the species have the ability of hibernating for either one or two winters.
The pale whitish or yellowish paper-like cocoons of some species are attached high up on the stems of grasses and other plants and are readily found, whereas those of other species are concealed amongst the herbage and are difficult to locate.

SUBFAMILY: PROCRIDINAE

Scarce Forester
Adscita globulariae Hübner
Plate **2** : *1–2*

Similar species. *A. statices*, pl. **2** and text. *A. geryon*, pl. **2** and text.
Imago. Male 24–30 mm, female 19–24 mm. Resident. Flies during the day in sunshine and is attracted to the flowers of knapweed, salad burnet and other downland plants. Single-brooded, flying in June, with the rather

short flight period varying according to season. Very local in southern England where it is found on the chalk downland of Sussex, from Findon to Eastbourne, southeast Kent, and in several localities on Salisbury Plain, Wiltshire. Recorded, but not recently, from West Gloucestershire.

Larva. July to May on common knapweed (*Centaurea nigra*) and greater knapweed (*C. scabiosa*).
Overwinters as a larva.

Cistus Forester
Adscita geryon Hübner
Plate **2** : *5–6*

Similar species. *A. globulariae*, pl. **2**, has the antenna pointed and is larger when comparing specimens of the same sex. *A. statices*, pl. **2** and text.

Imago. Male 23–25 mm, female 20–22 mm. Resident. Flies during the day in sunshine and is attracted to a variety of downland flowers such as thyme, rock-rose and trefoils. Single-brooded, flying in June and early July, inhabiting chalk downland and limestone hills. Local, but not uncommon, in parts of southern England and from the Midlands northwards to Cumbria and Co. Durham. Very local in Wales, mainly in the north, where the Great Orme, Caernarvonshire, is a well-known locality.

Larva. July to early May on common rock-rose.
Overwinters as a larva.

The Forester
Adscita statices Linnaeus
Plate **2** : *3–4*

Similar species. *A. globulariae*, pl. **2**, has the antenna pointed and the forewing distinctly broader. *A. geryon*, pl. **2**, is smaller when specimens of the same sex are compared.

Imago. Male 26–29 mm, female 24–26 mm. Resident. Flies by day in sunshine and is attracted to the flowers of ragged robin, viper's-bugloss, scabious, clover and other plants. Single-brooded, flying in June and July, inhabiting damp meadows, chalk downland, edges of woodland, waste ground, sandy heaths and breckland. Widespread, but local, in England, Wales, Ireland and parts of Scotland, including the Inner Hebrides.

Larva. July to April on common sorrel (*Rumex acetosa*).
Overwinters as a larva.

SUBFAMILY: ZYGAENINAE

Scotch Burnet
Zygaena exulans subochracea White
Plate **2** : *7*

Imago. 24–34 mm. Resident. Flies in sunshine and is attracted to the flowers of bird's-foot trefoil and mountain everlasting (*Antennaria dioica*). Single-brooded, flying from late June to mid-July. Very local,

the only known colonies occurring near Braemar, Aberdeenshire, where it is found above 600 m (2000 ft) on the higher slopes and summits of mountains.

Larva. August to June, mainly on crowberry, but also recorded from bilberry and cowberry.
Overwinters once or twice as a larva.

Slender Scotch Burnet
Zygaena loti scotica Rowland-Brown
Plate **2** : *10*

Similar Species. The combination of an extended outer spot on the forewing, a very narrow border on the hindwing and a hairy abdomen serve to distinguish this species from similar burnets.

Imago. 25–35 mm. Resident. Flies during the day in sunshine, visiting the flowers of bird's-foot trefoil. Very secretive and seldom located in dull weather. Single-brooded, flying from mid-June to early July. Locally common on the Hebridean islands of Mull and Ulva, where it inhabits grassy slopes and hillocks by the sea. Formerly found on the Scottish mainland in the Morven district of Argyllshire, but not since 1945. The records from Raasay and Rhum are considered to be erroneous.

Larva. August to early May on bird's-foot trefoil.
Overwinters once or twice as a larva.

New Forest Burnet
Zygaena viciae ytenensis Briggs
(*viciae anglica* Reiss)
Plate **2** : *9*

Similar Species. *Z. loti scotica*, pl. **2** and text.

Imago. 22–32 mm. Formerly resident, now extinct. Flies during the day in sunshine. Single-brooded, flying usually from mid-June to mid-July. First recorded in 1872 and subsequently found to occur in a number of localities in the New Forest, Hampshire, where it inhabited grassy rides and clearings. The species was last noted in 1927 and its demise has been attributed to the combined effects of conifer planting, forest fires and over-collecting.

Z. viciae argyllensis Tremewan, pl. **2** : *8*. This race differs from ssp. *ytenensis* in having the forewing broader, darker, and more deeply coloured with crimson; the border of the hindwing is broader and the thorax and abdomen strongly haired. Discovered in 1963, this race is only known from a single site in western Argyllshire, where it inhabits a steep grassy slope by the sea.

Larva. August to May on bird's-foot trefoil and meadow vetchling (*Lathyrus pratensis*).
Overwinters once or twice as a larva.

Six-spot Burnet
Zygaena filipendulae stephensi Dupont
(*filipendulae anglicola* Tremewan)
Plate **2** : *11–13*

Variation. A wide range of confluent forms has been described, but most of them are rare. Ab. *unitella* Crombrugghe (fig 13) has the two outer spots united and is the confluent form most frequently found. Ab. *chrysanthemi* Borkhausen has the red coloration of the forewing spots and the hindwing replaced by blackish-brown and has occurred, not uncommonly in the past, in northwest England. Ab. *flava* Robson (fig 12) has the red colour replaced by yellow and is a rare recessive form found in many parts of the species' range.

Imago. 25–40 mm. Resident. Flies during the day in sunshine and is attracted to a wide variety of downland and wayside flowers. Single-brooded, flying from late June to August, inhabiting chalk downland, flowery meadows, sandhills, sea-cliffs and woodland rides. Generally distributed and moderately common throughout England, Wales and Ireland. Widespread, but coastal, in Scotland, including the Hebrides.

Larva. September to May on bird's-foot trefoil and horseshoe vetch (*Hippocrepis comosa*).

Overwinters once or twice as a larva.

Five-spot Burnet
Zygaena trifolii decreta Verity
Plate **2** : *18–19*

Variation. As the following aberrations also occur in ssp. *palustrella*, this section will apply and refer to both races. Confluent forms are found regularly and are a characteristic feature of *Z. trifolii*. The typical form (figs 14 and 18) has the middle pair of spots united; ab. *orobi* Hübner (fig 19) has the middle spots separate and is often as common as the typical form; ab. *basalis* Selys-Longchamps (fig 15) has the inner and middle spots united and the outer spot separate; ab. *glycirrhizae* Hübner (fig 16) has the middle and outer spots confluent and separate from the inner spots which are also united; and ab. *minoides* Selys-Longchamps (fig 17) has all the spots confluent, forming an irregular patch. Specimens in which the red colour is replaced by yellow are referable to ab. *lutescens* Cockerell. This normally rare variety once occurred commonly around the end of the nineteenth century in a locality in West Sussex and was associated with ssp. *palustrella*.

Similar species. *Z. lonicerae*, pl. **2**, has, as a general rule, a rather longer forewing, the upper angle of the hindwing more pointed and the black border often narrower. If details of habitat and foodplant are known and an adequate series of specimens are available for examination, then the following rules can be applied: absence of confluent forms and larvae on any foodplant except *Lotus* indicate *Z. lonicerae*; absence of *Lotus uliginosus* as a foodplant precludes *Z. trifolii decreta*.

Imago. 32–40 mm. Resident. Single-brooded, flying in July and early August, inhabiting damp meadows, marshes, and the wetter parts of heathland. Widespread and locally common in southwest England as far east as the New Forest, Hampshire; North and South Wales; and the Isle of Man. Formerly local in southeast England

and East Anglia, but now extremely rare, if not extinct.

Larva. August to June on greater bird's-foot trefoil (*Lotus uliginosus*).

Pupa. The cocoons of this race are usually spun high up on the stems of rushes, grasses and other marsh plants and are easily found, whereas those of ssp. *palustrella* are concealed low down amongst the downland herbage.

Z. trifolii palustrella Verity, pl. **2** : *14–17*.

Imago. 30–36 mm. Resident. A smaller race inhabiting chalk downland. Single-brooded, flying in late May and June. Widespread, but local, along the North and South Downs from Kent to Hampshire and on Salisbury Plain, Wiltshire; also recorded from the Cotswolds, Gloucestershire.

Larva. July to early May on bird's-foot trefoil (*Lotus corniculatus*).

Both races overwinter once or twice as larvae.

Narrow-bordered Five-spot Burnet
Zygaena lonicerae latomarginata Tutt
(*lonicerae transferens* Verity)
Plate **2** : *20–22*

Variation. Ab. *centripuncta* Tutt (fig 22) has the middle pair of spots united and is an uncommon variety, except in ssp. *jocelynae*. Other confluent forms have been described, but these are even rarer. Ab. *citrina* Speyer (fig 21) has the red colour replaced by yellow and has occurred commonly in a locality in the Cotswolds, Gloucestershire, but rarely elsewhere. (Note: the large race occurring in northeast England, and named ssp. *latomarginata* Tutt, intergrades with ssp. *transferens* Verity; the name *latomarginata* should therefore be used for all the English populations and replaces *transferens* over which it has priority.)

Similar species. *Z. trifolii*, pl. **2** and text.

Imago. 30–46 mm. Resident. All the races are attracted to a variety of downland flowers and are single-brooded, flying in late June and July.

Ssp. *latomarginata* is found in a wide range of habitats such as downland, commons, marshes, undercliff, waste ground and open woodland. Generally distributed throughout most of England except the southwest; in Wales apparently confined to the southeast.

Z. lonicerae jocelynae Tremewan, pl. **2** : *24*. Separated from the English race by its longer and broader forewing, larger and frequently confluent forewing spots, longer and more slender antennae, and the thick blackish hair on the head, thorax, and abdomen.

Imago. 36–44 mm. Resident. Locally common on the Hebridean island of Skye, where it inhabits steep grassy and flowery slopes by the sea.

Z. lonicerae insularis Tremewan, pl. **2** : *23*. Separated from the English race by its larger size, larger and more elongate forewing spots, slender and very pointed antennae, and the dense blackish hair on the head, thorax, and abdomen.

Imago. 38–46 mm. Resident. Locally widespread in the northern half of Ireland, where it is found in a variety of inland and coastal habitats.

Larva. August to May, with all the races feeding on various species of trefoil, clover and vetch.

All races overwinter once or twice as larvae.

Transparent Burnet
Zygaena purpuralis segontii Tremewan
Plate **2** : *25*

Variation. Ab. *obscura* Tutt has the red markings of the forewing and the hindwing replaced by black; an uncommon form found also in ssp. *caledonensis* (fig 27). Ab. *lutescens* Tutt has the red colour replaced by yellow and is a rare form found in ssp. *sabulosa* and ssp. *caledonensis*. Specimens having the red colour replaced by orange (fig 28) are found in ssp. *caledonensis*.

Imago. 30–34 mm. Resident. All races fly during the day in warm weather, preferring sunshine and are single-brooded, flying in June and early July. Ssp. *segontii* is very local and confined to the sea-cliffs of the Lleyn Peninsula, Caernarvonshire. It has not been reported since 1962 and may possibly be extinct.

Z. purpuralis caledonensis Reiss, pl. **2** : *26–28*. Differs from the preceding race in having the first basal streak longer, all the streaks thicker and closer together, and the hindwing crimson, not scarlet.

Imago. 30–39 mm. Resident. Locally common on the Scottish mainland in Kintyre and parts of western Argyllshire, and on the Hebridean islands of Skye, Lismore, Kerrera, Mull, Ulva, Eigg, Canna, and Rhum. The species normally inhabits grassy slopes by the sea, but in the Oban district of Argyllshire it has been found inland and one of the colonies is over four miles from the coast.

Z. purpuralis sabulosa Tremewan, pl. **2** : *29*. Differs from the other races in the somewhat broader and more densely coloured forewing streaks and the generally brighter and warmer red coloration.

Imago. 29–36 mm. Resident. Locally common in the Burren District, Co. Clare, where it is found on the coast and up to seven miles inland. Elsewhere in Ireland it is found in Cos Galway and Mayo, and on Inishmore, Aran Islands. The three specimens supposedly taken in Co. Wexford in 1950 require confirmation.

Larva. August to May, with all the races feeding on thyme.

Overwinters once or twice as a larva.

Family: Limacodidae

The Festoon
Apoda limacodes Hufnagel
(*avellana* Linnaeus)
Plate **1** : *1–2*

Imago. 28–32 mm. Resident. Flies occasionally in sunshine around the tops of oak trees, but mostly at night when both sexes, especially the males, are attracted to light. Single-brooded, flying in June and July, inhabiting mature oak-woods. Locally distributed in the southern half of England as far north as Worcestershire and Northamptonshire, and recorded most frequently from Kent, Sussex, Surrey, Hampshire and Dorset. The Irish records from Co. Galway are considered to be unreliable.

Larva. Late August to early October on oak and beech. Overwinters as a larva within a cocoon in which it pupates in the spring.

The Triangle
Heterogenea asella Denis & Schiffermüller
Plate **1** : *3–4*

Imago. 16–22 mm. Resident. Flies occasionally in the afternoon sunshine, but more frequently at night when both sexes come to light. Single-brooded, flying from mid-June throughout July, inhabiting oak and beech woodland. A very local and scarce species found chiefly in Hampshire (New Forest, Alice Holt and Forest of Bere), southeast Kent (Hamstreet and Appledore), Sussex (Westbourne and Beckley), Wiltshire (Savernake), Oxfordshire (Goring Heath), Lincolnshire (Bardney) and Buckinghamshire (Marlow district). Has occurred in the past in Essex and Devon. Two larvae were found on poplar at Seaford, Sussex, c. 1930, and a specimen was taken near Looe, Cornwall, on 26.vi.1960.

Larva. Late August to early October on oak, beech and occasionally poplar.

Overwinters as a larva within a cocoon in which it pupates in the spring.

Family: Sesiidae

Thirteen definite and one possible resident species of this family are found in the British Isles.

The adults, which resemble Hymenoptera, fly during the day and are vary active in sunshine.

All the species have maggot-like larvae which feed for one or two years, either in the stems, branches, trunks, and roots of trees and shrubs or in the crowns and roots of low-growing plants. Before pupating, the larvae of the wood-feeding species bore to the outer surface of the host tree, but leave a thin membrane of bark to disguise the prospective exit hole. After the emergence of the adult, the empty pupal cases protrude from these holes and often remain in situ for several months. The larvae of those species associated with low plants, and which pupate in the roots, construct a silken exit tube leading up to the surface of the ground.

The moths usually emerge in early morning and whereas the males take off as soon as their wings have dried, the females often do not fly until after copulation.

Despite their diurnal habits the adults of this family are seldom seen in numbers and are best obtained in the larval or pupal stages.

Plants, stems, and sections of timber infected by the desired species should be collected in the winter or early spring, planted in damp sand and kept reasonably warm.

SUBFAMILY: SESIINAE

Hornet Moth
Sesia apiformis Clerck
Plate **2** : *32–33*

Similar species. *S. bembeciformis*, pl. **2** and text, has a black head, yellow patagial collar, and unicolorous dark brown tegulae.

Imago. 34–50 mm. Resident. Frequently found in early morning on the trunks of poplar and most easily obtained in this way. Single-brooded, flying from mid-June throughout July. Locally widespread in southeast England, Berkshire, Oxfordshire and East Anglia. Recorded, but not recently, from many other parts of Britain as far north as southern Scotland. Rare and very local in the south of Ireland.

Larva. September to May over two, possibly three, years in the lower trunks and upper roots of black poplar and occasionally other species of poplar. Overwinters as a larva.

Lunar Hornet Moth
Sesia bembeciformis Hübner
Plate **2** : *30–31*

Similar species. *S. apiformis*, pl. **2** and text, has a yellow head, a dark patagial collar, and the anterior halves of the tegulae are yellow.

Imago. 32–44 mm. Resident. Occasionally found on the trunks or stems of large sallows and poplars. Single-brooded, flying from July to early August, inhabiting open woodland, commons, wetter parts of moorland, and other marshy places. Widespread and locally common over much of the British Isles.

Larva. August to May for two years in the trunks and upper roots of well-grown sallow (*Salis caprea*) and occasionally poplar and willow. Overwinters as a larva.

SUBFAMILY: PARANTHRENINAE

Dusky Clearwing
Paranthrene tabaniformis Rottemburg
Plate **2** : *34*

Imago. 28–32 mm. Status uncertain, possible resident. Single-brooded on the Continent, occurring from late May to mid-July. A few specimens were reported during the nineteenth century from Kent, Sussex, Essex, Middlesex and Oxfordshire. Three others were recorded this century from near Portsmouth, Hampshire,

in July 1909, Totnes, South Devon, in July 1920 and at Tubney, Berkshire, in June 1924.

Larva. None of the immature stages have been found in Britain although some of the Kent specimens were apparently associated with poplar and the Essex ones with aspen. Abroad, the larva is found from September to May, feeding for two years in the shoots and main trunk of various species of poplar.* Other recorded foodplants are sallow and sea-buckthorn. Overwinters as a larva.

Currant Clearwing
Synanthedon tipuliformis Clerck
(*salmachus* Linnaeus)
Plate **2** : *35*

Similar species. *S. flaviventris*, pl. **2**, has both the tegulae and the underside of the patagial collar black, whereas in *S. tipuliformis* these features are yellow. (For differences in hindwing venation see text fig 1.)

Imago. 18–22 mm. Resident. Single-brooded, flying in June and July, inhabiting domestic and market gardens, allotments, etc. Widespread and moderately common in England and Wales; local and less frequent in Scotland and Ireland.

Larva. August to May in the stems and shoots of black currant, red currant and gooseberry Overwinters as a larva.

tipuliformis   flaviventris

Fig 1

Yellow-legged Clearwing
Synanthedon vespiformis Linnaeus
Plate **2** : *36–37*

Variation. Sexually dimorphic with the anal tuft of the male black and that of the female yellow. Occasionally specimens are found with the forewing bordered with red and these are referable to ab. *rufimarginata* Spuler.

Similar species. *S. andrenaeformis*, pl. **2** and text.

Imago. 19–27 mm. Resident. Sometimes seen as an adult in areas of felled woodland containing one- to three-year-old oak stumps where it occasionally comes to the flowers of bramble. Single-brooded, flying from May to August. Generally distributed and often common in southern England and the Midlands as far north as Yorkshire.

Larva. August to May under the bark of oak trees and stumps. Sometimes found in other trees such as birch, elm, cherry and sweet chestnut.

Overwinters as a larva.

White-barred Clearwing

Synanthedon spheciformis Denis & Schiffermüller

Plate **2** : *40*

Similar species. *S. scoliaeformis*, pl. **2**, has a broader discal spot, two abdominal bands, and a partly or completely orange anal tuft.

Imago. 28–32 mm. Resident. Single-brooded, flying from mid-May to early July, inhabiting heathland and marshy places. A local species, occurring in the southern half of Britain and found most frequently in central southern England and the west Midlands.

Larva. August to May in alder and birch. Most frequently found in suckers and young trees although both mature trees and stumps can be infected. A pile of sawdust-like frass at the base of the tree betrays the presence of a larva and the exit hole of this and the next species can be exposed by carefully abraiding the bark with a knife or wire brush.

Overwinters twice as a larva.

Welsh Clearwing

Synanthedon scoliaeformis Borkhausen

Plate **2** : *41–42*

Similar species. *S. spheciformis*, pl. **2** and text.

Imago. 27–38 mm. Resident. Newly emerged adults are sometimes found on birch-trunks. Single-brooded, flying in June and early July. Found locally in the Trossachs and near Rannoch, Perthshire; Glen Moriston and Glen Affric, Inverness-shire; Snowdonia, Merionethshire, and in the district between Killarney and Kenmare, Co. Kerry. Old larval workings have been noted in Sutherland and from 1854 to 1881 the species was recorded from Llangollen, Denbighshire. In 1913 an adult and a pupa were obtained from Cannock Chase, Staffordshire. There are also a few unconfirmed records from Herefordshire, Cheshire and Wiltshire.

Larva. August to May, feeding on the inner bark of old birch trees.

Overwinters twice as a larva.

Sallow Clearwing

Synanthedon flaviventris Staudinger

Plate **2** : *39*

Similar species. *S. tipuliformis*, pl. **2** and text.

Imago. 18–22 mm. Resident. Single-brooded, flying in July, inhabiting the wetter parts of open woodland and heathland. Widespread and locally common in southern England, except the southwest, and not reliably recorded north of Oxfordshire.

Larva. August to June in a small stem of sallow

that is usually from 8 to 15 mm in diameter. In its second year the larva causes a swelling in the stem and the resultant gall is similar to that formed by a beetle (*Saperda populnea*), although the beetle gall is often larger, bulbous and less evenly tapered at each end. In Britain this species has a biennial cycle and the galls should be searched for in the early spring of even years. The larvae are often heavily parasitized.

Overwinters twice as a larva.

Orange-tailed Clearwing

Synanthedon andrenaeformis Laspèyres (*anthraciniformis* Esper)

Plate **2** : *38*

Similar species. *S. vespiformis*, pl. **2**, has a red discal patch and bright yellow tibiae.

Imago. 19–25 mm. Resident. Single-brooded, flying from late May to early July, inhabiting downland and the edges of woods. Locally widespread in southern England as far north as Cambridgeshire and Huntingdonshire.

Larva. July to May in the stems of wayfaring-tree (*Viburnum lantana*) and guelder-rose (*V. opulus*). The exit hole is protected by a small disc of bark (5–6 mm in diameter) which sometimes falls off, but more often sinks a little below the level of the surrounding bark. The species has a two-year life-cycle and in some localities the pupae are only found in alternate years. The larvae are often heavily parasitized.

Overwinters twice as a larva.

Red-belted Clearwing

Synanthedon myopaeformis Borkhausen

Plate **2** : *43*

Similar species. *S. formicaeformis*, pl. **2**, has the forewing tipped with red. *S. culiciformis*, pl. **2**, has the base of the forewing dusted with red scales. (See text fig 2.)

Imago. 18–26 mm. Resident. Single-brooded, flying in June and July, inhabiting gardens, old orchards, tree-lined roads and open woodland. Locally common in the southern half of England and occasionally found as far north as Lancashire and Yorkshire. Doubtfully recorded from Ireland.

Larva. August to May under the old and cankerous bark of crab apple and cultivated apple; also found on rowan, pear, almond, and other fruit and ornamental trees. The cocoons are often attached to the inner surface of loose bark.

Overwinters as a larva.

Red-tipped Clearwing

Synanthedon formicaeformis Esper

Plate **2** : *45–46*

Similar species. *S. culiciformis*, pl. **2**, lacks the red-tipped forewing. *S. myopaeformis*, pl. **2** and text.

Imago. 18–26 mm. Resident. Single-brooded, flying from June to early August, inhabiting old osier beds, sallow-swamps, disused gravel pits and other marshy

places. Locally common in southern England and the Midlands. Less frequent in Wales and northern England. Scarce and local in Ireland with records from Cos Armagh, Kerry, Cork, Sligo and Louth.
Larva. August to May in the stems and trunks of osier and other species of willow and sallow.
Overwinters, probably twice, as a larva.

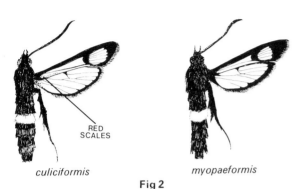

culiciformis   myopaeformis

Fig 2

Large Red-belted Clearwing
Synanthedon culiciformis Linnaeus
Plate **2** : *44*
Variation. Ab. *flavocingulata* Spuler is an uncommon form in which the red colour of the forewing and the abdominal band is replaced by yellow.
Similar species. *S myopaeformis*, pl. **2** and text. *S. formicaeformis*, pl. **2** and text.
Imago. 23–29 mm. Resident. The newly emerged adults are frequently found on birch-stumps. Single-brooded, flying in May and June, inhabiting heathland and open woodland. Widespread and generally common in England, Wales and much of Scotland. Recorded doubtfully from Ireland.
Larva. July to April under the bark of birch trees and stumps. Occasionally found in alder. The fibrous cocoon can be located in the upper section of one- to three-year-old birch-stumps by carefully prising off the bark.
Overwinters as a larva.

Six-belted Clearwing
Bembecia scopigera Scopoli
Plate **2** : *47*
Similar species. *B. muscaeformis*, pl. **2** and text.
Imago. 17–22 mm. Resident. This species is most easily obtained in the adult stage by searching or sweeping its foodplants and adjacent herbage. Single-brooded, flying from mid-June to early August, inhabiting downland, quarries, embankments, and sea-cliffs; most frequently found on chalky soils. A local species found in Wales, southern England and northwards to Yorkshire.
Larva. August to May in the roots of bird's-foot trefoil and kidney vetch (*Anthyllis vulneraria*).
Overwinters as a larva.

Thrift Clearwing
Bembecia muscaeformis Esper
Plate **2** : *48*
Similar species. *B. scopigera*, pl. **2**, has the discal spot and apical area suffused with orange, and the whitish abdominal bands are very distinct.
Imago. 16–20 mm. Resident. The adult is attracted to the flowers of thyme and thrift and can be obtained by searching or sweeping. Single-brooded, flying from mid-June throughout July, inhabiting cliffs and rocky places by the sea. Locally common along the coasts of Devon, Cornwall, Isles of Scilly, Wales, Cumbria and the Isle of Man. In Scotland it has been recorded from Kirkcudbrightshire, Angus and Aberdeenshire. Reported from Cos Dublin, Antrim, Cork, Clare and Wexford, but probably more widespread in Ireland than suggested by these records.
Larva. August to May in the crowns and roots of thrift. Small plants growing on almost bare rock are more likely to be infected than those forming large and luxuriant clumps. The workings of the larva are indicated by a small reddish-brown patch on the cushion of thrift.
Overwinters as a larva.

Fiery Clearwing
Bembecia chrysidiformis Esper
Plate **2** : *49–50*
Imago. 18–26 mm. Resident. In the days when this species was plentiful, it was frequently seen flying in sunshine over its foodplant. Single-brooded, flying in June and July, inhabiting rough ground and chalky slopes by the sea. As a resident it is confined to Folkestone Warren, Kent; and even here it is localized and by no means common. Occasional specimens have occurred elsewhere in Kent and also in Sussex, Hampshire and Essex.
Larva. August to May in the crowns and roots of dock and sorrel.
Overwinters twice as a larva

Family: Lasiocampidae

Eleven resident species represent this family in the British Isles. The general colour of these medium- to large-sized moths is some shade of brown. Two of the species have males that fly during the day; the rest are nocturnal and are attracted to light, but not to sugar or flowers.

The larvae, some of which are handsomely coloured, are covered with downy or short hairs, and certain species, in particular *E. lanestris*, should be handled with care as the larval hairs can severely irritate sensitive skin. Several species are notoriously difficult to rear and as a general rule the larvae of all the species thrive better if kept outdoors on their growing foodplant.

The cocoons are constructed at or above ground level with one exception; those of *L. trifolii* are frequently concealed under sand or stones.

December Moth
Poecilocampa populi Linnaeus
Plate **4** : *1–2*

Imago. 38–46 mm. Resident. Comes freely to light, especially the males. Single-brooded, flying from late October to mid-December in southern Britain, but appearing several weeks earlier in the north. Generally distributed and moderately common over much of the British Isles.

Larva. April to June on a variety of deciduous trees, including oak, birch, elm, hawthorn, poplar and lime. Overwinters as an egg.

Pale Eggar
Trichiura crataegi Linnaeus
Plate **4** : *5–7*

Variation. Geographically variable, with the darker forms predominating in northern Britain; this is particularly noticeable in the male which has the ground colour of the forewing ranging from whitish to blackish-grey.

Imago. 33–40 mm. Resident. Flies at night and both sexes are attracted to light. Single-brooded, flying from mid-August to late September, except in central and northern Scotland where it often appears in July. The species inhabits open woodland, hedgerows and heathland. Widespread and locally common throughout England, Wales and Scotland, including the Inner Hebrides. Apparently very local in Ireland and only recorded from Cos Fermanagh, Clare and Kerry.

Larva. April to June mainly on blackthorn, hawthorn and birch, but also found on sallow, oak, bramble, bilberry and heather.

Normally overwinters as an egg, except in the Highlands and other parts of Scotland where there exists a race which has a two-year cycle and passes the second winter in the larval stage. Both races are said frequently to occupy the same territory and at times interbreed. The relationship between them is therefore very complex and requires elucidation.

Small Eggar
Eriogaster lanestris Linnaeus
Plate **4** : *3–4*

Imago. 36–47 mm. Resident. Flies at night, but is rarely noticed in the wild, except very occasionally at light. Single-brooded, flying in February and March, inhabiting hedgerows and bushy places. A very local species nowadays, occurring in widely scattered colonies throughout England as far north as Yorkshire and Westmorland. The wholesale destruction and indiscriminate trimming of hedgerows, combined with the pollution caused by motor vehicles and the drift from agricultural insecticides, have all contributed to the serious decline of this species which was formerly widespread and moderately common over the whole of England, North Wales and parts of southeast Scotland. It is still, however, locally common in the northern half of Ireland.

Larva. April to early July mainly on blackthorn, hawthorn and occasionally wild rose, living gregariously, until the final instar, in a ball-shaped web of woven silk from which it emerges mostly at night to feed.

Overwinters from one to three, and in extremely rare instances up to seven, years as a pupa.

The Lackey
Malacosoma neustria Linnaeus
Plate **4** : *13–16*

Variation. Ground colour of male ranges from pale yellow to dark reddish-brown with the two median lines of the forewing varying in intensity and occasionally absent.

Similar species. *M. castrensis*, pl. **4** and text.

Imago. 30–41 mm. Resident. Both sexes come frequently to light. Single-brooded, flying in July and August. Generally distributed and moderately common in the southern half of England, Wales and Ireland. Very local in northern England as far north as Cumbria and Yorkshire.

Larva. April to June on a wide variety of trees and shrubs such as hawthorn, blackthorn, sallow, and various fruit trees, living in a communal silken web until nearly full-grown.

Overwinters as an egg.

Ground Lackey
Malacosoma castrensis Linnaeus
Plate **4** : *8–12*

Variation. Ground colour of male ranges from pale yellow to reddish-brown and that of the female from light brown to reddish-brown. A form in which the median lines are absent occurs frequently in both sexes.

Similar species. *M. neustria*, pl. **4**, has fringe of forewing chequered with ochreous-white.

Imago. 31–41 mm. Resident. Rarely seen in the wild except occasionally at light. Single-brooded, flying in July and August, inhabiting coastal and estuarine saltmarshes. Very local in southeast England where it is confined to north Kent, Essex and Suffolk. Also reported recently from South Devon.

Larva. April to July on sea plantain, common sea-lavender (*Limonium vulgare*), sea wormwood, and many other salt-marsh plants. The young larvae live gregariously in a silken web, constructed low down amongst the herbage. In captivity they will eat sallow, blackthorn and the leaves of various fruit trees and are best sleeved out. Overwinters as an egg.

Grass Eggar
Lasiocampa trifolii trifolii Denis & Schiffermüller
Plate 3 : *1–3*
Variation. Ground colour of both wings ranges from greyish-brown to almost blackish-brown with the dark forms predominating in northern and western England.
Imago. 46–76 mm. Resident. Flies at night and is attracted to light. Single-brooded, flying in August and early September. Very local, but not uncommon, inhabiting sandhills in Hampshire, Dorset, the Isles of Scilly, Glamorgan, Somerset, and Lancashire; sea-cliffs in South Devon and Cornwall; and inland heaths in Dorset.
L. trifolii flava Chalmers-Hunt, **Pale Grass Eggar**, pl. 3 : *4–6*. A yellowish race inhabiting shingle beaches at Dungeness, Kent and formerly near Eastbourne, East Sussex. Ab. *obsoleta* Tutt (fig 6) is an uncommon form occurring in both sexes.
Larva. Late March to mid-June on a variety of grasses and plants, but with distinct local preferences. The main foodplants are broom, creeping sallow, false oat-grass, tree lupin, marram, bramble and heather.
Overwinters as an egg.

Oak Eggar
Lasiocampa quercus quercus Linnaeus
Plate 3 : *7–8*
Imago. 58–90 mm. Resident. The male flies by day in sunshine and the female at night, when it is sometimes attracted to light. Single-brooded, flying in July and August, inhabiting woodland, commons, chalk downs, sandhills, hedgerows and sea-cliffs. Locally widespread throughout southern England and as far north as the coasts of Co. Durham and Lancashire.
Larva. September to early June on a wide range of trees and shrubs such as bramble, sallow, oak, sloe, broom, hazel and sea-buckthorn.
Overwinters as a larva in its third instar.
L. quercus callunae Palmer, **Northern Eggar**
Plate 3 : *9–12*
Variation. Ab. *olivacea* Tutt (figs 11–12) is a melanic form found commonly in Caithness and less frequently on the Yorkshire moors.
Imago. 68–96 mm. Resident. The male flies by day in sunshine and the female at night, when it occasionally comes to light. Single-brooded, flying in late May and June, inhabiting heathland and moorland. Locally widespread in southwest England, the Midlands, Wales, northern England, Scotland, including the Hebrides and Orkney, and Ireland.
Larva. July to August of the second year on heather and sometimes bilberry.

Overwinters the first year as a small larva and the second as a pupa.

Fox Moth
Macrothylacia rubi Linnaeus
Plate **4** : *17–18*
Variation. Female specimens from the Midlands and northern Britain are greyer and darker than those from southern England.
Imago. 48–72 mm. Resident. The male appears during the day flying rapidly in sunshine; the female flies at night and is frequently attracted to light. Single-brooded, flying in May and June, inhabiting downland, open woodland, sandhills, commons and waste ground. Generally distributed and locally common throughout the British Isles.
Larva. Late July to early spring on many plants including heather, heath, bramble, bilberry, and creeping willow.
Overwinters as a full-grown larva.

Pine Tree Lappet
Dendrolimus pini Linnaeus
Plate **43** : *16*
Imago. 60–92 mm. Suspected immigrant. The male comes to light. Single-brooded on the Continent, flying from June to August. The species inhabits conifer plantations where occasionally it can become a serious pest. There is a record for Richmond Park, Surrey, in 1748 and a male was taken in Norwich, Norfolk, on 22.vii.1809. The species did not appear again for almost two hundred years when a male was taken at light at Freshwater, Isle of Wight, on 12.viii.1996. On the Channel Islands single males have been taken at Forest, Guernsey, on 9.vii.1989 & 4.viii.1997. Abroad its extensive range covers much of Europe.
Larva. *August to May on various species of pine and spruce.
Overwinters as an almost full-grown larva.

The Drinker
Euthrix potatoria Linnaeus
Plate **4** : *19–20*
Imago. 50–70 mm. Resident. Both sexes come to light, the males sometimes in large numbers. Single-brooded, flying in July and August, inhabiting woodland rides, commons, fenland and the wetter parts of moorland. Generally distributed and common in England and Wales; less frequent, but widespread, in Ireland and western Scotland.
Larva. September to June on various grasses and reeds, including common reed, reed canary-grass, cock's foot, *Carex* spp., and *Calamagrostis* spp.
Overwinters as a small larva.

Small Lappet
Phyllodesma ilicifolia Linnaeus
Plate 5 : 4

Imago. 38–54 mm. Resident. Although this species flies at night and is attracted to light, most of the British specimens were found during the day at rest on the stems of heather and bilberry or bred from wild larvae. Single-brooded, flying in late April and May, inhabiting open woodland and moorland having an undergrowth of bilberry. Confined to central England where it occurred in several moorland localities in west Yorkshire from 1850 to *c.* 1880; on the Long Mynd, Shropshire, about 1889; and Cannock Chase, Staffordshire, from 1851 to *c.* 1900, with a single specimen in 1939. Elsewhere a specimen was reported from Weston-super-Mare, Somerset, on 15.v.1965, and there are unconfirmed records of two larvae: one from Lynton, North Devon, in 1864, and the other from Porlock, Somerset, in August 1938. *P. ilicifolia* has always been a local and uncommon species in Britain; it is easily overlooked and, despite the paucity of recent records, unlikely to be extinct.
Larva. June to mid-August on bilberry.
Overwinters as a pupa.

The Lappet
Gastropacha quercifolia Linnaeus
Plate 5 : 3

Imago. 56–88 mm. Resident. Comes to light in small numbers. Single-brooded, flying from late June to mid-August, inhabiting open woodland, hedgerows, orchards, and bushy places. Widespread and locally common in the southern half of Britain.
Larva. September to May on blackthorn, hawthorn, buckthorn, and sometimes apple and sallow. Mostly found on small trees and bushes, feeding at night and resting during the day on the lower stems.
Overwinters as a small larva.

Family: Saturniidae

Emperor Moth
Pavonia pavonia Linnaeus
Plate 5 : 1–2

Variation. Specimens from Scotland and the Northern Isles are brighter in colour than those from the south; this is particularly noticeable in the female, which has a distinct bluish-grey appearance.
Imago. 55–85 mm. Resident. The male flies rapidly in sunshine and the female at night when it occasionally comes to light. Single-brooded, flying in April and May, inhabiting heathland, moorland, open woodland, commons, mosses, and waste ground. Generally distributed and locally common throughout the British Isles, including Orkney and the Hebrides.
Larva. Late May to August on a variety of plants including heather, bramble, hawthorn, blackthorn, sallow, and meadowsweet.
Overwinters as a pupa within a tough, fibrous and pear-shaped cocoon spun up near the ground amongst the undergrowth.

Family: Endromidae

Kentish Glory
Endromis versicolora Linnaeus
Plate 4 : 21–22

Imago. 55–89 mm. Resident. The male flies in sunshine and the female from dusk onwards, when it is sometimes taken at light. Single-brooded, flying from late March to mid-May, inhabiting open woodland and moorland with birch. Very local in the Highland region of Scotland; recorded mostly from Inverness-shire, but also found in Aberdeenshire, Kincardineshire, Morayshire, and Perthshire. Formerly local in southeast England in the last century and until quite recently occurred in parts of the west Midlands, where the Wyre Forest, Worcestershire, was a well-known locality.
Larva. Late May to July on birch and sometimes alder, feeding when young in small clusters.
Overwinters as a pupa within a coarse netted cocoon spun up on the ground or just below the surface. Frequently a second winter and occasionally a third is passed in this stage.

Family: Drepanidae

Seven species of this family have occurred in the British Isles; one of them is a suspected immigrant and the rest are resident. The adults fly at night and both sexes come frequently to light, but not to sugar or flowers. The commoner species can be disturbed from their foodplants during the day and two of them have been noted flying of their own accord in sunshine.
The curious hump-backed larvae have a short horizontal pointed tail in place of the usual pair of anal claspers. The pupae are within thin silken cocoons spun between the leaves of the host tree.

Scalloped Hook-tip
Falcaria lacertinaria Linnaeus
Plate 5 : 30–31

Imago. 34–38 mm. Resident. Double-brooded in England, Wales and Ireland, flying in May and early June, and again in late July and August. Single-brooded in Scotland, flying in late May and June. The species inhabits woodland and heathland, and is widely distributed and moderately common over much of the British Isles.
Larva. June to July and August to September on birch.
Overwinters as a pupa.

Oak Hook-tip
Drepana binaria Hufnagel
Plate **5** : *25–26*

Similar species. *D. cultraria*, pl. **5**, has a dark central band on forewing and a single spot in the discal area. (See text fig 3.)

Imago. 28–35 mm. Resident. Occasionally flies around the upper branches of oak trees in the afternoon sunshine, but the usual time of flight is after dark when both sexes come readily to light. Double-brooded, flying in May and June, and again in late July and August, inhabiting woodland and parkland. Well distributed and fairly common in England, as far north as Yorkshire and Westmorland, and most of Wales.

Larva. June to July, and September on oak.
Overwinters as a pupa.

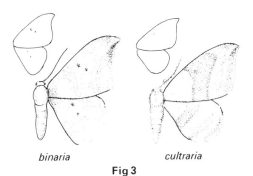

binaria   *cultraria*

Fig 3

Barred Hook-tip
Drepana cultraria Fabricius
Plate **5** : *24*

Similar species. *D. binaria*, pl. **5**, lacks the dark central band on the forewing and has two dark spots in the discal area.

Imago. 24–33 mm. Resident. Frequently seen in the afternoon sunshine flying around beech trees, and at night when both sexes come to light. Double-brooded, flying in May and June, and again in August. A locally common species inhabiting beech-woods and found in southern Britain as far north as Lincolnshire.

Larva. June to July, and September on beech.
Overwinters as a pupa.

Pebble Hook-tip
Drepana falcataria falcataria Linnaeus
Plate **5** : *28*

Similar species. *D. curvatula*, pl. **5** and text.

Imago. 36–40 mm. Resident. Double-brooded in England, Wales and Ireland, flying in May and June, and again in August. The species inhabits woodland and heathland, and is moderately common throughout

England and Wales. Local and generally uncommon in Ireland.

D. falcataria scotica Bytinski-Salz, pl. **5** : *29*. Differs from the typical form by having the ground colour of both wings ochreous-white. Single-brooded, occurring from mid-May to mid-June. Locally widespread in Scotland as far north as Caithness, but absent from the Northern Isles.

Larva. June to July, and September in the south; July to August in Scotland. Mostly found on birch, occasionally on alder.
Overwinters as a pupa.

Dusky Hook-tip
Drepana curvatula Borkhausen
Plate **5** : *27*

Similar species. *D. falcataria*, pl. **5**, has the costal half of the hindwing much paler and the outer discal spot much enlarged. (See text fig 4.)

Imago. 34–42 mm. Suspected immigrant. Double-brooded on the Continent, flying from late April to early July, and again in July and August. Recorded from Britain on eleven occasions, all at light: a female at Dover, Kent, on 13.viii.1960, from which a few specimens were reared; Petworth, West Sussex, on 14.viii.1965; Clay-next-to-Sea, Norfolk, on 19.viii.1971; Greatstone, Kent, on 21.viii.1991; Totton, Hampshire, on 22.viii.1991; Bradwell-on-Sea, Essex, on 28.v.1992; Pagham, West Sussex, on 24.v.1993; Dalby, Lincolnshire, on 30.vii.1993; Middleton-on-Sea, West Sussex, on 29.viii.1993; Stiffkey, Norfolk, on 2.viii.1995; and Dungeness, Kent, on 11.viii.1997. A specimen recorded on Guernsey on 10.viii.1996 would appear to be the only record from the Channel Islands so far. Abroad, the species is generally distributed throughout northern and central Europe.

Larva. *Mid-summer and early autumn on alder, birch and oak.
Overwinters as a pupa.

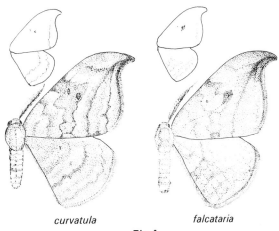

curvatula   *falcataria*

Fig 4

Scarce Hook-tip
Sabra harpagula Esper
Plate **5** : *23*

Imago. 36–42 mm. Resident. The male comes to light in moderate numbers, the female is much scarcer. Single-brooded, flying from mid-June to early July. Very local and confined to Monmouthshire and Gloucestershire where it inhabits the wooded areas of the Wye Valley. Formerly found in Leigh Woods, near Bristol, but not recorded from this locality since 1938.
Larva. Late July to September on small-leaved lime. Overwinters as a pupa.

Chinese Character
Cilix glaucata Scopoli
Plate **5** : *22*

Variation. First brood specimens are smaller and more richly marked than those of the second brood.
Imago. 22–27 mm. Resident. Both sexes come frequently to light. Double-brooded, flying in May and early June, and again in late July and August. The species inhabits hedgerows, commons, and bushy places and is moderately common throughout England, Wales and much of Ireland. Less frequent and local in southern Scotland.
Larva. June to July and September to October mainly on hawthorn and blackthorn, and occasionally bramble, rowan, apple and pear.
Overwinters as a pupa.

Family: Thyatiridae

Peach Blossom
Thyatira batis Linnaeus
Plate **5** : *6*

Imago. 39–44 mm. Resident. Comes to light and sugar. Single-brooded, flying from late May to late July; with a very small second generation occurring occasionally in southern England in late August and early September. A fairly common woodland species, found throughout the British Isles, except Orkney, Shetland and the Outer Hebrides.
Larva. July to September on bramble. Overwinters as a pupa.

Buff Arches
Habrosyne pyritoides Hufnagel
(*derasa* Linnaeus)
Plate **5** : *5*

Imago. 40–44 mm. Resident. Comes freely to light and sugar. Single-brooded normally, flying from late June to early August, inhabiting open woodland and commons. Generally distributed and not uncommon in England as far north as Cumbria and Yorkshire, throughout Wales, and most of Ireland. The only recent record from Scotland is a casual specimen found in Inverness-shire in 1958.

Larva. Mid-August to mid-October on bramble. Overwinters as a pupa.

Figure of Eighty
Tethea ocularis octogesimea Hübner
Plate **5** : *10*

Variation. Evidence suggests the origin of the melanic f. *fusca* Cockayne was the result of migration. This form, which varies in intensity, first appeared in southern and eastern Britain in the mid-1940s and increased rapidly to become dominant over much of the range of the species.
Similar species. *T. or*, pl. **5**, has four dark cross-lines in the basal half of the forewing. (See text fig 5.)
Imago. 36–44 mm. Resident and suspected immigrant. Comes to light and sugar. Single-brooded, flying from late May to July, inhabiting woodland, commons, and a variety of suburban localities including parks, edges of playing fields and waste ground. Widespread in southern England, the Midlands northwards to Cumbria and Yorkshire, and the eastern counties of Wales.
Larva. Late July and August on poplar and aspen. Overwinters as a pupa.

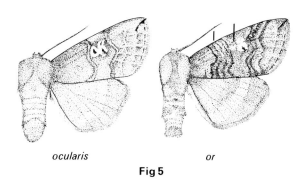

ocularis   *or*

Fig 5

Poplar Lutestring
Tethea or or Denis & Schiffermüller
Plate **5** : *11*

Similar species. *T. ocularis octogesimea*, pl. **5** and text.
Imago. 38–43 mm. Resident. Comes readily to light and sugar. Single-brooded, flying from late May to early August. Locally widespread in England and Wales.
T. or scotica Tutt, pl. **5** : *12*. Differs from typical race in having ground colour pale grey with strong violet tinge and the outer cross-lines more distinct. Single-brooded, flying in June. Moderately common in central, northern and western Scotland, including the Inner and Outer Hebrides.
T. or hibernica Turner, pl. **5** : *13*. Ground colour intermediate between typical and Scottish races; with the forewing stigmata either weakly defined or absent, and the two sets of cross-lines well defined and close together. Freshly emerged specimens of this race have a

deep violet tint which is unfortunately unstable and soon fades. Single-brooded, flying in June and early July, and found locally throughout Ireland.

Larva. All the races feed on aspen, but those of the English race are found occasionally on poplar.
Overwinters as a pupa.

Satin Lutestring
Tetheella fluctuosa Hübner
Plate **5** : *7–9*

Variation. The form *albilinea* Lempke (fig 9) occurs rarely, except in Scotland where it appears to be the normal form. Ab. *unicolor* Lempke (fig 8) is a melanic variety first taken in Hamstreet, Kent, in 1955 and now occurring annually in small numbers. The same or a similar form has occurred in Sussex, Surrey and Staffordshire.

Similar species. *Ochropacha duplaris*, pl. **5**, has two dark spots placed vertically in the discal area and lacks a subapical streak. (See text fig 6.)

Imago. 35–38 mm. Resident. Comes freely to light, but rarely to sugar. Single-brooded, flying from June to early August, inhabiting mature woodland. Very local and found mainly in southeast England, southwest Midlands, Wales and Cumbria. Recorded in Scotland from Inverness-shire, Perthshire, Argyllshire, and the islands of Arran and Mull. Scarce and local in Ireland; reported from Cos Kerry, Sligo, Galway, Mayo and Wexford.

Larva. August and September on birch.
Overwinters as a pupa.

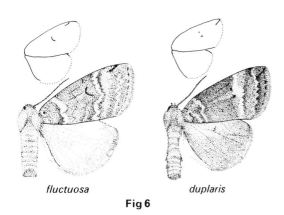

fluctuosa　　　　　*duplaris*

Fig 6

Common Lutestring
Ochropacha duplaris Linnaeus
Plate **5** : *18–19*

Variation. The melanic f. *obscura* Tutt (fig 19) is a common and often dominant form.

Similar species. *Tetheella fluctuosa*, pl. **5** and text.

Imago. 25–34 mm. Resident. Comes frequently to light. Single-brooded, flying from mid-June to mid-August, inhabiting woodland. Widely distributed and not uncommon throughout most of the British Isles.

Larva. August to early October on birch and occasionally oak and alder.
Overwinters as a pupa.

Oak Lutestring
Cymatophorima diluta hartwiegi Reisser
Plate **5** : *14–15*

Variation. Ab. *nubilata* Robson (fig 15) is found frequently in parts of northwest Sussex and has occurred in Yorkshire, Scotland and occasionally elsewhere.

Imago. 33–36 mm. Resident. Comes freely to light and sugar. Single-brooded, flying from late August throughout September, inhabiting mature oak woodland. Widely distributed and locally common in all of southern England, the Midlands and Wales. Local and less frequent in northern England and southern Scotland.

Larva. May and June on oak.
Overwinters as an egg.

Yellow Horned
Achlya flavicornis galbanus Tutt
Plate **5** : *16*

Imago. 39–44 mm. Resident. Comes freely to light, also to sugar and sallow blossom. Single-brooded, flying in March and April, inhabiting woodland, heathland and moorland. Generally distributed and common throughout England and Wales.

A. flavicornis scotica Tutt, pl. **5** : *17*. This race is larger (43–49 mm) than that from southern England, also darker and less greenish-grey, and with more pronounced forewing markings. Widespread over much of Scotland, including Orkney and the Inner Hebrides. Specimens from northern England tend to be intermediate between the two races. Local in Ireland.

Larva. Late May to mid-July on birch. Hides between spun leaves.
Overwinters once and sometimes twice as a pupa.

Frosted Green
Polyploca ridens Fabricius
Plate **5** : *20–21*

Variation. Melanic forms occur frequently over much of its range, and in some localities, especially those around London and in the Midlands, they predominate.

Imago. 36–40 mm. Resident. Comes readily to light. Single-brooded, flying from mid-April to mid-May, inhabiting mature oak woodland. Widespread and locally common in the southern half of England and Wales. Very local in the rest of England as far north as Lincolnshire and Cumbria.

Larva. Late May to mid-July on oak.
Overwinters as a pupa.

Family: Geometridae

This is the second largest family of macrolepidoptera in the British Isles and is represented by more than 300 species placed in six subfamilies: Archiearinae, Oenochrominae, Geometrinae, Sterrhinae, Larentiinae, and Ennominae.

Migration is not a strong feature of this group which includes only three regular visitors and a handful of casuals.

The adults of the Geometridae have mostly broad forewings and ample hindwings, and could be described in layman's terms as butterfly-like. The antennae, on the other hand, are very moth-like and are often feathered or pectinated in the male, but mostly simple in the female.

The majority of the species fly at night and frequently come to light, but only a small proportion have an appetite for sugar and natural attractions such as sallow and ivy blossoms. Many species fly slowly at dusk and are easily netted, while others may be disturbed during the day by gently tapping trees, bushes, etc.

The larvae of this large family are so variable in appearance that to generalize would serve little purpose. There is, however, one characteristic common to most of them and that is the absence of the first three pairs of prolegs. Progress is made by alternately arching and straightening the body, and this style of locomotion has led to the larvae being known colloquially as 'loopers' or 'inchworms'.

SUBFAMILY: ARCHIEARINAE

Orange Underwing
Archiearis parthenias Linnaeus
Plate **6** : *23–24*

Similar species. *A. notha*, pl. **6** and text.
Imago. 35–39 mm. Resident. Very active in sunshine, flying friskily and usually high up along the rides and edges of birchwoods. Occasionally visits sallow blossom. Single-brooded, flying in March and April. Widespread and locally common over much of England, Wales and the Scottish mainland.
Larva. May and June between spun leaves of birch and rowan. It requires soft wood or cork in which to pupate.
Overwinters as a pupa.

parthenias   *notha*

Fig 7

Light Orange Underwing
Archiearis notha Hübner
Plate **6** : *25–26*

Similar species. *A. parthenias*, pl. **6**, rather larger, forewing more variegated when comparing the same sexes, dark border on underside of hindwing notched, well broken, and sometimes almost absent. Antennae of male finely serrated, those of *notha* bipectinated. (See text fig 7.)
Imago. 33–36 mm. Resident. Flies in sunshine around the tops of aspen trees. Less active in the late afternoon and in dull weather may be dislodged by shaking the trees. Single-brooded, flying from late March to mid-April, but varying slightly according to season. Very local and found mainly in the southern half of England, although absent from the extreme southwest.
Larva. May and June between spun leaves of aspen. It requires soft wood or cork in which to pupate.
Overwinters from one to three times as a pupa.

SUBFAMILY: OENOCHROMINAE

March Moth
Alsophila aescularia Denis & Schiffermüller
Plate **6** : *27–28*

Imago. Male 34–38 mm, female wingless. Resident. After dark the males come freely to light and the females can be found on tree-trunks. Single-brooded, flying in March and April, but varying according to season. Generally distributed and common throughout England and Wales. Less frequent, but widespread in Ireland and much of Scotland, including the Inner Hebrides.
Larva. May and June on a wide variety of deciduous trees.
Overwinters as a pupa.

SUBFAMILY: GEOMETRINAE

Rest Harrow
Aplasta ononaria Fuessly
Plate **6** : *29–30*

Imago. 26–31 mm. Resident and suspected immigrant. Mainly single-brooded, flying in late June and July, with an occasional and partial second generation in late August and September. Confined as a resident to Kent, where it is found not uncommonly in Folkestone Warren and on the coastal sandhills between Deal and Sandwich. A small colony was reported in 1949 to exist between Dungeness and New Romney. As a suspected immigrant it has been recorded from: New Forest, Hampshire, in 1909 and 1924; southern England in 1923; Dungeness, Kent, on 20.viii.1932, and 6.viii.1934; Hastings, Sussex, in 1934; near Dover, Kent, on 18 and 22.viii.1947; Westerham, Kent, on 19.viii.1947; Tilgate, Sussex, on 23.viii.1947; Lydd-on-Sea, Kent, on 3.vii.1957; Southsea, Hampshire, on 15.vii.1959; Bradwell-on-Sea, Essex, on 2.ix.1961; Rowlands Castle,

Hampshire, on 9.vii.1962; Plaistow, Sussex, on 22.viii. 1976 and Littlestone, Kent, on 22.vii.1996.
Larva. September to May on common restharrow. Overwinters as a small larva.

Grass Emerald
Pseudoterpna pruinata atropunctaria Walker
Plate **6** : *2*

Variation. The bluish-green pigment of this species is very unstable and in the wild one frequently finds faded specimens having little or no trace of green colour, but otherwise appearing to be in good condition.
Imago. 35–40 mm. Resident. Comes to light in small numbers and during the day can be disturbed from its foodplants and adjacent undergrowth. Single-brooded, flying from mid-June to August, inhabiting heathland, commons, shingle beaches, and gravel pits. Widespread and common throughout England, Wales, southern Scotland, and the whole of Ireland.
Larva. September to May on gorse, broom and petty whin.
Overwinters as a very small larva.

Large Emerald
Geometra papilionaria Linnaeus
Plate **6** : *1*

Imago. 50–64 mm. Resident. Comes frequently to light, usually after midnight. Single-brooded, flying from late June to early August, inhabiting woodland and heathland. Generally distributed and moderately common throughout the British Isles.
Larva. September to May on birch and occasionally alder, hazel and beech.
Overwinters as a larva.

Blotched Emerald
Comibaena bajularia Denis & Schiffermüller
(*pustulata* Hufnagel)
Plate **6** : *8*

Imago. 29–33 mm. Resident. The males come freely to light, the females less frequently. Single-brooded, flying in late June and July, inhabiting oak woodland. Widespread and locally common in southern England, the eastern half of Wales, and the Midlands as far north as Yorkshire.
Larva. September to May on oak.
Overwinters as a very small larva.

Essex Emerald
Thetidia smaragdaria maritima Prout
Plate **6** : *7*

Imago. 33–35 mm. Resident. Rarely found as an adult except very occasionally at light. Single-brooded, flying from mid-June to early July, inhabiting the edges of salt-marshes. Formerly locally widespread in southeast Essex along the estuaries of the Thames, Crouch and Blackwater; also found in north Kent, mainly on the

Isle of Sheppey. Now much decreased, possibly to the point of extinction.
Larva. September to May on sea-wormwood. Overwinters as a small larva.

Common Emerald
Hemithea aestivaria Hübner
Plate **6** : *9*

Similar species. *Thalera fimbrialis*, pl. **6**, slightly larger, fringes of forewing chequered with red, margin of hindwing distinctly notched, colour of hindlegs bright red and antenna of male strongly bipectinate. (See text fig 8.)
Imago. 29–34 mm. Resident. Found frequently at dusk flying along hedgerows and over bushy places, and in small numbers at light. Single-brooded, flying in late June and throughout July. Generally distributed in England as far north as Co. Durham and Cumbria; Isle of Man, Wales and southern Ireland. Very local in northern Ireland, only from Fermanagh.
Larva. August to May on a variety of trees and shrubs such as hawthorn, blackthorn, birch, oak, and sallow. Overwinters as a larva.

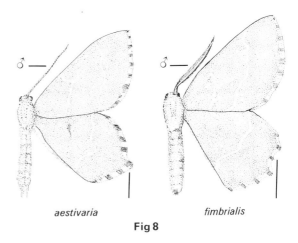

aestivaria   *fimbrialis*
Fig 8

Small Grass Emerald
Chlorissa viridata Linnaeus
Plate **6** : *5*

Similar species. *Jodis lactearia*, pl. **6**, has the postmedian line of the hindwing curved. (See text fig 9.)
Imago. 24–27 mm. Resident. Hides during the day amongst heather and is easily disturbed. Flies naturally from dusk onwards and is attracted sparingly to light. Single-brooded, flying in June and early July, inhabiting damp heathland and mosses. A very local and seemingly declining species found in Surrey, Sussex, Hampshire, Dorset, Devon and Cornwall. Formerly found in Cumbria, Wiltshire, Gloucestershire and Worcestershire.

In the last half of the twentieth century occasional and possibly vagrant examples have been reported from Lincolnshire, Kent, Isle of Wight and Wester Ross.
Larva. Late July and August on heather, birch and creeping willow.
Overwinters as a pupa.

Sussex Emerald
Thalera fimbrialis Scopoli
Plate **6** : *4*

Similar species. *Hemithea aestivaria*, pl. **6** and text.
Imago. 35–39 mm. Immigrant and transitory resident. Flies shortly after dark, comes to light and has been found frequently resting on the stems of false oat-grass. Single-brooded, flying in July and early August. Confined as a resident to the shingle beach of Dungeness, Kent, where it was discovered in 1950. Formerly resident on the Crumbles, near Eastbourne, Sussex, but not recorded since 1956. Other records are Beachy Head, Sussex, on 7.viii.1902; Swanage, Dorset, on 11.viii.1936; Bournemouth, Hampshire, on 29.vii.1946; Bradwell-on-Sea, Essex, on 8.viii.1946.
Larva. Late August to June on yarrow, common and hoary ragwort, and wild carrot (*Daucus carota*).
Overwinters as a larva.

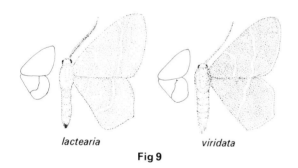

lactearia   viridata

Fig 9

Small Emerald
Hemistola chrysoprasaria Esper
(*immaculata* Thunberg)
Plate **6** : *3*

Imago. 33–40 mm. Resident. Comes to light in small numbers. Single-brooded, flying from late June to early August, inhabiting downland, hedgerows, and edges of woods; mainly found on chalk. Widely distributed and locally common in the southern half of Britain. Less frequent and very local from the Midlands northwards to Lincolnshire and Westmorland. The casual specimens reported from southern Scotland and Ireland were probably introduced on imported plants of *Clematis*.
Larva. September to early June on traveller's-joy.
Overwinters as a small larva.

Little Emerald
Jodis lactearia Linnaeus
Plate **6** : *6*

Variation. The delicate green tint displayed by newly emerged specimens is rarely present in wild-caught ones.
Similar species. *Chlorissa viridata*, pl. **6** and text.
Imago. 23–26 mm. Resident. Flies freely at dusk and is easily netted; also comes sparingly to light. Single-brooded, flying in May and June, inhabiting woodland. Generally distributed and moderately common throughout England, Wales and Ireland. Locally common in western Scotland from Clydesdale to Wester Ross.
Larva. August and September on various trees and plants including birch, oak, hawthorn, sweet chestnut, and bilberry.
Overwinters as a pupa.

SUBFAMILY: STERRHINAE
Dingy Mocha
Cyclophora pendularia Clerck
(*orbicularia* Hübner)
Plate **6** : *10*

Similar species. Dark forms of *C. albipunctata*, pl. **6** and text.
Imago. 26–29 mm. Resident. Both sexes come sparingly to light. Double-brooded, flying in May and early June, and again in July and early August. This very local and much decreased species inhabits damp heathland and occurs on the Purbeck heaths between Wareham and Studland, Dorset; the western edge of the New Forest, Hampshire; and single localities in Shropshire and South Wiltshire.
Larva. July and September on small-leaved *Salix* species, such as eared willow and sallow (*S. cinerea*).
Overwinters as a pupa.

The Mocha
Cyclophora annulata Schulze
Plate **6** : *21*

Imago. 22–26 mm. Resident. Both sexes come sparingly to light and during the day may be disturbed from the lower branches of maple. Double-brooded, flying from mid-May to mid-June and again in late July and August. A local woodland species found in small numbers throughout the southern half of Britain.
Larva. July and September on maple.
Overwinters as a pupa.

Birch Mocha
Cyclophora albipunctata Hufnagel
(*pendularia* auctt.)
Plate **6** : *11–13*

Variation. Ab. *subroseata* Woodforde (fig 12) is a dark grey form occurring in varying frequency over much of the range of this species. Scottish specimens are on the whole paler and slightly larger than those from elsewhere.

Similar species. *C. pendularia*, pl. **6**, has the post-median band of the forewing curved and scalloped; termen of forewing rounded with pointed apex; and margin of hindwing distinctly angled. (See text fig 10.)
Imago. 25–29 mm. Resident. Both sexes come to light and very occasionally to sugar and flowers. Double-brooded, flying in May and June and again in August. The second generation is only partial and does not occur in Scotland. This species inhabits woodland and heathland and is found throughout England as far north as Yorkshire; in much of Wales; central and northern Scotland and the whole of Ireland.
Larva. July and September on birch.
Overwinters as a pupa.

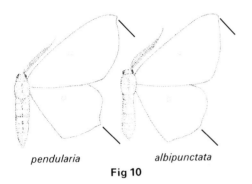

pendularia   albipunctata
Fig 10

Blair's Mocha
Cyclophora puppillaria Hübner
Plate **6** : *18–20*

Variation. Wild-caught specimens are usually dull red-brown in colour and unmarked except for the discal spots. Bred specimens, however, display a wide range of ground colour, from slate-brown to rich red-brown, and are frequently adorned with dark brown dots and cross-bands.
Similar species. Both *C. punctaria*, pl. **6**, and *C. linearia*, pl. **6**, lack the discal spot on hindwing. *C. porata*, pl. **6**, has a paler ground colour and the forewing lacks the pointed apex present in *C. puppillaria*.
Imago. 28–36 mm. Immigrant. Almost all the British specimens were taken at light, usually in August, September and especially October. First recorded in 1946, since when just over 100 specimens have been taken, mostly in southern England and occasionally inland as far as Warwickshire. The most favoured years were 1969 (25 specimens) and 1957 (14 specimens). It is possible that this species might be able to survive through a very mild winter and evidence suggests this may have happened on Tresco, Isles of Scilly, between 1956 and 1957. Not known in Ireland until 1982, when two specimens were recorded from Co. Cork. Abroad, its range includes southern Europe and North Africa.
Larva. Continuously brooded in captivity if provided with warmth and a fresh supply of tender oak leaves,

especially evergreen oak. On the Continent it has been found on *Cistus*, *Myrtus* and *Arbutus* spp.

False Mocha
Cyclophora porata Linnaeus
Plate **6** : *16–17*

Similar species. *C. punctaria*, pl. **6**, lacks the discal spots. *C. puppillaria*, pl. **6** and text.
Imago. 25–32 mm. Resident. Frequently found at dusk, also at light and occasionally sugar. Double-brooded, flying in May and June, with a partial second generation in late August and September. The species inhabits woodland and heathland, and is found locally throughout southern England, Wales, and parts of the Midlands.
Larva. July and from late September to early October on oak.
Overwinters as a pupa.

Maiden's Blush
Cyclophora punctaria Linnaeus
Plate **6** : *14–15*

Similar species. *C. porata*, pl. **6** and text. *C. puppillaria*, pl. **6** and text.
Imago. 25–32 mm. Resident. Both sexes come frequently to light. Double-brooded, flying in May and June, and again in August, inhabiting oak woodland. Generally distributed and locally common in southern England, Wales and the Midlands. Less frequent in northern England and southern Scotland. Local in Ireland, mainly in the west.
Larva. July and September on oak and perhaps occasionally birch.
Overwinters as a pupa.

Clay Triple-lines
Cyclophora linearia Hübner
Plate **6** : *22*

Similar species. *C. puppillaria*, pl. **6** and text.
Imago. 26–33 mm. Resident. Comes readily to light, with the males predominating. Mainly single-brooded, flying from late May to early July, with an occasional and partial second generation appearing at any time from mid-August to mid-October. Widespread and locally common in beech woods throughout southern England and parts of South Wales. Less frequent throughout the rest of its range which extends to Lincolnshire and Cheshire. Scarce in Ireland; from Cos Cork and Wicklow.
Larva. Mainly July and August on beech.
Overwinters as a pupa.

Blood-vein
Timandra griseata Petersen
(*amata* auctt.)
Plate **6** : *31*

Imago. 30–34 mm. Resident. Both sexes come frequently to light. Double-brooded, flying from late May to early July and again in August and September.

This species frequents a wide variety of habitats, the only requirement being an abundance of weeds. Widespread and moderately common in the southern half of England and Wales. Rather local in northern England, southern Scotland and southwest Ireland.

Larva. September to April, and during the summer on dock, sorrel, knotgrass and *Atriplex*.

Overwinters as a larva.

Lewes Wave

Scopula immorata Linnaeus

Plate **6** : *35*

Similar species. *S. marginepunctata*, pl. **6**. *Ematurga atomaria*, pl. **17**.

Imago. 25–29 mm. Formerly resident, presumed extinct. This species was easily disturbed from the undergrowth during the day and most of the British specimens were obtained in this way. Its normal flight is from dusk onwards when it is attracted to light. Single-brooded, flying from early June to mid-July. A very local species and known only from Vert Wood, East Sussex, where it inhabited a few acres of heathy ground. Extensive planting of conifers in the 1940s not only destroyed a large part of the habitat, but adversely affected the ecology of the remaining site which soon became overgrown with bracken and unsuitable for *immorata*. A few specimens were noted in 1958 and were the last to be seen in Britain, except for an unconfirmed sighting in 1961.

Larva. August to May in captivity on knotgrass and plantain.

Overwinters as a larva.

Sub-angled Wave

Scopula nigropunctata Hufnagel

Plate **6** : *32*

Similar species. The angled outer margin of the hindwing and the dark oblique fascia on both wings serve to separate this species from similar-looking 'waves'.

Imago. 29–34 mm. Resident and suspected immigrant. May be found during the day by beating; flies naturally at dusk and comes sparingly to light. Single-brooded, flying in July and early August. At present confined to Folkestone Warren, Kent, where in some years it can be locally common. Elsewhere it occurred at Hamstreet, Kent, from 1951 to 1986 and in Friston Forest, East Sussex, in 1984 and 1985. Single, probably migrant, specimens have been at Milton Street, East Sussex, on 27.vii.1970; Dungeness, Kent, on 22.vii.1980; Ninfield, East Sussex, on 17.vii.1983; Dungeness, on 30.vii.1992; Greatstone, Kent, on 14.vii.1995; Warehorne, Kent, on 16.vii.1995; Arne, Dorset, on 26.vii.1995; Dungeness on 22.vii.1996; Dymchurch, Kent, on 12.viii.1996 & 9.viii.1997; New Romney, Kent, on 12.viii. 1996 and Icklesham, East Sussex, on 7.viii.1996.

Larva. August to May in captivity on dandelion and *Clematis*.

Overwinters as a larva.

Lace Border

Scopula ornata Scopoli

Plate **6** : *42*

Imago. 23–26 mm. Resident. Frequently disturbed during the day in dry weather; flies from dusk onwards, comes sparingly to light and occasionally to sugar. Double-brooded, flying in May and June, and again from mid-July to early September. A downland species, occasionally found on railway embankments, which has apparently disappeared from many of its old haunts in southern England. It is still locally common on the North Downs of Surrey and north Kent. Even more local in Norfolk and Gloucestershire and only reported casually elsewhere.

Larva. September to April and June to July on thyme and marjoram (*Origanum vulgare*).

Overwinters as a larva.

Tawny Wave

Scopula rubiginata Hufnagel

Plate **6** : *43*

Imago. 20–23 mm. Resident and suspected immigrant. Easily put up during the day; flies from dusk onwards and comes to light. Double-brooded, flying from mid-June to mid-July, and again from mid-August to early September. As a resident confined to East Anglia where it is local, but not uncommon, in the Breck district and the coastal sandhills near Thorpeness, Suffolk. As a suspected immigrant it has been recorded this century as follows: three, Kingsgate, Kent, in 1914; Arundel, Sussex, on 18.viii. 1955; Studland, Dorset, on 7.viii.1969; Sandwich, Kent, on 9.viii.1969 and 15.viii.1980; Dungeness, Kent, on 5.viii.1981 and 31.vii.1982; Great Oakley, Essex, on 22.vii.1982; Bradwell-on-Sea, Essex, on 1.viii.1982 and 14.viii.1983; two at Kynance, Cornwall, on 22.viii.1984; Hornsey, Norfolk, on 23.vii.1989; Greatstone, Kent, on 17.viii.1989; Studland, Dorset, on 3.viii.1990; Gibraltar Point, Lincolnshire, on 1.viii.1992; Sholden, Kent, on 31.vii.1994; Burnt Lane, Guernsey, Channel Islands, on 2.viii.1994; Lydd, Kent, on 4.viii.1994; Christchurch, Hampshire, on 8.viii.1994; Portland, Dorset, on 11.viii.1994; Walberton, West Sussex, on 11.viii.1994; Dungeness on 12.viii.1994; Hethersett, Norfolk, on 26.vii.1995; Dungeness on 26.vii.1995; Greatstone on 26.vii. 1995; Stiffkey, Norfolk, on 27.vii.1995; Eastbourne, East Sussex, on 4.viii.1995; Birchington, Kent, on 31.viii.1995; and Beer, South Devon, on 18.viii.1996. The specimens occasionally found in the Norfolk Broads are either migrants or possibly wind-blown from an undiscovered colony on the nearby coastal sandhills.

Larva. September to May and July to August, feeding in captivity on dandelion and knotgrass.

Overwinters as a larva.

Mullein Wave
Scopula marginepunctata Goeze
(*conjugata* Borkhausen)
Plate **6** : *41*

Variation. Very variable in both ground colour and intensity of wing markings. Ab. *mundata* Prout has a pale, almost white, ground colour with fine cross-lines and is found in Sussex, Dorset and the Isle of Wight. Ab. *aniculosata* Rambur is a melanic form and has occurred in Scotland and southwest England.

Imago. 25–28 mm. Resident. Comes freely to light. Double-brooded, flying in June and July, and again in August and September, except in the most northerly part of its range. Found inland in the London area and the Home Counties, but mainly coastal elsewhere and occurring throughout southern England, Wales, Isle of Man and Ireland. Recorded in northern Britain from Cumbria, Yorkshire, Wigtownshire, and Ayrshire; and on the Isle of Arran, Buteshire.

Larva. September to May, and July on mugwort, yarrow, plantain, and other low plants.
Overwinters as a larva.

Small Blood-vein
Scopula imitaria Hübner
Plate **6** : *36*

Imago. 26–29 mm. Resident. May be found after dark flying or resting on the stems of grasses and weeds, and rather sparingly at light. Usually single-brooded, flying in July and August, inhabiting hedgerows, waste ground, weedy places, and coastal sandhills. In warm years a partial second generation has occurred in September and October. Widespread and frequent throughout southern England, Wales and the Midlands. Less frequent and local in northern England and the southern half of Ireland.

Larva. September to May on privet and probably a variety of low plants.
Overwinters as a larva.

Rosy Wave
Scopula emutaria Hübner
Plate **6** : *33–34*

Variation. Ground colour ranges from whitish-grey to almost white tinged with rose-pink.

Imago. 23–26 mm. Resident. Frequently found from dusk onwards resting on grass stems. Single-brooded, flying from late June throughout July, inhabiting the edges of coastal marshes and inland bogs. Locally common in southern and southeast England, and from Essex northwards to Yorkshire, and in parts of North and South Wales. Found inland on the Wareham heaths, Dorset, Whixall Moss, Shropshire, and in parts of the New Forest, Hampshire.

Larva. August to May on sea beet (*Beta maritima*) and in captivity on dandelion and knotgrass.
Overwinters as a larva.

Lesser Cream Wave
Scopula immutata Linnaeus
Plate **6** : *39*

Similar species. *S. floslactata*, pl. **6** and text.

Imago. 24–27 mm. Resident. Flies gently in damp meadows and marshes from dusk onwards and is easily netted, but is rarely seen at light May also be disturbed during the day. Single-brooded, flying from late June to early August. Widespread, but local, throughout England, Wales and Ireland.

Larva. September to May on meadowsweet and common valerian, and in captivity on groundsel, knotgrass and hawthorn.
Overwinters as a larva.

Cream Wave
Scopula floslactata floslactata Haworth
Plate **6** : *37*

Similar species. *S. immutata*, pl. **6**, has a more rounded forewing and a distinct black discal spot on both wings. *Cabera pusaria*, pl. **17**.

Imago. 29–33 mm. Resident. Frequently obtained during the day by beating the lower branches of broad-leaved deciduous trees. Comes also to light in small numbers. Single-brooded, flying in May and June, inhabiting woodland. Generally distributed and common throughout much of England, Wales and Ireland. *S. floslactata scotica* Cockayne, pl. **6** : *38*. This race is smaller, darker and usually more strongly marked than the typical form. Rather local in Scotland and recorded most frequently in the western half of the country.

Larva. July to April in captivity on dandelion, knotgrass and dock.
Overwinters as a full-grown larva.

Smoky Wave
Scopula ternata Schrank
Plate **6** : *40*

Variation. The female differs from the male by its smaller size and pointed forewing.

Similar species. *Cabera exanthemata*, pl. **17**, lacks a subterminal fascia.

Imago. 20–29 mm. Resident. Easily disturbed in the daytime and occasionally flies of its own accord in afternoon sunshine. Single-brooded, flying in June and July, inhabiting heathland and mosses. Widely distributed and locally common in Wales, the Midlands, northern England, and throughout Scotland, including the Inner Hebrides. Local and less frequent in southwest England, where Exmoor is the best-known locality.

Larva. August to May on heather and bilberry.
Overwinters as a half-grown larva.

Bright Wave
Idaea ochrata cantiata Prout
Plate **6** : *46*

Similar species. *I. serpentata*, pl. **6**, has a bright orange ground colour and a narrower forewing with finer and usually distinct cross-lines.

Imago. 21–24 mm. Resident and suspected immigrant. Rests during the day amongst low herbage or in small bushes from which it is easily disturbed. Single-brooded, flying from late June to early August, inhabiting coastal sandhills and sandy shingle beaches Very local in southeast England and found from Walmer to Sandwich, northeast Kent; near St Osyth, Essex; and between Aldeburgh and Thorpeness, Suffolk. As a suspected immigrant it has been reported as follows: near Bournemouth, Hampshire, on 19.vii.1900; Setley, Hampshire, in 1915/16; Harpenden, Hertfordshire, on 19.vii.1983; Axminster, South Devon, on 21.vii.1987; Portland, Dorset, on 15.vii.1994; and Rye Harbour, East Sussex, on 25.vii.1996.

Larva. August to May, possibly on the flowers of a variety of sandhill plants. In captivity it will accept dandelion and knotgrass and if kept warm will produce a second generation during the winter.

Overwinters as a larva.

Ochraceous Wave

Idaea serpentata Hufnagel

Plate **6** : *47*

Similar species. *I. ochrata cantiata*, pl. **6** and text.

Imago. 20–22 mm. Status unknown. Single-brooded, flying in the northern part of its European range in July. Of the few doubtfully genuine records the more acceptable are two from the Redhill area, Surrey, in 1865 and 1869, and one near Dartford, Kent, in 1909. A small colony was found on Jersey, Channel Islands, in 1941. Generally distributed throughout the rest of Europe.

Larva. *August to May on various grasses, and in captivity on dock and bedstraw.

Overwinters as a larva.

Purple-bordered Gold

Idaea muricata Hufnagel

Plate **6** : *44–45*

Variation. An almost entirely purple form f. *totarubra* Lambillion (fig 45) occurs chiefly in northern England and predominates in some localities.

Imago. 18–20 mm. Resident. Frequently put up from heather during the day. Flies naturally from dusk on-wards and is stated to fly freely around sunrise. Single-brooded, flying in late June and July, inhabiting fen-land, mosses and damp heathland. Found locally in the southern half of England, where it is well known from the New Forest, Hampshire; the heathlands of Dorset and Surrey; and the fenland of East Anglia, including the Norfolk Broads. Elsewhere it occurs locally in North and South Wales, Lincolnshire, North-East Yorkshire, and on the mosses of Shropshire, Lancashire and Westmorland. Very local in Ireland;

recorded from Cos Mayo, Galway, Offaly, Kerry and Cork.

Larva. August to May on marsh cinquefoil (*Potentilla palustris*); and in captivity on dandelion and knotgrass. Overwinters as a larva.

Least Carpet

Idaea vulpinaria atrosignaria Lempke

(*rusticata* auctt.)

Plate **6** : *48*

Imago. 19–21 mm. Resident. May be disturbed from hedges, especially elm, or found resting on fences and the upper surface of leaves. Flies naturally from dusk onwards and comes readily to light. Single-brooded, flying in July and early August, inhabiting hedgerows, gardens, scrub downland and chalk embankments. Moderately common in north Kent, South Essex, the London area, Surrey, and parts of East Sussex. In the past this species was resident on Portland, Dorset, between 1877 and 1890 and there was an unconfirmed report of its existence on the Hebridean island of St Kilda. It is possible that these colonies orginated from casual migrants, particularly as the occasional specimen continues to be reported from widely separated locali-ties along the coasts of southern England. 1991 was an especially prolific year for this species and subsequent records suggest it is established in scattered localities on the Isle of Wight and again on Portland.

Larva. August to May on ivy, traveller's-joy, *Alyssum saxatile* and probably many other plants. In captivity it will eat knotgrass and a second generation is easily obtained in the autumn.

Overwinters as a half-grown larva.

Strange Wave

Idaea laevigata Scopoli

(South, 1961, vol. 2, pl. **47**)

Imago. 19–21 mm. Suspected importation. Double-brooded on the Continent, flying in June and July, and again in September. Four larvae were discovered among coconut fibre at Durham in 1927 and reared on the shrivelled leaves of dandelion and sallow. Its range abroad includes southern and central Europe.

Larva. *July and August and from September to May mostly on dried plant material including moss.

Overwinters as a larva.

Dotted Border Wave

Idaea sylvestraria Hübner

Plate **6** : *57*

Variation. Ab. *circellata* Guenée is a deep brown form with distinct cross-lines found on the mosses of Lancashire and Cheshire. Specimens approaching this form have occurred in Kent, Hampshire and probably elsewhere.

Similar species. *I. subsericeata*, pl. **6** and text.

Imago. 20–23 mm. Resident. Occasionally put up from heather during the day. Flies naturally from dusk onwards and comes to light, usually in small numbers. Single-brooded, flying from late June to early August. Well established on heathland in Dorset, Hampshire, Surrey and Devon, with scattered colonies in Berkshire, Lincolnshire, Sussex, and from the West Midlands to Cumbria and Yorkshire.

Larva. September to May in captivity on the withered leaves of dandelion and knotgrass. A difficult larva to rear and best forced with heat from the egg stage. Overwinters as a larva.

Small Fan-footed Wave
Idaea biselata Hufnagel
Plate **6** : *54–55*

Variation. Ab. *fimbriolata* Stephens (fig 55) has a dark grey border on the outer area of both wings, intersected by a whitish irregular line; a frequent form found in many localities.

Imago. 22–25 mm. Resident. Commonly found by beating hedgerows and also at night when it comes readily to light. Usually single-brooded, flying from late June to mid-August, inhabiting woodland and hedgerows. Examples of a second generation in October have been reported on very rare occasions. Generally distributed and common throughout much of the British Isles.

Larva. August to May in captivity on knotgrass, dandelion, plantain, and bramble, preferring the withered leaves. Overwinters as a larva.

Rusty Wave
Idaea inquinata Scopoli
Plate **43** : *5*

Similar species. Superficially resembles a small brownish example of *I. contiguaria britanniae*, pl. **6**.

Imago. 16–19 mm. Suspected importation. A species normally found indoors with the ambient temperature determining the number of broods. Reported sporadically during the last half of the nineteenth century, mostly in or around the shops of central London, and probably imported in the larval stage in dried herbs or vegetable packing material. More recently it has been found to be associated with the dried flowers used in floral decoration especially *Nigella orientalis*. Its range abroad includes most of central and southern Europe, and North Africa.

Larva. *August to April on dried herbs and withered plants.

Silky Wave
Idaea dilutaria Hübner
Plate **6** : *58*

Similar species. *I. fuscovenosa*, pl. **6**, is paler and has a small, but distinct discal spot on the forewing.

Imago. 20–22 mm. Resident. Usually obtained in the daytime by gently tapping small bushes or disturbing the adjacent undergrowth. Single-brooded, flying in

July, inhabiting bushy places on limestone downland. This very local species was first noted in 1851 on Durdham Down, near Bristol; it still occurs there in small numbers, but is more easily found on the Great Orme, Caernarvonshire, where it is not uncommon. More recently a colony has been discovered on a south-facing limestone cliff on the Gower Peninsula, Glamorgan.

Larva. August to May on the withered and decaying leaves of common rock-rose. An easy species to rear in captivity; accepting dandelion and knotgrass and readily producing a second generation. Overwinters as a larva.

Dwarf Cream Wave
Idaea fuscovenosa Goeze
(*interjectaria* auctt.)
Plate **6** : *51*

Similar species. *I. dilutaria*, pl. **6** and text. *I. humiliata*, pl. **6**, has a darker and narrower forewing with a distinct reddish costa.

Imago. 19–22 mm. Resident. May be distributed from small bushes and hedgerows during the day. Flies at dusk onwards and comes to light in small numbers. Single-brooded, flying in late June and July, inhabiting a variety of weedy places. Widely distributed and moderately common in the southern half of England. Local and less frequent in the Midlands and northern England.

Larva. August to May in captivity on bramble and dandelion. Overwinters as a larva.

Isle of Wight Wave
Idaea humiliata Hufnagel
Plate **6** : *52*

Similar species. *I. fuscovenosa*, pl. **6** and text.

Imago. 19–22 mm. Resident. Flies just before dusk and again after sunrise. Single-brooded, flying in July, inhabiting grassy slopes by the sea. Its only known locality is along the chalk cliffs near Freshwater, Isle of Wight, where it was last recorded in 1931. A single specimen was reported in 1954 at Portsmouth, Hampshire.

Larva. *August to May in captivity on dandelion and dock. Overwinters as a larva.

Small Dusty Wave
Idaea seriata Schrank
Plate **6** : *49–50*

Variation. Ab. *bischoffaria* de la Harpe (fig 50) is a melanic variety which has occurred rarely in the London area and elsewhere.

Imago. 19–21 mm. Resident. Frequently obtained during the day by beating hedges or searching fences. Flies from dusk onwards and comes sparingly to light. Double-brooded, flying in late June and July, and again from mid-August to mid-September, except in northern Britain where it is single-brooded, flying in July and August. The species inhabits gardens, waste ground, hedgerows, etc, and is generally distributed throughout England, Wales and the eastern half of Scotland as far as Moray.

Larva. September to May, and during the summer on ivy, and probably various low plants.

Overwinters as a larva.

Single-dotted Wave
Idaea dimidiata Hufnagel
Plate **6** : *53*

Imago. 17–22 mm. Resident. Flies freely at dusk, comes to light and occasionally to sugar. Single-brooded, flying from late June to early August, inhabiting damp woodland, marshes, ditches and other wet places. Generally distributed throughout England, Wales and Ireland. Local in southwest Scotland.

Larva. September to May on cow parsley and burnet-saxifrage. In captivity will eat the withered leaves of dandelion.

Overwinters as a larva.

Satin Wave
Idaea subsericeata Haworth
Plate **6** : *59*

Similar species. *I. sylvestraria*, pl. **6**, is darker in colour and each wing has a small, but distinct, discal spot.

Imago. 22–25 mm. Resident. Comes to light in small numbers, but is most frequently seen at dusk when it is easily netted. Mainly single-brooded, flying in June and July, with an occasional and partial second genera-tion flying in late August and early September. The species inhabits woodland rides, downland, and other grassy places and is widely distributed and moder-ately common in the southern half of England. Rather local in the rest of Britain as far as Galloway. Locally common in Ireland, mainly in the southern half of the island.

Larva. August to May in captivity on dandelion, knotgrass and plantain.

Overwinters as a larva.

Weaver's Wave
Idaea contiguaria britanniae Müller, L.
(*eburnata* Wocke)
Plate **6** : *60*

Imago. 20–21 mm. Resident. Rests by day on rocks and stone walls, and is readily disturbed. Flies natur-ally soon after dark and comes frequently to light. Single-brooded, flying in late June and July. Very local and known only from northwest Wales, where it inhabits the heather-covered mountains and hills of Caernarvon-shire and Merionethshire.

Larva. August to May on heather, crowberry and

navelwort (*Umbilicus rupestris*). In captivity will thrive on knotgrass, dandelion and chickweed, and a second generation is easily obtained the same year.

Overwinters as a larva.

Treble Brown Spot
Idaea trigeminata Haworth
Plate **6** : *56*

Imago. 23–25 mm. Resident. Flies from dusk onwards, comes to light and occasionally to sugar. Mainly single-brooded, flying from mid-June to mid-July, with an occasional and partial second generation flying in late July and August. This species inhabits the edges of woodland, commons, downland, hedgerows, waste ground, etc, and is found locally throughout the southern half of England and parts of southeast Wales.

Larva. August to May in captivity on ivy, knotgrass and other low plants.

Overwinters as a larva.

Small Scallop
Idaea emarginata Linnaeus
Plate **6** : *61–62*

Imago. 24–27 mm. Resident. Frequently found at dusk and occasionally at light. Single-brooded, flying from late June to early August, inhabiting fenland, damp woodland, and other marshy places. Locally widespread throughout much of England and Wales as far north as Lancashire and Yorkshire.

Larva. September to May on bedstraw and probably other low plants. May be reared in captivity on dande-lion, preferring the withered leaves.

Overwinters as a very small larva.

Riband Wave
Idaea aversata Linnaeus
Plate **6** : *65–66*

Variation. The plain form, ab. *remutata* Linnaeus (fig 65), occurs as commonly as the banded typical form (fig 66).

Similar species. *I. straminata*, pl. **6**, is smaller, has a silky appearance, and the sub-terminal line is not indented towards the costa. (See text fig 11.)

Imago. 30–35 mm. Resident. Easily disturbed during the daytime from hedges and bushes. Comes to light in moderate numbers. Mainly single-brooded, flying from mid-June to mid-August, with an occasional and partial second generation occurring in southern England in September. Generally distributed and often common throughout the British Isles, including the Inner Hebrides.

Larva. September to May on a variety of low plants, such as bedstraw, chickweed and knotgrass.

Overwinters as a larva; about one-third grown.

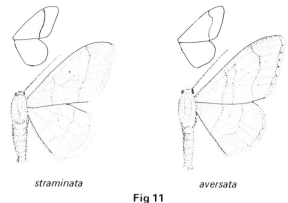

straminata   *aversata*

Fig 11

Plain Wave

Idaea straminata Borkhausen
(*inornata* Haworth)
Plate **6** : *64*

Similar species. *I. aversata*, pl. **6**.

Imago. 28–33 mm. Resident. Most frequently found flying from dusk onwards and at light. Single-brooded, flying in July, inhabiting woodland and heathland. A local and far from common species, but found in widely scattered localities throughout the British Isles.

Larva. August to May in captivity on dandelion and knotgrass.
Overwinters as a larva.

Portland Ribbon Wave

Idaea degeneraria Hübner
Plate **6** : *63*

Imago. 26–31 mm. Resident and suspected immigrant. The adult is not easily disturbed during the day and is best obtained at night, when it flies for an hour or so after dusk. Single-brooded, flying from mid-June to mid-July. The headquarters of this local species is an area of rough grassy and bushy undercliff on the Isle of Portland, Dorset. Elsewhere it has occurred near Torquay, South Devon and more recently on the Purbeck coast of Dorset. As a suspected immigrant it has been recorded at Sandown, Isle of Wight, on 5.ix.1902; Swanage, Dorset, on 17.ix.1936; Bodinnick, Cornwall, on 21.ix.1962; Brockenhurst, Hampshire, two in early October 1962; Walberton, West Sussex, on 22.ix.1981; Totton, Hampshire, on 26.viii.1990; St Agnes, Isles of Scilly, on 17.viii.1996; and Freshwater, Isle of Wight, on 11.viii.1997.

Larva. August to May in captivity on dandelion and knotgrass.
Overwinters as a half-grown larva.

The Vestal

Rhodometra sacraria Linnaeus
Plate **7** : *1–2*

Variation. Wild-caught specimens usually resemble one of the two forms figured; however, in captivity temperature experiments with the pupae will produce a wide range of dark brown and bright crimson colour forms.

Imago. 22–28 mm. Immigrant. Usually recorded at light, but in 1947 the species bred on knotgrass growing in wheat fields and during the day large numbers of adults could be disturbed from the stubble. A regular visitor in recent years to southern England with a varying number of specimens appearing almost annually. Both 1949 (*c.* 250 specimens) and 1983 (*c.* 1000 specimens) were favoured years, but the exceptional year, already referred to, was 1947 when well over 1000 specimens were reported from localities throughout the British Isles as far north as the Scottish Highlands. Abroad, the species is widely distributed in southern Europe and North Africa.

Larva. Continuously brooded in captivity on dock and knotgrass.

SUBFAMILY: LARENTIINAE

Oblique Striped

Phibalapteryx virgata Hufnagel
Plate **7** : *3–4*

Similar species. *Orthonama vittata*, pl. **7**, has a discal spot on hindwing and the outer line of forewing running to the apex. *Costaconvexa polygrammata*, pl. **7**, has the dorsal half of outer line either faint or absent. (See text fig 12.)

Imago. 22–25 mm. Resident. May be disturbed from its foodplant during the day or found at rest on fence posts, etc. Flies around sunset for an hour or so and comes sparingly to light. Double-brooded, flying in May and June, and again in August. A local species found in the Breck district of Suffolk and Norfolk; on chalk downland in Hampshire, Wiltshire, Berkshire and Sussex; and coastal sandhills in Kent, Essex, East Sussex, Hampshire, Isle of Wight, Dorset, Glamorgan, Lancashire and Yorkshire. Has occurred in Devon, Somerset and North Wales. The Irish records from Cos Down and Kerry are considered to be unreliable.

Larva. July and September on lady's bedstraw; and in captivity on other species of bedstraw.
Overwinters as a pupa.

Oblique Carpet

Orthonama vittata Borkhausen
(*lignata* Hübner)
Plate **7** : *5*

Similar species. *Phibalapteryx virgata*, pl. **7** and text. *Costaconvexa polygrammata*, pl. **7** and text.

Imago. 24–27 mm. Resident. Frequently found flying at dusk, but only sparingly at light. Double-brooded, flying in late May and June, and again in August and September, except in the north where it is only single-brooded. This species inhabits fenland and marshy places, and is locally widespread throughout much of the British Isles.

Larva. September to April, and July on various species of bedstraw, including *Galium palustre* and *G. saxatile*. Overwinters as a larva.

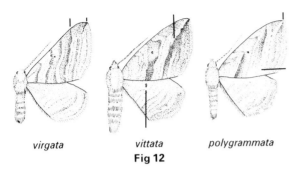

virgata *vittata* *polygrammata*

Fig 12

The Gem
Orthonama obstipata Fabricius
Plate 7 : 6–7

Imago. 18–21 mm. Immigrant. Mostly found at light. Recorded in most years in varying numbers, usually from the southern half of both England and Ireland, where it breeds in favourable summers. Abroad it has an immense range, occurring throughout Europe, Asia, Africa, and North and South America.

Larva. Continuously brooded in captivity, feeding on a variety of garden weeds such as knotgrass and groundsel.

Balsam Carpet
Xanthorhoe biriviata Borkhausen
Plate 7 : 8–9

Variation. Specimens of the second brood are darker in appearance than those of the earlier spring brood.

Imago. 27–30 mm. Resident. Flies from late afternoon until shortly after dusk. Double-brooded, flying in May and June, and again from mid-July to early September. This species inhabits lightly wooded water meadows bordering rivers and canals. Very local, but not uncommon in Middlesex, Surrey, Kent, Berkshire and North Hampshire; also recorded from Buckinghamshire, East Norfolk, Sussex and Cambridgeshire.

Larva. June and late summer on orange balsam; and in captivity on touch-me-not (*Impatiens noli-tangere*) and small balsam.
Overwinters as a pupa.

Flame Carpet
Xanthorhoe designata Hufnagel
Plate 7 : 10–11

Imago. 25–28 mm. Resident. Comes frequently to light. Double-brooded, flying in May and June, and again in August; in Scotland the second brood occurs only in favourable seasons. An inhabitant of damp woodland and hedgerows and found, not uncommonly, throughout the British Isles, including the Hebrides.

Larva. July and September in captivity on cabbage, wallflower, and other species of Cruciferae.
Overwinters as a pupa.

Red Carpet
Xanthorhoe munitata munitata Hübner
Plate 7 : 17–18

Variation. A form (fig 18) that lacks the dark red central band occurs frequently in parts of Yorkshire.

Imago. 30–34 mm. Resident. May be disturbed from rocks and stone walls during the day or netted at dusk. Single-brooded, flying from late June to mid-August, inhabiting mountain moorland and rocky hillsides. Rather local in Derbyshire, Staffordshire, Shropshire, Yorkshire and the northern half of Wales. Widespread and not uncommon in Cumbria and throughout much of Scotland, including Orkney and the Hebrides. Less frequent and local in the northern half of Ireland.

X. munitata hethlandica Prout, pl. 7 : 19. Differs from the typical race in having the ground colour of both wings ochreous and the central band a dull reddish-brown. Widespread and common throughout the Shetland Islands and, like the typical race on Orkney, inhabits a wide variety of habitats including coastal sandhills and roadside verges.

Larva. September to May on lady's-mantle (*Alchemilla* spp.) and probably other low plants. In captivity it has been reared on groundsel and chickweed.
Overwinters as a small larva.

Red Twin-spot Carpet
Xanthorhoe spadicearia Denis & Schiffermüller
Plate 7 : 14

Similar species. The red-banded form of *X. ferrugata*, pl. 7 and text.

Imago. 24–27 mm. Resident. Frequently disturbed during the day from bushes, hedges, etc; comes to light in small numbers. Double-brooded in southern England, flying from mid-May to mid-June, and again from late July throughout August. Mainly single-brooded elsewhere, flying from late May to early July. Generally common and found throughout the British Isles, including Orkney and the Inner Hebrides.

Larva. July and September on bedstraw and other low plants.
Overwinters as a pupa.

Dark-barred Twin-spot Carpet
Xanthorhoe ferrugata Clerck
Plate 7 : 15–16

Variation. Ab. *unidentaria* Haworth has a black central band and is much commoner than the typical red-banded form.

Similar species. *X. spadicearia*, pl. **7**, has the outer line of the central band usually edged with white, the inner line of the band is not notched at the costa, and in fresh specimens the central band is strongly tinged with violet.

Imago. 24–27 mm. Resident. Habits and flight times same as last species. Generally distributed throughout England, Wales and Ireland. Less frequent and rather local in Scotland including the Inner Hebrides.

Larva. July and September on unspecified low plants. In captivity will accept dock, groundsel and dandelion. Overwinters as a pupa.

Large Twin-spot Carpet
Xanthorhoe quadrifasiata Clerck
Plate **7** : *20*

Variation. A fairly frequent form has a solid black central band and is referable to ab. *thedenii* Lampa.

Imago. 29–32 mm. Resident. Most frequently seen at light in small numbers. Single-brooded, flying from mid-June throughout July, inhabiting woodland. Locally widespread in southern England, the Midlands as far north as Yorkshire, and southeast Wales.

Larva. August to May on bedstraw and other low plants, and possibly hawthorn. Overwinters as a larva about one-third-grown.

Silver-ground Carpet
Xanthorhoe montanata montanata Denis & Schiffermüller
Plate **7** : *21–22*

Imago. 29–33 mm. Resident. Readily disturbed during the day from grassy ditches, edges of woodland rides, etc. Flies freely at dusk, but is not strongly attracted to light. Single-brooded, flying from late May to mid-July, inhabiting downland, woodland rides and clearings, commons, and other damp grassy places. Generally distributed and common throughout the British Isles. *X. montanata shetlandica* Weir, pl. **7** : *23–24*. A small and variable race found throughout the Shetland Islands. Specimens similar to this race occur on Mount Brandon, Co. Kerry, and occasionally on Orkney and in northern Scotland.

Larva. August to April on bedstraw, primrose (*Primula vulgaris*), and probably many other low plants. Overwinters as a larva.

Garden Carpet
Xanthorhoe fluctuata Linnaeus
Plate **7** : *12–13*

Variation. Melanic specimens occur commonly in the Northern Isles and parts of Scotland and are referable to f. *thules* Prout (fig 13); similar forms are also found in the Midlands and the London area.

Similar species. *Epirrhoe galiata*, pl. **7**. *E. alternata*, pl. **7**.

Imago. 27–31 mm. Resident. Flies from dusk onwards, comes readily to light, and during the day may be found at rest on walls and fences. Normally double-brooded, with an occasional and partial third brood occurring in southern England. The adult often appears in every month from April to October. A common species, especially in suburban areas, and found throughout the British Isles.

Larva. June to October on perennial wall-rocket (*Diplotaxis tenuifolia*), garlic mustard (*Alliaria petiolata*) and other Cruciferae. Overwinters as a pupa.

Spanish Carpet
Scotopteryx peribolata Hübner
Plate **7** : *35*

Imago. 28–33 mm. Resident (Channel Islands) and suspected immigrant. Single-brooded, flying in late August and September. Well established on the Channel Islands and readily put up during the day from the prostrate form of broom that grows on the sea-cliffs. As a suspected immigrant it has occurred on the British mainland on seven occasions: Westward Ho, North Devon, in 1890; Fernhurst, West Sussex, on 26.viii.1951; Bishopsteignton, South Devon, on 6.ix.1962; Studland, Dorset, on 12.ix.1990, two on 29.viii.1991, three on 3.ix.1991; and Greatstone, Kent, on 6.ix.1994.

Larva. September to May probably on broom. *Also on gorse and *Genista* spp. Overwinters as a small larva.

Chalk Carpet
Scotopteryx bipunctaria cretata Prout
Plate **7** : *29*

Imago. 32–38 mm. Resident. Readily disturbed during the day and after dark comes freely to light. Single-brooded, flying in July and August, inhabiting chalk downland, embankments, and limestone hills. Widespread and common in southern England and parts of South Wales. Local in the Midlands, North Wales, Yorkshire and Co. Durham.

Larva. September to June on bird's-foot trefoil and other trefoils and clovers. Overwinters as a larva.

Shaded Broad-bar
Scotopteryx chenopodiata Linnaeus
(*limitata* Scopoli)
Plate **7** : *26–28*

Variation. Populations in northern England and Scotland contain a higher percentage of dark and melanic forms than those in the south.

Similar species. *Larentia clavaria*, pl. **7**, has a well-defined apical streak and a distinctly notched median line. (See text fig 13.)

Imago. 34–38 mm. Resident. Flies commonly from dusk onwards, visiting the flowers of ragwort, knapweed, marram, etc, but not strongly attracted to light. Single-brooded, flying in July and August, inhabiting

a wide range of habitats such as sandhills, downland, waste ground, and grassy embankments. Widespread and moderately common throughout the British Isles including Orkney and the Inner Hebrides.
Larva. September to June on vetches and clovers. Overwinters as a larva.

downland. Generally distributed and locally common over much of the British Isles.
Larva. Autumn to May on gorse and petty whin. Overwinters as a larva.

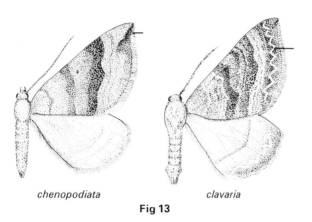

chenopodiata   clavaria

Fig 13

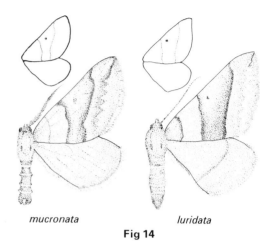

mucronata   luridata

Fig 14

Lead Belle
Scotopteryx mucronata umbrifera Heydemann
Plate **7** : *31–32*

Similar species. *S. luridata plumbaria*, pl. **7**, usually has the discal spot placed nearer the antemedian line than the post-median line (see text fig 14). In doubtful cases the only certain method of identification is to examine the genitalia.
Imago. 30–38 mm. Resident. Readily disturbed during the day from heather and gorse bushes. Single-brooded, flying from mid-May to mid-June, inhabiting mainly heathland and moorland. Locally common in southwest England and South Wales.
S. mucronata scotica Cockayne, pl. **7** : *33–34*. Generally darker than the typical race, otherwise very similar. Ab. *luridaria* Borkhausen (fig 34) is a melanic form found frequently in the Scottish populations, together with a wide range of intermediate forms. Locally common in North Wales, northern England, Isle of Man, Scotland, and Ireland.
Larva. September to March on gorse, broom, and *Genista*, feeding during mild periods throughout the winter.

July Belle
Scotopteryx luridata plumbaria Fabricius
Plate **7** : *30*
Similar species. *S. mucronata*, pl. **7** and text.
Imago. 32–38 mm. Resident. May be easily obtained during the day by beating gorse bushes. Single-brooded, flying from mid-June to early August, inhabiting heathland, moorland, commons, shingle beaches, and

Ruddy Carpet
Catarhoe rubidata Denis & Schiffermüller
Plate **7** : *36*

Imago. 26–31 mm. Resident. Flies slowly at dusk and is easily netted; also comes to light in small numbers. Single-brooded, flying in June and July, inhabiting downland, sea-cliffs, hedgerows, and bushy places. A local and on the whole uncommon species found mainly in the southern half of England and Wales.
Larva. July and August on hedge and lady's bedstraw. Overwinters as a pupa.

Royal Mantle
Catarhoe cuculata Hufnagel
Plate **7** : *37*

Imago. 26–30 mm. Resident. Flies at dusk and comes to light. Single-brooded, flying in late June and throughout July, inhabiting hedgerows, downland, sea-cliffs, breckland, etc. Locally common throughout southern England and parts of East Anglia; preferring localities on chalk or limestone. In Scotland it has been found locally in Perthshire, Fifeshire, and Angus, and in Ireland in the Burren district of Cos Clare and Galway.
Larva. July to early September on hedge and lady's bedstraw.
Overwinters as a pupa.

Small Argent and Sable
Epirrhoe tristata Linnaeus
Plate **7** : *42–43*
Similar species. *Rheumaptera hastata nigrescens*, pl. **9**.

Imago. 24–26 mm. Resident. Readily disturbed from its foodplant and frequently flies in afternoon sunshine as well as at dusk. Single-brooded, flying from late May to early July with a partial second generation appearing during August in southwest Britain and Ireland. This species inhabits mountain moorland, limestone hills, and sometimes grassy rides in conifer plantations. Locally common in southwest England, Wales, parts of the Midlands, northern England, Scotland, including Orkney and the Inner Hebrides, and from widely scattered localities in Ireland.

Larva. July and August on heath bedstraw (*Galium saxatile*). Will eat other species of bedstraw in captivity. Overwinters as a pupa.

Common Carpet
Epirrhoe alternata alternata Müller, O. F.
Plate 7 : *38*

Similar species. *E. rivata*, pl. 7, is larger and the outer white band of the forewing and the central white band of the hindwing are not bisected by a black wavy line. (See text fig 15.) *Xanthorhoe fluctuata*, pl. 7. *Euphyia unangulata*, pl. 9.

Imago. 27–30 mm. Resident. Appears in May and June with a partial second generation in August and September. Single-brooded in northern Britain, flying in June and July. Generally distributed and common throughout the British Isles including the Hebrides and Orkney.

E. alternata obscurata South, pl. 7 : *39–40*. A variable race found commonly in July in the Outer Hebrides.

Larva. June and July, and September on various species of bedstraw, including cleavers (*Galium aparine*). Overwinters as a pupa.

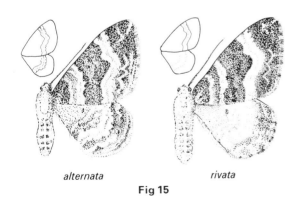

alternata   rivata

Fig 15

Wood Carpet
Epirrhoe rivata Hübner
Plate 7 : *41*

Similar species. *E. alternata*, pl. 7 and text.

Imago. 28–34 mm. Resident. Occasionally obtained by beating hedges and also at light. Single-brooded, flying from mid-June to early August, inhabiting downland, edges of woodland, sea-cliffs, and hedgebanks. Locally widespread in the southern half of Britain; very local in northern England and southern Scotland. Doubtfully recorded from Ireland.

Larva. August and September on hedge and lady's bedstraw.
Overwinters as a pupa.

Galium Carpet
Epirrhoe galiata Denis & Schiffermüller
Plate 7 : *44–45*

Variation. Specimens from coastal sandhills are distinctly ochreous and darker than the whitish forms found in chalk and limestone districts. The darkest forms of all frequent the rocky coasts of western Ireland and have jet-black bands on the forewings and dark grey hindwings.

Similar species. *Xanthorhoe fluctuata*, pl. 7.

Imago. 28–32 mm. Resident. Hides during the day low down among grasses and coarse herbage, but is easily disturbed. Very active around dusk and comes readily to light. Double-brooded in southern Britain and Ireland, flying from late May to mid-July, with a partial second generation in August. Elsewhere it is usually single-brooded, flying from June to early August. This species is found in a wide range of coastal habitats such as sandhills, shingle beaches, cliffs, rough grassy places, etc; also inland on chalk downland, limestone hills, and occasionally open moorland. Well distributed over much of England and Wales. Locally widespread and mainly coastal in Scotland and Ireland.

Larva. July to September on various species of bedstraw.
Overwinters as a pupa.

The Many-lined
Costaconvexa polygrammata Borkhausen
Plate 7 : *46*

Similar species. *Phibalapteryx virgata*, pl. 7, has both median bands well defined and complete, and a small, but distinct, black apical streak. *Orthonama vittata*, pl. 7 and text.

Imago. 25–27 mm. Extinct resident. Flies in the late afternoon and again from dusk onwards. Double-brooded, flying in April and June. Formerly found commonly in the Cambridgeshire fens, chiefly Burwell and Wicken, but not recorded here since around the middle of the last century. A specimen taken at Trinity, Jersey, Channel Islands, in late July 1984 was possibly an immigrant. The one reported from Hanworth, Middlesex, on 12.vi.1973 was recently re-examined and found to be *Costaconvexa centrostrigaria* Wollaston (The Traveller). Its distribution abroad includes Madeira and the other Atlantic Islands. [B. Goater, G.M. Haggett and M. R. Honey, *in press*]

Larva. During the summer on bedstraw.
*Overwinters as a pupa.

Yellow Shell

Camptogramma bilineata bilineata Linnaeus

Plate **7** : *47–48*

Variation. Specimens with the forewing suffused with dark brown predominate in many northern and western districts of Britain, and occur casually elsewhere.

Imago. 28–32 mm. Resident. Easily disturbed and found commonly in the daytime. Flies from dusk onwards when it may be found feeding on the flowers of ragwort, red valerian, and *Buddleia*; sometimes taken at sugar, but seldom at light. Single-brooded, flying from mid-June to mid-August, frequenting almost every conceivable type of lowland habitat. Generally distributed and common throughout the British Isles.

C. bilineata atlantica Staudinger, pl. **7** : *49–50*. A small dark race found in rocky places on Shetland. Similar forms also occur in the Outer Hebrides.

C. bilineata hibernica Tutt, pl. **7** : *51–52*. This normal-sized race has dark brown forewings and ochreous brown hindwings, inhabits sea-cliffs in western Ireland, and is found in west Co. Cork, including Dursey Island, Co. Clare and Co. Kerry. Specimens from the Inner Hebrides and parts of Orkney appear to relate more to this race than to ssp. *atlantica*.

C. bilineata isolata Kane, pl. **7** : *53*. A uniformly blackish-brown race confined to Inishvickilaun and Tearaght, the two outlying islands of the Blasket Islands, Co. Kerry.

Larva. September to May on dock, chickweed, and other low plants.

Overwinters as a larva.

Yellow-ringed Carpet

Entephria flavicinctata flavicinctata Hübner

Plate **7** : *54*

Variation. Specimens from Ireland and the Hebrides are slightly darker than those from England, but still generally conform to ssp. *flavicinctata*.

Similar species. *E. caesiata*, pl. **7** and text.

Imago. 34–39 mm. Resident. Rests by day on the surface or in the crevices of rock faces, and is readily disturbed, but not so easily secured. Flies naturally after dark, but shows little interest in light. Single-brooded in England, flying in July and early August, and found locally in the Yorkshire Dales, where its well-known locality is a limestone gorge near Grassington. Local in Herefordshire and there are unconfirmed records from North Wales, Lancashire and Derbyshire. Double-brooded in Scotland, flying in May and August, inhabiting rocky gullies and ravines by the sea. Found locally on the west coast of the mainland and on the Hebridean islands of Islay, Jura, Iona, Coll and Canna. Probably single-brooded in Ireland and found commonly at Fair Head, Co. Antrim; and also inland in Co. Fermanagh.

Larva. Autumn to spring, and, where it is double-brooded, again in June and July. Its recorded foodplants are mossy saxifrage (*Saxifraga hypnoides*) in England and Ireland; English stonecrop (*Sedum anglicum*) in western Scotland and the Hebrides.

E. flavicinctata ruficinctata Guenée, pl. **7** : *55*. A blackish-grey race inhabiting mountain ravines and occasionally old quarries. Single-brooded, flying in July and early August. Locally widespread in central and northwest Scotland.

Larva. September to early June on yellow saxifrage (*Saxifraga aizoides*), mossy saxifrage (*S. hypnoides*), purple saxifrage (*S. oppositifolia*), and occasionally roseroot (*Sedum rosea*).

All races overwinter in the larval stage.

Grey Mountain Carpet

Entephria caesiata Denis & Schiffermüller

Plate **7** : *56–57*

Variation. Very variable in the depth of the ground colour and in the extent of the blackish markings. Specimens almost totally suffused with black occur frequently on the Scottish mainland and islands.

Similar species. *E. flavicinctata*, pl. **7**, has the sub-terminal line and the central bands dusted with bright orange-yellow scales.

Imago. 32–41 mm. Resident. Rests by day on rocks, stone walls and tree-trunks, flying off at the slightest disturbance. Single-brooded, flying from late June to early August, inhabiting mountain and moorland districts. Local in South Wales and southwest Midlands. Widespread and common in North Wales, the Isle of Man, northern England, Scotland, the Hebrides, Orkney and Shetland. Widespread, but local, in Ireland.

Larva. Autumn to May on heather, heath and bilberry. In captivity it will accept sallow and knotgrass.

Overwinters as a small larva.

The Mallow

Larentia clavaria Haworth

Plate **7** : *25*

Similar species. *Scotopteryx chenopodiata*, pl. **7** and text.

Imago. 36–40 mm. Resident. Flies from dusk onwards and comes readily to light. Single-brooded, flying in September and October, inhabiting waste ground, marshes, river-banks, gardens and roadside verges. Widely distributed in England, Wales and the Isle of Man. Rather local in Ireland and southern Scotland.

Larva. April to June on common mallow, marsh-mallow, and occasionally garden hollyhock (*Alcea rosea*).

Overwinters as an egg.

Shoulder Stripe

Anticlea badiata Denis & Schiffermüller

Plate **8** : *1–2*

Imago. 31–35 mm. Resident. Most frequently seen at dusk. Single-brooded, flying in March and April, inhabiting hedgerows, open woodland, downland, and bushy places. Common and widespread in England and

Wales; local and less frequent in Scotland, including the Inner Hebrides, and Ireland.
Larva. May to July on wild rose.
Overwinters as a pupa.

The Streamer
Anticlea derivata Denis & Schiffermüller
Plate **8** : *3*

Imago. 30–34 mm. Resident. Mainly found at dusk. Single-brooded, flying in April and early May; inhabiting hedgerows, edges of woods, downland, and bushy places. Found throughout the greater part of the British Isles, being most frequent in the southern half of Britain.
Larva. June and July on the flowers and leaves of wild rose.
Overwinters as a pupa.

Beautiful Carpet
Mesoleuca albicillata Linnaeus
Plate **8** : *9*

Imago. 34–38 mm. Resident. Occasionally disturbed from trees and bushes during the daytime; also taken very sparingly at light. Single-brooded, flying in June and July, appearing early or later according to season. A woodland species found in small numbers throughout England, Wales, Ireland, and southern and western Scotland.
Larva. July to September on hazel, bramble and raspberry.
Overwinters as a pupa.

Dark Spinach
Pelurga comitata Linnaeus
Plate **8** : *10*

Imago. 33–39 mm. Resident. Frequently found at dusk or at light. Single-brooded, flying in July and August, inhabiting waste ground and other weedy places. Widespread and locally common in England, Wales, Ireland and southern Scotland.
Larva. September and October on goosefoot and orache.
Overwinters as a pupa.

Water Carpet
Lampropteryx suffumata Denis & Schiffermüller
Plate **8** : *7–8*

Variation. The melanic ab. *piceata* Stephens (fig 8) and intermediate forms occur frequently in northern England and Scotland. Ab. *porrittii* Robson has the ground colour of both wings white with the central band and basal patch blackish-brown. This variety is well known from Yorkshire, but rather uncommon elsewhere; although intermediate forms are not uncommon in many parts of the species' range.
Similar species. *L. otregiata*, pl. **8**, is smaller, has the termen of the forewing more rounded, and has a smooth whitish-grey hindwing almost devoid of markings.

Imago. 32–38 mm. Resident. Most frequently seen at dusk and is easily netted; also comes to light in small numbers. Single-brooded, flying in April and May, inhabiting woodland rides, downland, embankments, and bushy places. Widely distributed and generally common throughout much of the British Isles, as far north as Sutherland.
Larva. May and early June on various species of bedstraw.
Overwinters as a pupa.

Devon Carpet
Lampropteryx otregiata Metcalfe
Plate **8** : *6*

Similar species. *L. suffumata*, pl. **8** and text.
Imago. 27–30 mm. Resident. Rests by day on tree-trunks or in the adjacent undergrowth from which it may be disturbed; found also from dusk onwards and occasionally at light. Double-brooded, flying in May and June, and again in August and early September. An inhabitant of damp woodland and found locally in Berkshire, Sussex, Hampshire, southwest England, Gloucestershire, Herefordshire, and from the southern half of Wales northwards to Caernarvonshire. There is a single record for Derbyshire in 1984.
Larva. June to July and September to October on common marsh bedstraw (*Galium palustre*) and probably fen bedstraw (*G. uliginosum*).
Overwinters as a pupa.

Purple Bar
Cosmorhoe ocellata Linnaeus
Plate **8** : *4*

Imago. 28–30 mm. Resident. Readily disturbed from hedges and bushes; comes frequently to light. Double-brooded, except in the north, flying from late May to early July, with a partial second generation flying in late August and early September. This species occurs in a variety of habitats such as woodland, downland, sandhills, heathland, and commons, and is found commonly throughout the British Isles, including Orkney and the Hebrides.
Larva. Feeds during the summer and autumn on hedge bedstraw and other species of bedstraw.
Overwinters as a full-grown larva within an earthen cocoon in which it will pupate in the spring.

Striped Twin-spot Carpet
Nebula salicata latentaria Curtis
Plate **8** : *5*

Imago. 29–31 mm. Resident. Frequently disturbed from rocks and tree-trunks during the day, and at night is attracted to light in small numbers. Single-brooded, flying from mid-May to mid-July, but in some lowland localities it has a second generation in August and early September. Mainly a moorland species, but it also inhabits sandhills, waysides and open woodland.

Widespread and not uncommon in Ireland, Scotland, Inner and Outer Hebrides, Isle of Man, northern England and parts of North Wales. Less frequent and local in the rest of Wales and southwest England. Occasional specimens have occurred in Dorset, Sussex and Surrey, the origin of which is unknown.

Larva. Feeds during the summer and autumn on various species of bedstraw.

Overwinters as a full-grown larva within an earthen cocoon in which it will pupate in the spring.

The Phoenix
Eulithis prunata Linnaeus
Plate **8** : *11*

Imago. 37–42 mm. Resident. Mainly found at light. Single-brooded, flying in July and August, inhabiting gardens and allotments. A local species, rarely found commonly, but well distributed over the greater part of the British Isles.

Larva. April to early June on the leaves of black currant, red currant and gooseberry.

Overwinters as an egg.

The Chevron
Eulithis testata Linnaeus
Plate **8** : *12–16*

Variation. Sometimes very variable within a single locality, although as a general rule the yellowish forms predominate on sandy soils, whereas the dark varieties occur mainly on the moorlands of northern Britain.

Similar species. *E. populata*, pl. **8**, has the median lines of the forewing less acutely angled, ie, not chevron-shaped.

Imago. 34–40 mm. Resident. The male flies commonly at dusk and is easily netted. Later in the night both sexes may be found sitting on the stems of heather, grasses, or other low herbage. Single-brooded, flying in late July and August, inhabiting heathland, moorland, fenland, sandhills, open woodland, etc. Generally distributed and moderately common throughout the whole of the British Isles.

Larva. May to June on sallow, creeping willow, aspen, and birch.

Overwinters as an egg.

Northern Spinach
Eulithis populata Linnaeus
Plate **8** : *18–20*

Variation. Dark forms predominate in northern Britain, with the more extreme melanic forms occurring in the Northern Isles.

Similar species. *E. testata*, pl. **8** and text.

Imago. 33–40 mm. Resident. Occasionally disturbed during the day, but more easily found after dark sitting about on heather and bilberry. Single-brooded, flying in July and August, inhabiting open moorland. Generally distributed and locally common in southwest England,

Wales, Isle of Man, the Midlands, northern England, and the whole of Scotland including Orkney, Shetland and the Hebrides. Widely distributed throughout Ireland, except the extreme south.

Larva. April to June on bilberry.

Overwinters as an egg.

The Spinach
Eulithis mellinata Fabricius
Plate **8** : *17*

Similar species. *E. pyraliata*, pl. **8**.

Imago. 33–38 mm. Resident. Comes frequently to light. Single-brooded, flying from mid-June to early August, inhabiting gardens; and where its foodplants are present, on commons and in open woodland. Widespread and moderately common in England and Wales. Less frequent and very local in Scotland including the Inner Hebrides. Extremely rare in Ireland and found only in the Dublin area.

Larva. April to May on red currant and black currant.

Overwinters as an egg.

Barred Straw
Eulithis pyraliata Denis & Schiffermüller
Plate **8** : *21*

Similar species. *E. mellinata*, pl. **8**.

Imago. 33–38 mm. Resident. Comes frequently to light. Single-brooded, flying from mid-June to early August, inhabiting downland, commons and bushy places. Widely distributed and moderately common in England, Wales, Ireland and southern Scotland. Elsewhere in Scotland it is found mostly in the eastern half of the country, but also from Sutherland, Caithness, Argyllshire, Mull, Skye and Orkney.

Larva. April to June on various species of bedstraw, including cleavers (*Galium aparine*).

Overwinters as an egg.

Small Phoenix
Ecliptopera silaceata Denis & Schiffermüller
Plate **8** : *22*

Variation. In the typical form the dark central band of the forewing is complete, whereas in f. *insulata* Haworth (fig 22) the central band is interrupted by two white lines; both forms occur commonly.

Imago. 29–34 mm. Resident. May be disturbed from its foodplant during the day, and found after dark at light and occasionally at sugar and flowers. Mainly single-brooded, flying in May and June with a second generation occurring in southern England in late July and August. This species frequents a variety of habitats such as open woodland, downland, commons, gardens, and waste ground; and is found commonly throughout England and Wales. Widespread, but less frequent, in Ireland and Scotland, including Orkney and the Inner Hebrides. Apparently unrecorded from the Isle of Man and the Isles of Scilly.

Larva. July, and in the south in September on various species of willowherb, including rosebay and broad-leaved willowherb.
Overwinters as a pupa.

Red-green Carpet
Chloroclysta siterata Hufnagel
Plate **8** : *23–25*
Similar species. *C. miata*, pl. **8**, is larger and paler, especially the hindwing.
Imago. 30–36 mm. Resident. Comes frequently to light, and occasionally to sallow and ivy blossom. Single-brooded and found on the wing in September and October, and, after hibernation, in April and May. A woodland species found locally throughout the greater part of the British Isles, including Orkney.
Larva. June to August on oak, rowan and probably other deciduous trees.
The adults pair in the autumn and only the female moth overwinters.

Autumn Green Carpet
Chloroclysta miata Linnaeus
Plate **8** : *26*
Similar species. *C. siterata*, pl. **8** and text.
Imago. 34–40 mm. Resident. Comes to light, sallow and ivy blossom, and occasionally to sugar. Single-brooded, flying in September and October, and after hibernation, flying in March and April, inhabiting open woodland and bushy places. Widespread, but local, throughout the British Isles including Hoy, Orkney Islands.
Larva. June to August on sallow, rowan and other trees.
The adults pair in the autumn and only the female moth overwinters.

Dark Marbled Carpet
Chloroclysta citrata citrata Linnaeus
Plate **8** : *27–31*
Variation. Extremely variable throughout its range, except in the industrial areas of the Midlands and northern Britain where melanic forms tend to predominate.
Similar species. The acutly angled postmedian line of the hindwing, more obvious on the underside, serves to separate this species from *C. truncata*, pl. **8**, and *C. concinnata*, pl. **8**. (See text fig 16.)
Imago. 32–40 mm. Resident. Rests by day on tree-trunks, rocks and stone walls, and is easily disturbed. Single-brooded, flying in July and August, inhabiting moorland and woodland. Rather local in southern England, otherwise a widespread and moderately common species throughout the British Isles.
C. citrata pythonissata Millière, pl. **8** : *32*. A rather invariable race found throughout Shetland and Orkney.

Arran Carpet
Chloroclysta concinnata Stephens
Plate **8** : *40–41*
Similar species. *C. citrata*, pl. **8** and text.
Imago. 32–36 mm. Resident. Commonly found after dark sitting on heather. Single-brooded, flying in July and August, inhabiting high moorland. Locally common on the Isle of Arran, Buteshire, parts of Kintyre, and South Uist, Outer Hebrides.
Larva. September to June on heather. In captivity it will accept garden strawberry and a second generation is easily obtained.
Overwinters as a small larva.
(*Author's note:* I have followed recent check-lists and treated *C. concinnata* as a distinct species, although it is now accepted by most authorities as being only a single-brooded race of *C. truncata*.)

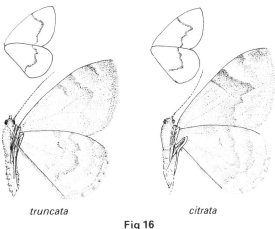

truncata   citrata

Fig 16

Common Marbled Carpet
Chloroclysta truncata Hufnagel
Plate **8** : *33–39*
Variation. The contrasting white forms are mostly found in northern Britain, and local races having similar characteristics occur in western Ireland and on the Scottish islands, otherwise this species is very variable throughout its range.
Similar species. *C. citrata*, pl. **8** and text.
Imago. 32–39 mm. Resident. Readily disturbed from trees, bushes, etc. Comes frequently to light, and sometimes to sugar, ivy blossom, and ripe blackberries. Normally double-brooded, flying in May and June, and again flying from late August to early November. Single-brooded races, appearing in July and August,

Larva. April to June on sallow, birch, bilberry and wild strawberry.
Overwinters as an egg.

occur in western Ireland and parts of Scotland. Usually these races frequent mountain moorland, but in western Scotland they may be found at lower elevations maintaining a complex relationship with the double-brooded race. This species frequents a wide range of rural and urban habitats, and occurs commonly throughout the British Isles, except Shetland where it is absent.

Larva. Autumn to May, and July and August on a variety of plants and trees such as sallow, birch, hawthorn, bilberry, bramble, privet, rose, strawberry, and dock.

Overwinters as a small larva.

Barred Yellow

Cidaria fulvata Forster

Plate **8** : *42*

Imago. 25–30 mm. Resident. Flies at dusk and comes sparingly to light. Single-brooded, flying in June and July, inhabiting downland, woodland, and bushy places. Locally widespread throughout the British Isles, including Orkney and the Inner Hebrides.

Larva. May and early June on wild rose.

Overwinters as an egg.

Blue-bordered Carpet

Plemyria rubiginata rubiginata Denis & Schiffermüller (*bicolorata* Hufnagel)

Plate **8** : *43*

Variation. Ab. *semifumosa* Cockayne (fig 45) rarely occurs in the typical race, but very frequently in ssp. *plumbata*.

Imago. 22–28 mm. Resident. Occasionally seen flying in the late afternoon, but more usually from dusk onwards, when it is attracted to light. Single-brooded, flying from late June to early August, inhabiting woodland, hedgerows, marshy places, and orchards. Widespread and locally common throughout England, Wales and Ireland.

P. rubiginata plumbata Curtis, pl. **8** : *44–45*. This race has the dark central band complete and the outer borders of both wings more heavily suffused with smoky-grey. Locally widespread in northern England and Scotland including the Inner Hebrides.

Larva. April to early June on alder, blackthorn and hawthorn, and probably birch, apple, plum and cherry. Overwinters as an egg. These are pinkish-white in colour and are deposited singly or in pairs on the twigs of alder, blackthorn, etc, usually where the stems fork, and are not too difficult to be found by the diligent searcher.

Pine Carpet

Thera firmata Hübner

Plate **8** : *52–53*

Similar species. Reddish forms of *T. obeliscata*, pl. **8** and text.

Imago. 30–34 mm. Resident. May be beaten out from its foodplant during the day; also comes readily to light.

On the wing from July to November, inhabiting pine-woods. Locally widespread over much of the British Isles.

Larva. Hatches in the autumn, feeding up the following year, sometimes not attaining full growth until September.

Overwinters as a very small larva.

Grey Pine Carpet

Thera obeliscata Hübner

Plate **8** : *48–51*

Variation. Extremely variable throughout its range with the reddish forms predominating in northern and western Britain.

Similar species. *T. firmata*, pl. **8**, has the median line deeply indented. (See text fig 17.) *T. britannica*, pl. **8**, is greyer in appearance and the forewing is variegated with whitish lines.

Imago. 28–36 mm. Resident. May be obtained, sometimes abundantly, by beating the lower branches of pine and spruce. Double-brooded, flying from late May to mid-July, and again flying in September and October. Generally distributed and common, especially in conifer plantations, throughout the British Isles, including Orkney and the Inner Hebrides.

Larva. Green with an ivory-white subspiracular stripe and pink thoracic legs. Autumn to spring, and during the summer on pine, Norway spruce, Douglas fir, and other species of conifer.

Overwinters as a larva.

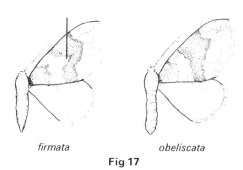

firmata   obeliscata

Fig 17

Spruce Carpet

Thera britannica Turner

(*variata* auctt.)

Plate **8** : *46–47*

Similar species. *T. obeliscata*, pl. **8** and text.

Imago. 30–36 mm. Resident. May be obtained by beating the lower branches of spruce; also comes to light. Double-brooded, flying from May to early July, and again flying in September and October. Widespread and locally common in spruce plantations over much of England and Wales. Less frequent and rather local in Scotland and Ireland.

Larva. Green with a deep yellow subspiracular stripe and usually greenish thoracic legs. Autumn to spring, and in June and July on Norway spruce, Douglas fir, and other species of *Picea*.

Overwinters as a small larva.

Chestnut-coloured Carpet
Thera cognata Thunberg
Plate **9** : *1–2*

Variation. When compared with specimens from mainland Britain, those from western Ireland are on average larger, paler, and richly tinged with violet; those from the Western and Northern Isles are darker and purplish-black in appearance, the darkest form occurring on Shetland.

Imago. 26–30 mm. Resident. Occasionally comes to light, but otherwise rarely seen as an adult and this species is best obtained in the larval stage. Single-brooded, flying in July and August, inhabiting moorland, sea-cliffs, and limestone hills. Locally widespread in central and northern Scotland, the Hebrides, and in western Ireland from Cos Clare, Galway, Sligo, Mayo, Donegal, and on Inishmore, Aran Islands. Elsewhere it is found locally in Yorkshire, Shetland, Co. Durham, Cumbria and on the Great Orme, Caernarvonshire; also recorded from Glamorgan, Pembrokeshire and Merionethshire.

Larva. September to June on juniper.

Overwinters as a small larva.

Juniper Carpet
Thera juniperata juniperata Linnaeus
Plate **9** : *3*

Similar species. *T. cupressata*, pl. **43** and text.

Imago. 26–29 mm. Resident. Usually found after dark, resting on the stems of juniper. Single-brooded from mid-October to mid-November, inhabiting chalk downland, limestone hills, and gardens. Very local in southern England and recorded mainly from Surrey, Hampshire and Berkshire. Elsewhere it is found in Caernarvonshire, Westmorland, Cumberland, and Co. Durham. Its association with cultivated foodplants probably accounts for the occasional and scattered records that have appeared in the rest of England.

T. juniperata scotica White, pl. **9** : *4*. A small (22–25 mm) and strongly marked race found locally in Scotland and the Inner Hebrides. On the wing in September and October.

T. juniperata orcadensis Cockayne. Another small race which differs from ssp. *scotica* in having the ground colour pale, the antemedian and postmedian lines blacker, and both the subterminal fascia of the fore-wing and the postmedian line of the hindwing more distinct. Recorded from Hoy, Orkney Islands, during the last century, but not recently.

T. juniperata Irish race. Specimens found in the Burren, Co. Clare, do not conform to either the English or Scottish races. They are intermediate in size (24–27 mm) and the ground colour is paler than in the typical race and in ssp. *scotica*. Similar in this aspect to ssp. *orcadensis*, but less strongly marked and larger. On the wing in September and October. Elsewhere in Ireland this species has been recorded from Connemara, Co. Galway.

Larva. From late August to late September in southern England, and from mid-July to mid-September in Scotland and Ireland, feeding on juniper and possibly cypress.

Overwinters as an egg.

Cypress Carpet
Thera cupressata Geyer
Plate **43** : *8*

Similar species. *T. juniperata*, pl. **9**, lacks the conspicuous black marks on the dorsum and the long apical streak.

Imago. 28–32 mm. Resident and suspected immigrant. Comes to light and after dark has been found resting on the foliage of its foodplants. Double-brooded, flying in late June and July, and again in October and November. Resident in the Isle of Wight, mainland Hampshire and along the Dorset coast where it is locally not uncommon. Elsewhere it has been reported from Cornwall and Surrey, and also from West Sussex, where the first specimen from England was taken in 1984. Some of these records may be the result of migration, but others could indicate the existence of undiscovered resident populations. It is well established in the Channel Islands where it was first noted in 1985.

Larva. November to May, and late July to September on Monterey cypress and the hybrid *Cupressocyparis* x *leylandii*.

Overwinters as a small larva.

Netted Carpet
Eustroma reticulatum Denis & Schiffermüller
Plate **9** : *14*

Imago. 24–28 mm. Resident. Most frequently found from dusk onwards flying in the vicinity of its foodplant. Single-brooded, flying from early July to mid-August, inhabiting the wetter parts of open or dense woodland, especially along the sides of streams. The headquarters of this very local species is the Lake District, where it is found in Westmorland (Lake Windermere, Coniston Water, and the Rusland Valley) and Cumberland (near Keswick). Elsewhere in Britain it has been reported from Merionethshire (near Bala in 1930, and near Dolgellau in 1973).

Larva. August and September on the flowers, seeds, and leaves of touch-me-not (*Impatiens noli-tangere*), and in captivity on orange balsam.

Overwinters as a pupa.

Broken-barred Carpet
Electrophaes corylata Thunberg
Plate **9** : *11–13*

Variation. Specimens from northern England and Scotland have a whiter ground colour than those from the south. Ab. *albocrenata* Curtis has the central band absent, except for an indistinct greyish outline; an uncommon form found in central and northern Scotland.
Imago. 27–31 mm. Resident. May be obtained during the day by beating hedges and bushes, or at night when it comes readily to light. Single-brooded, flying in May and June, inhabiting woodland and bushy places. Generally distributed and moderately common throughout the British Isles, but unrecorded from the Northern Isles.
Larva. July to September on birch, oak, hawthorn, blackthorn, and other trees.
Overwinters as a pupa.

Beech-green Carpet
Colostygia olivata Denis & Schiffermüller
Plate **9** : *5–6*

Variation. Specimens found in southern England, especially from coastal localities, are paler and less strongly marked than those from northern Britain. They are also on average larger in size. A particularly large form occurs in the Chilterns.
Similar species. *C. pectinataria*, pl. **9**.
Imago. 26–35 mm. Resident. Rests during the day on rocks, stone walls and the branches and trunks of trees, and is easily disturbed. Flies from dusk onwards and is attracted to light in small numbers. Single-brooded, flying in July and August, inhabiting woodland and coastal cliffs. In England it is usually found in chalk or limestone districts. Very local in southern England and most frequently recorded along the coast in Dorset and Devon; the Chiltern Hills, Oxfordshire and Buckinghamshire, and the Cotswold Hills, Gloucestershire. Widespread and not uncommon in North Wales, northern England, and much of mainland Scotland. In the Hebrides it has occurred on Mull and Rhum. Local and uncommon in the western half of Ireland.
Larva. September to May on bedstraw.
Overwinters as a larva.

Mottled Grey
Colostygia multistrigaria Haworth
Plate **9** : *8–10*

Variation. Melanic forms occur commonly in parts of the Midlands, the darkest of these being referable to ab. *nubilata* Tutt.
Imago. 26–31 mm. Resident. Usually found after dark resting on grasses and other low vegetation. Single-brooded, flying in March and April, inhabiting downland, heathland, moorland, and woodland rides and clearings. Generally distributed and locally common in England, Wales, and Scotland, including the Inner

Hebrides. Less frequent and local in the northern half of Ireland.
Larva. May to June on various species of bedstraw. Overwinters as a pupa.

Green Carpet
Colostygia pectinataria Knoch
Plate **9** : *7*

Similar species. *C. olivata*, pl. **9**.
Imago. 25–29 mm. Resident. Frequently seen flying at dusk, and also at light. Normally single-brooded, flying from late May to early July, with an occasional and partial second generation occurring in southern England. Generally distributed and common throughout the British Isles, including Orkney and the Hebrides.
Larva. August to May on various species of bedstraw. Overwinters as a larva.

July Highflyer
Hydriomena furcata Thunberg
Plate **9** : *19–30*

Variation. Extremely variable throughout its range; with the reddish forms predominating in western and northern Britain. The heather- and bilberry-feeding races are smaller in size than those associated with sallow, etc.
Similar species. *H. impluviata*, pl. **9**, lacks an apical streak and usually has a distinct discal mark or spot on the underside of the forewing. *H. ruberata*, pl. **9** and text.
Imago. 26–39 mm. Resident. Commonly found during the day by tapping hedges, bushes, and the lower branches of trees. Equally abundant from dusk onwards when it is attracted to light in moderate numbers and occasionally to flowering plants and grasses. Single-brooded, flying in July and August, inhabiting woodland, commons, bushy places, moorland, and fenland. A very common species found throughout the British Isles.
Larva. May and June on various species of sallow (including creeping willow), bilberry, heather and hazel. Overwinters as an egg.

May Highflyer
Hydriomena impluviata Denis & Schiffermüller
(*coerulata* Fabricius)
Plate **9** : *15–18*

Variation. Fig 15 represents the more typical and commoner form which predominates in rural districts throughout the southern half of Britain. Much greater variation in colour and markings is found in specimens from Scotland and western Britain. Melanic forms occur frequently in Scotland, the northern half of England and the London area.
Similar species. *H. ruberata*, pl. **9**, has a short black apical streak. *H. furcata*, pl. **9** and text.
Imago. 30–34 mm. Resident. Comes frequently to light. Single-brooded, flying from late May to early

July. Locally widespread throughout the greater part of the British Isles, its range being determined by the presence of its foodplant.

Larva. August to October on alder, concealed between spun leaves.

Overwinters as a pupa. The cocoons are frequently found under loose alder-bark.

Ruddy Highflyer

Hydriomena ruberata Freyer

Plate **9** : *31–34*

Variation. The ground colour ranges from pale grey to reddish-brown, with the forewing bands varying in both colour and intensity. A wide range of variation occurs in most districts, although it is usual for one of the forms to predominate.

Similar species. Greyish or reddish forms of *H. furcata*, pl. **9**, have the upperside of the hindwing darker, with the median fascia either faint or absent. *H. impluviata*, pl. **9** and text.

Imago. 32–37 mm. Resident. Easily disturbed from sallow bushes during the day, and also found at rest on nearby fence posts or tree-trunks. Flies commonly at dusk and is attracted to light. Single-brooded, flying in May and June, inhabiting open woodland, heathland, moorland, and marshy places. Locally widespread in North Wales, northern England, and Scotland, including the Inner Hebrides. Local and less frequent in South Wales, southwest England, and northern and western Ireland.

Larva. July to September on eared willow (*Salix aurita*), tea-leaved willow (*Salix phylicifolia*) and probably other species of *Salix*. Hides during the day between spun leaves.

Overwinters as a pupa.

Slender-striped Rufous

Coenocalpe lapidata Hübner

Plate **9** : *37–38*

Imago. 28–34 mm. Resident. In dry weather the females fly naturally during the afternoon. Both sexes, especially the males, fly from dusk onwards, but show little interest in light. Single-brooded, flying in September, inhabiting rough upland pasture and open moorland. Found locally in central and northern Scotland, the Inner Hebrides, and the northern half of Ireland.

Larva. April to early August. The natural foodplant is not known, but in captivity the larva will accept dandelion, buttercup, and traveller's-joy.

Overwinters as an egg.

Small Waved Umber

Horisme vitalbata Denis & Schiffermüller

Plate **9** : *36*

Imago. 30–35 mm. Resident. May be disturbed from its foodplant during the day; also comes to light in small numbers. Double-brooded, flying in May and June,

and again in August. An inhabitant of hedgerows and bushy places on chalky soils and found throughout southern England, East Anglia and parts of South Wales.

Larva. June to July and September to October on traveller's-joy.

Overwinters as a pupa.

The Fern

Horisme tersata Denis & Schiffermüller

Plate **9** : *35*

Imago. 31–36 mm. Resident. Occasionally disturbed from its foodplant, but more frequently taken at light. Single-brooded, flying from late June to early August, inhabiting hedgerows, edges of woodland, downland, and bushy places mainly on chalky soils. Widespread and not uncommon in the southern half of Britain.

Larva. August and September on traveller's-joy. Overwinters as a pupa.

Pretty Chalk Carpet

Melanthia procellata Denis & Schiffermüller

Plates **9** : *39* & **43** : *9*

Variation. Two melanistic forms which, although local and uncommon, do reoccur are: ab. *extrema* Schawerda, pl. **43**, in which all the white parts of the forewing are dark except for the square spot on the margin and has occurred for a number of years in the Chilgrove district, West Sussex; and ab. *nigrapicata* Cockayne, in which the white area between the costal blotch and outer margin is blackish and has been taken occasionally along the North Downs Way, near Snodland, Kent.

Imago. 35–43 mm. Resident. May be disturbed from its foodplant during the day. Flies from dusk onwards, when it is easily netted or taken at light. Single-brooded, flying from late June to early August, inhabiting hedgerows, edges of woods, and bushy places. Generally distributed and moderately common in southern Britain, ranging northwards to Lincolnshire and Caernarvonshire.

Larva. August and September on traveller's-joy. Overwinters as a pupa.

Barberry Carpet

Pareulype berberata Denis & Schiffermüller

Plate **9** : *40*

Imago. 27–32 mm. Resident and suspected immigrant. May be found after dark flying around its foodplant. Double-brooded, flying in May and early June, and again in August, inhabiting hedgerows. Extremely local and confined to single localities in West Suffolk, South Hampshire and West Gloucestershire. Elsewhere it has occurred at Blandford, Dorset, on 23.v.1926; Slapton, South Devon, on 17.vi.1959; several near Ifold, West Sussex, on 4 and 5.vi.1969; and single specimens at Faringdon, Oxfordshire, on 4.vi.1979, 19.viii.1979 and 31.v.1981. The individuals noted at Dungeness, Kent, on 17.viii.1996 and Greatstone, Kent, on 21.viii.1996 were most probably migrants.

Larva. Mid-June to mid-July, and late August and September on barberry.

Overwinters as a pupa.

White-banded Carpet
Spargania luctuata Denis & Schiffermüller
Plate **9** : *49*

Imago. 29–34 mm. Resident and suspected immigrant. Readily disturbed during the day. Flies soon after dark and is frequently taken at light. Double-brooded, flying from mid-May to mid-June, and again from mid-July to late August. A woodland species, preferring wide rides and clearings where its foodplant has been allowed to become well established. The first British specimen was noted in northwest Kent in 1924 and about the same time another was taken in Essex. No further examples were found until 1950 when one was taken at Hamstreet, Kent, and two were noted near Uckfield, Sussex. Since then the moth has become well established in several woods in southeast Kent and East Sussex. It is also found locally in West Sussex, West Norfolk and West Suffolk. A second specimen was recorded from Essex in 1974; at Usk, Monmouthshire, on 17.v.1975 and at Harpenden, Hertfordshire, on 31.v.1992.

Larva. July and September on rosebay willowherb.

Overwinters as a pupa.

Argent and Sable
Rheumaptera hastata hastata Linnaeus
Plate **9** : *42*

Imago. 34–38 mm. Resident. Flies during the day, preferring warm and sunny weather. Single-brooded, flying in May and June, inhabiting birch woodland. A local species occurring in widely scattered localities over the greater part of England, Wales and Ireland.

Larva. July and August in spun leaves of birch.

R. hastata nigrescens Prout, pl. **9** : *43*. A variable race both in size (30–36 mm) and in the extent of the black markings. Single-brooded, flying in June and early July, inhabiting boggy moorland and hillsides. Locally widespread in central, western and northern Scotland; also found in the Inner Hebrides. Specimens conforming to this race have been noted in North Wales, Yorkshire and parts of Ireland.

Larva. July to early September in the spun terminal leaves of bog myrtle. The larvae are often heavily parasitized.

Both races overwinter in the pupal stage.

Scarce Tissue
Rheumaptera cervinalis Scopoli
(*certata* Hübner)
Plate **9** : *44*

Similar species. *Triphosa dubitata*, pl. **9** and text.

Imago. 42–48 mm. Resident. Rarely noted in the adult stage, except occasionally at light. Single-brooded, flying from late April to early June, inhabiting hedgerows, bushy places, parks and gardens. Recorded from widely separated localities in England and Wales, but rarely found in numbers outside East Anglia.

Larva. June and July on barberry and cultivated species of *Berberis*.

Overwinters as a pupa.

Scallop Shell
Rheumaptera undulata Linnaeus
Plate **9** : *45*

Imago. 32–40 mm. Resident. Occasionally beaten out of sallow bushes, also comes to light. Single-brooded, flying in June and July, inhabiting woodland and marshy places. Locally widespread in England, Wales, southern Scotland and Ireland.

Larva. August to early October on sallow, aspen and bilberry.

Overwinters as a pupa.

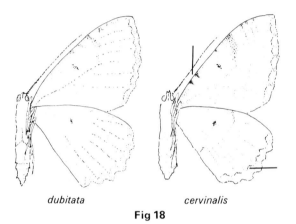

dubitata   cervinalis

Fig 18

The Tissue
Triphosa dubitata Linnaeus
Plate **9** : *41*

Similar species. *Rheumaptera cervinalis*, pl. **9**, has two dark marks on the costa on the underside of the forewing, and a dark wavy terminal line on the underside of the hindwing. (See text fig 18.)

Imago. 38–48 mm. Resident. Comes to light in small numbers and is attracted to various flowers, including sallow, ivy, ragwort, and heather. On the wing in August and early September, and after hibernation in April and May. This species inhabits chalk downland, limestone hills, woodland, heathland and bushy places. Widely distributed in England, Wales and Ireland, but rarely found commonly except in a few favoured localities.

Larva. Late May to early July on buckthorn and alder buckthorn.

Overwinters as an adult. Found in outbuildings and caves, sometimes in large numbers.

Brown Scallop

Philereme vetulata Denis & Schiffermüller

Plate **9** : *46*

Imago. 26–32 mm. Resident. Comes sparingly to light. Single-brooded, flying in July, inhabiting chalk downland, edges of woodland, and fenland. Generally distributed in the southern half of England, but absent from the southwest. Very local in South Wales and from the Midlands northwards to Yorkshire and Westmorland. In Ireland it is rare with a few larvae reported from Kenmare, Co. Kerry, in 1939 and single specimens from Crom Castle, Co. Fermanagh, and Lough Cutra, Co. Galway, in 1996.

Larva. May and early June on buckthorn.

Overwinters as an egg.

Dark Umber

Philereme transversata britannica Lempke

(*rhamnata* Denis & Schiffermüller)

Plate **9** : *47–48*

Imago. 31–40 mm. Resident. Comes to light in moderate numbers. Single-brooded, flying in July, inhabiting chalk downland, limestone hills, woodland, hedgerow, and fenland. Widespread and generally common in the southern half of England. Local and less frequent in the Midlands, northern England and South Wales. In Ireland it has been found in Co. Clare in both the larval and adult stages.

Larva. May and early June on buckthorn.

Overwinters as an egg.

Cloaked Carpet

Euphyia biangulata Haworth

(*picata* Hübner)

Plate **9** : *51*

Imago. 31–34 mm. Resident. May be disturbed from hedgerows during the day. Flies soon after dark and comes to light. Single-brooded, flying in July, inhabiting the edges of woodland and hedgerows. Very local in southern England, Wales and the Isle of Man. In recent years it is most frequently recorded from Somerset, South Devon, the Surrey/Hampshire border, Monmouthshire (Wye Valley) and southwest Wales. In Ireland it has been recorded from Cos Mayo, Wicklow, Tipperary, Cork, and Dublin.

Larva. August and September, in captivity on various species of chickweed and stitchwort.

Overwinters as a pupa.

Sharp-angled Carpet

Euphyia unangulata Haworth

Plate **9** : *50*

Similar species. *Epirrhoe alternata*, pl. **7**.

Imago. 27–30 mm. Resident. Comes frequently to light. Single-brooded, flying from late June to early August, inhabiting woodland and mature hedgerows.

Widely distributed, but rather local, in the southern half of England, Wales and Ireland.

Larva. August and September, in captivity on various species of chickweed and stitchwort.

Overwinters as a pupa.

Notes on the genus *Epirrita*:

The members of this genus are so alike that it is difficult, if not impossible, positively to identify the many forms without examining their genitalia. The one exception is *E. filigrammaria*, which is less variable and usually distinguishable by its smaller size. The other species, *E. dilutata*, *E. christyi* and *E. autumnata*, are extremely variable both in the ground colour, which ranges from whitish-grey to blackish-brown, and in the extent and intensity of the darker markings and crossbands. The range of variation, including the melanic form (illustrated on plate **11** : *3–10*), can be found in each of the three species. The shape of the post-median fascia (see text fig 19) should aid the identification of well-marked specimens, but it is of little use when this character is obscure or absent.

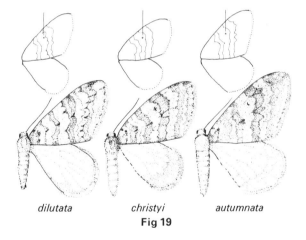

dilutata   christyi   autumnata

Fig 19

November Moth

Epirrita dilutata Denis & Schiffermüller

Plate **11** : *3–5*

Variation. Melanic forms occur commonly in the London area, the Midlands and northeast England, and in many localities constitute the total population.

Imago. 38–44 mm. Resident. Comes freely to light and is sometimes attracted to ivy blossom. Single-brooded, flying in October and November, except in northern Britain where it appears from mid-September. Widespread and generally common throughout the greater part of the British Isles.

Larva. April to June on a wide variety of trees and shrubs, such as hawthorn, oak, birch, elm, blackthorn, ash, apple, plum, and other fruit trees.

Overwinters as an egg.

Pale November Moth

Epirrita christyi Allen

Plate **11** : *6–8*

Variation. Melanic forms occur frequently in both industrial and rural districts, but rarely become dominant as in the last species.

Imago. 38–42 mm. Resident. Comes freely to light. Single-brooded, flying from late September to early November, inhabiting woodland. Widespread and locally common in England, Wales and southern Scotland. In Ireland it has been recorded from Cos Sligo, Tyrone, Fermanagh, Antrim and Kerry.

Larva. April to June on maple, blackthorn, oak, hawthorn, beech, elm, hazel, and other deciduous trees. Overwinters as an egg.

Autumnal Moth

Epirrita autumnata Borkhausen

Plate **11** : *9–10*

Variation. A little less variable than the two preceding species. Melanic forms occur regularly in the Home Counties and occasionally elsewhere.

Imago. 40–44 mm. Resident. Comes frequently to light. Single-brooded, flying in September and October, inhabiting woodland and heathland. This species appears to be widely distributed over much of the British Isles, but the lack of confirmed records makes it difficult to ascertain its true distribution.

Larva. April to June on birch and alder; also stated to feed on larch. Overwinters as an egg.

Small Autumnal Moth

Epirrita filigrammaria Herrich-Schäffer

Plate **11** : *1–2*

Imago. 30–38 mm. Resident. Found frequently after dark sitting on the stems of heather, and comes readily to light. Single-brooded, flying in August and early September, inhabiting moorland and mountain hillsides. Locally widespread in Scotland, including the Inner Hebrides, Isle of Arran, and Orkney, North and mid-Wales, the Isle of Man, and northern England as far south as Leicestershire. In Ireland it has been found in Cos Donegal, Derry, Antrim, Armagh, Fermanagh, Galway, Limerick, Down, Dublin and Wicklow.

Larva. April and May on heather and bilberry. The velvety, olive-green larva has a dark green dorsal stripe, a canary-yellow subdorsal stripe, and a pale yellow spiracular line, and is readily separable from the larvae of the other *Epirrita* species, which are very much alike. Overwinters as an egg.

Winter Moth

Operophtera brumata Linnaeus

Plate **9** : *52–53*

Similar species. *O. fagata*, pl. **9**, is larger, paler and more glossy.

Imago. Male 28–33 mm, female almost wingless. Resident. Both sexes may be found after dark sitting on the stems and trunks of trees. The male comes freely to light. Single-brooded, occurring from late autumn throughout the winter. A common to abundant species over much of the British Isles.

Larva. April to early June on most trees and shrubs; also recorded on heather and bog myrtle.

Northern Winter Moth

Operophtera fagata Scharfenberg (*boreata* Hübner)

Plate **9** : *54–55*

Similar species. *O. brumata*, pl. **9** and text.

Imago. Male 32–40 mm, female 10–12 mm. Resident. Both sexes may be found after dark sitting on tree trunks. The male frequently comes to light. Single-brooded, occurring from October to December, inhabiting woodland, commons, orchards, and heathland. Generally distributed and common in England, except the southwest. Less frequent, but widespread, in North Wales and much of mainland Scotland. Doubtfully recorded from Ireland.

Larva. April to June on birch, apple, plum, and cherry.

Barred Carpet

Perizoma taeniata Stephens

Plate **10** : *1–2*

Imago. 26–30 mm. Resident. May be disturbed during the day by beating the branches of trees and shrubs. Flies soon after dark and is attracted to the flowers of various rushes and grasses; also comes sparingly to light. Single-brooded, flying from late June to mid-August, inhabiting damp woodland. An uncommon species found locally in North Devon, Monmouthshire, North Wales, Derbyshire, Mid-west Yorkshire, Cumbria and Northumberland. In Scotland it occurs in Perthshire, Inverness-shire, Argyllshire, Dumfriesshire and Roxburghshire. In Ireland it has been recorded from Cos Kerry, Sligo, Donegal, Tyrone, Down, Mayo and Antrim.

Larva. September to May, possibly on a species of moss growing in wet places. In captivity it is said to eat the withered leaves of chickweed and other low plants. Overwinters as a small larva.

The Rivulet

Perizoma affinitata Stephens

Plate **10** : *4*

Similar species. *P. alchemillata*, pl. **10** and text.

Imago. 24–30 mm. Resident. Frequently found flying at dusk in the vicinity of its foodplant, and occasionally at light. Single-brooded, flying from late May to early July, inhabiting open woodland and roadside verges. Widely distributed in England, Wales and southern Scotland. Local elsewhere in Scotland, and in the northern half of Ireland.

Larva. July to September in the seed capsules of red campion.
Overwinters as a pupa.

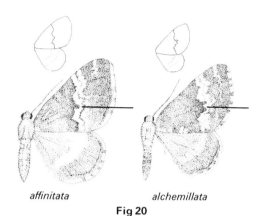

affinitata   alchemillata

Fig 20

Small Rivulet

Perizoma alchemillata Linnaeus
Plate **10** : *5*

Similar species. *P. affinitata*, pl. **10**, is larger, usually has a single (double in *P. alchemillata*) indentation halfway down the inner margin of the white central band, although this identification character is not one hundred percent reliable and should be used in conjunction with other differences, and has a more distinct whitish central band on the hindwing. (See text fig 20.)
Imago. 22–24 mm. Resident. Frequently found flying at dusk and also at light. Single-brooded, flying in June and July, inhabiting woodland, commons, marshes, waste ground, and downland. Generally distributed and moderately common throughout the British Isles, including the Hebrides and Orkney.
Larva. August and September on the flowers and seeds of hemp-nettle (*Galeopsis* spp.).
Overwinters as a pupa.

Barred Rivulet

Perizoma bifaciata Haworth
Plate **10** : *6*

Imago. 20–26 mm. Resident. Comes to light and occasionally visits flowers, such as ragwort. Single-brooded, flying in July and August, inhabiting downland, commons, rough pasture, and waste ground. Widespread and locally common in the southern half of England, Wales and northwest England. Elsewhere it is found locally in Yorkshire, northeast England, southern Scotland and Ireland.
Larva. September and October on the ripening seeds of red bartsia (*Odontites verna*) and at least on one occasion found on eyebright.

Overwinters as a pupa, sometimes remaining in this stage for up to five years.

Heath Rivulet

Perizoma minorata ericetata Stephens
Plate **10** : *10*

Imago. 18–20 mm. Resident. Flies during the afternoon and is very active in hot sunshine. Single-brooded, flying in July and August, inhabiting limestone hills, moorland and upland pasture. Widespread, but local, in Scotland. Extremely local in England (Yorkshire and Cumbria) and Ireland (Burren, Co. Clare).
Larva. September on the seeds of eyebright.
Overwinters as a pupa.

Pretty Pinion

Perizoma blandiata blandiata Denis & Schiffermüller
Plate **10** : *7*

Imago. 20–24 mm. Resident. Flies during dry weather from late afternoon to dusk. Single-brooded, flying in June and July, inhabiting moorland, limestone hills and grassy places. Widespread and not uncommon over the greater part of Scotland, including Orkney and the Hebrides. Less frequent in northern and western districts of Ireland. Very local in Cumbria and the southern half of Wales. Of unknown origin is a specimen taken near Midhurst, West Sussex, on 2.viii.1989.
P. blandiata perfasciata Prout. This race has the dark central band more or less complete, and is found in the Hebrides.
Larva. September on the flowers and seeds of eyebright.
Overwinters as a pupa.

Grass Rivulet

Perizoma albulata albulata Denis & Schiffermüller
Plate **10** : *8*

Imago. 20–26 mm. Resident. Flies during dry weather from late afternoon to early dusk. Single-brooded, flying from late May to early July, inhabiting downland, limestone hills, sandhills, shingle beaches, grassy embankments, and wet meadows. Widespread and locally common throughout the British Isles.
P. albulata subfasciaria Boheman, pl. **10** : *9*. A darker and often obscurely marked race occurring in Shetland.
Larva. July and August on the ripening seeds of yellow rattle.
Overwinters as a pupa.

Sandy Carpet

Perizoma flavofasciata Thunberg
Plate **10** : *3*

Imago. 26–32 mm. Resident. Frequently disturbed during the day. Flies naturally at dusk and occasionally comes to light. Single-brooded, flying in June and July, inhabiting open woodland, downland, commons, roadside verges, embankments, and sandhills. Generally distributed and not uncommon in England, Wales, northern

half of Ireland, and southern half of Scotland. Local in the rest of Scotland, as far north as East Sutherland.
Larva. July to early September in the seed-pods of red campion, and less frequently on white campion and bladder campion.
Overwinters as a pupa.

Twin-spot Carpet
Perizoma didymata didymata Linnaeus
Plate **10** : *11–12*

Variation. A blackish-brown form of the male occurs regularly on Mount Brandon, near Dingle, Co. Kerry, and is found occasionally in northern England and Scotland.
Imago. 24–32 mm. Resident. Both sexes rest by day on tree-trunks, rocks and stone walls; the male is easily disturbed and in dry warm weather flies of its own accord. Both sexes are found after dark, the male visiting the flowers of ragwort and various grasses, and coming to light, the less active female sitting about on heather and other herbage. Single-brooded, flying from late June to August, inhabiting woodland, moorland, mountain hill-sides, roadside verges, waste ground, etc. Generally distributed and locally common throughout the British Isles. *P. didymata hethlandica* Rebel, pl. **10** : *13*. In this race the ground colour is orange-brown in the male and ochreous-brown in the female. This race is found throughout the Shetland Islands in company with more typical forms.
Larva. April and May on a variety of low plants, such as willowherb, bilberry and sea campion.
Overwinters as an egg.

Marsh Carpet
Perizoma sagittata Fabricius
Plate **10** : *14*

Imago. 29–36 mm. Resident. Occasionally seen at dusk and at light. Single-brooded, flying in late June and July, inhabiting fenland, river banks, and other marshy places. Very local in England and confined to the counties of Huntingdonshire, Cambridgeshire, Nottinghamshire, Yorkshire and Norfolk.
Larva. August and September on the ripening seeds of common meadow-rue (*Thalictrum flavum*).
Overwinters as a pupa.

Slender Pug
Eupithecia tenuiata Hübner
Plate **10** : *15–16*

Variation. Ab. *johnsoni* Harrison (fig 16) is a melanic form found in the Midlands and northeast England.
Similar species. *E. inturbata*, pl. **10**, is paler, more ochreous, and has three dark brown patches in the terminal area of forewing. *E. haworthiata*, pl. **10**, *E. valerianata*, pl. **10**, and *E. plumbeolata*, pl. **10**, all lack a conspicuous discal spot on the forewing.
Imago. 14–16 mm. Resident. Single-brooded, flying in June and July, inhabiting damp woodland, fenland

and marshy places. Generally distributed and locally common over much of the British Isles.
Larva. March and April on the catkins of sallow.
Overwinters as an egg.

Maple Pug
Eupithecia inturbata Hübner
Plate **10** : *17*

Similar species. *E. haworthiata*, pl. **10**, is darker in appearance and the base of the abdomen is reddish-yellow. *E. tenuiata*, pl. **10** and text.
Imago. 13–15 mm. Resident. Single-brooded, flying in July and August, inhabiting woodland, downland and wherever maple is established. Well distributed over much of England and Wales.
Larva. May to early June on the flowers of field maple.
Overwinters as an egg.

Haworth's Pug
Eupithecia haworthiata Doubleday
Plate **10** : *18*

Similar species. Both *E. plumbeolata*, pl. **10**, and *E. valerianata*, pl. **10**, lack the reddish-yellow base of the abdomen. *E. tenuiata*, pl. **10** and text. *E. inturbata*, pl. **10** and text.
Imago. 12–14 mm. Resident. May be disturbed from its foodplant during the day and after dark comes freely to light. Single-brooded, flying in June and July, inhabiting open woodland and downland. Locally widespread over much of England and Wales. Generally local and scarce in Ireland, but likely to be found wherever the foodplant occurs.
Larva. July and August in the flower-buds of traveller's-joy.
Overwinters as a pupa.

Lead-coloured Pug
Eupithecia plumbeolata Haworth
Plate **10** : *19*

Similar species. *E. valerianata*, pl. **10**, is slightly smaller and has a conspicuous pale tornal spot. *E. tenuiata*, pl. **10** and text. *E. haworthiata*, pl. **10** and text.
Imago. 14–15 mm. Resident. Comes readily to light. Single-brooded, flying in late May and June, inhabiting woodland and occasionally sandhills. Locally distributed in England, Wales, southern Scotland and western Ireland.
Larva. July and August in the flowers of common cow-wheat (*Melampyrum pratense*) and occasionally yellow rattle.
Overwinters as a pupa.

Cloaked Pug
Eupithecia abietaria Goeze
(*pini* Retzius)
(*togata* Hübner)
Plate **10** : *20*

Imago. 21–25 mm. Resident and suspected immigrant. Comes sparingly to light and may be disturbed from the foliage of conifers. Single-brooded, flying in June and July, inhabiting spruce plantations. During the latter half of the nineteenth century this species was apparently well established in the New Forest, Hampshire, central Scotland and parts of Ireland. It then underwent a dramatic decline and for many years this century it went unrecorded. In 1984 it was found to be resident in North Northumberland and since then has been reported from over twenty widely separated localities in England, Wales and Scotland. Some of these records indicate the existence of resident populations, but others may well be the result of internal vagrancy or migration. Documentary evidence supporting the latter occurred in 1986 when within the space of a few weeks single specimens were reported from Kent, Sussex, Hampshire, Devon, Staffordshire, Lincolnshire and Aberdeenshire.

Larva. August and September in the cones of Norway spruce, noble fir (*Abies procera*) and silver fir (*Abies alba*). Overwinters as a pupa.

Toadflax Pug

Eupithecia linariata Denis & Schiffermüller
Plate **10** : *23*

Similar species. *E. pulchellata*, pl. **10**, is larger and has the outer line of the central band sharply angled.

Imago. 16–20 mm. Resident. Single-brooded, flying in July and August, inhabiting waste ground, roadside verges and downland. Widely distributed and locally common in England and Wales; local and less frequent in Scotland.

Larva. August and September in the flowers and seed capsules of common toadflax and occasionally the garden varieties of snapdragon (*Antirrhinum*). Overwinters as a pupa.

Foxglove Pug

Eupithecia pulchellata pulchellata Stephens
Plate **10** : *21*

Similar species. *E. linariata*, pl. **10** and text.

Imago. 18–22 mm. Resident. Single-brooded, flying from May to August, inhabiting downland, shingle beaches, woodland rides and clearings, commons, moorland, and sea-cliffs. Generally distributed and common throughout the British Isles.

E. pulchellata hebudium Sheldon, pl. **10** : *22*. A whitish-grey race found in parts of western Wales, the Hebrides, and western Ireland.

Larva. July and August in the flowers of foxglove. Overwinters as a pupa.

Marbled Pug

Eupithecia irriguata Hübner
Plate **10**: *24*

Imago. 18–20 mm. Resident. More frequently taken at light than in the larval stage. Single-brooded, flying in late April and May, inhabiting mature oak woodland. Very local in the southern half of England; recorded

most frequently from the New Forest, Hampshire, southwest Surrey, Northamptonshire, Oxfordshire and South Devon.

Larva. June and early July on the foliage of oak. Overwinters as a pupa.

Mottled Pug

Eupithecia exiguata exiguata Hübner
Plate **10** : *25*

Imago. 20–22 mm. Resident. Comes readily to light. Single-brooded, flying in May and June, inhabiting woodland and hedgerows. Generally distributed and not uncommon in England, Wales and Ireland. Very local in Scotland.

E. exiguata muricolor Prout. This race is deeper grey, and more strongly marked than the typical form and occurs locally in east Aberdeenshire. Specimens from northern England are intermediate in appearance.

Larva. Full-grown in September and October on the foliage of hawthorn, blackthorn and sycamore; and in Scotland on rowan. Overwinters as a pupa.

Pinion-spotted Pug

Eupithecia insigniata Hübner
Plate **10** : *26*

Imago. 18–22 mm. Resident. Single-brooded, flying in May, inhabiting hedgerows and bushy places. Local in the southern half of England, its range extending northwards to Yorkshire.

Larva. June to August on the leaves of hawthorn. Overwinters as a pupa.

Valerian Pug

Eupithecia valerianata Hübner
Plate **10** : *27*

Similar species. *E. tenuiata*, pl. **10** and text. *E. hawor-thiata*, pl. **10** and text. *E. plumbeolata*, pl. **10** and text.

Imago. 15–18 mm. Resident. Single-brooded, flying in June and July, inhabiting damp woodland, fenland and marshy places. Widespread, but local, in England, Wales and Scotland. In Ireland it has been reported from Cos Cavan, Galway, Clare, Cork, Donegal and Armagh.

Larva. July and August on the flowers and ripening seeds of common valerian. Overwinters as a pupa.

Marsh Pug

Eupithecia pygmaeata Hübner
(*palustraria* Doubleday)
Plate **10** : *28*

Imago. 14–16 mm. Resident. Occasionally found flying in sunshine over its foodplant. Single-brooded, flying in May and June, inhabiting fenland, coastal sandhills, waste ground, and other grassy places. A very local and rather uncommon species occurring in widely scattered localities in England from Bedfordshire, East Anglia and Warwickshire northwards to Cumbria and Yorkshire, North and South Wales, Isle of Man, Scotland including Orkney, and western and northern Ireland.

Larva. June and July on the flowers and seed capsules of field mouse-ear (*Cerastium arvense*).
Overwinters as a pupa.

Netted Pug
Eupithecia venosata venosata Fabricius
Plate **10** : *31*

Imago. 21–24 mm. Resident. Single-brooded, flying in May and June, inhabiting chalk downland, limestone hills, coastal cliffs, and rocky places by the sea. Locally widespread in England, Wales, Isle of Man and northeast Scotland.
E. venosata hebridensis W. P. Curtis. Described from Lewis, Outer Hebrides. All the Inner and Outer Hebridean specimens are more or less darker than the type and there is much variation throughout the Islands.
E. venosata fumosae Gregson, pl. **10** : *33*. A dark ochreous-brown race occurring in Shetland and Orkney.
E. venosata ochracae Gregson, pl. **10** : *32*. A pale ochreous-brown race occurring with ssp. *fumosae* in Orkney.
E. venosata plumbea Huggins, pl. **10** : *34*. A lead-grey race occurring on the western coast of Ireland. There is a record of a specimen conforming to this race from the Lizard, Cornwall.
Larva. June and July on the ripening seed-pods of bladder campion and in coastal habitats on sea campion. Overwinters as a pupa, sometimes lying over a second winter.

Pauper Pug
Eupithecia egenaria Herrich-Schäffer
Plate **10** : *30*

Variation. Specimens from Norfolk are slightly larger and more dusky than those from the Wye Valley.
Similar species. *E. lariciata*, pl. **10**, has the post-median line of the forewing sharply angulated and a small white metathoracic crest.
Imago. 21–24 mm. Resident. Occasionally disturbed during the day from its foodplant, but more often taken after dark when the males especially come readily to light. Single-brooded, flying in May and June, inhabiting woodland. Very local in Britain and known only from southwest Norfolk, near Bardney, Lincolnshire, Dorking district, Surrey, and the Wye Valley, in Monmouthshire and Gloucestershire. A single specimen was recorded from Walberton, West Sussex, on 1.vi.1987.
Larva. Late June and July on the flowers of small-leaved lime and large-leaved lime (*Tilia platyphyllos*). In captivity the larva will accept the flowers of the common hybrid lime.
Overwinters as a pupa.

Lime-speck Pug
Eupithecia centaureata Denis & Schiffermüller
Plate **10** : *29*

Imago. 20–24 mm. Resident. Comes frequently to light and flowers. Partially double-brooded and found throughout the summer and early autumn. A usually common species occurring in a wide variety of habitats and found over the greater part of the British Isles.
Larva. Summer and autumn on the flowers of many herbaceous plants.
Overwinters as a pupa.

Triple-spotted Pug
Eupithecia trisignaria Herrich-Schäffer
Plate **10** : *38–39*

Variation. Ab. *angelicata* Prout (fig 39) is a melanic form found commonly in many localities.
Imago. 15–20 mm. Resident. Single-brooded, flying in late June and July, inhabiting fenland, marshy places, woodland rides, and roadside verges. Widespread, but local, in England and Wales. Very local in southeast and southwest Scotland. In Ireland it has been reported from Cos Fermanagh, Dublin and Cork, but there are no recent records.
Larva. September on the ripening seeds of wild angelica and hogweed.
Overwinters as a pupa.

Freyer's Pug
Eupithecia intricata arceuthata Freyer
Plate **10** : *35*

Similar species. *E. pimpinellata*, pl. **10**, has a dove-grey appearance and a very distinct black discal spot.
Imago. 20–24 mm. Resident. May be disturbed from its foodplant during the day. Flies from dusk onwards and comes frequently to light. Single-brooded, flying in May and June. This race inhabits gardens and parks and is found in the southern half of England.
Larva. August to September on various species of cypress (*Cupressus* spp. and *Chamaecyparis* spp.).
E. intricata millieraria Wnukowsky, **Edinburgh Pug**, pl. **10** : *36*. More ochreous and less grey than the other two races and has less distinct cross-lines. A moorland race found in northwest England and much of Scotland.
Larva. August and September on juniper.
E. intricata hibernica Mere, **Mere's Pug**, pl. **10** : *37*. A small race distinguished from ssp. *arceuthata* and ssp. *millieraria* by its whitish-grey appearance, and by its well developed cross-lines. Very local in western Ireland and confined to the Burren, Co. Clare.
Larva. Late August and September on a prostrate form of juniper
All the races overwinter in the pupal stage.

Doubleday's Pug
Eupithecia cauchiata Duponchel

Similar species. Resembles a larger and more ochreous example of *E. satyrata*, pl. **10**.
Imago. 22–24 mm. Status unknown. Single-brooded on the Continent, flying in June and July, inhabiting

woodland rides and rocky places. The only specimen known from Britain was taken in Essex around the middle of the last century by Henry Doubleday.

Larva. *September on the leaves of goldenrod. Overwinters as a pupa.

Satyr Pug

Eupithecia satyrata satyrata Hübner

Plate **10** : *40*

Similar species. *E. vulgata*, pl. **10**, has costa of forewing arched, not straight, and has a distinct orange-brown appearance. *E. virgaureata*, pl. **10**, has costa of forewing arched, veins chequered black and brown, discal spot larger and blacker.

Imago. 21–23 mm. Resident. Single-brooded, occurring in May and June. This race inhabits open woodland, downland and fenland. Locally widespread in southern and eastern England.

E. satyrata callunaria Doubleday, pl. **10** : *41*. A variable race, browner and usually smaller than ssp. *satyrata*; and mainly associated with moorland. Rather local in Wales, the Midlands and northern England. Widespread in Scotland, the Inner Hebrides and Ireland.

E. satyrata curzoni Gregson, pl. **10** : *42*. A well-marked and banded race found commonly in Shetland. Very variable in Orkney where some of the population resembles this form, whilst the others conform to ssp. *callunaria*.

Larva. July to September on the flowers of a variety of downland and moorland plants including meadowsweet, devil's-bit scabious and knapweed. Overwinters as a pupa.

Wormwood Pug

Eupithecia absinthiata Clerck

Plate **10** : *43–44*

Similar species. *E. goossensiata*, pl. **10**, is smaller and greyer, and always associated with moorland or heathland. *E. assimilata*, pl. **10**, is shorter and broader, with a strongly arched costa, and a prominent white tornal spot. *E. expallidata*, pl. **10**, is paler and greyer with a large black discal spot on forewing and a small, but distinct, discal spot on hindwing. *E. denotata*, pl. **10** and text.

Imago. 21–23 mm. Resident. Single-brooded, flying in June and July, inhabiting woodland, gardens and waste ground. Widely distributed and generally common over much of the British Isles.

Larva. August to October on the flowers of mugwort, yarrow, ragwort, goldenrod, sea aster, and other plants. Overwinters as a pupa.

Ling Pug

Eupithecia goossensiata Mabille

Plate **10** : *45*

Similar species. *E. absinthiata*, pl. **10** and text.

Imago. 17–21 mm. Resident. Single-brooded, flying in June and July, inhabiting moorland and heathland. Widespread and locally common throughout much of the British Isles.

Larva. August and September on the flowers of heather. Overwinters as a pupa.

(*Author's note*: this species is considered by some authorities to be a moorland race of *E. absinthiata* and not specifically distinct.)

Currant Pug

Eupithecia assimilata Doubleday

Plate **10** : *46*

Similar species. *E. absinthiata*, pl. **10** and text.

Imago. 17–22 mm. Resident. Double-brooded, flying in May and June, and again in August, except in the northerly part of its range where it is single-brooded in June and July, inhabiting gardens, allotments and waste ground. Widespread and moderately common over much of the British Isles.

Larva. June and July, and September and October on wild hop, black currant and red currant. Overwinters as a pupa.

Bleached Pug

Eupithecia expallidata Doubleday

Plate **10** : *47*

Similar species. *E. absinthiata*, pl. **10** and text.

Imago. 20–24 mm. Resident. Single-brooded, flying in July and August, inhabiting woodland rides and clearings. Widespread, but local, in the southern half of England, and Wales. Very local in northwest England and southern Scotland as far north as Inverness-shire. In Ireland it has been reported from Cos Louth, Wicklow, Dublin, Westmeath and Londonderry.

Larva. September and October on the flowers of goldenrod. Overwinters as a pupa.

Common Pug

Eupithecia vulgata vulgata Haworth

Plate **10** : *50–51*

Variation. Ab. *atropicta* Dietze (fig 51) is a melanic form occurring not uncommonly in the London area and parts of northern England.

Similar species. *E. satyrata*, pl. **10** and text.

Imago. 18–21 mm. Resident. Frequently netted at dusk, and comes readily to light. Double-brooded, flying in May and June, and again in August. Generally distributed and common throughout England and Wales.

E. vulgata scotica Cockayne, pl. **10** : *52*. Paler and more strongly marked than the typical form. Widely distributed in Scotland, the Inner Hebrides and Ireland.

E. vulgata clarensis Huggins, pl. **10** : *53*. A pale whitish-brown form found on the open limestone areas of the Burren, Co. Clare. Both the races from Scotland and Ireland would appear to be single-brooded, flying in May and June.

Larva. Summer and autumn on the leaves of sallow, hawthorn, yarrow and bilberry, and the leaves and flowers of goldenrod, ragwort, and various other plants. Overwinters as a pupa.

White-spotted Pug
Eupithecia tripunctaria Herrich-Schäffer
(*albipunctata* Haworth)
Plate **10** : *48–49*

Variation. Ab. *angelicata* Barrett (fig 48) is a melanic form found in the London area, the Midlands and elsewhere.

Imago. 17–21 mm. Resident. The adult, which is taken sparingly at light, has been recorded in every month from May to September. This species inhabits woodland, river-banks, roadside verges, and marshy places. Widespread and locally common in England, Wales, the southern half of Scotland, and Ireland.

Larva. In July on the flowers of elder, and in August and September on the ripening seeds of wild angelica and wild parsnip (*Pastinaca sativa*).

Campanula Pug
Eupithecia denotata denotata Hübner
Plate **10** : *54*

Similar species. *E. absinthiata*, pl. **10**, texture of forewing smoother and more reddish in colour; costal spots more distinct.

Imago. 19–22 mm. Resident. Single-brooded, flying in July, inhabiting open woodland, downland and hedgebanks. Local, but not uncommon where found, in southern and eastern England as far north as Lincolnshire, and parts of South Wales.

Larva. August and September in the seed-heads of nettle-leaved bellflower (*Campanula trachelium*) and giant bellflower (*C. latifolia*).

E. denotata jasioneata Crewe, **Jasione Pug**, pl. **10** : *55*. A smaller and darker race than spp. *denotata* inhabiting hedgebanks and grass-covered stone walls on or near the coast. Found locally in southwest England, Wales, the Isle of Man, and in Ireland from Cos Cork, Kerry and Mayo.

Larva. August and September on the seed-heads of sheep's-bit (*Jasione montana*).
Both races overwinter in the pupal stage.

Grey Pug
Eupithecia subfuscata Haworth
(*castigata* Hübner)
Plate **10** : *56–57*

Variation. Ab. *obscurissima* Prout (fig 57). A melanic form found frequently in London and the Home Counties, the Midlands, and occasionally elsewhere.

Similar species. *E. virgaureata*, pl. **10**, frequently has a larger discal spot and chequered veins. The antenna of the male is biciliate, whereas that of *E. subfuscata* is

simple. Females are best separated by means of the genitalia.

Imago. 17–21 mm. Resident. Comes fairly frequently to light. Usually single-brooded, flying in May and June, with an occasional and partial second generation in August. Widely distributed and often common throughout most of the British Isles.

Larva. August to October on the flowers and leaves of a wide variety of trees and plants.
Overwinters as a pupa.

Tawny Speckled Pug
Eupithecia icterata subfulvata Haworth
Plate **10** : *58*

Imago. 20–24 mm. Resident. Comes frequently to the flowers of ragwort and marram, and also to light in small numbers. Single-brooded, flying in July and August, inhabiting waste ground, commons, roadside verges, sandhills, and downland. Widespread and moderately common in the British Isles, but absent from the Northern Isles.

E. icterata cognata Stephens, pl. **10** : *59–60*. A variable race, more whitish-grey than ssp. *subfulvata*, and without the reddish suffusion on the forewing. It is the predominant form in parts of Scotland and western Ireland; less frequent in northern England, Wales and southwest England.

Larva. September to October on the flowers and leaves of yarrow and sneezewort (*Achillea ptarmica*).
Overwinters as a pupa.

Bordered Pug
Eupithecia succenturiata Linnaeus
Plate **10** : *61–62*

Variation. Specimens heavily suffused with dark grey occur occasionally and refer to ab. *disparata* Hübner.

Imago. 21–24 mm. Resident. Single-brooded, flying in July and August, inhabiting commons, waste places and roadside verges. Widespread and common in the southern half of England. Less frequent in the rest of England and Wales; very local in Scotland and Ireland.

Larva. September and October on the leaves of mugwort; feeding at night and hiding during the day near the ground.
Overwinters as a pupa.

Shaded Pug
Eupithecia subumbrata Denis & Schiffermüller
Plate **10** : *63*

Imago. 16–20 mm. Resident. Frequently disturbed during the day; flies freely around dusk, but only comes to light in small numbers. Single-brooded, flying in June and early July, inhabiting salt-marshes, downland, grassy fields and banks, sea-cliffs, and fallow fields. Widespread and locally common in southern and eastern England. Less frequent and rather local elsewhere in Britain as far north as Yorkshire and Lancashire. Widespread and not uncommon in Ireland.

Larva. July to September on the flowers of field scabious, hawk's-beards, ragwort, St John's-wort, flixweed and other herbaceous plants.

Overwinters as a pupa.

Yarrow Pug

Eupithecia millefoliata Rössler

Plate **10** : *64*

Similar species. *E. subfuscata*, pl. **10**, is generally smaller and has a fuller and more rounded forewing without any trace of whitish-grey suffusion.

Imago. 19–23 mm. Resident. Single-brooded, flying in June and July, inhabiting shingle beaches, sandhills, waste ground, and roadside verges. Found locally along the coast from Dorset to Essex, and inland in Cambridgeshire and along both sides of the Thames estuary as far as the London area.

Larva. September to October on the seed-heads of yarrow.

Overwinters as a pupa.

Plain Pug

Eupithecia simpliciata Haworth

(*subnotata* Hübner)

Plate **10** : *65*

Imago. 21–23 mm. Resident. Flies from dusk onwards and is attracted to the flowers of ragwort and grasses. Single-brooded, flying from mid-June to early August, inhabiting salt-marshes, tidal river-banks and waste ground. Widely distributed and locally common over much of England, except the extreme north. Less frequent and very local in Wales and Ireland.

Larva. August and September on the ripening seed-heads of goosefoot and orache.

Overwinters as a pupa.

Goosefoot Pug

Eupithecia sinuosaria Eversmann

Plate **43** : *7*

Imago. 18–26 mm. Suspected immigrant. Abroad it is single-brooded flying from June to August inhabiting waste ground, edges of arable fields and roadside verges often near the coast. The only two British specimens, both males at light, were taken at Berrow, Somerset, on 13.vi.1992 and Harpenden, Hertfordshire, between 18 and 21.vi.1992. Its Continental range includes Scandinavia and the Netherlands.

Larva. *July to September on goosefoot and orache.

Overwinters as a pupa.

Thyme Pug

Eupithecia distinctaria constrictata Guenée

Plate **10** : *76*

Imago. 16–18 mm. Resident. Single-brooded, flying in June and July, inhabiting cliffs and rocky places by the sea, and limestone hills. Widespread, but very local, along the coasts of the Isle of Wight, Dorset, southwest England, Wales, Isle of Man, Westmorland, western Scotland, including the Hebrides, and northern and western Ireland. Inland it is found in Cumbria, the Staffordshire/Derbyshire Dales and central Scotland.

Larva. August and September on the flowers of thyme.

Overwinters as a pupa.

Ochreous Pug

Eupithecia indigata Hübner

Plate **10** : *77*

Imago. 15–18 mm. Resident. Flies actively at dusk and comes readily to light. Single-brooded, flying in April and May, inhabiting pine woodland. Locally widespread over much of mainland Britain and Ireland.

Larva. July to mid-September on the buds and young shoots of Scots pine.

Overwinters as a pupa.

Pimpinel Pug

Eupithecia pimpinellata Hübner

Plate **10** : *66*

Imago. 20–23 mm. Resident. Single-brooded, flying in June and July, inhabiting chalk downland, limestone hills, chalky embankments, and roadside verges. Locally widespread in southern and eastern England, and the Midlands as far north as Yorkshire. Uncommon in Ireland and recorded from Cos Derry, Cork, Kerry and Dublin.

Larva. Late August to early October on the ripening seed capsules of burnet-saxifrage.

Overwinters as a pupa.

Narrow-winged Pug

Eupithecia nanata angusta Prout

Plate **10** : *68–69*

Variation. Ab. *oliveri* Prout (fig 69) is a melanic form found regularly in the Midlands and occasionally elsewhere.

Imago. 17–20 mm. Resident. Readily disturbed from heather during the day. Mainly single-brooded, flying from late April to June, with a partial second brood in August in southern Britain. This species inhabits heathland and moorland, and is generally common throughout the British Isles.

Larva. July to September on the flowers of heather.

Overwinters as a pupa.

Scarce Pug

Eupithecia extensaria occidua Prout

Plate **10** : *67*

Imago. 22–25 mm. Resident. Single-brooded, flying in June and July, inhabiting the edges of coastal salt-marshes. Very local, but not uncommon where found, in north Norfolk, Lincolnshire and Southeast Yorkshire. Also recorded from a single site in Essex.

Larva. August and September on the leaves and flowers of sea wormwood.
Overwinters as a pupa.

Ash Pug
Eupithecia fraxinata Crewe
Plate **10** : *70*

Variation. Specimens of the spring brood are generally larger and darker. Ab. *unicolor* Prout is a melanic form found frequently in northern England and occasionally elsewhere.
Imago. 18–24 mm. Resident. Double-brooded, flying from late May to mid-June, and again in August. This species is found in two distinct types of habitat: in woodland and hedgerows, where the larva feeds on ash, and on coastal sandhills, where the larva feeds on sea-buckthorn. The ash-feeding race occurs, usually in small numbers, over a greater part of the British Isles. The sea-buckthorn race, which in the past has been referred to in error as *E. innotata* Hufnagel, Angle-barred Pug, occurs locally on the east and southeast coasts of England.
Larva. June and July, and again in September.
Overwinters as a pupa.

Golden-rod Pug
Eupithecia virgaureata Doubleday
Plate **10** : *71–72*

Variation. Ab. *nigra* Lempke (fig 72) is a melanic form predominating in the Midlands and occurring occasionally elsewhere.
Similar species. *E. subfuscata*, pl. **10** and text.
Imago. 17–20 mm. Resident. Double-brooded, flying in May and June, and again in August, although apparently only single-brooded in parts of Scotland where it appears in May and June. This species inhabits woodland rides and clearings, grassy hillsides, waste ground, and roadside verges. Widespread, but local, over much of the British Isles; most frequently found in western England, the Midlands, western Scotland and Ireland.
Larva. June and July, and again in September and October. A single larva on grey sallow (*Salix cinerea*) is the only record of a foodplant of the first brood larva in the wild. In captivity the larva will accept hawthorn and blackthorn. Those of the second brood are found on the flowers of goldenrod and ragwort.
Overwinters as a pupa.

Brindled Pug
Eupithecia abbreviata Stephens
Plate **10** : *73–74*

Variation. Ab. *hirschkei* Bastelberger (fig 74) is a melanic form found commonly in many parts of Britain.
Similar species. *E. dodoneata*, pl. **10**, is a smaller, paler, and more greyish in appearance; with a blacker and more distinct discal spot on the forewing.
Imago. 19–22 mm. Resident. Comes freely to light. Single-brooded, flying in April and May, inhabiting

woodland. Commonly distributed in England, Wales and Ireland. Locally widespread over much of Scotland, but absent from the extreme north and the Northern and Western Isles.
Larva. June and July on the leaves of oak and hawthorn.
Overwinters as a pupa.

Oak-tree Pug
Eupithecia dodoneata Guenée
Plate **10** : *75*

Similar species. *E. abbreviata*, pl. **10** and text.
Imago. 19–22 mm. Resident. Flies from dusk onwards along hawthorn hedges and is easily netted; also comes to light in small numbers. Single-brooded, flying in May and early June, inhabiting open woodland, hedgerows and copses. Widespread, but local, in England, Wales and Ireland.
Larva. Late June to early August on the calyx of the hips of hawthorn.
Overwinters as a pupa.

Juniper Pug
Eupithecia pusillata pusillata Denis & Schiffermüller (*sobrinata* Hübner)
Plate **10** : *78–80*

Variation. Specimens from Scotland are paler, and frequently variegated with whitish-grey. Melanic forms (fig 79) are found in northern England.
Imago. 17–21 mm. Resident. Single-brooded, flying from July to September, inhabiting chalk downland, limestone hills, gardens, and parkland. Widely distributed throughout the British Isles, occurring commonly where its foodplants are well established.
Larva. April to early June on juniper, and various species of cultivated conifers such as *Juniperus*, *Thuya* and *Chamaecyparis*.
Overwinters as an egg.
E. pusillata anglicata Herrich-Schäffer. A whitish-grey race formerly found on the coastal chalk cliffs at Dover, Kent, but not recorded since 1915 and presumed extinct. The adults were on the wing in August and September, but little else is known about the origin or life history of this distinctive race.

Cypress Pug
Eupithecia phoeniceata Rambur
Plate **10** : *81*

Imago. 18–22 mm. Resident. May be found after dark flying around its foodplant or resting openly on the foliage. Single-brooded, flying in August and September, with the occasional specimen appearing as early as May, or as late as October. Since the first British specimen was recorded from Cornwall in 1959, this species has spread along the southern coast to Kent; and inland to Surrey, the London area and Essex. It has been recorded as far north as Rugby, Warwickshire. In Ireland it is locally well established in Co. Cork.

Larva. Late autumn to early summer on the foliage of Monterey cypress; feeding throughout the winter during mild weather. In captivity it will eat Lawson's cypress and the hybrid *Cupressocyparis* x *leylandii*, and probably does so in the wild.

Channel Islands Pug
Eupithecia ultimaria Boisduval
Plate **43** : *6*

Similar species. *E. distinctaria*, pl. **10**, lacks the elongated discal spot on the forewing.
Imago. 13–17 mm. Suspected immigrant and recent colonist. So far all the adults taken in Britain have appeared at light. Single-brooded, flying from late June to early August. Occasional specimens noted in the autumn are probably the result of premature emergence and not a viable second generation. It is well established on Guernsey, Channel Islands, from where it was first reported in 1984. The first record for the English mainland was from Hertfordshire in 1988 and remains the only inland one to date. Single specimens were reported from West Sussex in 1990 and 1992, and others from West Sussex and Hampshire in 1995. The species is now known to be established in parts of the Isle of Wight and along the south coast from East Sussex to southeast Hampshire, although a wider range in the future could be reasonably predicted.
Larva. Late July and August on tamarisk (*Tamarix gallica*). As in the wild, but more so in captivity, pupae may emerge prematurely in September and October.
Overwinters as a pupa.

Larch Pug
Eupithecia lariciata Freyer
Plate **10** : *82–83*

Variation. Ab. *nigra* Prout (fig 83) is a melanic form found commonly over much of Britain.
Similar species. *E. egenaria*, pl. **10** and text.
Imago. 19–22 mm. Resident. May be dislodged from the lower branches of larch during the day; also comes freely to light. Single-brooded, flying in May and June, inhabiting larch plantations. Widely distributed and locally common throughout the British Isles, except that it is not found in the Northern Isles.
Larva. Late June to early August on larch.
Overwinters as a pupa.

Dwarf Pug
Eupithecia tantillaria Boisduval
(*pusillata* auctt.)
Plate **10** : *84*

Imago. 16–19 mm. Resident. Readily disturbed from the lower branches of spruce and fir; also comes readily to light. Single-brooded, flying in May and June, inhabiting conifer plantations, parks and gardens. Widely distributed but local throughout England, Wales and

much of Scotland. Uncommon in Ireland and reported only from Cos Armagh, Kerry, Cork and Clare.
Larva. July and August on Norway spruce and Douglas fir.
Overwinters as a pupa.

The V-Pug
Chloroclystis v-ata Haworth
(*coronata* Hübner)
Plate **10** : *85*

Similar species. The black v-shaped mark on the forewing distinguishes this species from other green-coloured pugs.
Imago. 14–19 mm. Resident. Comes frequently to light. Double-brooded in southern England, flying in May and June, and again from mid-July to mid-August; with the flight period varying each year according to season. Single-brooded in the north, flying in June and July. Widespread and not uncommon in England, except the northwest, Wales and Ireland. Less frequent and local in northwest England and southern Scotland.
Larva. Summer and autumn on the flowers of a wide variety of plants, such as hemp-agrimony, elder, bramble, traveller's-joy, goldenrod, mugwort, and wild angelica.
Overwinters as a pupa.

Sloe Pug
Chloroclystis chloerata Mabille
Plate **10** : *86*

Variation. Dark and obscurely marked specimens occur in Epping Forest, Essex, but extreme melanism as found in *C. rectangulata* is unknown in this species.
Similar species. *C. rectangulata*, pl. **10**, has the postmedian line strongly toothed near costa.
Imago. 17–19 mm. Resident. Single-brooded, flying in May and June, inhabiting hedgerows, edges of woodland and bushy places. Overlooked in Britain until 1971 when larvae were found in Surrey. Now known to be locally common in southern England; its range extending westwards to Gloucestershire, and northwards to Yorkshire and Westmorland.
Larva. Late March and April on the flowers of blackthorn.
Overwinters as an egg.

Green Pug
Chloroclystis rectangulata Linnaeus
Plate **10** : *87–88*

Variation. Ab. *anthrax* Dietze (fig 88) is one of a variety of melanic forms found commonly in London and the Home Counties, the Midlands, and northern England. In many districts these black forms make up the entire population.
Similar species. *C. chloerata*, pl. **10** and text. *C. debiliata*, pl. **10**, is paler, weakly marked, and has the postmedian line usually composed of a row of small dark dots.

Imago. 17–21 mm. Resident. Frequently found at light. Single-brooded, flying in June and July, inhabiting orchards, gardens, woodland, and commons. Generally distributed and common in England, Wales and Ireland. Widespread, but local, in Scotland.
Larva. April and May on the flowers of wild and cultivated apple, pear, cherry, and blackthorn.
Overwinters as an egg.

Bilberry Pug
Chloroclystis debiliata Hübner
Plate **10** : *89*
Similar species. *C. rectangulata*, pl. **10** and text.
Imago. 17–19 mm. Resident. Frequently found after dark flying amongst bilberry, and also at light. Single-brooded, flying in June and July, inhabiting woodland. Very local in southern and western England where it is most frequently recorded from Surrey, Hampshire, Devon and Staffordshire. In Wales it is known from Monmouthshire, Merioneth, Carmarthenshire, Pembrokeshire, Caernarvonshire and Denbighshire; and in Ireland from Cos Sligo, Galway, Wicklow, Waterford, Cork and Kerry.
Larva. April and May on the leaves of bilberry.
Overwinters as an egg.

Double-striped Pug
Gymnoscelis rufifasciata Haworth
Plate **10** : *90–91*
Variation. Both ground colour and wing markings very variable, with the brightest and most sharply defined examples occurring in western and northern Britain, and Ireland.
Imago. 15–19 mm. Resident. Frequently disturbed during the day, especially from holly, gorse and heather. Flies from dusk onwards visiting various flowers, including those of its foodplants. Comes to light in small numbers. Double-brooded, flying in April and May, and again in July and August, with an occasional and partial autumn generation occurring in southern England. In the north, including parts of Scotland, it is only single-brooded, appearing in June and July. Found commonly in a wide variety of habitats throughout the British Isles, including the Inner Hebrides.
Larva. During the summer and autumn on the flowers of holly, gorse, broom, traveller's-joy, ragwort, wild and cultivated heathers, rowan, and many other wild and garden plants.
Overwinters as a pupa.

Dentated Pug
Anticollix sparsata Treitschke
Plate **10** : *92*
Imago. 20–24 mm. Resident. Rarely found as an adult, except occasionally at light. Single-brooded, flying in June and July, inhabiting the wetter parts of woodland, shady river-banks, fenland, and other marshy places.

Locally widespread in Surrey, Hampshire, and East Anglia. Very local in Lincolnshire, Yorkshire, Staffordshire, Somerset, Berkshire, Dorset and Kent.
Larva. August and September on the leaves, and sometimes the flowers, of yellow loosestrife. Usually found on plants growing in shade.
Overwinters as a pupa.

The Streak
Chesias legatella Denis & Schiffermüller
(*spartiata* Herbst)
Plate **11** : *11–12*
Imago. 35–38 mm. Resident. Flies for a short time at dusk, and afterwards may be found sitting on the stems of broom. Single-brooded, flying in September and October, inhabiting commons, downland, heathland, moorland, and occasionally sandhills. Generally distributed and common throughout much of mainland Britain. Local and less frequent in the northern counties of Ireland.
Larva. May and June on broom, and recently found in one locality in Hampshire on tree lupin.
Overwinters as an egg.

Broom-tip
Chesias rufata rufata Fabricius
Plate **11** : *13*
Imago. 34–36 mm. Resident. Usually found after dark flying around or resting on well-established broom bushes. Single-brooded, flying from April to July, inhabiting much the same range of habitats as the last species. Locally widespread over much of England and Wales.
C. rufata scotica Richardson, pl. **11** : *14*. A bluish-grey race found mainly in central Scotland from the Forth to Moray.
Larva. July to September on broom. Frequently highly parasitized.
Overwinters as a pupa; sometimes remaining in this stage for two winters.

Manchester Treble-bar
Carsia sororiata anglica Prout
(*paludata* Thunberg)
Plate **11** : *15*
Imago. 24–30 mm. Resident. Readily disturbed during the day in warm weather. Flies actively from dusk visiting various moorland flowers. Single-brooded, flying in July and August, inhabiting damp heathland, moorland and mosses. Found locally in England from Leicestershire and Staffordshire, ranging northwards to Cumbria and Northumberland. More widespread in Scotland, including the Hebrides, Orkney and Shetland. There is a single record from the Isle of Man, and in Ireland it is found in Cos Tyrone, Galway, Westmeath and Offaly.

Larva. April to June on the flowers and leaves of bilberry, cowberry and cranberry (*Vaccinium oxycoccus*). Overwinters as an egg.

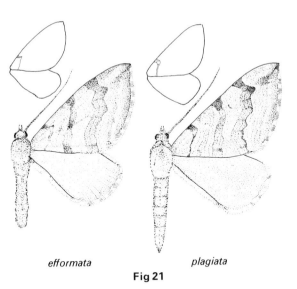

efformata　　　　*plagiata*

Fig 21

Treble-bar
Aplocera plagiata plagiata Linnaeus
Plate **II** : *16*

Similar species. *A. praeformata*, pl. **43** and text. *A. efformata*, pl. **II**, is slightly smaller, duller in appearance, and has the antemedian line acutely angled. (See text fig 21.)

Imago. 37–43 mm. Resident. Readily disturbed during the day. Comes to light in small numbers. Double-brooded in southern Britain and Ireland, flying in May and June, and again in August and September. Single-brooded in northern England and Scotland, flying in July and August. An inhabitant of downland, moorland and woodland; and found not uncommonly over the greater part of the British Isles.
A. plagiata scotica Richardson, pl. **II** : *17*. A variable race, differing from specimens found in southern Britain by its bluish-grey colouring. Specimens conforming to this race occur in central and northern Scotland, the Hebrides, and Orkney.

Larva. Autumn and spring, and in July and early August in the south, on various species of St John's-wort. Overwinters as a third-grown larva.

Lesser Treble-bar
Aplocera efformata Guenée
Plate **II** : *18*

Similar species. *A. plagiata*, pl. **II** and text. *A. praeformata*, pl. **43** and text.

Imago. 35–41 mm. Resident. Readily disturbed during the day from its foodplant and surrounding herbage. Double-brooded, flying in May and June, and again in August and September, inhabiting downland, woodland clearings, commons, and waste ground. Widespread and common in southern England; less frequent in the rest of England and Wales, but found as far north as Cumbria and Co. Durham.

Larva. Autumn to spring, and in July on various species of St John's-wort. Overwinters as a larva.

Purple Treble-bar
Aplocera praeformata Hübner
Plate **43** : *1*

Similar species. *A. plagiata*, pl. **II** and *A. efformata*, pl. **II** are both smaller and lack the wider dark band on the upper half of the antemedian fascia.

Imago. 34–44 mm. Suspected immigrant or accidental introduction. Abroad it is single-brooded, flying from June to August, inhabiting woodland clearings, meadows and gardens and is found throughout much of Europe. Only twice recorded from Britain; on the Oxfordshire/Buckinghamshire border in 1919 and at Lawrenny Park, Pembrokeshire, in 1946.

Larva. *August to June on various species of St John's-wort. Overwinters as a larva.

Chimney Sweeper
Odezia atrata Linnaeus
Plate **II** : *19*

Imago. 27–30 mm. Resident. Flies during the day, especially in sunshine. Single-brooded, flying in June and July, inhabiting chalk downland, limestone hills, and damp grassy meadows. Very local in southern England and East Anglia; widespread and not locally uncommon throughout the rest of mainland Britain and much of Ireland. Also found in the Inner Hebrides on Mull and Rhum.

Larva. April to early June on the flowers of pignut (*Conopodium majus*). Overwinters as an egg.

Grey Carpet
Lithostege griseata Denis & Schiffermüller
Plate **II** : *20*

Imago. 29–33 mm. Resident. Frequently disturbed from its foodplant during the day. Flies from dusk onwards, but is rarely attracted to light. Single-brooded, flying from late May to early July. Very local and confined to the Breck district of Norfolk and Suffolk. A single and possible immigrant example was recorded at Bradwell-on-Sea, Essex, on 15.vi.1995.

Larva. July and August on the seed-pods of flixweed and treacle mustard (*Erysimum cheiranthoides*). Overwinters as a pupa, sometimes remaining in this stage over two winters.

Blomer's Rivulet
Discoloxia blomeri Curtis
Plate **II** : *21*

Imago. 24–28 mm. Resident. Flies gently at dusk and is easily netted; also comes readily to light. Also found on tree-trunks. Single-brooded, flying from late May to early July, inhabiting woodland containing wych elm. A local species found mainly in Oxfordshire, Buckinghamshire, southwest England, North and South Wales, the Midlands, Cumbria, Yorkshire and Co. Durham.
Larva. August and September on wych elm.
Overwinters as a pupa.

Welsh Wave
Venusia cambrica Curtis
Plate **II** : *22–23*

Variation. Ab. *bradyi* Prout (fig 23) is a melanic form found frequently in Derbyshire and Yorkshire.
Similar species. *Hydrelia sylvata*, pl. **II**.
Imago. 28–31 mm. Resident. May be found during the day on the trunks of its foodplant. Comes to light in small numbers. Single-brooded, flying from late June to mid-August, inhabiting woodland and mountain moorland. Locally widespread in southwest England, Wales, the Midlands, northern England, Scotland, the Inner Hebrides and Ireland.
Larva. August and September on rowan and occasionally birch.
Overwinters as a pupa.

Dingy Shell
Euchoeca nebulata Scopoli
Plate **II** : *24*

Imago. 23–25 mm. Resident. Frequently disturbed from its foodplant during the day. Flies from dusk onwards and comes to light in small numbers. Single-brooded, flying in June and early July, inhabiting damp woodland, commons, fenland, and marshy places. Locally widespread and not uncommon over the greater part of England and Wales. In Scotland it has been reported from Aberdeenshire, Dunbartonshire and Perthshire.
Larva. July and August on alder.
Overwinters as a pupa.

Small White Wave
Asthena albulata Hufnagel
(*candidata* Denis & Schiffermüller)
Plate **II** : *25*

Similar species. The pure white colour and silky appearance of both wings and body should distinguish this species from the similar looking 'waves' figured on plate **6**.
Imago. 20–22 mm. Resident. Flies during the hour before dusk, and is therefore rarely taken at light. Normally single-brooded, flying from mid-May to early July, with an occasional and partial generation occurring in southern England during August. A woodland species found over much of England and Wales. Thinly scattered in western Scotland as far north as Wester Ross. Locally widespread in northern and western Ireland.
Larva. July and August on hazel, birch, hornbeam, and probably other trees.
Overwinters as a pupa.

Small Yellow Wave
Hydrelia flammeolaria Hufnagel
Plate **II** : *28*

Imago. 20–22 mm. Resident. Can be obtained during the day by tapping the foliage of maple and alder, and also after dark when it comes frequently to light. Single-brooded, flying in June and early July, inhabiting woodland, commons and hedgerows. Generally distributed and not uncommon in the southern half of England, the Midlands and Wales. Less frequent and local in northwest England and western Scotland, its range extending northwards to Argyllshire and Inverness-shire. A specimen taken at Killarney, Co. Kerry, in 1953 appears to be the only record from Ireland to date.
Larva. August and September on maple, and in northern districts on alder.
Overwinters as a pupa.

Waved Carpet
Hydrelia sylvata Denis & Schiffermüller
(*testaceata* Donovan)
Plate **II** : *26–27*

Variation. Ab. *goodwini* Bankes (fig 27) is a dusky brown form found locally near Maidstone, Kent, and near Arundel, Sussex.
Similar species. *Venusia cambrica*, pl. **II**.
Imago. 27–30 mm. Resident. Comes to light in small numbers. Single-brooded, flying in June and July, inhabiting woodland. A rather uncommon species found locally in southern and southwest England, Wales, northwest Midlands and Cumbria. In Ireland it is stated to have been found in Cos Sligo, Galway, Wicklow and Kerry.
Larva. July and August on alder, birch, sallow, and sweet chestnut.
Overwinters as a pupa.

Drab Looper
Minoa murinata Scopoli
Plate **II** : *29*

Imago. 18–23 mm. Resident. May be found on the wing in sunshine or disturbed from its foodplant during dull weather. Normally single-brooded, flying in May and June, with the occasional second brood specimen occurring in August. This species inhabits woodland rides and clearings and occurs locally in southern England, the southwest Midlands and southeast Wales.
Larva. July to early September on wood spurge (*Euphorbia amygdaloides*).
Overwinters as a pupa.

The Seraphim

Lobophora halterata Hufnagel

Plate **II** : *30–32*

Variation. Variable throughout its range, with both the yellowish and the more contrasting forms occurring more frequently in Scotland than elsewhere.

Imago. 29–32 mm. Resident. Rests by day on the trunks of its foodplants. Comes to light in moderate numbers. Single-brooded, flying in May and June, inhabiting woodland. Well established in the southern half of Britain and central Scotland; thinly scattered over the rest of the British Isles.

Larva. Late June and July on aspen, and occasionally other species of poplar.

Overwinters as a pupa.

Barred Tooth-striped

Trichopteryx polycommata Denis & Schiffermüller

Plate **II** : *35*

Variation. A melanic form recorded rarely in West Sussex is referable to ab. *caliginosa* Cockayne. Specimens from Cumbria and Scotland have the broad cross band of the forewing darker and thereby contrasting strongly with the paler and whiter ground colour.

Imago. 33–36 mm. Resident. May be found after dark flying around or resting upon its foodplants; also comes to light in small numbers. Single-brooded, flying from mid-March to mid-April, except in northern Britain where it appears a week or so later. This species inhabits open woodland, downland and bushy places, and occurs locally in southern England from Kent to Dorset, and northwards to Staffordshire; in Yorkshire and Cumbria; and in western Scotland from Galloway to Inverness-shire.

Larva. May and June on wild privet and ash.

Overwinters as a pupa.

Early Tooth-striped

Trichopteryx carpinata Borkhausen

Plate **II** : *36–38*

Variation. Ground colour of forewing ranges from whitish-grey to brownish-grey. Ab. *fasciata* Prout (fig 38) has blackish cross-bands, and occurs not uncommonly in Scotland and Wales.

Imago. 30–34 mm. Resident. Frequently found at rest on tree-trunks, fences, and telegraph poles; and after dark at light and sallow blossom. Single-brooded, flying in April and May. A woodland species found more or less commonly over most of the British Isles, but unrecorded from the Isle of Man, Outer Hebrides, Orkney and Shetland.

Larva. June and July on honeysuckle, sallow, birch, and alder.

Overwinters as a pupa.

Small Seraphim

Pterapherapteryx sexalata Retzius

Plate **II** : *33*

Imago. 22–26 mm. Resident. Usually found after dark flying around sallow bushes or at light. Double-brooded in southern England, flying in May and June, and again in July and early August. Single-brooded elsewhere in June and July. The species inhabits damp woodland, commons, fenland, and marshy places, and is locally widespread in southern England and East Anglia. Elsewhere it has a sporadic distribution and is found locally in North and South Wales, the Midlands, Cumbria, Perthshire, and the western half of Ireland.

Larva. June and August to September on sallow.

Overwinters as a pupa.

Yellow-barred Brindle

Acasis viretata Hübner

Plate **II** : *34*

Variation. The olive-green colour of fresh specimens is rather unstable and in wild-caught specimens has often faded to yellow.

Imago. 25–29 mm. Resident. Sometimes found on tree-trunks, but mostly noted at light. Single-brooded, flying in May and June, with a second generation occurring in southern Britain from July to early September. It inhabits woodland, hedgerows, and bushy places. Widespread, but rarely common, in the southern half of England, Wales and Ireland. Very local in north-west England and western Scotland.

Larva. June to July and in the south from September to October on the flowers and leaves of holly, ivy, wild privet, dogwood and guelder-rose (*Viburnum opulus*).

Overwinters as a pupa.

SUBFAMILY: ENNOMINAE

The Magpie

Abraxas grossulariata Linnaeus

Plate **II** : *40–43*

Variation. A wide range of variation is possible and the aberrant specimens illustrated (figs 41–43) are but three of the many named forms. Most of these are genetically recessive and are obtained in captivity by selective breeding from minor aberrant parents; they are rarely found in the wild.

Imago. 42–48 mm. Resident. Comes freely to light. Single-brooded, flying in July and August, inhabiting woodland, commons, gardens, hedgerows, sandhills, etc. Generally distributed and common in England, Wales and Ireland. Widespread, but less frequent, in Scotland, including the Hebrides.

Larva. September to early June on currant, gooseberry, blackthorn, hawthorn, hazel, *Euonymus* spp., and other plants and shrubs. In the Hebrides it is stated to feed on heather.

Overwinters as a small larva.

Clouded Magpie

Abraxas sylvata Scopoli

Plate **II** : *39*

Variation. Specimens with either the forewing or both wings suffused with dark grey have occurred in Yorkshire and elsewhere.

Imago. 38–48 mm. Resident and a suspected occasional immigrant. Occasionally found during the day sitting on the upper surface of the leaves of woodland plants, but most frequently taken at light. Single-brooded, flying from late May to July, inhabiting woodland and parkland. Widespread, but local, over much of Britain; its range extending to Dumfriesshire. In Ireland it is well established in Co. Kerry, and also recorded from Cos Down, Carlow, Antrim, Tyrone and Wicklow.

Larva. August to October on wych elm and English elm.

Overwinters as a pupa.

Clouded Border

Lomaspilis marginata Linnaeus

Plate **12** : *1–2*

Variation. Very variable in the extent of the black markings. Extreme aberrations in which the wings are either entirely white or black have occurred, but are very rare.

Imago. 24–28 mm. Resident. Occasionally disturbed during the day, but most frequently seen at light. Single-brooded, flying in June and July, inhabiting woodland, commons, heathland, fenland, and marshy places. Generally distributed and moderately common in England, Wales and Ireland. Locally widespread over much of Scotland, including the Hebrides.

Larva. August and September on sallow and aspen; also occasionally found on poplar and hazel.

Overwinters as a pupa. Sometimes remaining in this stage over two to four winters.

Scorched Carpet

Ligdia adustata Denis & Schiffermüller

Plate **12** : *3*

Imago. 25–30 mm. Resident. Flies freely at dusk, also comes to light in small numbers. In southern England it is double-brooded, flying in May and June, and again in August, earlier or later according to season. In the north it is single-brooded, flying in June. This species inhabits woodland, hedgerows and bushy places. Widespread and not uncommon in the southern half of both England and Wales. Local and less frequent in the rest of Wales, northwest England and Ireland. Extremely local in the Midlands and northeast England.

Larva. Mid-June to July, and late August to September on spindle (*Euonymus europaeus*).

Overwinters as a pupa.

Dorset Cream Wave

Stegania trimaculata de Villers

Similar species. Not unlike a small example of *Lomographa bimaculata*, pl. **17**, except that in *S. trimaculata* the ground colour is creamy yellow and the postmedian

line of the forewing is sharply angled towards the costa.

Imago. 26–28 mm. Suspected immigrant. Double-brooded on the Continent, flying in April and May, and again in August. The only British specimen was attracted to light at Stoborough, Dorset, on 13/14.vi.1978. Abroad the species is widespread in southern Europe.

Larva. *June and September on various species of poplar.

Overwinters as a pupa.

Peacock Moth

Semiothisa notata Linnaeus

Plate **12** : *7*

Similar species. *S. alternaria*, pl. **12**. (See text fig 22.)

Imago. 28–32 mm. Resident. Comes to light in small numbers. Single-brooded, flying in late May and June, except in southern England where a second generation occurs in August. A woodland species found locally in southern England, East Anglia, Wales, west Midlands, Yorkshire, and central and western Scotland, including the Inner Hebrides. In Ireland it is found in Cos Kerry and Cork.

Larva. July, and in the south during September usually on birch.

Overwinters as a pupa.

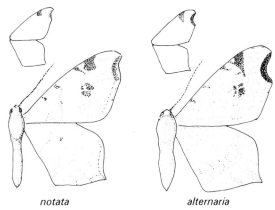

notata   alternaria

Fig 22

Sharp-angled Peacock

Semiothisa alternaria Hübner

Plate **12** : *8*

Similar species. *S. notata*, pl. **12**. (See text fig 22.)

Imago. 27–32 mm. Resident. Comes to light in small numbers. Double-brooded, flying in late May and June, and as a partial generation flying in August, inhabiting woodland and sandhills. Locally widespread in southern England from Kent to Cornwall, and in South Wales from Monmouthshire to Pembrokeshire. Elsewhere it has been recorded from Essex, Norfolk, Suffolk, Yorkshire and Westmorland. In Ireland it was found in Co. Wexford in July 1969.

Larva. July and September on sallow, blackthorn, alder, and sea-buckthorn.
Overwinters as a pupa.

Dusky Peacock
Semiothisa signaria Hübner
Plate **12** : *9*

Similar species. *S. liturata*, pl. **12**, has the sub-terminal band reddish-orange without a dark square-shaped blotch. *S. notata*, pl. **12**, has the termen of the forewing notched.

Imago. 30–32 mm. Suspected immigrant. On the Continent it can be obtained during the day by beating the lower branches of its foodplants from late May to mid-July. All the thirteen British specimens to date have been taken at light. These are at: Danbury, Essex, on 20.vi.1970; Hamstreet, Kent, on 31.vii.1984; Worthing, West Sussex, on 28.vi.1986; Steyning, West Sussex, on 3.vii.1986, two at Hamstreet on 15.vii.1986; St Osyth, Essex, on 6.vii.1991; Strumpshaw, Norfolk, on 7.vii.1991; Kingsgate, Kent, on 29.v.1992, two at Dover, Kent, on 1.vi.1992; Harpenden, Hertfordshire, on 2.vii.1992 and Beckley, East Sussex, on 21.vii.1996. Abroad the species is widespread in central Europe.

Larva. *August and September on Norway spruce, Scots pine and other species of conifer.
Overwinters as a pupa.

Tawny-barred Angle
Semiothisa liturata Clerck
Plate **12** : *10–11*

Variation. The melanic f. *nigrofulvata* Collins (fig 11) is found over much of England and Wales; and in some localities in the northern half of England it occurs as commonly as the typical form.

Imago. 28–34 mm. Resident. Readily disturbed from pine trees during the day, and after dark comes frequently to light. Single-brooded, flying in June and July, except in southern England where it flies from late May to early June, and again in August and early September. The species is found commonly in conifer plantations and occurs over the greater part of the British Isles.

Larva. Summer and autumn on Scots pine, Norway spruce, and probably other species of pine.
Overwinters as a pupa.

Latticed Heath
Semiothisa clathrata clathrata Linnaeus
Plate **12** : *12–14*

Variation. Ab. *aboguttata* Fettig (fig 14) is a melanic form occurring frequently in small numbers in the southern half of England.

Similar species. *Ematurga atomaria*, pl. **17**.

Imago. 26–32 mm. Resident. Flies in sunshine and also at night when it is attracted to light. Double-brooded over much of its range, appearing in May and June, and again from July to September. The species inhabits downland, embankments, heathland, commons, under-cliff, open woodland, and waste ground. Widespread and locally common in England, Wales and southern Scotland. In the Hebrides it has been reported from Canna, Rhum, Mull, Islay and Colonsay.

S. clathrata hugginsi Baynes, pl. **12** : *15*. This race has a white ground colour very noticeable in fresh specimens. Normally single-brooded, flying in May and June, and found locally in northern and western Ireland.

Larva. Summer and autumn on lucerne and various species of clover and trefoil.
Overwinters as a pupa.

Netted Mountain Moth
Semiothisa carbonaria Clerck
Plate **12** : *16–17*

Similar species. *Ematurga atomaria*, pl. **17**, is larger and both the median fasciae converge and unite before reaching the dorsum.

Imago. 23–25 mm. Resident. Both sexes fly actively in sunshine and are attracted to the flowers of moorland plants such as bearberry. Single-brooded, flying from April to early June; its time of appearance varying according to season and altitude of locality. The species inhabits moorland and mountain hillsides, and is found locally in the Scottish Highlands.

Larva. June and July on bearberry. In captivity it will feed on sallow, birch and bilberry.
Overwinters as a pupa.

Rannoch Looper
Semiothisa brunneata Thunberg
Plate **12** : *4–5*

Imago. 25–30 mm. Resident and suspected immigrant. The male may be found flying in hot sunshine or in dull weather by disturbing its foodplant. Single-brooded, flying in late June and July, inhabiting bilberry-covered clearings in old pine and birch woodland. Found locally in central Scotland from Perthshire northwards to East Ross, and eastwards to Aberdeenshire. As a suspected immigrant about 40 specimens have been recorded, mostly from the eastern half of England and southeast Scotland. The highest numbers were noted in 1920 (10), 1956 (8), and 1960 (8). Over half of the total number of specimens recorded were taken at light.

Larva. August to May on bilberry.
Overwinters the first year as an egg, but having pupated in June will sometimes remain in this stage for up to four years.

The V-Moth
Semiothisa wauaria Linnaeus
Plate **12** : *6*

Imago. 27–34 mm. Resident. May be disturbed from currant and gooseberry bushes during the day. Flies actively from dusk onwards and is attracted to light in small numbers. Single-brooded, flying in July and

August, inhabiting gardens, orchards, allotments, and other places where its foodplants are cultivated. Widely distributed at low density and apparently becoming much scarcer in England, Wales, Ireland, and Scotland as far as Moray.

Larva. April to June on the leaves of black currant, red currant and gooseberry.

Overwinters as an egg.

Frosted Yellow
Isturgia limbaria Fabricius
Plate **12** : *18–19*

Variation. Specimens taken from Ross-shire are stated to be larger and paler than those from southern England.

Imago. 26–30 mm. Extinct resident. Flies in sunshine, but in dull weather may be disturbed from its foodplant. Double-brooded in England, flying in May and early June, and again in late July and August. The few preserved Scottish specimens were taken in June and it is probable that this race is or was single-brooded. The species inhabited mature stands of broom and during the last century was found locally in north and north-west Kent, Essex, Suffolk, Norfolk, Ross-shire and Perthshire. The reason for its decline and possible extinction are not known, but it has not been recorded from Kent since 1873, Scotland since 1901, and East Anglia since 1914.

Larva. June and September on broom.

Overwinters as a pupa, sometimes remaining in this stage for up to four years.

Little Thorn
Cepphis advenaria Hübner
Plate **12** : *20*

Variation. A unicolorous dark brown form occasionally found in Kent and Surrey is referable to ab. *fulva* Gillmer.

Imago. 27–30 mm. Resident. Flies gently in sunshine and is easily disturbed in dull weather. Single-brooded, flying in late May and June, inhabiting open woodland. Widespread and locally common in Surrey, West Sussex, Hampshire, Gloucestershire and Monmouthshire. Very local in Kent, Dorset, Wiltshire, Somerset, Glamorgan, Berkshire, Oxfordshire, Herefordshire and formerly Southwest Yorkshire. In Ireland it has been recorded from Cos Clare and Tipperary.

Larva. July and August usually on bilberry, but in some localities where this plant is absent it must have an alternative foodplant and among those suggested are bramble, wild rose and dogwood.

Overwinters as a pupa.

Brown Silver-line
Petrophora chlorosata Scopoli
Plate **11** : *47*

Imago. 31–37 mm. Resident. Frequently disturbed during the day from bracken and adjacent herbage. Flies commonly at dusk when it is attracted to light. Single-brooded, flying in May and June, inhabiting woodland, commons and heathland. Generally distributed and common over much of the British Isles.

Larva. July to September on bracken.

Overwinters as a pupa.

Barred Umber
Plagodis pulveraria Linnaeus
Plate **11** : *44–45*

Imago. 32–38 mm. Resident. Usually found flying at dusk or at light. Single-brooded, flying in May and June, inhabiting woodland. Widely distributed at low density over the greater part of the British Isles, including the Inner Hebrides.

Larva. June to August on sallow, hazel, hawthorn and birch.

Overwinters as a pupa.

Scorched Wing
Plagodis dolabraria Linnaeus
Plate **11** : *46*

Imago. 34–38 mm. Resident. The male comes to light in moderate numbers, but the female is seldom seen, except at sugar. Single-brooded, flying in late May and June, inhabiting woodland. Generally distributed and not uncommon over much of England and Wales. Local in Scotland from Galloway to north Argyllshire; also recorded from Perthshire. Locally widespread in Ireland.

Larva. July to September on oak, birch, and sallow; and occasionally on beech and sweet chestnut.

Overwinters as a pupa.

Horse Chestnut
Pachycnemia hippocastanaria Hübner
Plate **12** : *24–25*

Imago. 28–32 mm. Resident. Occasionally put up from heather during the day, but more frequently found flying at dusk or at light. Double-brooded, flying in April and May, and again as a partial generation in August. Well established and not uncommon on the heaths of Surrey, Hampshire, Dorset, Somerset and South Devon, but very local or casual elsewhere in southern Britain.

Larva. June to July, and September on heather.

Overwinters as a pupa.

Brimstone Moth
Opisthograptis luteolata Linnaeus
Plate **11** : *48*

Imago. 33–46 mm. Resident. Frequently disturbed from hedgerows during the day. Flies commonly at dusk and is also attracted to light. In southern Britain the species produces three broods over two years with the result that the adult appears in every month from April to October. In northern districts it is usually single-brooded, flying in June and July. Generally distributed and common throughout the British Isles including the Inner Hebrides. Also recorded occasionally from the Outer Hebrides and Orkney.

Larva. Spring to autumn on hawthorn, blackthorn, rowan, plum, and other trees.

Overwinters either as a larva or pupa.

Bordered Beauty

Epione repandaria Hufnagel

Plate **12** : *21*

Similar species. *E. paralellaria*, pl. **12**. (See text fig 23.)

Imago. 28–31 mm. Resident. Frequently found flying at dusk and in small numbers at light. Single-brooded, flying from July to September, inhabiting damp woodland, fenland, commons, and marshy places. Widespread and not uncommon in England and Wales. Locally widespread in Scotland, including the Inner Hebrides, and Ireland.

Larva. May to July on sallow.

Overwinters as an egg.

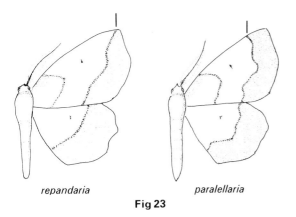

repandaria   paralellaria

Fig 23

Dark Bordered Beauty

Epione paralellaria Denis & Schiffermüller

(*vespertaria* Fabricius)

Plate **12** : *22–23*

Similar species. *E. repandaria*, pl. **12**. (See text fig 23.)

Imago. 26–29 mm. Resident. Both sexes are occasionally disturbed during the day. The male flies naturally for an hour or so after sunrise and again from dusk onwards when it is attracted to light in small numbers. The rather sluggish female is seldom seen. Single-brooded, flying in late July and August, inhabiting wet and lightly wooded heathland. A very local species found at Strensall Common, Northeast Yorkshire; Newham Bog, Northumberland; Adderstonlee Moss, Roxburghshire; near Balmoral, Aberdeenshire; and several localities in east Inverness-shire.

Larva. May to early July on creeping willow and aspen. Other foodplants given include tea-leaved willow (*Salix phylicifolia*) and birch.

Overwinters as an egg.

Speckled Yellow

Pseudopanthera macularia Linnaeus

Plate **12** : *26*

Imago. 28–30 mm. Resident. Flies in sunshine. Single-brooded, flying from mid-May to late June, inhabiting woodland and bushy places. Widely distributed and generally common in the southern half of England, Wales and much of Ireland. Locally widespread in northwest England and western Scotland, including the Inner Hebrides. Elsewhere in Scotland it has occurred occasionally in many widely separated localities.

Larva. July and August on wood sage. Other foodplants given are woundwort (*Stachys* spp.), yellow archangel (*Lamiastrum galeobdolon*), and dead-nettle.

Overwinters, sometimes twice, as a pupa.

Lilac Beauty

Apeira syringaria Linnaeus

Plate **13** : *12–13*

Imago. 38–42 mm. Resident. Frequently obtained flying along woodland rides at dusk and also at light. Single-brooded, flying in late June and July, inhabiting woodland rides and clearings, and wooded heathland. Locally widespread in England as far north as Cumbria and Co. Durham; Wales, and much of Ireland.

Larva. September to May on honeysuckle, wild privet and ash.

Overwinters as a small larva.

Large Thorn

Ennomos autumnaria Werneburg

Plate **13** : *2–3*

Variation. The ground colour ranges from pale to deep ochreous yellow and the purplish-brown freckling varies in extent. Specimens heavily suffused with blackish-brown rarely occur in the wild and are usually obtained in captivity by selective breeding.

Imago. 49–64 mm. Resident and suspected immigrant. The adult is seldom seen except at light. Single-brooded, flying in September and early October, inhabiting woodland and bushy places. A local species, probably reinforced by immigration, and found regularly in southeast Hampshire, Sussex, Kent, Essex, Suffolk, Norfolk, Hertfordshire, Cambridgeshire and Bedfordshire. A single specimen from Co. Wexford in 1931 appears to be the only Irish record.

Larva. May to early August on a variety of trees, including birch, alder, oak, sycamore, hazel, and hawthorn.

Overwinters as an egg.

August Thorn
Ennomos quercinaria Hufnagel
Plate **13** : *4–6*

Variation. Specimens with outer half of the wings suffused with blackish-brown occur frequently in some localities. Melanic specimens have occurred in industrial areas, but are very rare.

Similar species. This species is less robust; it has the postmedian line angled inwards around the discal spot, and then slightly outwards at the costa, and the median line more acutely angled; these characters distinguish it from both *E. alniaria*, pl. **13**, and *E. erosaria*, pl. **13**. (See text fig 24.)

Imago. 42–50 mm. Resident. Occasionally found on tree-trunks, but more frequently taken at light. Single-brooded, flying from mid-August to mid-September, inhabiting woodland, gardens, parkland, and wooded downland. Locally widespread in England as far north as Cumbria and Yorkshire, Wales and the Isle of Man. Thinly scattered in Scotland from Clydesdale to Ross-shire. Widespread and generally common in Ireland.

Larva. May to July on oak, beech, birch, hawthorn, and other trees.

Overwinters as an egg.

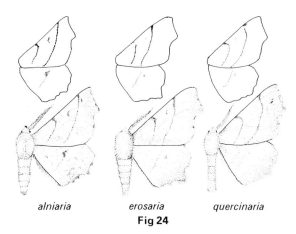

alniaria   erosaria   quercinaria

Fig 24

Canary-shouldered Thorn
Ennomos alniaria Linnaeus
Plate **13** : *8–9*

Similar species. *E. erosaria*, pl. **13** and text. *E. quercinaria*, pl. **13** and text.

Imago. 38–42 mm. Resident. Comes readily to light. Single-brooded, flying from late July to early October; varying according to the season. It inhabits woodland, fenland, gardens, commons, sandhills, etc, and is found, not uncommonly, over much of the British Isles.

Larva. May to July on a variety of trees such as birch, sallow, alder, and lime.

Overwinters as an egg.

Dusky Thorn
Ennomos fuscantaria Haworth
Plate **13** : *7*

Variation. Ab. *perfuscata* Rebel has both wings totally suffused with dark brown and occurs regularly in many localities.

Imago. 38–42 mm. Resident. Comes frequently to light. Single-brooded, flying from late July to early October; varying according to season. It inhabits woodland and parkland, and occurs, not uncommonly, throughout England and Wales, its range extending northwards to Lancashire and Co. Durham.

Larva. May to July on ash.

Overwinters as an egg.

September Thorn
Ennomos erosaria Denis & Schiffermüller
Plate **13** : *10–11*

Variation. The ground colour ranges from pale yellow to dark ochreous-brown. Specimens appearing in July and early August are smaller and paler than those of the later emergence and it is possible that two ecologically separate races are involved. More research is therefore needed to clarify the relationship between these two forms.

Similar species. *E. alniaria*, pl. **13**, each wing has a dark spot or dash in the discal area. *E. quercinaria*, pl. **13** and text.

Imago. 38–42 mm. Resident. Comes frequently to light. Single-brooded, flying from July to October, inhabiting woodland, parkland, commons, gardens, etc. Generally distributed and moderately common in the southern half of England and Wales. Local and less frequent in northern England and the southern half of Scotland, its range extending northwards to Inverness-shire. The only confirmed records from Ireland are three specimens taken in Killarney, Co. Kerry, in 1966, 1970 and 1988. Those from Co. Kildare in 1931 and 1938 are considered to be erroneous.

Larva. May to July on oak, lime and birch.

Overwinters as an egg.

Early Thorn
Selenia dentaria Fabricius
(*bilunaria* Esper)
Plate **13** : *16–19*

Variation. Specimens of the second generation (fig 19) are smaller and usually paler than those of the earlier brood. Ab. *harrisoni* Wagner (fig 18) has occurred in Yorkshire and Co. Durham, and is one of a number of melanic forms found mostly in industrial districts.

Imago. Spring brood 46–51 mm, summer brood 40–44 mm. Resident. Found frequently flying from dusk onwards also at light. Double-brooded, flying in April and May, and again in August and September, except in northern Britain where it is single-brooded, flying in May and June. Generally distributed and common in England, Wales and Ireland. Widespread, but less frequent, in Scotland; also found in the Inner Hebrides and Orkney.

Larva. May to June and August to September on a variety of trees and shrubs, including hawthorn, birch, alder, sallow and blackthorn. A third generation is easily obtained in captivity.

Overwinters as a pupa.

Lunar Thorn
Selenia lunularia Hübner
(*lunaria* Denis & Schiffermüller)
Plate **13** : *20–23*

Variation. Very variable in the extent of both the dark brown freckling and the purplish-red colour of the central band. Of the many local forms, some from Scotland are richly marked with purplish-red and easily confused with *S. tetralunaria*. Specimens from western Ireland have a brighter and cleaner appearance, and contrast strongly with the melanistic forms found in parts of the Midlands.

Similar species. *S. tetralunaria*, pl. **13**, has the post-median line angled towards both the costa and dorsum, and a dark spot on the hindwing equidistant between the discal crescent and the termen.

Imago. 39–44 mm. Resident. Comes to light in moderate numbers, usually after midnight. Single-brooded, flying in May and June, inhabiting woodland. Widely distributed, but local, over the greater part of the British Isles. Second generation specimens are sometimes produced in captivity and on even rarer occasions may occur in the wild.

Larva. July to September on oak, ash, birch, and other trees.

Overwinters as a pupa.

Purple Thorn
Selenia tetralunaria Hufnagel
Plate **13** : *14–15*

Variation. Specimens of the second generation (fig 15) are smaller and lack the whitish suffusion in the marginal area of both wings.

Similar species. *S. lunularia*, pl. **13** and text.

Imago. Spring brood 46–52 mm, summer brood 44–46 mm. Comes regularly to light in small numbers. Double-brooded, flying in April and May and again in July and August, except in northern Britain where it is single-brooded, flying in May. The species inhabits woodland, commons, downland and heathland, and occurs not uncommonly throughout the southern half of England and Wales. Less frequent and very local in northern England and Scotland where its range extends from Galloway to Ross-shire.

Larva. June to July and August to September on birch, oak, alder, and other trees.

Overwinters as a pupa.

Scalloped Hazel
Odontopera bidentata Clerck
Plate **13** : *24–27*

Variation. The ground colour ranges from pale whitish-brown through various shades of brown to black, and is expressed in a variety of local forms. Specimens richly variegated with blackish-brown occur commonly in Scotland and the Hebrides, whereas those from southern and western Britain frequently have a pale forewing with an ochreous-red central band. Melanic forms occur regularly in the London area, northern England, and parts of the Midlands.

Imago. 46–50 mm. Resident. Found frequently at rest on walls and fences, also at light. Single-brooded, flying in May and June, inhabiting woodland, parkland, commons, gardens, heathland, etc. Generally distributed and not uncommon in England, Wales, Scotland, the Hebrides and Ireland. Also recorded from Orkney.

Larva. July to September on oak, birch, garden privet, larch, pine, hawthorn, and other deciduous and coniferous trees.

Overwinters as a pupa.

Scalloped Oak
Crocallis elinguaria Linnaeus
Plate **12** : *27–28*

Variation. Ground colour ranges from pale yellow to reddish-buff, with the central band, usually darker than the surrounding area, varying from yellow to dark brown. Ab. *fusca* Reutti has both wings suffused with blackish-brown and has occurred in Scotland and Ireland and the Hebrides. Ab. *unicolor* Prout (fig 28) has the cross-lines very faint or absent, and occurs commonly in some Scottish localities and occasionally elsewhere.

Imago. 40–46 mm. Resident. Comes readily to light. Single-brooded, flying in July and August, earlier or later according to season. This species frequents a wide variety of habitats and is found more or less commonly throughout the British Isles, except that it is not known to reside in Orkney or Shetland.

Larva. April to early July on most deciduous trees and shrubs.

Overwinters as an egg.

Dusky Scalloped Oak
Crocalis dardoinaria Donzel
Plate **43** : *2*

Similar species. *C. elinguaria*, pl. **12**.

Imago. 46–52 mm. Suspected immigrant. Single-brooded on the Continent, flying from July to September. It has not been reported from mainland Britain, but two specimens were recorded on Guernsey, Channel Islands, at Icart, on 4.ix.1990 and Petit Bot, on 11.ix.1990. Abroad it is a widespread species occurring in southern and central France, and Spain.

Larva. *October to June on the flowers and leaves of gorse, broom and juniper.
Overwinters as a small larva.

Swallow-tailed Moth
Ourapteryx sambucaria Linnaeus
Plate **13** : *1*

Imago. 50–62 mm. Resident. Comes frequently to light. Single-brooded, flying in late June and July, inhabiting woodland, gardens, commons, etc. Generally distributed and moderately common in England, Wales, Ireland and southern Scotland. Elsewhere in Scotland it is found locally as far north as Ross-shire.
Larva. August to June on ivy, and a variety of trees and shrubs.
Overwinters as a larva.

Feathered Thorn
Colotois pennaria Linnaeus
Plate **12** : *29–32*

Variation. Very variable throughout its range. Specimens from northern and western parts of the British Isles appear to be more reddish and richly coloured.
Imago. 46–50 mm. Resident. The males fly actively after dark and are readily attracted to light. The females are rather sluggish and are usually found sitting on the twigs, branches and trunks of trees. Single-brooded, flying from mid-September to mid-November, inhabiting woodland, commons, heathland, and bushy places. Generally distributed and common in England, Wales and Ireland. Locally widespread in Scotland and the Inner Hebrides.
Larva. April to June on various trees and shrubs, including oak, birch, sallow, hawthorn, elm and blackthorn.
Overwinters as an egg.

Orange Moth
Angerona prunaria Linnaeus
Plate **12** : *33–38*

Variation. The banded form f. *corylaria* Thunberg (figs 36–38) is found throughout the range of this species and in many localities occurs as frequently as the plain typical form. The ground colour of both forms ranges from pale yellow to orange, and the brown banding of f. *corylaria* varies both in extent and intensity.
Imago. 42–56 mm. Resident. The male flies from dusk onwards and comes readily to light. The elusive female appears to fly later in the night and is only occasionally taken at light. Single-brooded, flying in late June and July, inhabiting woodland and heathland. Widely distributed and locally common in the southern half of England, ranging northwards to Shropshire and Lincolnshire. Also found locally in southeast Wales and the southern half of Ireland.
Larva. August to May on a variety of plants and trees, including birch, heather, hawthorn, blackthorn and traveller's-joy. In captivity it thrives on garden privet and lilac.
Overwinters as a third-grown larva.

Small Brindled Beauty
Apocheima hispidaria Denis & Schiffermüller
Plate **14** : *19–21*

Imago. Male 35–37 mm, female wingless. Resident. Both sexes have been found in the daytime on oak-trunks. After dark the male comes readily to light and the female is occasionally obtained by searching tree-trunks. Single-brooded, occurring in late February and March, inhabiting woodland and parkland. Widespread and locally common in the southern half of England and South Wales. Elsewhere in Britain it is found sporadically as far north as Cumbria and Yorkshire.
Larva. Late April to mid-June on oak, and sometimes hazel, elm and sweet chestnut.
Overwinters as a pupa.

Pale Brindled Beauty
Apocheima pilosaria Denis & Schiffermüller
(*pedaria* Fabricius)
Plate **14** : *15–18*

Variation. The melanic form f. *monacharia* Staudinger (fig 17) occurs with varying frequency over much of Britain. It is common in the London area, and in parts of the Midlands and northern England it has become the dominant form.
Imago. Male 45–50 mm, female wingless. During the day the male may be found on fences and tree-trunks, and after dark at light. The female is usually obtained by searching tree-trunks after dark. Single-brooded and normally on the wing from January to March, although in mild weather the first specimens can appear in late autumn. Generally distributed and common in England and Wales. Widespread, but less frequent, in Scotland, the Hebrides and Ireland.
Larva. April to June on a variety of trees and shrubs, including oak, birch, hawthorn, lime, elm, sallow, apple and blackthorn.
Overwinters as a pupa.

Brindled Beauty
Lycia hirtaria Clerck
Plate **14** : *11–14*

Variation. Specimens from northern Scotland and the Highlands are larger and brighter in appearance than those from southern Britain, and some examples of this race have a white ground colour. Ab. *nigra* Cockayne (fig 14) is a recessive melanic form found occasionally in London and the Home Counties.
Imago. 42–52 mm. Resident. The male flies late at night, but comes freely to light. The female is not strongly attracted to light and is more easily obtained during the day when both sexes may be found resting on tree-trunks, fences and walls. Single-brooded, flying in March and April, inhabiting woodland, parkland,

tree-lined streets, and gardens. Generally distributed and locally common in the southern half of England, South Wales, and the Midlands, but very local in North Wales, northern England and Scotland. Evidently rare and local in Ireland, with records from Cos Sligo, Cavan, Westmeath, Galway, Wicklow, Dublin, Tyrone, Fermanagh and Clare.

Larva. May to July on lime, birch, alder, hawthorn, beech, and other deciduous trees.
Overwinters as a pupa.

Belted Beauty
Lycia zonaria britannica Harrison
Plate **14** : *8–9*

Imago. Male 28–35 mm, female wingless. Resident. Both sexes may be found during the day or night sitting on low herbage or fence posts. The males are attracted to light. Single-brooded, occurring in March and April, inhabiting coastal sandhills. A local species, but not uncommon where it occurs, and found at Conway, Caernarvonshire; the Wirral, Cheshire; Sanna Point, western Argyllshire; the Hebrides; and in Ireland from Cos Mayo, Antrim, and Galway. In the past it has occurred at Formby, Lancashire, and on the Flintshire sandhills.
L. zonaria atlantica Harrison, pl. **14** : *10*. A somewhat anomalous race described from the Isle of Baleshare and stated to occur on many of the other Hebridean islands. Specimens from the type locality are smaller in size (24–29 mm) and this appears to be the only tangible character on which this subspecies was based. Elsewhere in the Hebrides it is variable in size and some of the races, as on Canna, are as large if not larger than the mainland race.
Larva. May to July on bird's-foot trefoil, plantain, clover, yellow iris, creeping willow, burnet rose (*Rosa pimpinellifolia*), and other low plants.
Overwinters as a pupa, sometimes remaining in this stage for up to four years.

Rannoch Brindled Beauty
Lycia lapponaria scotica Harrison
Plate **14** : *6–7*

Imago. Male 31–34 mm, female wingless. Resident. Both sexes may be found during the day at rest on fence posts or the stems of heather or bog myrtle. Single-brooded, occurring in April, inhabiting boggy moorland. A local species found mainly in Perthshire and Inverness-shire, but also recorded from Argyllshire, Banffshire, Aberdeenshire, West Ross and Stirlingshire.
Larva. May to August on bog myrtle, sallow, heather, bell heather and cross-leaved heath. In confinement it will accept birch.
Overwinters as a pupa, remaining in this stage for up to four years.

Oak Beauty
Biston strataria Hufnagel
Plate **14** : *4–5*

Variation. Ab. *melanaria* Koch is a rare unicolorous black variety recorded from Kent, Surrey and Hampshire. Less extreme forms in which both wings are suffused with dark brown occur more frequently.
Imago. 51–56 mm. Resident. The male comes readily to light, the female rarely so. Single-brooded, flying in March and April, inhabiting woodland and parkland. Widespread and not uncommon over much of England and Wales. Sporadically distributed and less frequent in Ireland and southern Scotland.
Larva. May to July on oak, elm, hazel, aspen, alder and other trees.
Overwinters as a pupa.

Peppered Moth
Biston betularia Linnaeus
Plate **14** : *1–3*

Variation. The melanic f. *carbonaria* Jordan (fig 3) occurs with varying frequency in southern England (except the southwest), the Midlands, northern England, southern Scotland, and northern Ireland. It is dominant over much of its range and in the industrial areas of northern England forms the total population. F. *insularia* Thierry-Mieg (fig 2), although intermediate in appearance, is genetically unrelated to f. *carbonaria* and can never be produced by crossing pure f. *carbonaria* with the typical form. Its distribution is similar to f. *carbonaria*, but in many industrial areas its presence is overshadowed by the dominant melanic form.
Imago. 45–62 mm. Resident. Both sexes come readily to light. Single-brooded, flying from mid-May to mid-August. Commonly distributed throughout England, Wales and Ireland. Locally widespread in Scotland and the Inner Hebrides.
Larva. July to September on many trees and a wide variety of plants. Some of the recorded foodplants are lime, sallow, birch, hawthorn, mugwort, goldenrod and hop.
Overwinters as a pupa.

Spring Usher
Agriopis leucophaearia Denis & Schiffermüller
Plate **14** : *22–27*

Variation. Extremely variable throughout its range with little geographical significance.
Imago. Male 31–37 mm, female wingless. Resident. The male rests by day on fences and tree-trunks, and at night comes freely to light. The spider-like female may be found after dark scuttling up oak-trunks. Single-brooded, occurring from mid-February to mid-March, inhabiting woodland, parkland, and occasionally orchards. Widespread and generally common over much of England and Wales. Widely scattered and local in

southern Scotland ranging northwards to Inverness-shire. A stray specimen from Co. Wicklow appears to be the only Irish record.

Larva. April to early June normally on oak, but on at least one occasion the larvae have been found on apple. Overwinters as a pupa.

Scarce Umber
Agriopis aurantiaria Hübner
Plate **14** : *28–29*

Variation. Ab. *fumipennaria* Hellweger has both wings suffused with dark brown and occurs locally in Yorkshire and Surrey.

Imago. Male 40–44 mm, female almost wingless. Resident. After dark the male comes readily to light, and the female may be found on the trunks of birch, oak and other trees. Single-brooded, occurring in October and November, inhabiting woodland, parkland and bushy places. Generally distributed and moderately common throughout England and Wales. Locally widespread in Scotland and mainly in the northern half of Ireland although it has been recorded from Co. Kerry. Also recorded from the Inner Hebrides and Orkney.

Larva. April to June on birch, oak, hazel, and many other trees. Overwinters as an egg.

Dotted Border
Agriopis marginaria Fabricius
Plate **14** : *30–34*

Variation. Ab. *fuscata* Mosley (fig 31) is the darkest of a wide range of melanic forms found commonly in the London area, the Home Counties, the Midlands, and northern England.

Similar species. *Erannis defoliaria*, pl. **14** and text.

Imago. Male 36–42 mm, female 10–14 mm. Resident. The male is not strongly attracted to light and is more readily found sitting on the stems of bushes and the lower branches of trees. The flightless female may be found, sometimes commonly, by searching the trunks of oak and other trees. Single-brooded, occurring from mid-February to April, inhabiting woodland, commons, heathland, hedgerows, and bushy places. Widespread and more or less common over the greater part of the British Isles.

Larva. April to June on a variety of trees and shrubs, including oak, hawthorn, hazel, sallow, elm and birch. Overwinters as a pupa.

Mottled Umber
Erannis defoliaria Clerck
Plate **14** : *35–40*

Variation. Extremely variable throughout its range, with the darker and more obscurely marked forms predominating in industrial areas. The darkest of these is

ab. *nigra* Bandermann (fig 38) which is well known from Epping Forest, Essex. A melanic form of the female (fig 40) is also found in this locality.

Similar species. *Agriopis marginaria*, pl. **14**, has a row of distinct dots around the margin of the hindwing.

Imago. Male 40–45 mm, female wingless. Resident. After dark the female may be found on tree-trunks, and the male sitting about on the stems of trees and bushes, and also at light. Single-brooded, occurring from October to December with the occasional specimen emerging in September or even earlier. Widely distributed over the greater part of the British Isles and frequently abundant in southern Britain.

Larva. April to June on oak, birch, hawthorn, sallow, and many other deciduous trees and shrubs. Overwinters as an egg.

Waved Umber
Menophra abruptaria Thunberg
Plate **15** : *1–4*

Variation. Ab. *fuscata* Tutt (fig 4) is a melanic form found frequently in the London area and occasionally in the Midlands and elsewhere in the southern half of England.

Imago. 36–42 mm. Resident. May be found during the day on fences and tree-trunks, and after dark in small numbers at light. Single-brooded, flying from mid-April to early June, inhabiting woodland, commons, parkland, and gardens. Widespread and not uncommon in the southern half of England and much of Wales. Less frequent from the Midlands northwards to Cumbria and Co. Durham. In Ireland there are unconfirmed records from Cos Wicklow and Fermanagh.

Larva. June to September on garden privet and lilac. Its foodplant in rural districts is not recorded, but in captivity it will accept wild privet, ash and birch. Overwinters as a pupa within a tough silken cocoon attached to a stem of its foodplant.

Willow Beauty
Peribatodes rhomboidaria Denis & Schiffermüller
Plate **15** : *9–11*

Variation. The slate-grey f. *perfumaria* Newman (fig 10) occurs in many parts of Britain and is dominant in most industrial areas. A widespread, but much less frequent, melanic form is ab. *rebeli* Aigner (fig 11).

Similar species. *P. secundaria*, pl. **15** and text. *P. ilicaria*, pl. **43** and text.

Imago. 40–48 mm. Resident. Both sexes come readily to light. Normally single-brooded, flying from late June to August, with an occasional and partial second generation occurring in southern England in September. Generally distributed and more or less common in England, Wales, Ireland and southern Scotland. Local and less frequent over the rest of Scotland and not found in Orkney, Shetland or the Outer Hebrides.

Larva. Autumn to May on a wide variety of trees such as hawthorn, birch, garden privet, yew, and plum; also on ivy and traveller's-joy.
Overwinters as a quarter-grown larva.

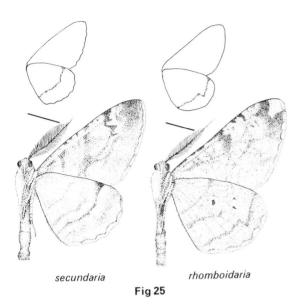

secundaria   *rhomboidaria*

Fig 25

Feathered Beauty
Peribatodes secundaria Esper
Plate **15** : *5–8*

Variation. Ab. *nigrata* Sterneck (fig 8) is a melanic form found occasionally in its Kentish locality.
Similar species. *P. ilicaria*, pl. **43** and text. *P. rhomboidaria*, pl. **15**, has a pale apical patch on the underside of forewing, and an angulated postmedian line on the underside of hindwing. Pectinations of antenna much shorter. (See text fig 25.)
Imago. 38–44 mm. Resident and suspected immigrant. A few specimens have been disturbed from the lower branches of conifers during the day, but it is more readily obtained at light. Single-brooded, flying in July and early August, inhabiting coniferous woodland. The species appears to be well established at Hamstreet, Kent, where it was first taken in July 1981. Elsewhere it has been recorded from West and East Sussex, Surrey, and as single specimens from Bradwell-on-Sea, Essex, on 7.vii.1987, Greatstone, Kent, on 15.vi.1994 and Kirby-le-Soken, Essex, on 27.vii.1997. Abroad it is well distributed in central and southern Europe, including France and Denmark.
Larva. September to early June on Norway spruce and probably other conifers. In captivity it has been reared from the egg on Douglas fir, Scots pine, western red cedar (*Thuja plicata*), Lawson's cypress and western hemlock (*Tsuga heterophylla*).
Overwinters as a small larva.

Lydd Beauty
Peribatodes ilicaria Geyer
(*manuelaria* Herrich-Schäffer)
Plate **43** : *3*

Similar species. *P. rhomboidaria*, pl. **15**, has a pale apical patch on the underside of the forewing. *P. secundaria*, pl. **15**, lacks the distinctly curved postmedian line on the hindwing.
Imago. 28–32 mm. Suspected immigrant. Abroad it is single-brooded, flying from July to September, inhabiting woodland and sometimes gardens. The first specimen to be taken in Britain was a male at Lydd, Kent, on 27.viii.1990 and the second, a female from which a second generation was reared in captivity, at New Romney, Kent, on 4.viii.1994. Two more were captured at Ninham, Isle of Wight, on 14 & 18.viii.1996. All four specimens have appeared at light. Its Continental range includes central and southwest Europe.
Larva. *September to July on oak, evergreen oak, pine, privet and blackthorn. In captivity it will accept birch and can be forced to emerge the same year.
Overwinters as a small larva.

Bordered Grey
Selidosema brunnearia scandinaviaria Staudinger
(*ericetaria* de Villers)
(*plumaria* auctt.)
Plate **15** : *15–16*

Imago. 37–43 mm. Resident. May be disturbed from heather during the day, and in hot sunshine the male will fly of its own accord. Both sexes fly from dusk onwards and are attracted to light, but rarely in large numbers. Single-brooded, flying in July and August, inhabiting heathland, mosses, downland, and coastal sandhills. A local species with a very complex distribution. It is well known from the larger heaths of northwest Surrey, northeast Hampshire, the New Forest, and southeast Dorset; but it also occurs on the sandhills of Hayling Island, Hampshire, on chalk downland at Swanage and Lulworth, Dorset; and locally in the Isle of Wight, in South Devon, Wiltshire and Berkshire. In the rest of England it is well established on the mosses of Westmorland (Meathop, Holker, etc), and Shropshire (Whixall). In Scotland it occurs in Kincardineshire (St Cyrus), Argyllshire (Ardnamurchan), and on the Hebridean islands of Canna and Rhum. Elsewhere in Britain it has been recorded from Caernarvonshire, Cheshire and the Isle of Man. In Ireland it is locally not uncommon on heaths and bogs from north to south.
S. brunnearia tyronensis Cockayne. This race is characterized by its small size (30–34 mm) and by having the dark marginal shade narrower and the darker median shade much fainter in both sexes. Evidently this race is extinct as its only locality, a bog near Lough Neagh, Co. Tyrone, no longer exists.
Larva. September to early June on heather and in some localities on bird's-foot trefoil. Abroad it is stated to

feed on broom, *Genista* spp., clover, restharrow, and dock.

Overwinters as a larva.

Ringed Carpet
Cleora cinctaria cinctaria Denis & Schiffermüller
Plate **16** : *1–2*

Imago. 36–42 mm. Resident. Both sexes may be found during the day at rest on tree-trunks and fence-posts, and after dark in small numbers coming to light. Single-brooded, flying in late April and May, inhabiting lightly wooded heathland. The headquarters of this species is the New Forest, Hampshire, where it is well established and locally common. Elsewhere it is found locally in southeast Dorset, South Wiltshire, Berkshire, and in Ireland from Cos Kerry, Cork, Down, Donegal, Sligo, Galway, Meath, Offaly and Mayo.

C. cinctaria bowesi Richardson, pl. **16** : *3–4*. This race has a silvery-white ground colour and blackish-grey markings, and occurs locally in Perthshire, Inverness-shire, Argyllshire, Wigtownshire, Dumfriesshire and Kirkcudbrightshire. Specimens conforming more to this race than to the typical form have been recorded from the Portmadoc district, Caernarvonshire.

Larva. June to August on bog myrtle, birch, bilberry and heath.

Overwinters as a pupa.

Satin Beauty
Deileptenia ribeata Clerck
Plate **15** : *12–14*

Variation. f. *nigra* Cockayne (fig 14) is a dominant melanic form occurring not uncommonly at Boxhill, Surrey, its larvae feeding mostly on yew. f. *sericearia* Curtis (fig 13) is a dark, variable, and often dominant form found over much of the species' range.

Imago. 42–48 mm. Resident. May be obtained during the day by beating the lower branches of yew, spruce, etc, or after dark in small numbers at light. Single-brooded, flying from late June to mid-August, inhabiting deciduous and coniferous woodland. Locally widespread in the southern half of England, and much of Wales. Elsewhere in Britain it is found locally in Cumbria, Yorkshire and southern Scotland, as far north as Perthshire. Scarce and local in Ireland and known only from Cos Kildare, Wicklow and Leix.

Larva. August to May on yew, spruce and Douglas fir. Overwinters as a small larva.

Mottled Beauty
Alcis repandata repandata Linnaeus
Plate **16** : *13–21*

Variation. Geographically variable, with the paler forms predominating in northern and western Britain, and much of Ireland. Melanic forms occur commonly, especially in industrial areas where they are often dominant. The banded form ab. *conversaria* Hübner

(figs *17–18*) exists as a variable percentage in most populations.

Imago. 43–56 mm. Resident. Both sexes come readily to light, and occasionally to sugar. Single-brooded, flying in June and July, inhabiting woodland, bushy places, gardens, and commons. Widespread and generally common throughout the greater part of the British Isles.

A. repandata muraria Curtis, pl. **16** : *22–24*. Many of the whitish-grey and often weakly marked specimens found on open moorland in Scotland and western Ireland vaguely conform to this race. The larvae are usually associated with bilberry.

A. repandata sodorensium Weir. A small and lead-grey coloured race described from specimens taken on the Isle of Lewis, Outer Hebrides.

Larva. August to May on birch, bilberry, bramble, honeysuckle, hawthorn, oak, broom, dock, and many other trees and plants. In early spring it frequently comes out of hibernation well before the leaves have formed and in these circumstances will eat the skin or soft bark of its foodplant. Therefore, in captivity the larva is best sleeved out-of-doors on a living plant, both birch and garden privet being well suited for this purpose.

Overwinters as a quarter-grown larva.

Dotted Carpet
Alcis jubata Thunberg
(*glabraria* Hübner)
Plate **16** : *25*

Variation. Specimens suffused with dark brown occur occasionally in Hampshire and western Scotland, and are referable to ab. *obscura* Fuchs.

Imago. 28–33 mm. Resident. May be obtained by jarring the lichen-covered branches of oak or in varying numbers at light. Single-brooded, flying from mid-July to mid-August, inhabiting ancient woodland. Locally widespread in southwest England, Wales, and from southern Scotland northwards to Ross-shire. Very local elsewhere, namely the New Forest, Hampshire, Dorset, Gloucestershire, Northumberland, Isle of Arran, and on the Hebridean islands of Islay and Mull. Only one Irish record, from Co. Kerry in June 1941.

Larva. September to early June on beard lichen (*Usnea barbata*) and probably other lichens.

Overwinters as a larva.

Great Oak Beauty
Hypomecis roboraria Denis & Schiffermüller
Plate **15** : *24–26*

Variation. f. *infuscata* Staudinger (fig 25) a common and frequently dominant melanic form found in many localities.

Similar species. *Serraca punctinalis*, pl. **15**, is usually smaller in size, and lacks the pale apical patch on the underside of the forewing. (See fig 26.)

Imago. 60–68 mm. Resident. Comes regularly to light and occasionally to sugar. Single-brooded, flying from mid-June to mid-July, inhabiting oak woodland. A local species found not uncommonly in southern England and southeast Wales, its range extending westwards to Devon and northwards to Nottinghamshire and Shropshire.

Larva. August to May on oak.

Overwinters as a larva.

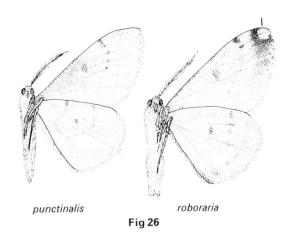

punctinalis　　　　　*roboraria*

Fig 26

Pale Oak Beauty

Serraca punctinalis Scopoli

Plate **15** : *21–23*

Variation. Melanism is common in this species and is very variable in its expression. Ab. *humperti* Humpert (fig 22) is one of the darker forms occurring regularly over much of the species' range.

Similar species. *Boarmia roboraria*, pl. **15** and text.

Imago. 46–55 mm. Resident. May be found on the trunks of oak and fir trees, and after dark comes readily to light and occasionally to sugar. Single-brooded, flying from late May to mid-July, with the occasional specimen appearing in the autumn possibly representing a partial second generation. A woodland species found not uncommonly in southern and southeast England, and locally in southwest England and parts of Wales. Two specimens from Glengariff, Co. Cork, in 1914 constitute the only Irish records.

Larva. July and August on oak, birch, and occasionally sallow and sycamore.

Overwinters as a pupa.

Brussels Lace

Cleorodes lichenaria Hufnagel

Plate **16** : *26–27*

Imago. 31–38 mm. Resident. Comes regularly to light in varying numbers. Single-brooded, flying from June to early August, inhabiting woods and copses. Wide-spread and locally common in southwest England, Wales and much of Ireland. Local and thinly scattered in the rest of southern England, and from southern Scotland to Ross-shire. Also recorded from the Hebridean island of Mull.

Larva. September to May on lichen growing on oak, blackthorn, old fences and in some coastal localities on rocks.

Overwinters as a larva.

Speckled Beauty

Fagivorina arenaria Hufnagel

Plate **16** : *28*

Imago. 35–39 mm. Extinct resident. The adults were usually obtained at rest on tree-trunks or by sweeping the higher branches of oak trees. Single-brooded, flying in July and early August, inhabiting mature woodland. Formerly found during the last century in the New Forest, Hampshire, Tilgate Forest and other localities in Sussex, but not recorded from either county since 1898.

Larva. *August–September on lichens growing on oak and beech.

Overwinters as a pupa.

The Engrailed

Ectropis bistortata Goeze

(*biundulata* de Villers)

Plate **16** : *5–8*

Variation. Specimens of the second brood are smaller, and more weakly marked. A variety of melanic forms are found in this species and occur with varying frequency in many English and Welsh localities. Specimens from the Scottish Highlands are consistently larger and more richly marked with reddish-brown than those from elsewhere.

Similar species. *E. crepuscularia*, pl. **16**. Typical specimens have a whiter ground colour, with the well-defined blackish-brown cross-lines frequently edged with yellow, never ochreous or brown; otherwise virtually indistinguishable from pale-coloured, first brood, form of *E. bistortata*. The date of capture is an important guide to identification; furthermore *E. crepuscularia* is nearly always single-brooded, even in captivity.

Imago. 38–45 mm. Resident. Occasionally found on tree-trunks and fences, but more frequently obtained after dark at light. Double-brooded, flying in March and April, and again from late June to early August, except in northern Britain where it is single-brooded, flying from mid-April to mid-May. On rare occasions specimens of a suspected third generation have been reported in southern England in October. The species inhabits woodland, parkland and bushy places, and is found more or less commonly throughout England and Wales. Widespread, but less frequent, in Scotland, including the Inner Hebrides. In Ireland it has been reported from the southwest and the north, but the situation is complex and awaits clarification.

Larva. May to June, and August on a wide variety of trees and shrubs, including oak, birch, sallow, broom and buckthorn.

Overwinters as a pupa.

Small Engrailed

Ectropis crepuscularia Denis & Schiffermüller

Plate **16** : *9–11*

Variation. Melanic forms are found commonly in the industrial districts of northeast England, the Midlands, and South Wales.

Similar species. *E. bistortata*, pl. **16** and text.

Imago. 38–44 mm. Resident. Frequently found at rest on tree-trunks, but rarely taken commonly at light. Single-brooded, flying from mid-May to mid-June, appearing slightly earlier or later according to the season. It inhabits woodland and bushy places. Locally widespread in England, Wales and Ireland. Its distribution in Scotland other than in the extreme south is uncertain and requires further investigation.

Larva. July and August on birch, larch, sallow, and probably other trees and shrubs.

Overwinters as a pupa.

Square Spot

Paradarisa consonaria Hübner

Plate **15** : *17–20*

Variation. Geographically variable, with a number of local forms. The majority of specimens found in southern and western Britain more or less conform to the typical example illustrated (fig 18). Specimens from southwest Ireland are distinctly ochreous in appearance, and those from parts of Surrey (Leith Hill and Abinger) are tinged with ochreous-brown and often obscurely marked (fig 17). There are two melanic forms, namely, f. *nigra* Bankes (fig 20) which occurs near Maidstone, Kent, near Uckfield, East Sussex, and in the Cotswolds, Gloucestershire; and ab. *waiensis* Richardson (fig 19) which is found in the Wye Valley and other parts of Monmouthshire, and in the Forest of Dean, Gloucestershire.

Imago. 40–45 mm. Resident. May be found on tree-trunks during the day, and after dark in moderate numbers at light. Single-brooded, flying from late April to early June, inhabiting woodland. Local, but not uncommon, throughout southern England ranging northwards to Leicestershire, much of Wales, Westmorland, and southwest Ireland (Cos Kerry and West Cork).

Larva. Late June to August on oak, birch, pine, yew, beech, and probably larch and other trees.

Overwinters as a pupa.

Brindled White-spot

Paradarisa extersaria Hübner

(*luridata* Borkhausen)

Plates **16** : *12* & **43** : *12*

Variation. A melanic form occurring locally in north-west Kent is referable to ab. *variegata* Raebel (pl. **43** : *12*).

Imago. 33–39 mm. Resident. Occasionally disturbed during the day from the trunks or branches of trees, but more readily obtained after dark at light or sugar. Single-brooded, flying in late May and June, inhabiting woodland. Locally widespread in southern Britain, ranging northeastwards to Norfolk, and northwestwards to Denbighshire.

Larva. July to September mainly on oak and birch.

Overwinters as a pupa.

Grey Birch

Aethalura punctulata Denis & Schiffermüller

Plate **16** : *29*

Variation. Ground colour variable, ranging from light to dark grey. Extreme melanism is rare and has only occurred in Surrey.

Imago. 30–35 mm. Resident. Frequently found on tree-trunks and fences, and also at light. Single-brooded, flying in May and June, inhabiting woodland. Widespread and not uncommon over much of England and Wales. Rather scarce and sporadically distributed in Ireland and the southern half of Scotland.

Larva. July and August mainly on birch, but sometimes on alder.

Overwinters as a pupa.

Common Heath

Ematurga atomaria atomaria Linnaeus

Plates **17** : *1–6* & **43** : *10–11*

Variation. The ground colour in the male ranges from pale yellow to blackish-brown, and extreme unicolorous examples of both colour forms are occasionally reported. Ab. *unicoloraria* Staudinger (pl. **43**) is an extreme melanic form reported from Yorkshire and Lancashire.

Similar species. *Semiothisa carbonaria*, pl. **12** and text. *Semiothisa clathrata*, pl. **12**. *Scopula immorata*, pl. **6**.

Imago. 22–34 mm. Resident. Flies on dry and sunny days. Double-brooded, flying in May and June, with a partial second generation in August occurring regularly in southern Britain and occasionally in the north. This species inhabits heathland, moorland, downland, and open woodland, and occurs commonly over much of the British Isles.

E. atomaria minuta Heydemann refers to a small race occurring on northern heathlands.

Larva. July to September on heather, heath, clovers and trefoils.

Overwinters as a pupa.

Bordered White

Bupalus piniaria Linnaeus

Plate **16** : *30–34*

Variation. The ground colour of the male varies from yellow in southern England to white in northern England and Scotland. The female displays a similar south to north cline varying from orange to brown. Male specimens from Ireland are predominantly white.

Imago. 34–40 mm. Resident. Has been noted flying high up in the sunshine and may be obtained, sometimes in profusion, by beating the lower branches of pine and other conifers. Single-brooded, flying in May and June, later in the north, inhabiting coniferous woodland. Generally distributed and locally abundant over the greater part of the British Isles, but as yet unrecorded from the Outer Hebrides, Orkney and Shetland.

Larva. July to September on Scots pine, Corsican pine (*Pinus nigra*) and probably other species of pine.
Overwinters as a pupa.

Common White Wave
Cabera pusaria Linnaeus
Plate **17** : 7

Similar species. *C. exanthemata*, pl. **17**, has the forewing dusted with ochreous-grey, and the outer cross-line distinctly curved. *Scopula floslactata*, pl. **6**.

Imago. 32–35 mm. Resident. Frequently disturbed from trees and bushes during the day. Flies from dusk onwards and comes regularly to light. Double-brooded in the southern half of Britain, flying in May and June, and again in late July and August. Single-brooded in the north, flying from May to July. It inhabits woodland and bushy places and occurs more or less commonly throughout the British Isles, except the Northern Isles.

Larva. July to September on birch, sallow, alder, oak, and other trees and shrubs.
Overwinters as a pupa.

Common Wave
Cabera exanthemata Scopoli
Plate **17** : 8

Similar species. *C. pusaria*, pl. **17** and text. *Scopula ternata*, pl. **6**.

Imago. 30–35 mm. Resident. May be beaten out from sallow bushes during the day. Flies at dusk and comes regularly to light in small numbers. Single-brooded, flying from May to July, with a partial second brood occurring in most years in southern England from late July to mid-August. The species inhabits damp woodland, fenland and sallow carr, and is found not uncommonly throughout the British Isles, but not recorded from the Outer Hebrides and the Northern Isles.

Larva. July to September on sallow and aspen.
Overwinters as a pupa.

White-pinion Spotted
Lomographa bimaculata Fabricius
Plate **17** : 9

Imago. 27–31 mm. Resident. Flies from dusk onwards and comes to light, usually in small numbers. Single-brooded, flying in May and June, inhabiting woodland and hedgerows. Widespread and not uncommon in the southern half of England, East Anglia, west and east Midlands, Lincolnshire and South Wales. Apparently absent from most of North Wales, but surprisingly well established locally in Westmorland and Cumberland. In Ireland it is found in Cos Wicklow, Cork and Kerry.

Larva. Late June to August on hawthorn, blackthorn and probably other trees.
Overwinters as a pupa.

Clouded Silver
Lomographa temerata Denis & Schiffermüller
Plate **17** : 10–11

Imago. 27–34 mm. Resident and suspected immigrant. Comes frequently to light. Single-brooded, flying in May and June, inhabiting woodland, hedgerows and bushy places. Occasionally noted on the south coast in the autumn during periods of migrant activity. Generally distributed and not uncommon over much of England, Wales and Ireland. Thinly scattered in Scotland from the south to western Argyllshire.

Larva. July and August on hawthorn, blackthorn, plum, wild cherry, apple and aspen.
Overwinters as a pupa.

Sloe Carpet
Aleucis distinctata Herrich-Schäffer
Plate **17** : 12

Similar species. Male *Theria primaria*, pl. **17**, is larger, has a less angulated outer cross-line, and the antennae are distinctly pectinated.

Imago. 27–31 mm. Resident. Flies from dusk onwards around blackthorn bushes, settling and resting on the stems and twigs. Single-brooded, flying in April, inhabiting blackthorn hedges and thickets. A local species found in South Hampshire, Sussex, Surrey, Berkshire, Essex and Suffolk. Occasionally reported from Kent, Buckinghamshire and Hertfordshire.

Larva. June to early July on blackthorn.
Overwinters as a pupa.

Early Moth
Theria primaria Haworth
(*rupicapraria* auctt.)
Plate **17** : 13–14

Similar species. *Aleucis distinctata*, pl. **17** and text.

Imago. Male 32–37 mm, female 9–11 mm. Resident. The males fly at dusk and afterwards may be found with the almost wingless females sitting on the stems and twigs of hawthorn and blackthorn. Single-brooded, occurring in January and February, inhabiting the edges of woods, hedgerows and bushy places. Widespread and locally common over much of England, Wales and the northern half of Ireland. Very local and sporadically distributed in southern Scotland.

Larva. April to May on hawthorn and blackthorn.
Overwinters as a pupa.

Light Emerald

Campaea margaritata Linnaeus
Plate **17** : *20–21*

Imago. 42–54 mm. Resident. Comes to light in moderate numbers. Normally single-brooded, flying from late May to early August, with a partial second generation occurring in southern England in most years in late August and September. A woodland species found fairly commonly throughout the British Isles, but unrecorded from Shetland.
Larva. September to May on oak, birch, beech, hawthorn, elm, and many other deciduous trees.
Overwinters as a larva.

Barred Red

Hylaea fasciaria Linnaeus
Plate **17** : *15–19*

Variation. Ab. *prasinaria* Denis & Schiffermüller (figs 18–19) is an uncommon green form found regularly at Hamstreet, Kent, and occasionally elsewhere. Ab. *grisearia* Fuchs (fig 17) is a brownish-grey form found frequently in the Midlands, northern England and parts of Scotland.
Imago. 32–44 mm. Resident and suspected immigrant. Comes to light in moderate numbers. Single-brooded, flying from mid-June to early August, inhabiting coniferous woodland. Widespread and not uncommon throughout the British Isles, but apparently absent from the Outer Hebrides and the Northern Isles.
Larva. September to May on Scots pine, Norway spruce, Douglas fir, lodgepole pine (*Pinus contorta*) and probably other conifers.
Overwinters as a small larva.

Scotch Annulet

Gnophos obfuscata Denis & Schiffermüller
(*myrtillata* Thunberg)
Plate **17** : *27–28*

Similar species. *G. obsurata*, pl. **17**, is smaller and the termen of the hindwing is distinctly dentate. *Odontonophos dumetata hibernica*, pl. **43** : *11*.
Imago. 41–46 mm. Resident. Occasionally disturbed from rocks during the day, but more usually netted at dusk or taken at light. Single-brooded, flying in July and August, inhabiting mountain hillsides, moorland, rocky gullies, and old quarries. Locally widespread in northern and central Scotland as far south as Renfrewshire; the Isle of Arran, and the Hebrides. In Ireland it occurs locally in Cos Galway, Clare, Donegal and Mayo.
Larva. September to early June on heather and other low plants. In captivity it will accept knotgrass.
Overwinters as a larva.

The Annulet

Gnophos obscurata Denis & Schiffermüller
Plate **17** : *22–26*

Variation. The ground colour strongly reflects the type of locality in which the adult occurs; with the lightest forms frequenting chalky districts, and the darkest forms inhabiting peaty heathland or dark rocky terrain.
Imago. 32–39 mm. Resident. Rests by day on bare patches of ground, under rocky ledges and overhanging vegetation, and on cliff faces. It is readily disturbed, but not so easily netted, especially on windy days. Single-brooded, flying in July and August, inhabiting heathland, moorland, downland, and rocky places by the sea. Locally widespread in coastal localities throughout the British Isles, and on inland heaths and downland in the southern half of England and Wales.
Larva. September to May on heather, bird's-foot trefoil, common rock-rose, *Potentilla* spp., salad burnet, shining crane's-bill (*Geranium lucidum*), and probably other low plants. In captivity it will accept garden strawberry, but it is a difficult species to get through hibernation.
Overwinters as a small larva.

Irish Annulet

Odontognophos dumetata hibernica Forder
Plate **43** : *4*

Similar species. *Gnophos obfuscata*, pl. **17**.
Imago. 24–28 mm. Resident. May be found after dark flying around buckthorn bushes when it is attracted both to light and the flowers of scabious and knapweed. Single-brooded, flying in August, inhabiting limestone pavement. Locally well established in the Burren, Co. Clare, where it was first found in 1991.
Larva. April to early July on buckthorn.
Overwinters as an egg.

Black Mountain Moth

Psodos coracina Esper
Plate **17** : *29–30*

Imago. 21–28 mm. Resident. Flies in sunshine. Single-brooded, flying in July, inhabiting the higher plateaux and summits of mountains, and rarely found below 600 m (2000 ft). Widespread and locally common in the central Highlands of Scotland; also recorded from Ross-shire and Sutherland.
Larva. Evidence suggests that this species has a two-year life-cycle, and overwinters twice in the larval stage. The only recorded foodplant is crowberry.

Black-veined Moth

Siona lineata Scopoli
Plate **17** : *31*

Imago. 38–48 mm. Resident. The moth rests during the day in long grass and is readily disturbed. In hot sunshine it will fly of its own accord. Single-brooded, flying in late May and June, inhabiting downland and grassy embankments where the female has been noted depositing eggs on tor-grass. A very local species, confined to a few localities in southeast Kent.
Larva. July to May on marjoram and knapweed. In captivity on knotgrass, dock and bird's-foot trefoil.
Overwinters as a larva.

Straw Belle

Aspitates gilvaria gilvaria Denis & Schiffermüller
Plate **17** : *32–33*

Similar species. *A. ochrearia*, pl. **17**, has a more rounded forewing and a distinct antemedian fascia.

Imago. 32–39 mm. Resident. Flies naturally at dusk, but is readily disturbed and more easily obtained during the day. Single-brooded, flying in July and August, inhabiting chalk downland. Very local in southeast England, and confined to the North Downs of Surrey and Kent.

A. gilvaria burrenensis Cockayne, pl. **17** : *34–35*. This race differs from the typical form by its darker appearance and by having the oblique stripe of the hindwing extending almost to the hind margin. Well established and locally common in the Burren, Co. Clare. Elsewhere in Ireland the species has been reported from Cos Derry, Galway, Dublin and Wicklow, but in the absence of specimens it is not known to which race these records relate.

Larva. September to June on thyme, cinquefoil (*Potentilla* spp.), wild parsnip (*Pastinaca sativa*), and other low plants.
Overwinters as a very small larva.

Yellow Belle

Aspitates ochrearia Rossi
Plate **17** : *36*

Similar species. *A. gilvaria*, pl. **17** and text.

Imago. 28–36 mm. Resident. Frequently disturbed during the day from long grass and low herbage. The male occasionally flies in hot sunshine, but the normal time of flight is from dusk onwards when it is attracted to light. The less active female is more readily found at rest than at light. Double-brooded, flying in May and June, and again in August and September, inhabiting sandhills, shingle beaches, waste ground, edges of salt-marshes, and other rough grassy places. Widespread and locally common in all the seaboard counties of southern England, ranging up the west coast to Pembrokeshire, and the east coast to Lincolnshire. It is well established in the Breck district of Norfolk and Suffolk, and along the Thames estuary, otherwise it is rarely found far inland.

Larva. September to May, and June to July on wild carrot (*Daucus carota*), buck's-horn plantain (*Plantago coronopus*), beaked hawk's-beard (*Crepis vesicaria*), and probably other low plants. In confinement it will eat knotgrass.
Overwinters as a larva.

Grey Scalloped Bar

Dyscia fagaria Thunberg
Plate **17** : *37–39*

Variation. Rather variable in both size and ground colour, the latter ranging from white to dark grey. Light-coloured forms occur frequently in Scotland and the New Forest, Hampshire, and very dark specimens have occurred in Surrey and Cheshire. A lead-coloured and obscurely marked race occurs in southwest Ireland.

Imago. 31–40 mm. Resident. Occasionally put up during the day, but more frequently seen after dark resting on heather, and to a lesser extent at light. Single-brooded, flying from late May to July, sometimes later in the north, inhabiting heathland, moorland, and mosses. Locally widespread in the northern half of Wales, west Midlands, northern England, much of Scotland, including the Inner Hebrides and Orkney, and Ireland. Elsewhere it is found locally in southern England from Surrey to Cornwall.

Larva. Autumn to spring on heather, heath and cross-leaved heath.
Overwinters as a small larva.

Grass Wave

Perconia strigillaria Hübner
Plate **17** : *40–41*

Variation. Locally variable, but with very little geographical significance, except that the lighter forms appear to predominate in western Britain and Ireland. Very dark specimens are found commonly in one Yorkshire locality and occasionally elsewhere.

Imago. 36–41 mm. Resident. Flies naturally from dusk onwards, but in dry weather is readily disturbed during the day. Single-brooded, flying in June and July, inhabiting heathland, moorland, commons, woodland rides and clearings. Widespread and locally common in Surrey, Sussex and Hampshire. Sporadically distributed in the rest of England, Wales, southern Scotland and Ireland.

Larva. August to May on heather, heath, broom, and the flowers of gorse.
Overwinters as a small larva.

Family: Sphingidae

Nine resident and eight confirmed migrant species represent this medium- to large-sized family in the British Isles. Several other species have been reported in Britain, but the origin of most of them is doubtful, and only one of these is included as a possible immigrant. All but the three smallest members of the family fly at night and are attracted to light.

The rounded and greenish eggs are usually laid singly on the leaves of the foodplant.

The larvae are generally smooth in appearance, and are usually adorned with brightly coloured lateral stripes or eye-like spots and a horn-like projection on the twelfth segment. Most of the resident species may be found by searching the foodplants by day.

Pupation takes place on or under the surface of the ground, and the pupae of the tree-feeding species may be obtained by digging the soil around the base of their respective foodplants.

SUBFAMILY: SPHINGINAE

Convolvulus Hawk-moth
Agrius convolvuli Linnaeus
Plate **18** : *4*

Imago. 94–120 mm. Immigrant. Frequently found at dusk visiting the flowers of garden plants such as *Nicotiana* and *Petunia*, and also at light. It is seen in most years, sometimes in large numbers as in 1945 when more than 500 specimens were reported. It appears from mid-summer to mid-autumn and has been noted from most parts of the British Isles. Widespread in southern Europe, Asia and Africa.
Larva. Occasionally found in Britain feeding on field bindweed and other species of Convolvulaceae.

Death's-head Hawk-moth
Acherontia atropos Linnaeus
Plate **18** : *1*

Imago. 102–135 mm. Immigrant. Is attracted to light and is known to visit beehives in search of honey. Recorded in small numbers in most years, mostly as adults and larvae, sometimes as pupae. The greatest number recorded in one year was almost 400 of all stages in 1956. May to September are the usual months of appearance and although favouring southern and eastern England it has been noted from most parts of the British Isles. Abroad its range includes southern Europe, Africa and the Middle East.
Larva. August to October usually feeding on the leaves of potato (*Solanum tuberosum*) and occasionally on other species of Solanaceae. In captivity it has been successfully reared on garden privet.
Pupa. Has been found in the ground when potatoes are lifted, sometimes in large numbers in the days before crop spraying and mechanical harvesting became common practice.

Privet Hawk-moth
Sphinx ligustri Linnaeus
Plate **18** : *9*

Imago. 100–120 mm. Resident and occasional immigrant. Flies at night and is attracted to light. Single-brooded, flying in June and July, inhabiting woodland, fenland, gardens, etc. Widely distributed, but not common in the southern half of the British Isles.
Larva. July to August on garden and wild privet, lilac, holly and ash.
Overwinters as a pupa.

Wild Cherry Sphinx
Sphinx drupiferarum Smith

Similar species. *S. ligustri*, pl. **18**, has the hindwing and abdomen more intensively marked with pink.

Imago. 100–120 mm. Status uncertain, possible immigrant. The only British specimen was taken at light at Weston-super-Mare, Somerset, on 21.v.1970. The species is an inhabitant of North America, where it flies from May to July.
Larva. *July to September on apple, plum, wild cherry and lilac.
Overwinters as a pupa.

Pine Hawk-moth
Hyloicus pinastri Linnaeus
Plate **19** : *10*

Imago. 72–80 mm. Resident. Comes frequently to light. Single-brooded, flying in May and June. Confined to southern and eastern England and not uncommon in parts of Dorset, Hampshire, Surrey, Sussex and the Breckland of Norfolk and Suffolk.
Larva. August to September on Scots pine.
Overwinters as a pupa.

Lime Hawk-moth
Mimas tiliae Linnaeus
Plate **19** : *4–6*

Variation. The ground colour of the males varies from pale salmon-pink to dark olive-green and in the females from light pink to reddish-brown. The median fascia of the forewing varies in size and shape as illustrated in figs 4–5.
Imago. 70–80 mm. Resident. Comes regularly to light. Single-brooded, flying in May and June. Generally distributed in the southern half of England, but rarely seen in large numbers except in parts of the London area.
Larva. July to September on lime, English elm, alder and birch.
Overwinters as a pupa and is often found in this stage at the roots of lime and elm just below the surface of the soil.

Eyed Hawk-moth
Smerinthus ocellata Linnaeus
Plate **19** : *3*

Imago. 75–95 mm. Resident. Comes to light in moderate numbers. Single-brooded, flying from May to July, although a partial second generation may occasionally occur in late summer. Generally distributed and not uncommon throughout England and Wales; somewhat local in Ireland.
Larva. June to September on willow, aspen, sallow, apple and occasionally on poplar.
Overwinters as a pupa.

Poplar Hawk-moth
Laothoe populi Linnaeus
Plate **19** : *1–2*

Variation. The buff form (fig 2), which occurs more frequently in the female, exists as a small percentage of the total population in some localities such as the London area.

Imago. 72–92 mm. Resident. Comes freely to light. Usually single-brooded, flying from May to July, with an occasional second generation in August and September. Generally distributed and often common throughout much of the British Isles.

Larva. July to September on poplar, aspen, sallow and willow.

Overwinters as a pupa.

SUBFAMILY: MACROGLOSSINAE

Narrow-bordered Bee Hawk-moth
Hemaris tityus Linnaeus
Plate **18** : *7*

Similar species. *H. fuciformis*, pl. **18**, has a large brown discal spot and a broader terminal fascia, particularly noticeable on the hindwing.

Imago. 41–46 mm. Resident. Flies in sunshine and visits the flowers of bugle, bird's-foot trefoil, red valerian, *Rhododendron*, and lousewort (*Pedicularis* spp.). Single-brooded, flying from mid-May to mid-June, inhabiting woodland, marshland and the wetter parts of moorland. Distributed throughout much of the British Isles, but very local and on the whole uncommon.

Larva. July to August on devil's-bit scabious.

Overwinters as a pupa.

Broad-bordered Bee Hawk-moth
Hemaris fuciformis Linnaeus
Plate **18** : *8*

Similar species. *H. tityus*, pl. **18** and text.

Imago. 46–52 mm. Resident. Flies in sunshine and visits a variety of woodland and garden flowers such as bugle, honeysuckle, ragged-robin and *Rhododendron*. Single-brooded, flying in May and June, although in the exceptionally hot summer of 1976 a partial second generation occurred in Hampshire during August. Abroad the species is regularly double-brooded. Locally distributed in the southern half of England where it inhabits woodland rides and clearings.

Larva. July to August on honeysuckle.

Overwinters as a pupa.

Humming-bird Hawk-moth
Macroglossum stellatarum Linnaeus
Plate **18** : *10*

Imago. 50–58 mm. Immigrant. Usually seen by day in sunshine visiting the flowers of many wild and garden plants such as red valerian, honeysuckle, *Petunia*, *Escallonia*, *Buddleia* and *Jasminia*. Occurring from spring to autumn in most years in varying numbers. The greatest number recorded was more than 4000 in 1947. The species is distributed over most of the Palaearctic region.

Larva. July to August on hedge bedstraw, lady's bedstraw and wild madder (*Rubia peregrina*).

Overwinters as an adult, but rarely, if ever, in Britain.

Willowherb Hawk-moth
Proserpinus proserpina Pallas
Plate **43** : *13*

Imago. 48–54 mm. Suspected immigrant or accidental introduction. Single-brooded on the Continent, flying from May to July, inhabiting waste ground, railway embankments and river-banks. The two specimens recorded in Britain are at light at Newhaven, East Sussex, on 25.v.1985 and at rest on a stone pillar at St Katharine's Dock, East London, on 18.vii.1995. Abroad it is known from central Europe where its range extends northwards to the Ardennes.

Larva. *July and August on willowherb, evening primrose (*Oenothera biennis*) and purple loosestrife (*Lythrum salicaria*).

Overwinters as a pupa.

Oleander Hawk-moth
Daphnis nerii Linnaeus
Plate **18** : *6*

Imago. 80–120 mm. Immigrant. Mostly recorded at light. Rare and absent in many years, the maximum reported for any one year being 13 in 1953. Usually occurs from August to October, mainly in southern England, with the occasional record from Scotland and Ireland. Abroad it is an inhabitant of North Africa extending eastwards into Asia.

Larva. *Feeds on oleander (*Nerium oleander*) and periwinkle (*Vinca* spp.). In captivity it has been reared on garden privet.

Spurge Hawk-moth
Hyles euphorbiae Linnaeus
Plate **19** : *8*

Similar species. *H. gallii*, pl. **19**. *H. lineata livornica*, pl. **19**.

Imago. 64–77 mm. Immigrant. Is attracted to light and occasionally visits flowers. A very rare visitor to southern England, the most recent records being at Selsdon, Surrey, on 26.v.1973; East End of London on 13.x.1976; at Feltham, Middlesex, on 20.viii.1977; Brentwood, Essex, on 28.vii.1979; Smeeth, Kent, on 24.vii.1981; Newton Abbot, Devon, on 17.vi.1991; Dungeness, Kent, on 12.viii.1993; a full-grown larva at Hastings, East Sussex, on 22.viii.1994; and Dungeness, on 12.vi.1997. Its distribution abroad extends through central and southern Europe into Asia.

Larva. August to September on spurge (*Euphorbia* spp.). Rarely found in Britain.

Bedstraw Hawk-moth
Hyles gallii Rottemburg
Plate **19** : *7*

Similar species. *H. euphorbiae*, pl. **19**. *H. lineata livornica*, pl. **19**.

Imago. 64–78 mm. Immigrant. Comes regularly to light, and occasionally visits flowers. An erratic visitor;

absent for many years and then appearing in good numbers as in 1870, 1888, 1955 and 1973, then becoming temporarily established for a few years. It has been recorded from many parts of the British Isles as far north as the Shetland Islands, usually appearing from May to August. Its range abroad extends from western Europe to Japan.

Larva. August to September on various species of bedstraw and willowherb, and on one occasion on garden *Godetia*. Large numbers of larvae occurred in 1888 in Lancashire, Cheshire, and southeast England; from 1955 to 1958 in Norfolk; and in 1973 in many localities in England and Scotland.

Overwinters as a pupa.

Striped Hawk-moth
Hyles livornica Esper
Plate **19** : 9

Similar species. *H. euphorbiae*, pl. **19**. *H. gallii*, pl. **19**. *H. lineata* Fabr. (*Author's note*: *H. lineata* has the tegula bordered with white, surrounding a central white stripe; and a central white stripe the length of the patagium to the base of the head. An American species with one reputed British specimen from Yorkshire in 1897 in the Natural History Museum, London.)

Imago. 78–90 mm. Immigrant. Flies usually at night, is attracted to light and at dusk visits the flowers of red valerian and garden plants such as *Petunia*. Occurs from May to October in most years, usually in small numbers although in 1943 over 500 were recorded. Reported from many parts of the British Isles as far north as central Scotland. Widely distributed abroad extending to southern Europe and Africa.

Larva. June to July on hedge bedstraw, willowherb, knotgrass and snapdragon (*Antirrhinum majus*), and in captivity on dock, *Fuchsia* and grape-vine.

Elephant Hawk-moth
Deilephila elpenor Linnaeus
Plate **18** : 3

Imago. 62–72 mm. Resident. Comes readily to light, and visits flowers, especially honeysuckle and *Rhododendron*. Usually single-brooded, flying from May to July with a very occasional and partial second generation in late summer. A widely distributed and often common species throughout England, Wales and many parts of Ireland. Rather local in Scotland, mainly in the south and west.

Larva. July to September on willowherb, bedstraw, *Fuchsia* and many other plants.

Overwinters as a pupa.

Small Elephant Hawk-moth
Deilephila porcellus Linnaeus
Plate **18** : 2

Imago. 47–56 mm. Resident. Flies from dusk onwards, is attracted to light, and visits the flowers of honeysuckle

and *Rhododendron*. Single-brooded, flying from May to July, inhabiting chalk downland, heathland, golf-courses, shingle beaches and coastal sandhills. Widely distributed, but rarely common, over most of the British Isles.

Larva. July to early September, mainly on bedstraw. Overwinters as a pupa.

Silver-striped Hawk-moth
Hippotion celerio Linnaeus
Plate **18** : 5

Imago. 72–80 mm. Immigrant. It is attracted to light and has been recorded visiting the flowers of ivy and *Verbena*. A rare visitor to Britain, absent in some years and rarely seen in numbers; the 41 specimens reported in 1885 were exceptional, and the best total in recent years was 14 in 1963. Has occurred throughout England, sometimes as early as May, but more often from August to November. Widely distributed abroad extending to southern Europe.

Larva. *Foodplants given are bedstraw, willowherb, grape-vine, *Fuchsia* and Virginia creeper (*Parthenocissus* spp.). The few British larvae to be reported have been found in October.

Family: Notodontidae

Twenty-seven species, of which 23 are resident, represent this family in the British Isles.

The adults are seldom found during the day, but after dark the males of most species come readily to light. The females' response to light varies with each species, but they never appear so frequently as the males, and those of a few species are rarely ever seen. Both sexes are unable to feed and so are never attracted to sugar or flowers. Male specimens required for preservation should be killed or refrigerated at once as they seldom settle down in confinement and soon damage themselves.

The larvae are smooth in appearance, except those of the *Phalera*, *Clostera* and *Diloba* genera which are slightly hairy, and very variable in form; most have fleshy dorsal humps and the *Cerura*, *Furcula* and *Stauropus* genera have the hind claspers modified into tail-like appendages. All feed on trees and shrubs; the *Clostera* genus between spun leaves, and the others openly, usually resting with the head and anal segments raised.

The pupae are either subterranean, usually in a silken cocoon, or within a tough cocoon constructed of chewed wood.

Buff-tip
Phalera bucephala Linnaeus
Plate **20** : 1

Imago. 55–68 mm. Resident. Comes to light in small numbers, usually after midnight. Single-brooded, flying in June and July, inhabiting woodland and commons. Generally distributed throughout the British Isles and usually a common species in England and Wales.

Larva. July to September on elm, sallow, lime, oak and many other deciduous trees and shrubs.

Overwinters as a pupa.

Puss Moth

Cerura vinula Linnaeus

Plate **20** : *5*

Imago. 62–80 mm. Resident. Both sexes come to light in small numbers. Single-brooded, flying from May to July. Widely distributed throughout the British Isles as far north as the Orkney Islands. Generally a moderately common species.

Larva. July to September on poplar, sallow and aspen.

Overwinters as a pupa enclosed in a tough cocoon on the trunk of its foodplant or a nearby wooden post.

Alder Kitten

Furcula bicuspis Borkhausen

Plate **20** : *4*

Similar species. *F. furcula*, pl. **20**, and *F. bifida*, pl. **20**, both have a grey central band on the forewing, the inner line of this band being almost straight. (See text fig 27.)

Imago. 40–48 mm. Resident. Both sexes come regularly to light. Single-brooded, flying from mid-May to early July, inhabiting woodland. Rather local in the southern half of England, mainly in the southwest, southeast, Wales, Norfolk and parts of the Midlands.

Larva. July to September on birch and alder.

Overwinters as a pupa enclosed in a tough cocoon on a branch or the trunk of its foodplant.

Sallow Kitten

Furcula furcula Clerck

Plate **20** : *2*

Similar species. *F. bicuspis*, pl. **20** and text. *F. bifida*, pl. **20**, is larger and the outer margin of the central band of the forewing does not angle towards costa and is not dentate.

Imago. 35–42 mm. Resident. Both sexes come readily to light. Double-brooded in England and Wales, flying in May and June and again in August; single-brooded in Scotland and Ireland, flying in June and early July. Widely distributed and generally common throughout much of the British Isles.

Larva. First brood from mid-June to mid-July and the second brood in August and September on sallow, aspen and occasionally poplar.

Overwinters as a pupa in a cocoon constructed on a stem of the foodplant.

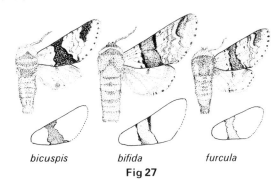

bicuspis   bifida   furcula

Fig 27

Poplar Kitten

Furcula bifida Brahm

Plate **20** : *3*

Similar species. *F. bicuspis*, pl. **20** and text. *F. furcula*, pl. **20** and text.

Imago. 44–48 mm. Resident. Comes to light in small numbers. Single-brooded, flying from late May to July. Widely distributed in England and parts of Wales, rarely seen commonly outside well-established poplar plantations in southern England. Rare in Ireland and, with the exception of Co. Galway, recorded only from the northern counties.

Larva. July to September on aspen, poplar and occasionally sallow.

Overwinters as a pupa enclosed in a tough cocoon on the trunk of its foodplant.

Lobster Moth

Stauropus fagi Linnaeus

Plate **20** : *9–10*

Variation. The melanic form *obscura* Rebel (fig 10) occurs in many localities, and in those nearer to London it represents the dominant form. Irish specimens are lighter and larger than the normal typical form found in Britain.

Imago. 55–70 mm. Resident. The male comes readily to light, but the female is seldom seen. Single-brooded, flying from mid-May to July, inhabiting mature woodland. Widely distributed and not uncommon in southern England, parts of Wales, and southwest Ireland.

Larva. July to September on oak, hazel, birch and beech.

Overwinters as a pupa.

Iron Prominent

Notodonta dromedarius Linnaeus

Plate **20** : *6–7*

Variation. Specimens from northern England and Scotland tend to be darker and more slate-grey in colour (fig 7).

Imago. 42–50 mm. Resident. Both sexes come readily to light. Double-brooded, flying in May and June and

again in August except in the north where it is usually single-brooded, flying in June and July. Widespread and often common throughout much of the British Isles.
Larva. July and August to September on birch, alder, hazel and oak.
Overwinters as a pupa.

Large Dark Prominent

Notodonta torva Hübner
Plate **20** : *8*

Similar species. The smaller and usually darker male might be confused with a large pale example of *N. dromedarius*, pl. **20**, which has a conspicuous pale basal patch on the forewing and a short whitish-yellow streak along the lower part of the postmedian fascia.
Imago. 46–50 mm. Immigrant. Double-brooded on the Continent, flying from May to June and again in August. There are only two British records; the first was bred from either an egg or larva found in Norfolk in the summer of 1882 and the second came to light at Eastbourne, Sussex, on 29.v.1979. Abroad it is widely distributed in central Europe.
Larva. *June to July and September on aspen and poplar.
Overwinters as a pupa.

Three-humped Prominent

Tritophia tritophus Denis & Schiffermüller
Plate **20** : *12*

Imago. 54–62 mm. Immigrant. Most of the adults recorded have been at light. Double-brooded on the Continent, flying from May to June and July to August. A few specimens of this very rare visitor were reported during the latter half of the nineteenth century, either as adults or as larvae. Since then there have been only seven additional records, all of adults. These are Bedford on 13.v.1907; Havant, Hampshire, on 20.v.1920; Waterlooville, Hampshire, in July 1920; Folkestone, Kent, on 21.viii.1955; Freshwater, Isle of Wight, on 19.viii.1956; Cranmore, Isle of Wight, on 2.viii.1960 and Walberswick, Suffolk, on 24.vii.1992. Abroad it is widely distributed throughout much of Europe.
Larva. *June and September on poplar, willow, aspen and birch.
Overwinters as a pupa.

Pebble Prominent

Eligmodonta ziczac Linnaeus
Plate **20** : *13*

Imago. 42–52 mm. Resident. Comes regularly to light. Double-brooded in the south, flying in May and June and again in August. Single-brooded in the north, flying in June and July. Widely distributed and common throughout the British Isles.

Larva. June to July and late August to September on sallow, willow, aspen and poplar.
Overwinters as a pupa.

Tawny Prominent

Harpyia milhauseri Fabricius
Plate **43** : *14*

Imago. 50–60 mm. Immigrant. Single-brooded in central Europe, flying in May and June. The two British specimens to date, both at light, were Aldwick Bay, West Sussex, on 11.vi.1966 and Dungeness, Kent, on 24.v.1993. Widely distributed, but local in central and southern Europe, its range including Denmark and northern France.
Larva. *June to August on various species of oak and occasionally beech.
Overwinters as a pupa.

Great Prominent

Peridea anceps Goeze
Plate **20** : *11*

Variation. The melanic form *fusca* Cockayne has occurred in the Lake District and a similar form is occasionally found in Surrey.
Imago. 52–72 mm. Resident. The male comes readily to light. Single-brooded, flying from late April to June, inhabiting mature woodland. Widely distributed and moderately common in the southern half of Britain and the Lake District. Local elsewhere, occurring as far north as West Perthshire.
Larva. June to August on oak.
Overwinters as a pupa.

Lesser Swallow Prominent

Pheosia gnoma Fabricius
Plate **20** : *14–15*

Variation. In specimens from Scotland the ground colour of the forewing is clearer white and the colour of the thorax is either dark brown or light grey; Irish specimens have a grey thorax and in southern England it is light brown.
Similar species. *P. tremula*, pl. **20**, has a white, slightly wavy, line running through the dark anal patch of the hindwing and the forewing lacks the distinct white wedge-shaped tornal streak of *P. gnoma*. (See text fig 28.)
Imago. 46–58 mm. Resident. Both sexes come to light. Double-brooded, flying in May and June and again in August. Widely distributed and generally common throughout most of the British Isles.
Larva. June to July and late August to September on birch.
Overwinters as a pupa.

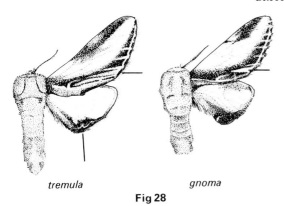

tremula   *gnoma*

Fig 28

Swallow Prominent
Pheosia tremula Clerck
Plate **20** : *16*

Similar species. *P. gnoma*, pl. **20** and text.
Imago. 50–64 mm. Resident. Both sexes come to light. Double-brooded in the south, flying in May and June and again in August, single-brooded in the north, flying in June and July. Widely distributed and generally common throughout most of the British Isles.
Larva. June to July and September on poplar, aspen, willow and sallow.
Overwinters as a pupa.

Coxcomb Prominent
Ptilodon capucina Linnaeus
Plate **20** : *18*

Variation. Ground colour can vary from pale yellowish-brown to dark purple-brown; the darkest form being ab. *nigra* Riesen.
Similar species. *Ptilodontella cucullina*, pl. **20**.
Imago. 40–50 mm. Resident. Both sexes come to light. Double-brooded, flying in May and June and again in August and September. Widely distributed and common throughout most of the British Isles.
Larva. June to July and August to September on hawthorn, birch, hazel, alder, oak and many other deciduous trees.
Overwinters as a pupa.

Maple Prominent
Ptilodontella cucullina Denis & Schiffermüller
Plate **20** : *17*

Similar species. *Ptilodon capucina*, pl. **20**.
Imago. 37–46 mm. Resident. The male, especially, comes regularly to light. Single-brooded, flying from mid-May to July, inhabiting downland and woodland mainly on calcareous soils. Widespread, but seldom abundant, in East Anglia, and the southern and south-eastern counties of England. Also found locally in Devon and Somerset.

Larva. July to September on field maple and occasionally on sycamore.
Overwinters as a pupa.

Scarce Prominent
Odontosia carmelita Esper
Plate **20** : *19–20*

Variation. Specimens from Scotland are darker and purplish-grey in colour (fig 20).
Imago. 44–52 mm. Resident. The male comes regularly to light, the female less often. Single-brooded, flying in April and early May, inhabiting mature birch woods. Widely distributed in southern and southeast England, northern England and central Scotland. Isolated colonies exist in the Forest of Dean, Gloucestershire, and in Sherwood Forest, Nottinghamshire; and it has been recently recorded from South Devon. In Ireland it has been found in Cos Kerry, Cork, Tipperary, Fermanagh and Wicklow.
Larva. May to July on birch.
Overwinters as a pupa.

Pale Prominent
Pterostoma palpina Clerck
Plate **20** : *21*

Imago. 42–60 mm. Resident. Comes readily to light. Double-brooded in the south, flying from May to June and again in August. Single-brooded in the north, flying in May and June. Generally distributed throughout the British Isles, commoner in the southern half of England.
Larva. July and late August to September on poplar, aspen and sallow.
Overwinters as a pupa.

White Prominent
Leucodonta bicoloria Denis & Schiffermüller
Plate **21** : *1*

Imago. 38–42 mm. Resident. Comes freely to light on the Continent. Single-brooded, flying from mid-May to early July. A few specimens were claimed to have been taken in Burnt Wood, Staffordshire, in the middle of the nineteenth century and these remain the only English records. In Ireland it occurs in the mature birch woods of Co. Kerry, where it has been found in small numbers both as adults and larvae, both stages having been obtained by beating the lower branches of birch trees. It has not been recorded since 1938, but there is no reason to assume that this species is extinct.
Larva. June to August on birch.
Overwinters as a pupa.

Plumed Prominent
Ptilophora plumigera Denis & Schiffermüller
Plate **20** : *22–24*

Variation. Male specimens from southeast Kent have the forewing a unicolorous light orange-brown (fig 24).

Imago. 33–44 mm. Resident. Comes regularly to light, the males appearing about an hour after dusk, the females usually not until much later. Single-brooded, flying in November and December, inhabiting woodland on calcareous soils. Very local in southern England from Devon to Suffolk, also in the Cotswolds and Chilterns.

Larva. Late April to early June mainly on field maple, also on sycamore.

Overwinters as an egg.

Marbled Brown

Drymonia dodonaea Denis & Schiffermüller

Plate **21** : *5–6*

Variation. The melanic form *nigrescens* Lempke (fig 6) occurs regularly in the Norfolk Broads and occasionally elsewhere.

Similar species. *D. ruficornis*, pl. **21**, has a conspicuous black crescent in the discal area of the forewing.

Imago. 39–44 mm. Resident. The male comes readily to light, the female rarely so. Single-brooded, flying in late May and June, inhabiting oak woods. Locally common in many parts of Britain as far north as west Scotland. In Ireland it has occurred in Cos Cork and Kerry.

Larva. July to September mainly on oak.

Overwinters as a pupa.

Lunar Marbled Brown

Drymonia ruficornis Hufnagel

Plate **21** : *2–4*

Variation. Specimens from Ireland are stated to be darker and larger than those from Britain. Melanic examples occasionally occur in the New Forest, north Surrey and elsewhere (fig 3).

Similar species. *D. dodonaea*, pl. **21** and text.

Imago. 38–46 mm. Resident. Both sexes come regularly to light. Single-brooded, flying in April and May. Widely distributed and moderately common in the southern half of England and Wales; rather less common in northern England, southern Scotland and Ireland.

Larva. July to August on oak.

Overwinters as a pupa.

Dusky Marbled Brown

Gluphisia crenata vertunea Bray

Plate **43** : *15*

Imago. 30–38 mm. Status uncertain, possible former resident now extinct. Flies at night and on the Continent is attracted to light. Double-brooded in central Europe, flying in April and again in June and July. The three reputedly authentic records are as follows: a female in Ongar Park Wood, Essex, in June 1839; another female in the same locality in June 1841; and a larva beaten from poplar at Halton, Buckinghamshire, in August 1853. The only recent record is of a male taken at light at Gorey, Jersey, Channel Islands, on 28.vii.1995. Abroad the species is found in central and southern Europe.

Larva. May and August to September on poplar.

Overwinters as a pupa.

Small Chocolate-tip

Clostera pigra Hufnagel

Plate **21** : *7–8*

Variation. Specimens from Ireland and Scotland are more brightly marked than those from southern England.

Imago. 24–28 mm. Occasionally flies during the day in sunshine, but more usually late at night when it is attracted to light. Double-brooded in the south of Britain and in Ireland, flying in May and August. Single-brooded in the north, flying in June and July. A locally common species occurring in many parts of the British Isles.

Larva. June and September in the south, August to mid-September in Scotland mainly on aspen, creeping willow, eared willow and sallow, hiding by day between spun leaves.

Overwinters as a pupa.

Scarce Chocolate-tip

Clostera anachoreta Denis & Schiffermüller

Plate **21** : *9*

Similar species. *C. curtula*, pl. **21**, from which it differs in having the brown apical patch of the forewing intersected by the white postmedian line and the presence of two dark spots above the tornus. (See text fig 29.)

Imago. 36–38 mm. Suspected immigrant and transitory resident. The males and to a lesser extent the females are attracted to light. Double-brooded, flying in April and May and again in August. The species was first noted in southeast Kent in 1858 and for the next 54 years was found at regular intervals, this fact indicating that it was probably resident, particularly as most of the records were of larvae. There appear to be no records after 1912 until 1951, when a specimen was taken at Dover on 8 August. Thenceforth the records for Kent have been Lydd on 9.viii.1953; Dover on 26.vii.1964; Hamstreet on 21.viii.1968; and Dungeness, on 16.viii.1974 and 18.viii.1978. In August 1979 more than 20 specimens were seen at Dungeness, followed in September by the discovery of wild larvae. Since 1979 it has been noted annually in both stages. Outside Kent it has been noted in the egg stage at St Leonards, Sussex, on 23.viii.1893; Ipswich, Suffolk, in 1898; as larvae at Dovercourt, Essex, in 1907; Clacton, Essex, on 8.viii.1908; in the egg stage at Canford Cliffs, Dorset, in 1909; Waldringfield, Suffolk, on 3.viii.1956; Bradwell-on-Sea, Essex, on 9.v.1976 and 16.vii.1976; Southwold, Suffolk, on 4.viii.1976; and Bradwell-on-Sea on 2.vi.1981; all as adults unless stated otherwise.

Larva. June to July and September on sallow, poplar, aspen and willow.
Overwinters as a pupa.

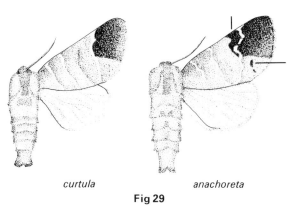

curtula   anachoreta
Fig 29

Chocolate-tip
Clostera curtula Linnaeus
Plate **21** : *10*

Similar species. *C. anachoreta*, pl. **21** and text.
Imago. 36–38 mm. Resident. Both sexes come to light in small numbers, but rarely before midnight. Double-brooded in England, flying in April and May, and again in August and September. Apparently only single-brooded in Scotland, flying in June. Widely distributed in southern and southeast England, ranging northwards to Lincolnshire. Resident also in Scotland, occurring locally in Aberdeenshire and Inverness-shire.
Larva. May to June and August to September in England; July to August in Scotland, feeding on aspen, poplar and willow, hiding by day between spun leaves.
Overwinters as a pupa.

Figure of Eight
Diloba caeruleocephala Linnaeus
Plate **21** : *11*

Imago. 34–40 mm. Resident. Comes to light in small numbers. Single-brooded, flying in October and early November, inhabiting woodland, commons and hedgerows. Widely distributed and not uncommon over much of England and Wales. Thinly scattered and rather scarce in Scotland and Ireland.
Larva. May to July on hawthorn, blackthorn, apple, and other trees.
Overwinters as an egg.

Family: Thaumetopoeidae

Oak Processionary
Thaumetopoea processionea Linnaeus
Plate **43** : *17*

Imago. 31–41 mm. Resident (Channel Islands) and immigrant. Single-brooded on the Continent, flying in July and August. In Britain male specimens have been recorded at light as follows: Mawnan Smith, Cornwall, on 19.viii.1983; two at Dungeness, Kent, on 9.viii.1992; Greatstone, Kent, on 10.viii.1992; two at Languard, Suffolk, on 4.viii.1995; two at Bradwell-on-Sea, Essex, on 3.viii.1995; two at Sholden, Kent, on 10.viii.1995; Ramsgate, Kent, on 10.viii.1995; Helpston, Northamptonshire, on 11.viii.1995; Languard on 12.viii.1995; Sea Palling, Norfolk, on 12.viii.1995; Meldreth, Cambridgeshire, on 13.viii.1995 and Worth Matravers, Dorset, on 18.viii.1996. It was first noted in the Channel Islands, on Jersey, in 1984, and is now considered to be resident. On neighbouring Guernsey it was reported once on 18.viii.1983 and twice on 18.viii.1996. Abroad it is a widespread and locally abundant species occurring in central and southern Europe.
Larva. *May and June, living gregariously on oak, and often causing considerable damage to the foliage. The hairs of the larva are extremely irritant to sensitive skin.
Overwinters as an egg.

Family: Lymantriidae

Eleven moderate-sized species represent this family in the British Isles.
The males of the *Orgyia* genus fly in sunshine, whereas those of the other species fly at night and come readily to light. The adults of this family are not attracted to sugar or flowers. The eggs are laid in batches, usually covered by hairs from the anal tuft of the female.
The larvae are very hairy and some species are adorned with long dorsal tufts. The larval hairs of a few species can cause a severe skin-rash; all the stages should be handled with care as the irritant hairs are transferred to the cocoon, and to the egg-batch via the anal tuft of the female.
The pupae are stout and hairy, and spun up in silken cocoons usually amongst the foliage of the foodplant, but sometimes on tree-trunks or fences.

Reed Tussock
Laelia coenosa Hübner
(South 1961, vol. 1, plate 36).

Imago. 46–50 mm. Extinct resident. The male comes readily to light. Single-brooded, flying in July and August. First reported in 1819 from Whittlesea Mere, Huntingdonshire, and later found in the Fens of Yaxley, Huntingdonshire, Burwell and Wicken, Cambridgeshire; being quite abundant in these latter localities, especially in the larval stage. By 1855 all its habitats had been drained and ploughed up except Wicken Fen, where it throve until 1873 and then declined rapidly, the last specimen being recorded in 1879. The species

is still widespread, but local, in the rest of Europe, occurring in France, Denmark and northern Germany.
Larva. Autumn to spring on branched bur-reed, great fen-sedge and common reed.
Overwinters as a larva.

Scarce Vapourer
Orgyia recens Hübner
Plate **21** : *14–15*

Similar species. *O. antiqua*, pl. **21**, lacks the white mark on the apex of the forewing.
Imago. Male 34–40 mm, female wingless. Resident. The males fly by day. Mainly single-brooded, occurring in June and July, with a partial second generation in late summer and early autumn. Formerly widespread in the southern half of England and parts of Wales, now extremely local and confined to the counties of Yorkshire, Lincolnshire and Norfolk.
Larva. August to June on hawthorn, sallow, oak and other deciduous trees and shrubs. Has also been found on meadowsweet and water dock.
Overwinters as a larva.

The Vapourer
Orgyia antiqua Linnaeus
Plate **21** : *12–13*

Similar species. *O. recens*, pl. **21** and text.
Imago. Male 35–38 mm, female wingless. Resident. The males fly by day. Mainly single-brooded, occurring from July to September, with a rare partial second brood in October. Generally distributed throughout much of the British Isles, often common in suburban areas including central London.
Larva. May to August on most deciduous trees and shrubs.
Overwinters as an egg, attached amongst several hundred others, on the outside of the female's cocoon. These are often found on tree-trunks, fences and under the window-sills or eaves of buildings.

Dark Tussock
Dicallomera fascelina Linnaeus
Plate **21** : *23–25*

Variation. The ground colour in specimens from northern England and Scotland is darker than in those from the south and examples of the sooty-grey form illustrated (fig 24) are not uncommon. An exceptionally large race occurs at Dungeness, Kent.
Similar species. *Calliteara pudibunda*, pl. **21**.
Imago. 40–53 mm. Resident. Both sexes come regularly to light. Single-brooded, flying in July and August, inhabiting moorland, coastal sandhills and shingle beaches. Widespread, but local in southern England, the coastal sandhills of Cheshire and Lancashire, northern England, and central Scotland. Rare and local in the northern half of Ireland.

Larva. September to May on a wide variety of plants including heather, sallow, broom, hawthorn, bramble and birch saplings.
Overwinters, sometimes twice in Scotland, as a larva.

Pale Tussock
Calliteara pudibunda Linnaeus
Plate **21** : *20–22*

Variation. The melanic form *concolor* Staudinger (fig 21) occurs in both sexes and has been noted mainly in the London area and the Home Counties, where it seems to be on the increase.
Similar species. *Dicallomera fascelina*, pl. **21**.
Imago. 50–70 mm. Resident. Comes to light. Single-brooded, flying in May and June. Widespread and generally common in England and Wales. Locally common in the southern half of Ireland.
Larva. July to September on birch, oak, elm, lime and many other deciduous trees. In the days before insecticides it was a caterpillar common in hop fields, being locally known as the 'hop-dog'.
Overwinters as a pupa.

Brown-tail
Euproctis chrysorrhoea Linnaeus
Plate **21** : *18*

Similar species. *E. similis*, pl. **21**.
Imago. 36–42 mm. Resident. Both sexes come freely to light. Usually single-brooded, flying in July and August, although following a very warm summer a partial second generation has occurred in October. A locally abundant species in eastern and southern England extending northwards to Yorkshire and westwards to the Scilly Isles. Essentially a coastal species outside Essex, Suffolk, Kent, Surrey and Hertfordshire. In the latter half of the nineteenth century it was occasionally reported from coastal localities in Northumberland and Co. Durham. More recently a male was taken at light at Lunan Bay, Angus, on 7.viii.1996.
Larva. September to May on hawthorn, blackthorn, sallow, sea-buckthorn, bramble and many other trees and shrubs. The larval hairs can cause severe and prolonged irritation if they come in contact with the human skin.
Overwinters as a larva within a communal web of tough silk.

Yellow-tail
Euproctis similis Fuessly
Plate **21** : *16–17*

Similar species. *E. chrysorrhoea*, pl. **21**.
Imago. 35–45 mm. Resident. Both sexes come regularly to light. Single-brooded, flying in July and August. Widely distributed and often common throughout England, but local and scarce in southern Scotland. In Ireland it has not been recorded outside Cos Down, Kildare, Galway, Dublin, Mayo and Wicklow.

Larva. September to May on hawthorn, oak, black-thorn, sallow and many other trees. Overwinters as a larva.

White Satin Moth
Leucoma salicis Linnaeus
Plate **21** : *19*
Similar species. *Arctornis l-nigrum*, pl. **21**.
Imago. 43–60 mm. Resident and immigrant. Comes to light in moderate numbers. Single-brooded, flying in July and August. Widely distributed in England and the eastern counties of Wales, but rarely abundant except in the London area and parts of Essex and Kent. The occasional records from Scotland, and from the Orkney and Shetland Islands, are considered to be of migrants. The only confirmed breeding site of this species in Ireland is near Newcastle, Co. Wicklow.
Larva. September to June on sallow, poplar and willow. Overwinters as a larva.

Black V Moth
Arctornis l-nigrum Müller
Plate **21** : *28*
Similar species. *Leucoma salicis*, pl. **21**.
Imago. 52–60 mm. Suspected immigrant and transitory resident. Both sexes, but mostly males, come to light. Single-brooded, flying in late June and July. During the early part of the nineteenth century several specimens were reported from near Sheffield, Yorkshire, and three from Kent. It was not recorded again until July 1904 at Chelmsford, Essex; a second occurred at Arundel, Sussex, on 7.vii.1946 and in June 1947 several were reported from Bradwell-on-Sea, Essex. There for the next 13 years it was noted annually, a total of 102 adults and one wild larva having been observed. The last record was July 1960. Abroad the species is wide-spread in central and southern Europe.
Larva. *August to May on a wide range of deciduous trees including elm, lime and sallow. Overwinters as a larva.

Black Arches
Lymantria monacha Linnaeus
Plate **21** : *29–31*
Variation. Specimens suffused with black have been noted from many localities including the New Forest, Hampshire, where it is not an uncommon form (fig 30). Extreme examples wholly suffused with black are referable to f. *eremita* Ochsenheimer.
Imago. 44–54 mm. Resident. Occasionally found on tree-trunks. The males in particular come readily to light. Single-brooded, flying in late July and August, inhabiting woodland. Distributed throughout the southern half of Britain. Rarely and not recently recorded from Ireland.
Larva. April to June, mainly on oak. Overwinters as an egg.

Gypsy Moth
Lymantria dispar Linnaeus
Plate **21** : *26–27*
Imago. 48–65 mm. Extinct resident and probable immigrant. The male flies by day and also at dusk. The female does not fly and seldom moves far from its cocoon. Single-brooded, flying in August. During the first half of the nineteenth century the species was relatively abundant in the fens of Huntingdonshire, Cambridgeshire and Norfolk. The exact date of its demise is obscured by unpublished attempts at reintroduction; the last accepted record is from Wennington Wood, Huntingdonshire, in 1907. Occasional male specimens continue to be reported at light, mainly from southern England, and these are presumed to be migrants. Some of the more recent sightings are from Margate, Kent, on 10.vii.1950; Dover, Kent, on 31.vii.1951; Salcombe, Devon, on 22.viii. 1954; Alverstoke, Hampshire, on 16.viii.1955; Lexden, Essex, on 10.vii.1959; Aldwick Bay, Sussex, on 29.vii. 1960; Folkestone, Kent, on 29.vii.1961; Deal, Kent, on 13.viii.1965; Sevenoaks, Kent, on 2.vii.1966; Alderley Edge, Cheshire, on 12.vii.1968; Mayland, Essex, on 4.viii. 1971; Ringmer, Sussex, on 3.ix.1973; Sevenoaks, Kent, on 4.viii.1982; Mawnan Smith, Cornwall, on 19.viii. 1983; Highcliffe, Hampshire, on 29.viii.1985; Aylesford, Kent, on 1.ix.1985; Portland, Dorset, on 10.ix.1986; Godshill, Isle of Wight, on 8.viii.1991; Brockenhurst, Hampshire, on 21.viii.1991; Greatstone, Kent, on 21.viii. 1991; Crowborough, East Sussex, on 21.viii.1991; Kingsbury Escopi, Somerset, on 18.viii.1992; Greatstone, on 25.viii.1992; Chale Green, Isle of Wight, on 4.ix. 1993; Dungeness, Kent, on 4.viii.1994; New Forest, Hampshire, on 5.viii.1994; Plymouth, Devon, on 10.viii. 1994; Ringmer, on 19.viii.1996 and Chardstock, Devon, on 22.viii.1996. Recorded fairly regularly on the Channel Islands. A widespread species in the rest of Europe and a major forest pest throughout much of its range.
Larva. April to June feeding, on the Continent, on a wide variety of wild and cultivated trees. In its English haunts it was associated with bog myrtle and creeping willow, suggesting that our native race was biotopically distinct. Dispersal is effected by the young hairy larva which can be carried by a strong breeze for many miles. Overwinters as an egg.

Family: Arctiidae

Thirty-three species, of which 30 are resident, represent this family in the British Isles. These are placed into two subfamilies, the Lithosiinae and Arctiinae.
The Lithosiinae is a group of small- to medium-sized species with elongate forewings which fold down along or around the body when the moth is resting. Most of the species are greyish or buff in colour. In general the

adults are rarely seen during the day, but after dark they come regularly to light and a few of the species have been found on sugar.

The slightly hairy larvae feed in the wild on lichens and algae, but in captivity some species will accept cultivated lettuce.

The glabrous pupae are spun up in silken cocoons placed mostly near or on the ground amongst tree-litter, dead leaves, or rocks.

The Arctiinae is a more variable group of medium- to large-sized moths, containing many brilliantly coloured species. Most members of this subfamily are not attracted to flowers or sugar, but those which fly at night come readily to light.

The larvae, usually very hairy and known popularly as 'woolly bears', feed on a variety of herbaceous plants. The pupae are spun up in silken cocoons amongst herbage or on the ground.

SUBFAMILY: LITHOSIINAE

Round-winged Muslin
Thumatha senex Hübner
Plate **22** : *1*

Similar species. *Nudaria mundana*, pl. **22**, has the wings less rounded, almost transparent, and the discal spot on the hindwing is either faint or absent.
Imago. 20–22 mm. Resident. Flies from dusk onwards and is attracted to light. Single-brooded, flying in July and August, inhabiting fens and marshy places. Widely distributed in England, Wales and northern Ireland. Local in Scotland and a few of the southern counties of Ireland.
Larva. September to May on various lichens and mosses, including *Peltigera canina*.
Overwinters as a larva.

Dew Moth
Setina irrorella Linnaeus
Plate **22** : *4–5*

Imago. 26–32 mm. Resident. The male flies at dawn, in the afternoon, and again at dusk when it comes to light in small numbers. The less active female is more usually found after dark sitting on grass stems. Single-brooded, flying from June to July, inhabiting shingle beaches, rocky cliffs and chalk and limestone hills. Mainly coastal but reported inland from the North Downs, Surrey; the Cotswolds, Gloucestershire; and the Black Hills, Breconshire. The coastal sites from which it has been recorded recently are at Dungeness and Folkestone Warren, Kent; Hurst Beach, Hampshire; Freshwater, Isle of Wight; Pembroke, and elsewhere along the west coast of Wales; parts of western Argyllshire; and the Hebridean islands of Skye, Canna and Rhum. Found also on the Isle of Man and in the Burren district of Cos Clare and Galway.

Larva. August to May on various lichens growing on rocks.
Overwinters as a larva.

Rosy Footman
Miltochrista miniata Forster
Plate **22** : *6*

Variation. Ab. *flava* Bigneau is an uncommon variety in which both wings are yellow without any trace of red.
Imago. 25–33 mm. Resident. Comes freely to light. Single-brooded, flying from late June to early August, inhabiting woodland. Generally distributed in the southern half of Britain as far north as Lincolnshire and Caernarvonshire, although absent from the Midlands. In Ireland it has been recorded from Co. Waterford.
Larva. September to May on *Peltigera canina* and other lichens growing on the stems and branches of trees. In captivity will feed on lettuce.
Overwinters as a larva.

Muslin Footman
Nudaria mundana Linnaeus
Plate **22** : *2*

Similar species. *Thumatha senex*, pl. **22** and text.
Imago. 19–23 mm. Resident. The male comes regularly to light. Single-brooded, flying from late June to early August. It occurs locally in many parts of the British Isles as far north as Aberdeenshire.
Larva. September to May on various small lichens growing on stone walls, fences and bushes.
Overwinters as a larva.

Red-necked Footman
Atolmis rubricollis Linnaeus
Plate **22** : *3*

Imago. 28–36 mm. Resident and suspected immigrant. Comes to light in small numbers. Also found by day, when it has been seen flying around the tops of trees in hot sunshine. When at rest it sits exposed on bracken and other low herbage. Single-brooded, flying in June and July, inhabiting deciduous and coniferous woodland. Widely distributed, but local, in Wales, the southern counties of England, the Isles of Scilly, and Ireland. It is also very occasionally reported from Suffolk, Lincolnshire and Staffordshire. Occasional specimens have been noted in western Scotland and other localities way outside the normal breeding range of this species; these are probably immigrants.
Larva. August to October on lichens and algae growing on the trunks and branches of oak, beech, larch and several species of conifer.
Overwinters as a pupa within a silken cocoon; these can sometimes be found in numbers attached to leaf and twig debris of the tree on which the larva has been feeding.

Four-dotted Footman

Cybosia mesomella Linnaeus

Plate **22** : *20–21*

Variation. The form *flava* de Graaf, fig **21**, has a uni-colorous yellow forewing and occurs throughout the species' range.

Imago. 29–34 mm. Resident. Flies from dusk onwards and is attracted to light. It hides by day in the heather and small bushes from which it is easily flushed. Single-brooded, flying from mid-June to early August, inhab-iting heathland and open woodland. Widespread in southern England and Wales. More local in northern England and Scotland as far north as Morayshire. The only record to date for Ireland appears to be a specimen taken on the outskirts of Belfast, Co. Down, on 4.vii.1991.

Larva. August to May on lichens and algae.

Overwinters as a larva.

Dotted Footman

Pelosia muscerda Hufnagel

Plate **22** : *8*

Similar species. *P. obtusa*, pl. **22**, has shorter and more rounded wings and the ground colour of the forewing is browner and the transverse spots are arranged differently. (See text fig 30.)

Imago. 30–34 mm. Resident and immigrant. Both sexes come readily to light. Single-brooded, flying from mid-July to mid-August. Resident in the Norfolk Broads where it is not uncommon. It seems to prefer fenland carrs and is usually scarce or absent in pure reed-beds. It was resident in Ham Fen, Kent, from 1891–1911, and possibly in the New Forest, Hampshire, during the nineteenth century. Odd specimens have occurred in Cambridgeshire, Sussex, Suffolk, Lincolnshire, Essex, Dorset, Yorkshire and southeast Kent, and were probably immigrants.

Larva. Autumn to spring, probably on algae growing on small bushes.

Overwinters as a larva.

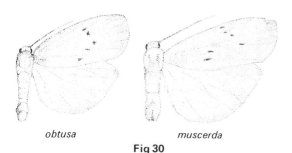

obtusa   *muscerda*

Fig 30

Small Dotted Footman

Pelosia obtusa Herrich-Schäffer

Plate **22** : *7*

Similar species. *P. muscerda*, pl. **22** and text.

Imago. 24–26 mm. Resident. The male comes spar-ingly to light. Single-brooded, flying in July, inhabiting old and undisturbed reed-beds. First recorded in Britain in 1961 and apparently confined to one small area in the Norfolk Broads.

Larva. Autumn to spring probably on algae attached to reed litter. In captivity it will accept the green algae, *Desmococcus* (*Pleurococcus*), commonly found growing on fallen twigs and branches.

Overwinters as a larva.

Orange Footman

Eilema sororcula Hufnagel

Plate **22** : *19*

Similar species. *E. griseola* f. *stramineola*, pl. **22**, is much larger and less orange in colour.

Imago. 27–30 mm. Resident. Comes to light, sometimes in numbers. Single-brooded, flying in late May and June, inhabiting mature oak woodland. Generally distributed in the southern and southeast counties of England, and parts of South Wales. Elsewhere it is found locally in East Anglia and very occasionally in Lincolnshire.

Larva. July to September on various lichens associated with oak and beech.

Overwinters as a pupa.

Dingy Footman

Eilema griseola Hübner

Plate **22** : *12–13*

Variation. The form *stramineola* Doubleday (fig 13) has a yellow abdomen and pale straw-coloured wings, and occurs frequently in some localities but is absent from others. This form has not occurred outside Britain.

Similar species. The much broader forewing and the strongly arched costa should distinguish this footman from other similar-looking species. *E. caniola*, pl. **22**. *E. sericea*, pl. **22**. *E. complana*, pl. **22**. *E. lurideola*, pl. **22**. *E. deplana*, pl. **22**.

Imago. 32–40 mm. Resident. Comes readily to light. Single-brooded, flying in July and August, inhabiting fenland, damp woodland and coastal cliffs. Widely dis-tributed and locally common in the southern half of the British Isles. The only record for Ireland, a specimen taken in Co. Cork, in 1984, was possibly an immigrant.

Larva. September to June on various unspecified lichens.

Overwinters as a larva.

Hoary Footman

Eilema caniola Hübner

Plate **22** : *11*

Similar species. The whitish-grey almost silky fore-wing, the pale hindwing and the weakly marked pale yellow costa should distinguish this footman from other similar-looking species.

Imago. 28–35 mm. Resident and possible immigrant. Comes to light in small numbers. Single-brooded, flying from late July to early September, inhabiting sea-cliffs and shingle beaches. Locally common along the coasts of North and South Devon, Cornwall, Pembrokeshire, and the other seaboard counties in west Wales. Inland it was found to be not uncommon in a quarry in the Wye Valley, Monmouthshire, in 1981; further records of single specimens have occurred in 1989 and 1991. In Ireland there are very old records from Co. Dublin and recent single examples from Cos Waterford and Cork. A handful of specimens have been reported in the last 20 years from East Sussex, Dorset and southeast Kent and these may have been immigrants.

Larva. Autumn to spring on lichens growing on rocks. Overwinters as a larva.

Pigmy Footman
Eilema pygmaeola pygmaeola Doubleday
Plate **22** : *14*

Imago. 24–28 mm. Resident and suspected immigrant. Comes readily to light, sometimes in large numbers. Also found between flights resting on the stems of grasses. Single-brooded, flying from mid-July to August, inhabiting coastal sandhills. Locally common from Deal to Sandwich, Kent; and from Winterton to Waxham, Norfolk. Single and probably migrant specimens have been reported from Exmouth, Devon, in 1937; Bradwell-on-Sea, Essex, in 1958 and 1961; Walberswick and Minsmere, Suffolk, in 1976; and Thorpeness, Suffolk, in 1983. Two specimens were recorded on Sheppey, Kent, in 1976, since when it has occurred fairly regularly and may possibly be resident.

E. pygmaeola pallifrons Zeller, pl. **22** : *15*. This race differs from the typical form in having a pale yellow forewing and a yellow abdomen. It is well established and not uncommon on the shingle beach at Dungeness, Kent. Specimens conforming to ssp. *pygmaeola* also occur here.

Larva. September to June on unspecified lichens. Overwinters as a larva.

Scarce Footman
Eilema complana Linnaeus
Plate **22** : *17*

Similar species. *E. griseola*, pl. **22** and text. *E. caniola*, pl. **22** and text. *E. sericea*, pl. **22**, has the hindwing suffused with dark grey. *E. lurideola*, pl. **22**, has the costal streak tapering towards the apex (see text fig 31).

Imago. 30–36 mm. Resident. Flies at dusk onwards, is attracted to light and is said to visit the flowers of knapweed, thistles and field scabious. Single-brooded, flying in July and August, inhabiting heathland, woodland, downland, salt-marshes and sandhills. Widely distributed in central and southern England, Wales and the Isle of Man. In Scotland it has been recently recorded from Kirkcudbrightshire, Wigtownshire and Kintyre. Uncommon in Ireland where it is coastal in the south and west.

Larva. September to June on unspecified lichens. Overwinters as a larva.

Northern Footman
Eilema sericea Gregson
Plate **22** : *18*

Similar species. *E. complana*, pl. **22** and text.

Imago. 32–36 mm. Resident. Comes to light, but is more often found after dark resting on grass stems. Single-brooded, flying in July, inhabiting peat bogs and marshy places on moorland. Outside its best known locality, Whixall Moss, Shropshire, it has been reported from Lancashire, Cheshire, Merionethshire and the Isle of Man.

Larva. September to June on unspecified lichens. Overwinters as a larva.

(*Author's note*: this species, which is unknown outside Britain, is considered by some authorities to be a form or race of *Eilema complana* as they cannot be separated by means of the genitalia. Although I tend to agree with this opinion I have, to keep in line with recent checklists, credited *E. sericea* with specific status.)

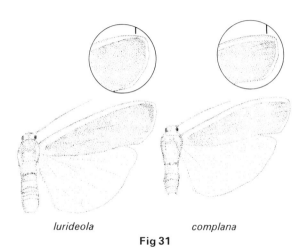

lurideola   *complana*

Fig 31

Buff Footman
Eilema deplana Esper
Plate **22** : *9–10*

Similar species. *E. griseola*, pl. **22** and text.

Imago. 28–36 mm. Resident. Both sexes come regularly to light. Single-brooded, flying in July and August, inhabiting woodland and scrub-covered downland. Local but not uncommon in southern England, parts of Wales, and the southwest of Ireland.

Larva. Autumn to May on lichens and algae growing on the trunks and branches of yew, hawthorn and other trees and shrubs.
Overwinters as a larva.

Common Footman
Eilema lurideola Zincken
Plate **22** : *16*

Similar species. *E. complana*, pl. **22** and text. *E. caniola*, pl. **22** and text. *E. griseola*, pl. **22** and text.

Imago. 31–38 mm. Resident. Comes readily to light and is known to visit the flowers of wild plants. Single-brooded, flying in July and August. Widely distributed in England and Wales. Local in Scotland, mainly along the east coast. Widespread in Ireland.

Larva. September to June on various lichens growing on trees, fences and rocks.

Overwinters as a larva.

Four-spotted Footman

Lithosia quadra Linnaeus

Plate **22** : *22–23*

Imago. 35–55 mm. Resident and immigrant. Both sexes are attracted to light. Single-brooded, flying from July to September. Resident populations appear to exist in Hampshire, Dorset, Devon, Cornwall and the Scilly Isles. Also in Ireland in Cos Cork, Kerry, Galway and Clare. As an immigrant it has occurred in many parts of the British Isles although it is by no means a common one.

Larva. Autumn to June on *Peltigera canina* and other lichens growing on the trunks and branches of oak and other trees.

Overwinters as a larva.

SUBFAMILY: ARCTIINAE

Feathered Footman

Spiris striata Linnaeus

Plate **22** : *28*

Imago. 33–42 mm. Status uncertain. Flies in sunshine and can be readily put up in dull weather. On the Continent it is single-brooded, flying in June and July, inhabiting dry heathland and clearings in woods on limestone soils. Of the seven British records, the two from Windsor, Berkshire, in 1815 and the one from Essex in 1859 emanated from unreliable sources and are therefore suspect. The remaining four are from Manachty, Anglesey, before 1803; Wharfedale, Yorkshire, c. 1836; Bettws-y-Coed, Caernarvonshire, in June 1859; and near Wrexham, Denbighshire, on 28.vii.1859. Abroad the species is widespread and common in many parts of Europe and its range includes Denmark, Belgium, and northern France.

Larva. *August to May on a wide variety of herbaceous plants.

Overwinters as a larva in a communal web.

Speckled Footman

Coscinia cribraria bivittata South

Plate **22** : *25–26*

Variation. The intensity of the blackish-grey markings of the forewing is very variable and in extreme cases both unicolorous grey and almost spotless white examples can occur.

Similar species. *Myelois cribrella* Hübner (Family Pyralidae), has a much paler hindwing with a pure white fringe.

Imago. 33–40 mm. Resident. The males regularly, the females occasionally come to light. During the day it rests among the heather and can sometimes be disturbed in hot weather. Single-brooded, flying in July and August. A very local species found in the Wareham district, Dorset, and formerly the New Forest, Hampshire, where it was last reported in 1960. A specimen conforming to ssp. *bivittata* was taken on Portland, Dorset, on 1.vii.1993.

Larva. September to June and stated to feed on dandelion and other herbaceous plants.

Overwinters as a small larva. In captivity some larvae have overwintered twice.

C. cribraria arenaria Lempke, pl. **22** : *27*. A rare migrant occasionally reported from southern England. Records this century are: Sandwich, Kent, in July 1914 and July 1922; Dungeness, Kent, on 21.viii.1934; Sandwich, Kent, on 7.viii.1937; Chandlers Ford, Hampshire, on 2.vi.1945; Thorpeness, Suffolk, on 6.viii.1965; St Peters, Kent, on 13.viii.1965; Midrips, Sussex, on 26.vi.1967; East Waldringford, Suffolk, on 25.vi.1973; Minster in Sheppey, Kent, on 6.vi.1977; Dungeness, on 26.vii.1995; Ongar, Essex, on 6.viii.1996 and Kingsgate, Kent, on 8.viii.1997. It was reported from Guernsey, Channel Islands, on 4 & 16.vii.1992.

Crimson Speckled

Utetheisa pulchella Linnaeus

Plate **22** : *24*

Imago. 28–40 mm. Immigrant. Flies by day in sunshine, resting in dull weather and at night in low herbage from which it can be easily disturbed. Occurs from March to October, but mainly in the autumn. A rare visitor to the British Isles and absent in many years. Between 1900 and 1960 about 40 specimens were reported, the most in one year being 10 in 1923. In 1961 more than 30 were recorded over a wide area of the British Isles including Scotland and Ireland. From 1962 to 1989 the records have been: Kingswear, Devon, on 17.viii.1962; Minstead, Hampshire, on 4.vi.1964; La Moye, Jersey, on 11.vii.1968; Anglesey, North Wales, in March 1977; Walberton, Sussex, on 18.ix.1980; and Fenit, Co. Kerry, on 29.x.1982. In 1990 twenty-five were reported from mainland Britain: Isles of Scilly (3), Cornwall (9), Devon (6), Dorset (4), Berkshire (1), Surrey (1) and Essex (1); and from the Channel Islands: Jersey (5) and Guernsey (1). Since then the records have been Kingsbury Episcopi, Somerset, on 17.ix.1992; Hayling Island, Hampshire, on 19.ix.1992; Walberton, on 21.ix.1992; Dymchurch, Kent, on 26.ix.1992; Kynance, Cornwall, on 15.x.1995; St Agnes, Isles of Scilly, on 15 & 17.x.1995; Annet, Isles of Scilly, on 18.x.1995; Bryher, Isles of Scilly, on 19.x.1995; Pleinmont, Guernsey, on 28.x.1995; two at Lower Lanner, Cornwall, on 29.x.1995; Poltesco,

Cornwall, on 9 & 15.vi.1996; Lower Lanner on 29.vi. & 13.vii.1996; Poltesco on 3.viii.1996; Ventongimps, Cornwall, on 1.viii.1996; Lower Lanner on 2.ix.1997; and Carlyon Bay, Cornwall, on 20.ix.1997.

Larva. Continuously brooded in captivity on a wide variety of herbaceous plants including forget-me-not (*Myosotis* spp.) and borage.

Beautiful Utetheisa
Utetheisa bella Linnaeus
(South 1961, vol. 2, pl. 35)

Similar species. *U. pulchella*, pl. **22**, lacks the pink ground colour of the hindwing.

Imago. 46–50 mm. Importation or possible immigrant. The only British specimen of this North American species was taken on Skokholm Island, Pembrokeshire, at the end of July 1948.

Wood Tiger
Parasemia plantaginis plantaginis Linnaeus
Plate **22** : *33–35*

Variation. In ab. *hospita* Denis & Schiffermüller (fig 35) the yellow ground colour of the male is replaced with white. This form occurs regularly in northern England and Scotland.

Imago. 34–42 mm. Resident. During the day both sexes can be disturbed from heather, long grasses and other herbage. In hot weather the male flies freely in search of the rather sluggish female which seldom moves about until late afternoon or after dark. Single-brooded, flying from late May to July, inhabiting moorland, downland and open woodland. Widely distributed, but local, over the whole of the British Isles except in southeast England where it has almost disappeared in recent years.

P. plantaginis insularum Seitz, pl. **22** : *36*. In the male the ground colour of the hindwing is darker and the black markings more extensive. This race occurs in northern Scotland, Orkney and Shetland.

Larva. August to April on a wide variety of herbaceous plants. In captivity it thrives on a mixture of groundsel, dandelion and plantain and if kept warm will pupate and emerge in late autumn.

Overwinters as a larva.

Garden Tiger
Arctia caja Linnaeus
Plate **23** : *2–4*

Variation. Exceedingly variable both in the colour of the hindwing and the extent of the chocolate markings on the forewing. The more extreme aberrations rarely occur in the wild and are more usually obtained by selective breeding.

Similar species. *Euplagia quadripunctaria*, pl. **23** : *5*.

Imago. 50–78 mm. Resident. Both sexes come regularly to light. Single-brooded, flying in July and August.

Widespread and often common throughout the British Isles as far north as Orkney.

Larva. September to June on a wide variety of wild and garden plants. In captivity it can be bred continuously if kept warm.

Overwinters as a small larva.

Cream-spot Tiger
Arctia villica britannica Oberthür
Plate **23** : *1*

Variation. The black markings of both forewing and hindwing can vary extensively although extreme aberrations are rarely found in the wild.

Imago. 50–66 mm. Resident. Both sexes are regularly taken at light and during the day may sometimes be found sitting exposed on low herbage. Single-brooded, flying in May and June, inhabiting woodland, downland, coastal cliffs and sandhills. Locally common in the southern counties of England, extending northwards to Norfolk. In Wales it occurs mainly in the south with the occasional record from the north.

Larva. August to early spring on a wide variety of herbaceous plants.

Overwinters as a larva, feeding during mild periods. In captivity it can be reared without trouble on potted foxglove kept in a cool outhouse.

Clouded Buff
Diacrisia sannio Linnaeus
Plate **22** : *29–30*

Imago. 35–50 mm. Resident. During the day both sexes rest among the heather and other low herbage; the males are easily disturbed and in hot weather will fly of their own accord. The sluggish female is seldom active before dark and even then is more often found sitting about on the stems of heather and grasses than in flight. Single-brooded, occurring in June and July, inhabiting heathland, chalk downland and woodland clearings. Widely distributed and locally common over much of the British Isles.

Larva. August to May on many low plants including heather, heath and *Hieracium* spp.

Overwinters as a larva.

White Ermine
Spilosoma lubricipeda Linnaeus
(*menthastri* Denis & Schiffermüller)
Plate **23** : *9–10*

Variation. The extent of the black spotting of the forewing varies considerably. In extreme cases the spots can be almost absent or joined together to form streaks. Examples with yellowish-buff forewings occur frequently in Scotland and Ireland.

Similar species. *S. urticae*, pl. **23**, has pure white wings and thorax, and lacks the distinct discal spot on the hindwing which is present on even the most immaculate forms of *S. lubricipeda*.

Imago. 34–48 mm. Resident. Comes to light. Single-brooded, flying from late May to July; occasionally there is a partial second generation in the autumn. Widespread and common throughout the British Isles as far north as Orkney.
Larva. August to September on various wild and garden plants.
Overwinters as a pupa.

Buff Ermine
Spilosoma luteum Hufnagel
Plate **23** : *11–14*

Variation. The ground colour ranges from yellowish-buff in the male to cream in the female. The extent of the black markings varies considerably from almost spotless examples to the extreme melanistic ab. *zatima* Stoll (fig 14). This latter form and its heterozygote ab. *intermedia* Standfuss (fig 13) has been obtained in recent years by inbreeding from well-marked females taken in Lincolnshire.
Similar species. Yellowish-buff forms of *S. lubricipeda*, pl. **23**.
Imago. 34–42 mm. Resident. Comes readily to light. Single-brooded, flying from mid-May to mid-July. Widespread and generally common throughout much of the British Isles.
Larva. August to September, feeding on a variety of wild and garden plants and on trees and shrubs including birch and elder.
Overwinters as a pupa.

Water Ermine
Spilosoma urticae Esper
Plate **23** : *15*

Similar species. *S. lubricipeda*, pl. **23** and text. *Diaphora mendica* ♀, pl. **23**.
Imago. 38–46 mm. Resident. Comes to light in small numbers. Single-brooded, flying in June and July, inhabiting fenland and marshy meadows. Rather local, occurring mainly in southeast England including East Anglia.
Larva. July–August on various marsh plants including mint, yellow loosestrife, water dock, lousewort (*Pedicularis sylvatica*) and yellow iris.
Overwinters as a pupa.

Muslin Moth
Diaphora mendica Clerck
Plate **23** : *16–18*

Variation. In Ireland the ground colour of the male ranges from white to creamy-yellow and refers to f. *rustica* Hübner (fig 18). Specimens approaching this form have been reported from Kintyre.
Imago. 30–43 mm. Resident. The males fly at night and are attracted to light. The females are occasionally seen flying in sunshine. Single-brooded, flying in May and early June, inhabiting gardens, downland and open woodland. Generally distributed throughout the British Isles as far north as Sutherland.
Larva. July to September on dock, chickweed, plantain, dandelion and other herbaceous plants. A second generation can be obtained in captivity.
Overwinters as a pupa.

Ruby Tiger
Phragmatobia fuliginosa fuliginosa Linnaeus
Plate **23** : *7*

Imago. 28–38 mm. Resident. Flies occasionally in sunshine, as well as at night, when, mainly the second generation, it comes to light. Double-brooded, from April to June and again from mid-July to early September. Widespread and locally common throughout the British Isles including Orkney.
P. fuliginosa borealis Straudinger, pl. **23** : *8*. The forewing is darkened with brown and the hindwing is almost totally suffused with dark grey. This race occurs in Scotland where it flies in June as a single brood. Specimens from northern England and Ireland are intermediate in appearance. Aberrant specimens conforming to ssp. *borealis* can occasionally appear outside of Scotland.
Larva. July to April on a variety of plants including dock, dandelion, heather, purple moor-grass and eared sallow (*Salix aurita*).
Overwinters as a final-instar larva.

Jersey Tiger
Euplagia quadripunctaria Poda
(*hera* Linnaeus)
Plate **23** : *5–6*

Variation. Ab. *lutescens* Staudinger (fig 6) has the ground colour of the hindwing yellow and is not an uncommon form.
Similar species. *Arctia caja*, pl. **23**.
Imago. 52–65 mm. Resident and occasionally immigrant. Comes regularly to light and may also be found feeding on the flowers of *Buddleia*. During the day it will fly in hot sunshine and again visit the flowers of *Buddleia* and other garden plants, and in dull weather can be flushed from hedgerows, bushes and ivy-covered walls. Single-brooded, flying from mid-July to early September, inhabiting suburban gardens and waste ground as well as the open countryside. Common in the Channel Islands and along the south coast of Devon from Brixham eastwards to Seaton, spreading inland to the edge of Dartmoor. Recently established coastally in West Dorset and on the Isle of Wight.
Larva. September to May on common nettle, hemp-agrimony, plantain and other low plants.
Overwinters as a small larva.

Scarlet Tiger
Callimorpha dominula Linnaeus
Plate **22** : *37–39*

Variation. In ab. *rossica* Kolenati (fig 39) the ground colour of the hindwing is yellow. Most other aberrations relate to the extent of the black markings on both the forewing and hindwing.

Imago. 52–58 mm. Resident. Flies freely in sunshine. Single-brooded, flying in June and July, inhabiting water-meadows, river-banks, marshy hillsides and coastal undercliff. Apart from two colonies in east Kent, this very local species is confined to the southern and western counties of England and to parts of southern and western Wales.

Larva. August to May on comfrey (*Symphytum* spp.), common nettle, bramble, meadowsweet, hemp-agrimony and many other plants.

Overwinters as a larva.

The Cinnabar
Tyria jacobaeae Linnaeus
Plate **22** : *31–32*

Variation. In ab. *flavescens* Thierry-Mieg the red markings are replaced with yellow; in ab. *negrana* Cabeau the wings are unicolorous black; and in ab. *coneyi* Waston (fig 32) the wings are unicolorous red. These varieties are rarely seen in the wild, although large numbers of some of them have been reared in captivity.

Imago. 35–45 mm. Resident. Flies late at night and comes occasionally to light. Rests by day in low herbage from which it is easily disturbed. Single-brooded, flying from late May to July. Widespread and often common throughout most of England, Wales and Ireland. Rather local and mainly coastal in the southern half of Scotland. A single specimen was recorded from Orkney in 1985.

Larva. July–August on common ragwort, groundsel, and other wild and garden varieties of *Senecio*. Less frequent on colt's-foot (*Tussilago farfara*).

Overwinters as a pupa.

Family: Nolidae

Five species represent this family in the British Isles. All the adults are small in size, and characterized by small tufts of raised scales on the forewing. They fly at night and come to light, but *Meganola strigula* appears to be the only species recorded at sugar.

The larvae are covered with short tufts of hair, and have the first pair of prolegs absent.

The pupae are spun up in tough silken, spindle-shaped or boat-shaped cocoons, attached to bark, stems or sometimes fences.

Small Black Arches
Meganola strigula Denis & Schiffermüller
Plate **23** : *19*

Similar species. *Nola confusalis*, pl. **23**, has a narrower and more pointed forewing, and much paler hindwing.

Imago. 18–24 mm. Resident. Comes to light in moderate numbers. Single-brooded, flying from late June to July, inhabiting mature oak woods. A local and declining species confined to a few counties in southern Britain, namely Sussex, Hampshire, Kent, Surrey, Oxfordshire, Buckinghamshire, Wiltshire, Monmouthshire and Gloucestershire.

Larva. Autumn to spring. Foodplant unspecified, possibly oak.

Overwinters as a larva.

Kent Black Arches
Meganola albula Denis & Schiffermüller
Plate **23** : *20*

Imago. 18–24 mm. Resident. Flies from dusk onwards and is attracted to light. Single-brooded, flying from late June to early August. Generally distributed, but local, in southern and eastern England and parts of Wales, frequenting a variety of coastal habitats. Inland it has occurred in Hampshire, Surrey and Berkshire where it inhabits woodland clearings.

Larva. September to May on dewberry (*Rubus caesius*)

Overwinters as a small larva.

Short-cloaked Moth
Nola cucullatella Linnaeus
Plate **23** : *21–22*

Imago. 15–20 mm. Resident. Both sexes come readily to light. Single-brooded, flying in June and July, inhabiting woodlands, commons and hedgerows. Generally distributed throughout England and Wales.

Larva. August to May on hawthorn, blackthorn, apple and plum.

Overwinters as a small larva.

Least Black Arches
Nola confusalis Herrich-Schäffer
Plate **23** : *23*

Variation. Ab. *columbina* Image is a dark grey form occurring not uncommonly in Epping Forest, Essex.

Similar species. *Meganola strigula*, pl. **23** and text.

Imago. 16–24 mm. Resident. Comes regularly to light. During the day it is occasionally found on tree-trunks. Single-brooded, flying in May and June, inhabiting woodland, orchards and parkland. Widely distributed but rather local, throughout the British Isles.

Larva. July to August on the leaves of several species of lime; also on evergreen oak and probably other trees. Overwinters as a pupa in a rounded cocoon attached to bark.

Scarce Black Arches
Nola aerugula Hübner
(*centonalis* Hübner)
Plate **23** : *24–26*

Imago. 15–20 mm. Immigrant and transitory resident. Most of the recent records have been at light. Single brooded, flying from late June to early August. Formerly resident on the sandhills at Deal, Kent, from 1858 to 1898, where it could be found after dark resting on the stems of grass and other low herbage. As a migrant it has been recorded 51 times this century, mainly along the coasts of eastern and southeastern England. A summary of records is: Dorset (2), Sussex (4), Kent (20), Essex (7), Suffolk (7), Norfolk (3) and Yorkshire (8), the best years yielding eight in 1982, six in 1964 and five in both 1957 and 1995. Abroad the species is widespread in Europe, its range including France, Belgium and Denmark.

Larva. *September to June on bird's-foot trefoil and various species of clover.
Overwinters as a larva.

Family: Noctuidae

The largest family of macrolepidoptera in the British Isles, and represented by more than 400 species placed in 14 subfamilies.

The adults are mostly medium sized and dull coloured. In many species the sex can be determined by the shape of the antenna, which may be ciliate or bipectinate in the male, but always almost simple in the female. Of the nocturnal species, all come to light, the majority are attracted to sugar, and many are attracted to various flowers.

The larvae, usually fleshy and cylindrical, mostly feed at night, hiding during the day on the ground, in spun leaves, or in a crevice of a tree. Those of most species pupate in the ground.

SUBFAMILY: NOCTUINAE

Square-spot Dart
Euxoa obelisca grisea Tutt
Plate **24** : *1–2*

Similar species. *E. tritici*, pl. **24**, has the area between the postmedian line and the termen more variegated, and there is often a series of wedge-shaped marks present. The other distinguishing feature is the shape of the postmedian line in relation to the reniform stigma – in *E. tritici* this line curves around and barely touches the stigma, whereas in *E. obelisca* it merges with the entire outer edge of the stigma. (See text fig 32.)

Imago. 35–40 mm. Resident. Most frequently taken at light, but also comes to sugar and visits the flowers of ragwort and heather. Single-brooded, flying from mid-August to September, inhabiting coastal cliffs. Locally common near Eastbourne, East Sussex, and from the Isle of Wight westwards to Cornwall and the Scilly Isles, and then northwards through North Devon, along the Welsh coastline to Lancashire. In Scotland it has occurred on the east coast in Berwickshire, Midlothian, Kincardineshire and Aberdeenshire, and from a number of localities in the west including the

Hebrides. Inland it has been reported from Warwickshire and on rare occasions elsewhere. It is stated to occur in Ireland mainly along the southern and western coasts. The life history of the larva in the wild is apparently unknown.

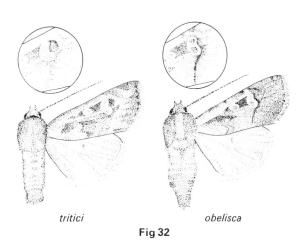

tritici   obelisca

Fig 32

White-line Dart
Euxoa tritici Linnaeus
Plate **24** : *3–8*

Variation. Although specimens from moorland localities tend to be darker than those from coastal sandhills it is difficult to classify geographical forms because of the great variation that often occurs in a single population.

Similar species. *E. obelisca*, pl. **24** and text. *E. nigricans*, pl. **24**, is less variegated, usually of some shade of sepia brown, with the claviform stigma indistinct or absent, lacking the subterminal series of wedge-shaped marks and the pale costal stripe which is often present in *E. tritici*.

Imago. 28–40 mm. Resident. Comes readily to light, sugar, and the flowers of ragwort, marram and heather. Single-brooded, flying from July to early August, inhabiting coastal sandhills and heathland. Generally distributed throughout the British Isles as far north as Shetland. In Ireland it is mainly coastal.

Larva. March to June on various small herbaceous plants.
Overwinters as an egg.

Garden Dart
Euxoa nigricans Linnaeus
Plate **24** : *9–12*

Similar species. *E. tritici*, pl. **24** and text.

Imago. 32–40 mm. Resident. Comes readily to light and sugar, and is attracted to the flowers of ragwort, marram and other wild and garden plants. Single-brooded, flying in July and August, inhabiting commons, waste ground, gardens, sandhills, marshes, etc. Generally distributed throughout most of the British Isles.

Larva. March to June on a wide variety of wild and cultivated plants including clover, plantain, lettuce and onion (*Allium* spp.).

Overwinters as an egg.

Coast Dart
Euxoa cursoria Hufnagel
Plate **24** : *13–24*

Variation. Extremely variable often within a single population. As a general rule those from the southern part of its range are light sand-coloured, the darker forms appearing in Northumberland and northwards to Shetland.

Similar species. *Agrotis ripae*, pl. **24**, has a much smaller reniform stigma and the hindwing lacks a discal spot and the grey terminal shading.

Imago. 34–38 mm. Resident and suspected occasional immigrant. Comes to light, but more frequently seen at sugar, and at the flowers of ragwort and marram. Single-brooded, flying in late July and August, inhabiting coastal sandhills. In England it occurs on the east coast northwards from Suffolk to Northumberland and on the west coast from Cheshire to Cumberland. Widespread in Scotland including parts of the Hebrides. It has not been recorded recently from Orkney although it still exists on Unst, Shetland. In Ireland it has been recorded from Cos Kerry, Clare, Sligo, Donegal, Antrim, Derry and Down. During the last forty years it has been reported from Essex and Kent on twelve occasions. These are: Dover, Kent, on 6.viii.1957; Dovercourt, Essex, on 13 & 16.viii.1979; Dover, on 14 & 16.viii.1979; Newington, Kent, on 3.viii.1982; Dovercourt, on 22.ix.1985; Fingringhoe Wick, Essex, on 15.viii.1987; Bradwell-on-Sea, Essex, on 27.vii. 1991; Ramsgate, Kent, on 13.viii.1994 & 27.vii.1997 and Beltinge, Kent, on 27.vii.1996. Many of these specimens are paler and whiter than any of the forms found in Britain; this evidence and an analysis of the 1979 records suggest they were immigrants.

Larva. Has been found in the spring and early summer feeding on sea sandwort (*Honkenya peploides*), sand-couch, and other sandhill plants, hiding in the sand by day.

Overwinters as an egg.

Light Feathered Rustic
Agrotis cinerea Denis & Schiffermüller
(*denticulatus* Haworth)
Plate **24** : *25–30*

Variation. Geographical, but often very variable within a single locality. When compared with the more usual brownish-grey form, the males from southwest England and South Wales are larger, paler and more obscurely marked; those from the old spoil heaps in the Forest of Dean, Gloucestershire, are distinctly browner; those from Dungeness, Kent, are paler and bluish-grey in colour; and those from the Derbyshire and Staffordshire Dales vary from slate-grey to blackish-brown and are frequently strongly banded.

Imago. 33–40 mm. Resident. Both sexes fly at dusk and visit the flowers of red valerian, and also come to light (the males readily, the females very occasionally). Single-brooded, flying in May to June, inhabiting chalk and limestone downland, sea-cliffs, shingle beaches, mountain hillsides, quarries, and old spoil heaps. Widespread, but local in the southern half of England, ranging northwards to Derbyshire; and in South Wales ranging northwards to Anglesey. In Ireland the only recent records are from Cos Antrim and Kerry.

Larva. Feeds from July to September on wild thyme and other unspecified low plants.

Overwinters as a full-grown larva.

Archer's Dart
Agrotis vestigialis Hufnagel
Plate **24** : *33–36*

Variation. Geographically variable with many distinct forms; the darkest of these occurring on the heaths of Surrey, Dorset and Hampshire.

Imago. 30–40 mm. Resident. Comes readily to light and sugar, and visits the flowers of ragwort, marram and heather. Single-brooded, flying from July to September, inhabiting coastal sandhills, breckland and a few inland heaths. Widely distributed around the coastline of the British Isles, but very local inland.

Larva. September to May on a variety of grasses and low plants.

Overwinters as a larva.

Turnip Moth
Agrotis segetum Denis & Schiffermüller
Plate **25** : *9–12*

Similar species. *A. ipsilon*, pl. **25**. *Peridroma saucia*, pl. **26**.

Imago. 32–42 mm. Resident, reinforced by immigration. Comes readily to light and to sugar. Double-brooded, flying in May and June with a partial second generation flying from late August to September. Local in Scotland, but widespread and often common throughout the rest of the British Isles.

Larva. Autumn to spring, and during the summer, on the roots and lower parts of the stems of root vegetables and other wild and cultivated plants.

Overwinters as a full-grown larva.

Heart and Club
Agrotis clavis Hufnagel
(*corticea* Denis & Schiffermüller)
Plate **25** : *1–6*

Similar species. *A. exclamationis*, pl. **25**, has a dark bar on the patagia.

Imago. 35–40 mm. Resident. Comes readily to light and to sugar. Single-brooded, flying in late June and

July, inhabiting coastal sandhills and waste ground. Generally distributed and locally common in the southern half of England. Rather local in the rest of the British Isles.

Larva. Feeds from August to November on the leaves, and later the roots, of dock, clover, knotgrass and many other herbaceous plants.

Overwinters as a full-grown larva in an earthen cell in which it will pupate in the spring.

Heart and Dart

Agrotis exclamationis Linnaeus

Plate **25** : *13–20*

Variation. The ground colour of the forewing varies from pale whitish-brown through shades of grey and red-brown to sooty-grey. Specimens with confluent markings are not uncommon and some of these forms are illustrated.

Similar species. *A. clavis*, pl. **25** and text.

Imago. 35–44 mm. Resident. Comes commonly to light and to sugar, and visits the flowers of *Buddleia*, red valerian and ragwort. Mainly single-brooded, flying from mid-May to July. Generally distributed and often common throughout most of the British Isles.

Larva. July to October on a wide variety of wild and cultivated plants.

Overwinters as a full-grown larva in an earthen cell in which it will pupate in the spring.

Crescent Dart

Agrotis trux lunigera Stephens

Plate **24** : *31–32*

Imago. 35–42 mm. Resident. Comes to light and sugar in moderate numbers. Usually single-brooded, flying in July and August, inhabiting coastal cliffs. A rare and very partial second generation has occurred in October. Locally common from the Isle of Wight westwards to Cornwall and then northwards to North Wales. Well established in the Isle of Man. In Ireland it has been recorded from Cos Louth, Dublin, Waterford, Cork and Kerry. Outside its usual range it has been recorded from Sussex and Morayshire.

Larva. August to November on various low plants. In captivity it will eat dandelion, knotgrass, plantain and sliced carrot, and may be induced to feed up quickly and produce moths in the autumn.

Overwinters as a full-grown larva.

Dark Sword-grass

Agrotis ipsilon Hufnagel

Plate **25** : *7–8*

Similar species. *Agrotis segetum*, pl. **25**. *Peridroma saucia*, pl. **26**.

Imago. 40–55 mm. Immigrant and transitory resident. Comes readily to light and to sugar. A common immigrant, possibly surviving the occasional mild winter, although there is no evidence of this. It has occurred from March to November and been noted from most parts of the British Isles including Shetland and the Outer Hebrides.

Larva. Probably feeds on the leaves and roots of many wild and cultivated plants. In parts of its Continental range it is a pest on wheat and cotton.

Spalding's Dart

Agrotis herzogi Rebel

(Atropos 1997, no. 1, pl. 1)

Imago. 32–50 mm. Suspected immigrant. A single male was taken at light at Praze-an-Beeble, near Camborne, Cornwall, on 22.xi.1995. This species, which is similar to a large male specimen of *A. puta*, pl. **25**, with pure white hindwings, is resident from North Africa eastwards to India and has occasionally occurred, perhaps as a migrant, in southern Europe.

Shuttle-shaped Dart

Agrotis puta puta Hübner

Plate **25** : *21–23*

Variation. Ground colour of forewing in the male varies from ochreous-white to brownish-grey. Specimens from parts of South Devon have a distinct reddish-brown appearance.

Imago. 30–32 mm. Resident. Comes readily to light and to sugar, and visits the flowers of ragwort and *Buddleia*. Can be on the wing any time from late April to early October, there being two or three protracted and overlapping broods. Widespread and often common in Wales and the southern half of England. In Ireland it has been reported on three occasions: Co. Fermanagh (1893), Co. Down (*c*. 1944) and Co. Cork (1984).

A. puta insula Richardson, pl. **25** : *24–25*. This is the normal form found on the Isles of Scilly. A melanic form of the male, having both wings dark brown, occurs occasionally in this race, but rarely in ssp. *puta*.

Larva. September to March and during the summer on dock, dandelion, knotgrass, lettuce and many other herbaceous plants.

Overwinters as a larva, probably feeding during mild weather.

Sand Dart

Agrotis ripae Hübner

Plate **24** : *37–40*

Variation. Most geographical races are distinctive in appearance, despite the variation that can occur within a single population.

Similar species. *Euxoa cursoria*, pl. **24** and text.

Imago. 32–42 mm. Resident. Comes readily to light, sugar and the flowers of marram, ragwort and lyme-grass. Single-brooded, flying in June and July, inhabiting coastal sandhills. Occurring in suitable localities throughout England including the Isle of Wight and the Isles of Scilly, Wales, the Isle of Man. In Scotland it is known on the west coast from Wigtownshire and on the east coast from East Lothian northwards to Aberdeenshire. In Ireland it has been recorded from Cos Dublin, Wicklow, Waterford, Wexford, Cork and Kerry.

Larva. August to October on a variety of sandhill plants including prickly saltwort, sea rocket and orache; hiding in the sand during the day. In captivity it can be reared on sliced carrots.

Overwinters as a full-grown larva within a silken cocoon in which it will pupate in the spring.

Great Dart
Agrotis crassa Hübner
Plate **25** : *26*

Similar species. *A. clavis*, pl. **25**. *A segetum*, pl. **25**. *A. trux* ♂, pl. **24**.

Imago. 40–48 mm. Resident (Channel Islands) and immigrant. Comes readily to light. Single-brooded, flying in August. In the nineteenth century it was recorded from Epping, Essex, on 9.vii.1841; at Plumstead, Kent, on 8.viii.1841; at Lewisham, Kent, in 1845; and near Dover, Kent, in 1873. Most authors doubt the origin or identification of these records although this apparently retiring species might have been part of the rich fauna which at one time inhabited the now almost extinct marshland of East London. As a suspected immigrant eighteen specimens have been recorded this century. Half of these have been at the Old Light Bird Observatory, Portland, Dorset, on 18.viii. 1987, 6.viii.1989, 2.viii.1991, 30.vii.1992, 4.viii.1994, 27.vii. & 8.viii.1995, 5.viii.1996 and 11.viii.1997. The remaining nine have been at Fountainstown, Co. Cork, on 20.viii.1984; Playden, East Sussex, on 7.viii.1986; Saffron Walden, Essex, on 13.viii.1995; St Marys, Isles of Scilly, on 24.viii.1995; Beaulieu, Hampshire, on 8.viii.1996; Freshwater, Isle of Wight, on 12.viii.1996 and three on St Agnes, Isles of Scilly, on 10.viii.1997.

Larva. *Autumn to spring feeding on the roots of grasses and low plants.

Overwinters as a larva.

Purple Cloud
Actinotia polyodon Clerck
Plate **25** : *27*

Imago. 31–36 mm. Immigrant. Comes to light and sugar, and on the Continent is frequently attracted to various flowers. Double-brooded over much of Europe, flying in May and June and again in August. Excluding the doubtful and unconfirmed report of a specimen from Co. Galway in 1891 the twenty British records to date are as follows: Yarmouth, Norfolk, in June 1839; Ashdown Forest, Sussex, on 2.vi.1843; Ashford, Hampshire, pre-1855; Folkestone, Kent, on 4.vi.1892; Norwich, Norfolk, in 1892; Brockenhurst, Hampshire, in July 1918; Worthing, East Sussex, on 15.v.1919; St

Nicholas lightship, off Gorleston, Norfolk, in 1938; Tilgate, Sussex, on 5.vi.1954; Bradwell-on-Sea, Essex, on 27.v.1954; Hailsham, East Sussex, on 30.v.1954; Bradwell-on-Sea, on 16.v.1960; Hamstreet, Kent, on 1.vi.1967; Bradwell-on-Sea, on 17.vi.1986 & 31.v.1992; Littlestone, Kent, on 24.v.1995; Crowborough, East Sussex, on 11.vi.1996; Dungeness, Kent, on 18.viii. 1996; North Foreland, Kent, on 20.v.1997 and Eccles on Sea, Norfolk, on 7.viii.1997. Widely distributed throughout the rest of Europe including France, Belgium and Denmark.

Larva. *July to August on the flowers and seeds of St John's-wort.

Overwinters as a pupa.

Pale-shouldered Cloud
Chloantha hyperici Denis & Schiffermüller
Plate **43** : *19*

Imago. 30–40 mm. Suspected immigrant. In southern Europe it is treble-brooded, occurring from April to October, but in northern Europe, where it is represented by the bluish-grey ssp. *svendseni* Fibiger, it is on the wing in June and August. Although the only British specimen was taken at light at Dungeness, Kent, on 20.viii.1996 it is known to be expanding its range elsewhere in Europe and now resides in all our neighbouring countries.

Larva. *Probably could be found any time from May to November on St John's-wort.

Overwinters as a pupa.

The Flame
Axylia putris Linnaeus
Plate **25** : *36*

Imago. 30–36 mm. Resident. Comes to light in moderate numbers. Mainly single-brooded, flying in June and July, with an occasional and partial second generation flying in September. Generally distributed and often common throughout England, Wales and Ireland. Local in Scotland, mainly in the south, and the Hebrides.

Larva. July to September on a wide variety of low plants including dock, dandelion, common nettle and bedstraw.

Overwinters as a pupa.

Portland Moth
Actebia praecox Linnaeus
Plate **25** : *28*

Imago. 40–46 mm. Resident. Comes, sometimes commonly, to light and visits the flowers of ragwort and other coastal plants. Single-brooded, flying in late August and September, inhabiting coastal sandhills, sandy heathland and the fine shingle banks of rivers.

Coastal colonies exist in Kent, Sussex, Dorset, South and North Devon, Somerset, South and North Wales, Isle of Man, Cheshire, Lancashire, Cumbria, Northumberland, western Scotland, including parts of the Hebrides, and in a number of places in eastern Scotland. Single examples have occurred at Bodinnick, Cornwall in 1956 and at Bradwell-on-Sea, Essex, in 1978 and 1982. Inland sites exist in Lincolnshire, Nottinghamshire and along the river Spey in Morayshire and Inverness-shire. In Ireland it occurs on the coasts of Cos Donegal, Down, Antrim, Mayo, Galway, Clare, Kerry and Cork.

Larva. September to June on creeping willow, tree-lupin and other sandhill plants; hiding in the sand during the day.
Overwinters as a larva.

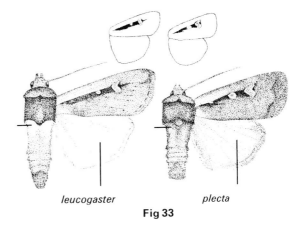

leucogaster   *plecta*

Fig 33

Eversmann's Rustic

Actebia fennica Tauscher
Plate **25** : *29*

Variation. The orange stripe along the dorsum of the forewing, which is a characteristic feature of the male, is absent in the female.

Imago. 38–44 mm. Immigrant. Comes to light, and abroad is attracted to sugar and the flowers of *Spiraea*. Single-brooded on the Continent, flying in July and August. This rare British visitor has only been recorded on six occasions – Chesterfield, Derbyshire, in August 1850; Shepperton, Middlesex, in early August 1972; Mapperley, Nottinghamshire, on 9.viii.1972; Newcastle upon Tyne on 15.viii.1972; Barthol Chapel, Aberdeenshire, on 20.viii.1977; and Rugby, Warwickshire, on 14.viii.1983. Its range abroad includes northern Europe, western Siberia and North America.

Larva. *September to early June on various herbaceous plants including *Corydalis gigantea* and *Epilobium* spp.
Overwinters as a larva.

Black Collar

Ochropleura flammatra Denis & Schiffermüller
Plate **43** : *18*

Imago. 42–52 mm. Immigrant. Comes to light and sugar, and visits various flowers. Single-brooded on the Continent, flying in June and July. Three specimens were reported in the nineteenth century; two at Freshwater, Isle of Wight, in 1859 and 1876; and at Cromer Lighthouse, Norfolk, on 10.viii.1875. Almost a century had elapsed before another example was recorded, this time from Huntley, Gloucestershire, in June 1968. The fifth and most recent specimen was taken at sugar at Eswick, Shetland, on 28.vi.1997. Widely distributed, but rarely common, in central and southern Europe, extending eastwards to central Asia.

Larva. *Autumn to spring on dandelion, strawberry and other low plants.
Overwinters as a larva.

Flame Shoulder

Ochropleura plecta Linnaeus
Plate **25** : *30*

Similar species. *O. leucogaster*, text fig 33 and text.

Imago. 28–34 mm. Resident. Comes regularly to light and sugar, and visits the flowers of ragwort. Double-brooded, flying from late April to June and again in August and September, except in the northerly part of its range, which includes Scotland and the Isles, it is only single-brooded, flying in June and July. Generally distributed throughout the British Isles including Orkney and the Outer Hebrides.

Larva. Summer and late autumn on plantain, dock, groundsel and many other wild and cultivated plants.
Overwinters as a pupa.

Radford's Flame Shoulder

Ochropleura leucogaster Freyer
Plate **43** : *20*

Similar species. *O. plecta*, pl. **25**, lacks the following characters: the silky white hairs which cover the anterior abdominal segments, the narrower and usually longer forewing, the smaller reniform and orbicular stigmata, the pale brown abdomen and the purer white colour of the hindwing. (See text fig 33.)

Imago. 34–37 mm. Suspected immigrant. Abroad it is frequently double-brooded, occurring from May to September, but appearing earlier or later according to locality or season. The seven records to date from Britain are at Walberton, West Sussex, on 17.x.1983; Swanage, Dorset, on 17.x.1990; Ladock Wood, near Truro, Cornwall, on 17.x.1990; Dungeness, Kent, on 11.x.1993; the Lizard, Cornwall, on 31.x.1995; and St Agnes, Isles of Scilly, on 30.x. & 21.xi.1997. Its European range includes France (as far north as Brittany), Spain, Portugal, Greece and Italy.

Larva. *November to March, and probably during the summer on various species of trefoil and other low plants.
Overwinters as a larva.

Plain Clay

Eugnorisma depuncta Linnaeus

Plate **25** : *37*

Imago. 36–44 mm. Resident. Comes to light and to sugar, and visits the flowers of ragwort. Single-brooded, flying from July to early September, inhabiting the edges of deciduous woodland. Local, generally uncommon, in Wales and southwest and northern England. Widespread and more frequent in central and east Scotland.

Larva. September to May on nettle, stitchwort, dock and probably any herbaceous plant growing in its chosen habitat.

Overwinters as a very small larva.

Northern Rustic

Standfussiana lucernea Linnaeus

Plate **25** : *31–33*

Similar species. *Rhyacia simulans* f. *suffusa*, pl. **25**.

Imago. 36–46 mm. Resident. Comes to light and to sugar, and visits the flowers of heather, red valerian, ragwort, wood sage and sea rocket. It also flies in hot sunshine, careering wildly over its rocky haunts. Single-brooded, flying from late June to September. It is possible that the female of this species spends part of the summer in a state of aestivation, having paired soon after emergence. Mainly coastal, inhabiting cliffs and rocky places from Sussex and the Isle of Wight westwards to Cornwall and North Devon and thence northwards through Wales to Cumbria. Apparently absent from the eastern coasts of England, except in Kent where it occurs in Folkestone Warren. Inland in inhabits mountain scree and quarries from the Derbyshire moors northwards to Lancashire. Widespread along the coasts of Scotland, the Hebrides, Orkney, Shetland, the Isle of Man and Ireland.

Larva. October to early spring on grasses and herbaceous plants.

Overwinters as a larva.

Dotted Rustic

Rhyacia simulans Hufnagel

Plate **25** : *34–35*

Variation. The dark race f. *suffusa* Tutt (fig 35) occurs in Orkney, Shetland, the Hebrides and Co. Donegal. Intermediate forms occur in mainland Scotland.

Similar species. *Spaelotis ravida*, pl. **26**. *Standfussiana lucernea*, pl. **25**.

Imago. 42–54 mm. Resident, perhaps reinforced in the south by immigration. Comes sparingly to light, preferring the attractions of sugar and the flowers of red valerian, *Buddleia* and sweet-william. Single-brooded. In England the moths emerge in June and July, fly for a short period, then aestivate in outhouses and other buildings and reappear from late August to October. Elsewhere there appears to be one flight period from mid-July to late August. Subject to great fluctuation,

this species has just gone through a most prolific phase, appearing in many new localities in the southern half of England. A reverse trend is now evident and it is certainly less frequent. Elsewhere it has been recorded from Lincolnshire, Yorkshire, North Wales, Lancashire, the Isle of Arran and the Scottish Highlands.

Larva. September to spring on unspecified plants. The larva has not been found in the wild. In captivity the larva will accept dandelion and couch grass, but it is rarely reared to maturity.

Southern Rustic

Rhyacia lucipeta Denis & Schiffermüller
(*Entomologist's Gazette* 1978, vol. 29, pl. 2.)

Similar species. *R. simulans*, pl. **25**, is smaller and lacks the pale-ringed orbicular stigma which is a striking forewing character of *R. lucipeta*.

Imago. 56–64 mm. Probable immigrant. Abroad it is single-brooded, flying from mid-June to mid-August. The only British specimen, a female, was taken at light at Pulborough, Sussex, on 15.vii.1968. It occurs in western Europe, and has a range that includes France, Belgium and the Netherlands.

Larva. *September to May on a variety of plants; specifically mentioned are *Petasites*, *Euphorbia* and *Tussilago* spp.

Overwinters as a larva.

Large Yellow Underwing

Noctua pronuba Linnaeus

Plate **26** : *2–4*

Variation. Sexually dimorphic, the ground colour of the male varying from medium brown to almost black, and that of the female varying from pale reddish-brown through ochreous-brown to greyish-brown.

Similar species. *N. fimbriata*, pl. **26**.

Imago. 50–60 mm. Resident and immigrant. Comes commonly to light and to the flowers of *Buddleia*, red valerian, ragwort and many other wild and garden plants. Single-brooded, flying from July to September. Widespread and often abundant throughout the British Isles. The vast numbers that occasionally and suddenly appear in southern England during high summer are presumed to be migrants.

Larva. September to April on a wide range of plants and grasses.

Overwinters as a larva, feeding during the winter in mild weather.

Lunar Yellow Underwing

Noctua orbona Hufnagel

Plate **26** : *1*

Similar species. *N. comes*, pl. **26**, lacks the well-defined black apical mark. *N. pronuba*, pl. **26**, is larger and lacks the large discal spot on the hindwing.

Imago. 38–45 mm. Resident. Comes to light and sugar

in small numbers, and occasionally to the flowers of heather. Single-brooded, emerging in late June, aestivating, then reappearing in late August and September. A declining species formerly local, but widespread, in the southern half of Britain. It still exists locally in Wiltshire, Hampshire, the Breck district of East Anglia, the eastern border counties of England and Scotland including the sandhills of Northumberland, and the Findhorn sandhills in Morayshire. The only confirmed records for Ireland are Lough Neagh, Co. Londonderry, on 1.viii.1977 and Killard Point, Co. Down, on 29.viii.1996.

Larva. October to April on fine grasses and small herbaceous plants. Mortality is high in the young larvae due to parasitism. In captivity the larvae prefer broadleaved grasses such as cock's-foot and reed canary-grass. Overwinters as a small larva.

Lesser Yellow Underwing
Noctua comes Hübner
Plate **26** : *5–9*

Variation. The form ab. *sagittifer* Cockayne (fig 6) has well-defined cross-lines and occurs commonly in the Isles of Scilly, on Lundy, North Devon, and occasionally elsewhere. A wide range of reddish-brown and dark forms occur in Scotland, resulting in an equally wide range of aberrational names.
Similar species. *N. orbona*, pl. **26** and text.
Imago. 38–48 mm. Resident. Comes regularly to light and to sugar, and visits the flowers of marram, ragwort, heather and many other plants. Single-brooded, flying from July to September. Generally distributed and often common throughout the British Isles.
Larva. September to April on blackthorn, hawthorn, sallow, heather, dock, foxglove and many other trees, shrubs and plants.
Overwinters as a larva.

Broad-bordered Yellow Underwing
Noctua fimbriata Schreber
Plate **26** : *12–13*

Variation. Sexually dimorphic, the forewing ground colour of the male varying from medium brown to almost black, and that of the female varying from pale to dark olive-brown.
Similar species. *N. pronuba*, pl. **26**.
Imago. 50–58 mm. Resident. Comes regularly to light and sugar. Single-brooded, flying from July to September, spending part of this period in a state of aestivation. Widely distributed over much of the British Isles.
Larva. September to April on blackthorn, sallow, dock and other shrubs and low plants. Can be forced in captivity if exposed to at least fifteen hours of natural or artificial light per day.
Overwinters as a young larva.

Lesser Broad-bordered Yellow Underwing
Noctua janthe Borkhausen
(*janthina* sensu auctt.)
Plate **26** : *11*

Imago. 34–44 mm. Resident. Comes to light in moderate numbers and visits the flowers of ragwort, *Buddleia* and other plants. Single-brooded, flying from late July to early September. Widely distributed and often common throughout the British Isles.
Larva. September to April on dock, blackthorn, sallow and a wide variety of shrubs and plants.
Overwinters as a half-grown larva.
(*Author's note*: In 1991 it was found that *N. janthina* comprised two separate species. Only one of these has been found in the British Isles and for nomenclatural reasons our resident species has been designated *N. janthe*.)

Least Yellow Underwing
Noctua interjecta caliginosa Schawerda
Plate **26** : *10*

Imago. 31–36 mm. Resident. Comes to light regularly in small numbers and visits the flowers of ragwort. Single-brooded, flying in July and August, inhabiting fenland, sandhills, waste ground, etc. Widespread, but local, in England, Wales, Scotland and Ireland.
Larva. September to May on various grasses and herbaceous plants.
Overwinters as a larva.

Stout Dart
Spaelotis ravida Denis & Schiffermüller
Plate **26** : *14–15*

Similar species. *Rhyacia simulans*, pl. **25**. *Graphiphora augur*, pl. **26**. Possibly a large example of *Euxoa nigricans*, pl. **24**.
Imago. 42–50 mm. Resident, possibly reinforced by immigration. Comes to light and sugar, and visits the flowers of red valerian and common reed. Singlebrooded, flying from July to September, aestivating during this period in houses, garden sheds and under loose bark. Subject to great fluctuation, this species is now flourishing in many parts of southern, central and eastern England with a few records from Lancashire, Cumbria, central Wales and southeast Scotland.
Larva. September to May. The natural foodplants are apparently unknown; in captivity it will eat dandelion, dock and *Sonchus* spp.; it is a difficult species to rear.
Overwinters as a larva.

Double Dart
Graphiphora augur Fabricius
Plate **26** : *18*

Similar species. *Spaelotis ravida*, pl. **26**.
Imago. 38–48 mm. Resident. Comes to light and more frequently to sugar. Single-brooded, flying in June and July, inhabiting woodland, commons and bushy places.

Widely distributed, but seldom common, throughout the British Isles.
Larva. August to April on blackthorn, sallow, hawthorn, birch, elm and occasionally dock.
Overwinters as a larva.

Rosy Marsh Moth
Eugraphe subrosea Stephens
Plate **26** : *19–20*

Similar species. *Diarsia mendica*, pl. **27**. *Diarsia brunnea*, pl. **27**. Both these species have a conspicuous dot-like subclaviform stigma.
Imago. 36–40 mm. Resident. Comes readily to light. Single-brooded, flying in late July and August, inhabiting acid bog and fenland. Originally resident in the fenland of Huntingdonshire up to the middle of the nineteenth century, it became extinct when its habitats were destroyed. A chance capture of a specimen in North Wales in 1965 eventually led to its discovery in Borth Bog, Cardiganshire, where is was found to be well established. Since then it has been reported from Tregarron Bog, Cardiganshire and the Glaslyn marshes, Caernarvonshire.
Larva. September to May on bog myrtle. In captivity it will eat willow.
Overwinters as a small larva.

Cousin German
Paradiarsia sobrina Duponchel
Plate **26** : *21*

Similar species. Dark forms of *Diarsa mendica*, pl. **27**. *D. dahlii*, pl. **27**. Both these species have a distinct subclaviform stigma.
Imago. 34–39 mm. Resident. Comes to light and to sugar, usually in numbers, also visits the flowers of heather. Single-brooded, flying in July and August, inhabiting birch woodland with a bilberry undergrowth. A very local species occurring in the Highlands and adjacent counties in central Scotland.
Larva. September to May on bilberry and the leaves of the lower branches of young birches.
Overwinters as a larva.

Autumnal Rustic
Paradiarsia glareosa glareosa Esper
Plate **26** : *22–24*

Variation. The usual ground colour is light grey (fig 24); specimens from Scotland tend to be darker, and those from southeast Kent are ochreous and slightly larger (fig 22). Specimens tinged with pink occur in Devon and Cornwall, and less frequently elsewhere (fig 23); the more extreme examples of this form are referable to ab. *rosea* Tutt.
Imago. 32–38 mm. Resident. Comes readily to light and also visits the flowers of heather and heath. Single-brooded, flying in August and September, inhabiting heathland, moorland, shingle beaches, chalky places

and the edges of woodland. Generally distributed throughout the British Isles.
P. glareosa edda Staudinger, pl. **26** : *25*. This nearly black form occurs in Shetland as a varying percentage of the total population: from two per cent in South Mainland to 97 per cent in Unst. Forms approaching ssp. *edda* have been taken in Orkney and Caithness.
Larva. October to early May on a wide variety of plants and grasses. In captivity it readily accepts sallow.
Overwinters as a very small larva.

True Lover's Knot
Lycophotia porphyrea Denis & Schiffermüller
(*varia* Villers)
Plate **26** : *16–17*

Variation. Several small specimens were bred from pupae found near Braemar, Aberdeenshire, at an altitude of 670 m (2200 ft). (See fig 17.)
Imago. 26–34 mm. Resident. Found regularly at light and on the flowers of heather. Single-brooded, flying from June to August, inhabiting heathland and mountain moorland. Generally distributed and common throughout the British Isles.
Larva. August to May on heather and bell heather.
Overwinters as a larva.

Pearly Underwing
Peridroma saucia Hübner
Plate **26** : *26–28*

Similar species. *Agrotis segetum*, pl. **25**. *Agrotis ipsilon*, pl. **25**.
Imago. 45–56 mm. Immigrant. Comes readily to light and to sugar, and visits the flowers of red valerian, ivy and common reed. Although it has been recorded in every month of the year, it is usually most numerous in September and October. This annual and often common migrant has been noted throughout the British Isles, although it is much more frequent in southern England.
Larva. During the summer on wild and cultivated herbaceous plants. It is said to be an occasional pest of lettuces in glasshouses. In captivity it is easily reared on dock.
There is no evidence to suggest this species can survive our winter in any stage.

Ingrailed Clay
Diarsia mendica mendica Fabricius
(*festiva* Denis & Schiffermüller)
Plate **27** : *1–6*

Variation. If both of the northern races are included, then this species must rate the most variable of the Noctuidae. It is perhaps sufficient to state that the straw-coloured forms from southern England and the smaller dark brown ones from Shetland represent each end of a south to north cline.
Similar species. *Diarsia rubi*, pl. **27** and text. *Diarsia*

brunnea, pl. **27** and text. *Xestia xanthographa*, pl. **28** and text. *Eugraphe subrosea*, pl. **26** and text.

Imago. 28–36 mm. Resident. Comes commonly to light and occasionally to sugar. Single-brooded, flying from late June to August. Widespread and generally common throughout the British Isles.

D. mendica orkneyensis Bytinski-Salz, pl. **27** : *7–10*. Described from specimens occurring on Orkney.

D. mendica thulei Staudinger, pl. **27** : *11–15*. Described from specimens from Shetland. Very variable with some examples indistinguishable from those inhabiting Orkney, Scotland and northern England.

Larva. September to April on bilberry, bramble, sallow, hawthorn, heather, dock and probably many other plants. Overwinters as a larva.

Barred Chestnut

Diarsia dahlii Hübner

Plate **27** : *17–18*

Variation. Sexually dimorphic, the dark purplish-brown specimens being female (although dark examples of the male occur in Ireland and parts of the Midlands).

Similar species. *D. mendica*, pl. **27**, has the costa of the forewing less strongly arched. *D. brunnea*, pl. **27**, usually has a blackish patch or bar linking reniform and orbicular stigmata.

Imago. 32–42 mm. Resident. Comes frequently to light, and commonly to sugar; also visits the flowers of heather and ragwort. Single-brooded, flying in August and September, inhabiting moorland and deciduous woodland. Widely distributed in Scotland, including the Inner Hebrides, Wales, northern and central England. In the south it is locally common in parts of Surrey, but rare elsewhere. Reported from a number of counties in Ireland where it is possibly more widespread than the records suggest.

Larva. September to early spring on birch, bilberry and probably other trees and plants. In captivity it thrives on dock and if kept warm will pupate and emerge during the winter. Overwinters as a larva.

Purple Clay

Diarsia brunnea Denis & Schiffermüller

Plate **27** : *16*

Similar species. *D. dahlii*, pl. **27** and text. *D. mendica*, pl. **27**, in which the outer edge of subterminal fascia of forewing is not angulated below costa. *Eugraphe subrosea*, pl. **26** and text; and *Xestia rhomboidea*, pl. **27**.

Imago. 36–45 mm. Resident. Comes frequently to light and sugar. Single-brooded, flying from mid-June to early August, inhabiting deciduous woodland. Widespread and common throughout the British Isles as far north as Orkney, although as yet unrecorded from the Hebrides.

Larva. September to April on bilberry, sallow, birch, dock and other trees and plants. Overwinters as a larva.

Small Square-spot

Diarsia rubi Vieweg

Plate **27** : *21–24*

Variation. The second brood is smaller and generally darker than the earlier brood. Specimens from Shetland are stated to be larger and duller in appearance than those from elsewhere.

Imago. 30–38 mm. Resident. Comes readily to light and to sugar, and visits the flowers of ragwort and heather. Double-brooded in southern Britain and Ireland, flying in May and June and again in August and September. Single-brooded in Scotland and the northern islands, flying in July and August. Widespread and often common throughout the British Isles.

Larva. Autumn to spring and during the summer on a wide variety of herbaceous plants. Three to four generations a year can be obtained in captivity. Overwinters as a larva.

Fen Square-spot

Diarsia florida Schmidt

Plate **27** : *19–20*

Variation. The pale yellow ab. *ochracea* Walker (fig 20), and the more extreme ab. *flava* Walker are rare recessive forms bred from Yorkshire.

Similar species. In those localities listed below, *D. florida* can be separated from the *D. rubi* that share its habitat by its larger size, paler hindwing and brighter and more orange forewing; it is superficially not unlike a southern form of *D. mendica*, pl. **27**. It is also single-brooded, appearing between the two generations of *D. rubi*. Another important biological difference is the flight-times of the two species, which in *D. florida* is usually from 0030 hrs to 0200 hrs BST, whereas *D. rubi* often appears soon after dusk. Elsewhere in Britain, particularly in the north, these distinctions do not apply. They cannot be separated by means of the genitalia and fertile hybrids are readily obtained in captivity. Further research is therefore needed to clarify this complex situation.

Imago. 30–38 mm. Resident. Flies late at night and is attracted to light. Single-brooded, flying in late June and July, inhabiting fenland and marshy places. Recorded with certainty from Wicken Fen and Chippenham Fen, Cambridgeshire; Askham Bog, Skipwith Common and elsewhere in Yorkshire; the Broads and Lopham Fen, Norfolk; and Borth Bog, Cardiganshire. Probably occurring in other parts of Wales and in the Lake District.

Larva. Has not been found in the wild; in captivity it will eat dock and dandelion, pupating and emerging in the autumn.

Northern Dart

Xestia alpicola alpina Humphreys & Westwood

Plate **27** : *28–32*

Imago. 34–40 mm. Resident. Has occasionally been noted flying during the day in hot sunshine, but its usual time of flight is very late at night when it is attracted to light. Single-brooded, flying from late June to August, inhabiting the higher slopes and summits of mountains and rarely occurring below 460 m (1500 ft), except in Shetland where it has been found near sea-level. Evidence suggests the species has a biennial rhythm, and is more commonly found in alternate years. The favoured year is given in brackets after each county; a date signifies that it has only been found on one occasion. In Scotland it occurs in Perthshire (even years), Inverness-shire (even years), Aberdeenshire (even years), Ross-shire (odd years). Recently it has been reported from Lewis, Outer Hebrides, and as a single specimen from Orkney Mainland in 1986. In England in the Pennines (odd years), Northumberland (1975) and a single specimen from Cumbria (1950). In Ireland it has been noted from Co. Mayo (1972) and Co. Donegal (1973).

Larva. It has a two-year cycle, hatching in August and overwintering twice as a larva. It is found on crowberry and possibly on heather.

Pupa. Late May and early June at ground-level under lichen and moss.

Setaceous Hebrew Character

Xestia c-nigrum Linnaeus

Plate **27** : *33*

Imago. 35–45 mm. Resident, probably reinforced by immigration. Comes to light and sugar in varying numbers; also visits the flowers of ragwort, *Buddleia*, ivy and many other plants. Probably double-brooded, appearing from May to July and again, more abundantly, from late August to October. In northern England and Scotland it is evidently only single-brooded, appearing from early July to mid-August. This species, which often occurs commonly in southern Britain, has been reported from most parts of the British Isles including Shetland and the Hebrides.

Larva. Autumn to early spring and during the summer on common nettle and probably many other herbaceous plants.

Overwinters as a larva, feeding during mild weather.

Triple-spotted Clay

Xestia ditrapezium Denis & Schiffermüller

Plate **27** : *34*

Similar species. *X. triangulum*, pl. **27**. *X. rhomboidea*, pl. **27**.

Imago. 39–46 mm. Resident. Comes to light and sugar in small numbers and also visits the flowers of ragwort and wood sage. Single-brooded, flying from late June to early August, inhabiting parkland and deciduous woodland. Locally widespread throughout much of Britain. In Ireland it has been recorded from Cos Dublin, Clare and Galway.

Larva. September to April on birch, sallow, bramble, hazel, honeysuckle and other trees and plants.

Overwinters as a larva.

Double Square-spot

Xestia triangulum Hufnagel

Plate **27** : *35*

Similar species. *X. ditrapezium*, pl. **27**. *X. rhomboidea*, pl. **27**.

Imago. 36–46 mm. Resident. Comes regularly to light and sugar; also visits the flowers of wood sage. Single-brooded, flying in June and July, inhabiting deciduous woodland. Generally distributed throughout much of the British Isles.

Larva. September to April on blackthorn, hawthorn, bramble, raspberry, sallow, birch, dock, and other trees and plants.

Overwinters as a larva.

Ashworth's Rustic

Xestia ashworthii Doubleday

Plate **28** : *1–2*

Imago. 35–40 mm. Resident. Comes readily to light. Single-brooded, flying from mid-June to August, inhabiting slate and limestone hills and mountains. Locally common in Caernarvonshire, Merionethshire, Montgomeryshire, Denbighshire, and in smaller numbers in Cardiganshire. Stray specimens are occasionally recorded outside this area of North Wales.

Larva. September to May on many herbaceous plants including heather and foxglove. Feeds at night, but can be found during the day in mild weather resting high up on its foodplant. In captivity it thrives on the leaves and especially the catkins of sallow.

Overwinters as a larva.

Dotted Clay

Xestia baja Denis & Schiffermüller

Plate **28** : *10–11*

Imago. 38–44 mm. Resident. Comes regularly to light and to sugar. Single-brooded, flying in late July and August, inhabiting heathland and woodland. Generally distributed and often common throughout the British Isles as far north as Orkney.

Larva. September to May on birch, bramble, bog myrtle, blackthorn, dock and many other trees and plants.

Overwinters as a larva.

Square-spotted Clay

Xestia rhomboidea Esper

(*stigmatica* Hübner)

Plate **27** : *36*

Similar species. *X. triangulum*, pl. **27**. *X. ditrapezium*, pl. **27**. *Diarsia brunnea*, pl. **27**.

Imago. 37–44 mm. Resident. Comes to light and sugar, and is especially fond of the flowers of burdock (*Arctium* spp.), wood sage and willowherb. Single-brooded, flying in August, inhabiting deciduous woodland. A very local species, found mainly in the southern half of Britain, Yorkshire and a few widely scattered localities in western and central Scotland.

Larva. September to May on birch, bramble and probably other trees and herbaceous plants. In captivity it will eat dock and sliced carrots, and is easily forced. The larva remains in the soil for several weeks before pupating and should not be disturbed during this time. Overwinters as a larva.

Neglected Rustic
Xestia castanea Esper
(*neglecta* Hübner)
Plate **28** : *3–4*

Variation. There are two basic colour forms, ochreous-grey, f. *neglecta* Hübner (fig 3), and reddish-orange. The latter, which is the type form, predominates in northern England and Scotland, but is less common in the south. A rare yellowish form, referable as ab. *xanthe* Woodforde, has occurred in Surrey, Staffordshire, Hampshire and Co. Kerry.

Similar species. *X. xanthographa*, pl. **28**, has a paler hindwing and lacks the dark dot in the reniform stigma.

Imago. 36–42 mm. Resident. Comes to light and to sugar, and is very fond of the flowers of heather. Single-brooded, flying in August and September, inhabiting heathland and moorland. Widely distributed and locally common throughout much of the British Isles, including Orkney and the Hebrides.

Larva. October to May on heather and *Erica* spp. In captivity it will accept sallow and hawthorn and like the last species rests in the ground for several weeks before pupating.
Overwinters as a small larva.

Six-striped Rustic
Xestia sexstrigata Haworth
Plate **28** : *9*

Imago. 36–38 mm. Resident. Comes in moderate numbers to light and sugar, and visits freely the flowers of ragwort. Single-brooded, flying in July and August. Generally distributed throughout the British Isles, including Orkney and the Hebrides.

Larva. Autumn to April on a variety of herbaceous plants. In captivity it will readily accept dock and plantain.
Overwinters as a larva.

Square-spot Rustic
Xestia xanthographa Denis & Schiffermüller
Plate **28** : *5–8*

Variation. Ground colour varies from pale ochreous-grey through many shades of brown to almost black. These melanistic forms are not uncommon in Shetland, Orkney and parts of London.

Similar species. *X. castanea*, pl. **28** and text. The pale reniform stigma, 'square-spot', of *X. xanthographa* should preclude confusion with any other species.

Imago. 30–40 mm. Resident. Comes readily to light and sugar, and visits the flowers of many plants such as ragwort, marram and heather. Single-brooded, flying from late July to September. A common species and found throughout the British Isles.

Larva. September to April, feeding throughout the winter on grasses and low plants.
Overwinters as a larva.

Heath Rustic
Xestia agathina agathina Duponchel
Plate **27** : *25–26*

Variation. Reddish forms occur in southwest England, Wales and elsewhere and are referable to ab. *rosea* Tutt. Blackish forms occur in parts of northern England and are referable to ab. *scopariae* Millière.

Similar species. *Lycophotia porphyrea*, pl. **26**.

Imago. 28–36 mm. Resident. Comes to light in moderate numbers, and visits the flowers of heather and *Erica* spp. Single-brooded, flying in September, inhabiting moorland and heathland. Widespread throughout the British Isles, including Orkney and the Hebrides. *X. agathina hebridicola* Staudinger, pl. **27** : *27*. Has the ground colour of forewing pale grey. Described from the Hebrides, with allied forms occurring on the Scottish mainland.

Larva. October to May, feeding on the young shoots of heather. Can be reared in captivity on a mixture of young heather and sallow.
Overwinters as a small larva.

The Gothic
Naenia typica Linnaeus
Plate **28** : *12*

Similar species. Both *Heliophobus reticulata*, pl. **29**, and *Tholera decimalis*, pl. **30**, have narrower forewings, and lack the dark ground colour between the reniform and orbicular stigmata.

Imago. 36–46 mm. Resident. Comes frequently to sugar, honey-dew and various flowers, and in small numbers to light. Single-brooded, flying in June and July, inhabiting waste ground, gardens, and marshy places. Widespread over much of the British Isles, but rarely found commonly, except on the old slag heaps in parts of the Midlands.

Larva. August to March on a wide variety of plants and trees, including willowherb, dandelion, dock, and sallow. Before hibernation the small larvae live gregariously on the underside of leaves.
Overwinters as a larva.

Great Brocade
Eurois occulta Linnaeus
Plate **28** : *13–14*

Variation. Ground colour ranges from pale grey to almost black. Immigrant specimens are invariably light grey.

Similar species. *Polia nebulosa*, pl. **28**.

Imago. 52–64 mm. Resident and immigrant. Comes to light and sugar. Single-brooded, flying in July and early August, inhabiting the wetter parts of mountain moorland. As a resident it is widespread and locally common in the central and western Scottish Highlands. As a immigrant it appears most years in varying numbers from late July to September. A rare visitor to southern Britain and mostly reported from the eastern counties. In northern Britain, including Orkney and Shetland, it is stated to occur more frequently. Abroad its range includes Scandinavia, Belgium and the rest of northern Europe.

Larva. September to May, mainly on bog myrtle. In April, soon after hibernation, the very small larvae may be found during the day high up on the leafless food-plant; as they increase in size they become nocturnal and are then rarely found in numbers until several hours after dark.

Green Arches
Anaplectoides prasina Denis & Schiffermüller
Plate **28** : *15*
Variation. Ab. *demuthi* Richardson is a melanic form which has been bred from Cannock Chase, Staffordshire. Less extreme forms have occurred in Derbyshire and other parts of the Midlands.
Imago. 43–53 mm. Resident. Comes to light in small numbers, and readily to sugar. Single-brooded, flying from mid-June to mid-July, inhabiting deciduous woodland. Widely distributed and locally common over much of the British Isles.
Larva. August to April on a variety of plants, especially honeysuckle and bilberry. A second generation can be obtained in captivity, with the larvae accepting dock and sliced carrots.
Overwinters as a larva.

Red Chestnut
Cerastis rubricosa Denis & Schiffermüller
Plate **28** : *19–20*
Variation. Specimens from Scotland are darker than those from southern England and vary from slaty-brown to slaty-grey (fig 20).
Similar species. *C. leucographa*, pl. **28**, has pale yellowish-grey stigmata and a much paler hindwing.
Imago. 32–38 mm. Resident. Comes regularly to light, sugar, and sallow catkins. Single-brooded, flying in March and April, inhabiting woodland and boggy moorland. Generally distributed and common throughout the British Isles as far north as Orkney.
Larva. May to June on a variety of herbaceous plants. In captivity will readily accept dock and sallow.
Overwinters as a pupa.

White-marked
Cerastis leucographa Denis & Schiffermüller
Plate **28** : *21*
Similar species. *C. rubricosa*, pl. **28** and text.

Imago. 35–39 mm. Resident. Comes to light and is frequently taken at sallow blossom. Single-brooded, flying in late March and April, inhabiting open woodland. Rather local, occurring in southern England, south and west Midlands, Nottinghamshire, Yorkshire, the Lake District and the southern half of Wales.
Larva. May to June. In captivity it will eat sallow, dock, stitchwort and chickweed, preferring a mixed diet.
Overwinters as a pupa.

Pale Stigma
Mesogona acetosellae Denis & Schiffermüller
(South 1961, vol. 1, pl. 46)
Imago. 36–46 mm. Immigrant. Single-brooded on the Continent, flying from August to October. The only British specimen, a female, was taken at sugar at Arlington, Sussex, on 26.x.1895 at a time of much migrant activity. Widely distributed in central and southern Europe, its range extending eastwards into Asia.
Larva. *May to July on scrub-oak, blackthorn and other shrubs and small trees.
Overwinters as an egg.

SUBFAMILY: HADENINAE
Beautiful Yellow Underwing
Anarta myrtilli Linnaeus
Plate **28** : *16*
Similar species. *A. cordigera*, pl. **28**.
Imago. 24–28 mm. Resident. Flies rapidly during the day preferring hot sunshine. There are probably two overlapping broods between late April and August except in the north where it is only one, occurring in June and early July. The species inhabits heathland and moorland, and occurs throughout the British Isles including Orkney and the Hebrides.
Larva. Has been found from April to October feeding on heather and heath, preferring the terminal shoots.
It is not known for certain how this species overwinters. Evidence suggests it might be capable of diapause in both the larval and pupal stages.

Small Dark Yellow Underwing
Anarta cordigera Thunberg
Plate **28** : *17*
Similar species. *A. myrtilli*, pl. **28**.
Imago. 24–28 mm. Resident. Flies in sunshine and is attracted to the flowers of bearberry. Single-brooded, flying from mid-May to mid-June, inhabiting heather moorland between 200 m and 600 m (600 and 2000 ft). Occurring locally in Inverness-shire, Perthshire, Aberdeenshire, Angus, Morayshire, and Banffshire.
Larva. June to July on bearberry.
Overwinters as a pupa.

Broad-bordered White Underwing
Anarta melanopa Thunberg
Plate **28** : *18*

Imago. 26–32 mm. Resident. Flies by day in sunshine and is attracted to the flowers of various mountain plants. Single-brooded, flying in late May and June, inhabiting the higher slopes and summits of mountains and rarely occurring below 600 m (2000 ft). In Scotland it occurs from Galloway through Argyllshire and the Highlands to Caithness, and old specimens exist from the Hebrides. A single specimen was reported on Shetland Mainland in 1992 after many years' absence. In England it has been found recently in the Cheviot Hills, Northumberland.
Larva. July to August on crowberry, cowberry, bilberry and bearberry. In captivity it is said to eat sallow and knotgrass.
Overwinters as a pupa.

The Nutmeg
Discestra trifolii Hufnagel
Plate **28** : *22–24*

Variation. Specimens from the Breck district of East Anglia have a distinct reddish-brown appearance (fig 23). In the Midlands and the London area dark grey forms are not uncommon (fig 24).
Similar species. *Mamestra brassicae*, pl. **29**, is larger and has the outer edge of reniform stigma outlined with white. *Sideridis albicolon*, pl. **29**, is larger and has two white marks on the lower and outer edges of the reniform stigma. *Apamea anceps*, pl. **37**. *A. remissa*, pl. **37** and text.
Imago. 23–39 mm. Resident and suspected immigrant. Comes to light and to sugar, and visits the flowers of many wild and cultivated plants. Double-brooded in the south, flying May to June and August to September. Single-brooded from the Midlands northwards, flying in late June and July. Generally distributed and often common in the southern half of Britain. Has occurred in Scotland, Orkney, Shetland and Ireland, but most of these specimens are presumed migrants or transitory residents.
Larva. July and late September and October mainly on goosefoot and orache.
Overwinters as a pupa.

The Shears
Hada plebeja Linnaeus
(*nana* Hufnagel)
Plate **29** : *1–3*

Variation. The species tends to become progressively darker from south to north although great variation can occur within a single locality.
Imago. 28–38 mm. Resident. Flies occasionally in hot sunshine, but the normal flight is from dusk onwards when it visits the flowers of wood sage, red valerian, viper's-bugloss and campions (*Silene* spp.). Mainly single-brooded, flying from late May to early July, with a partial second brood in the south in August. Widespread and generally common throughout the British Isles.
Larva. July to August, and September in the south, on hawk's-beard, hawkweed, dandelion, and chickweed. Overwinters as a pupa.

Pale Shining Brown
Polia bombycina Hufnagel
(*nitens* Haworth)
Plate **29** : *4*

Imago. 47–52 mm. Resident and suspected immigrant. Comes to light and sugar in small numbers, and has been found feeding on the flowers of red valerian, campions (*Silene* spp.) and various garden plants. Single-brooded, flying from mid-June to mid-July, inhabiting downland and open country mainly on chalk. A local and possibly declining species now rarely recorded outside of southern and southeastern England. A few specimens having a silvery-grey appearance have been recorded from southeast Kent and these were probably immigrants.
Larva. Life history in the wild is apparently unknown. In captivity the larva will eat dock, dandelion and sliced carrot, and if kept warm will mature and produce moths during the winter.
Probably overwinters as a larva.

Silvery Arches
Polia hepatica Clerck
(*tincta* Brahm)
Plate **28** : *25–26*

Variation. Specimens from Scotland have a strong bluish tinge, very noticeable in freshly emerged specimens, but fading slowly with age.
Similar species. *P. nebulosa*, pl. **28**.
Imago. 43–52 mm. Resident and suspected immigrant. Comes sparingly to light, but readily to sugar. Single-brooded, flying in June and July, inhabiting woodland and heathland. Common in parts of southern England except the extreme southwest, the Lake District and central Scotland. Rather local elsewhere with a scattered distribution throughout Great Britain. Specimens occasionally appearing unexpectedly in coastal localities in southern and southeastern England are presumed immigrants.
Larva. Late summer to May mainly on birch, but also bog myrtle, sallow and hawthorn.
Overwinters as a small larva.

Grey Arches
Polia nebulosa Hufnagel
Plate **28** : *27–30*

Variation. The pale cream or white forms occur in western England, most of Scotland, Wales and Ireland. Dark grey and melanic forms predominate in the industrial areas of the Midland counties and parts of the London area. A striking melanic form having white fringes, ab. *thompsoni* Arkle (fig 30), occurred frequently in Delamere Forest, Cheshire, but has not been noted in recent years.

Similar species. *P. hepatica*, pl. **28**. *Eurois occulta*, pl. **28**. *Apamea monoglypha*, pl. **37**.

Imago. 46–58 mm. Resident. Comes to light in small numbers, but more frequently to sugar. Single-brooded, flying in June and July. Generally distributed and not uncommon throughout mainland Britain and Ireland.

Larva. August to May on a variety of plants and trees such as birch, sallow, honeysuckle, bramble, hawthorn and dock.

Overwinters as a larva.

Feathered Ear

Pachetra sagittigera britannica Turner
(*leucophaea* Denis & Schiffermüller)
Plate **29** : *5*

Imago. 38–50 mm. Resident. Comes to light, sugar, and the flowers of privet. Single-brooded, flying in late May and June, inhabiting chalk downland. Old records exist from Wiltshire, Buckinghamshire, Gloucestershire and Hampshire, but the headquarters of this species was always the North Downs of Surrey and Kent where it was local, but not uncommon. In recent years it has declined to the point of extinction and even in its most favoured localities has not been seen since 1963.

Larva. July to March on various grasses. It is stated to prefer meadow-grass. Normally found in the wild in early February.

Overwinters as a larva.

White Colon

Sideridis albicolon Hübner
Plate **29** : 6

Variation. Dark, almost blackish, forms have been recorded from the heaths of east Hampshire and from northeast Scotland.

Similar species. *Discestra trifolii*, pl. **28** and text. *Mamestra brassicae*, pl. **29**, is usually darker, has the entire outer edge of the reniform stigma outlined with white and has the subterminal line of forewing with white ≥-mark. *Apamesa remissa*, pl. **37**, is smaller, lacks the small white c-mark in reniform stigma and has subterminal line of forewing with ≥-mark. *Apamea oblonga*, pl. **37**, has a darker and glossy forewing and lacks the whitish subterminal line.

Imago. 38–44 mm. Resident. Comes to light and sugar, and the flowers of viper's-bugloss, marram and other grasses. Has occasionally been seen flying and visiting flowers in sunshine. Mainly single-brooded, flying in late May and June, with a partial second generation in southern England in late July and August. It inhabits heathland in east Hampshire, parts of Surrey and the Breckland area of East Anglia. Elsewhere it frequents coastal sandhills and is widely distributed in England,

Wales and eastern Scotland. Local and rather uncommon in Ireland.

Larva. July and September on the leaves and flowers of a wide variety of plants such as goosefoot, orache, sea bindweed (*Calystegia soldanella*), and sea rocket. Hides by day in sand.

Overwinters as a pupa.

Bordered Gothic

Heliophobus reticulata marginosa Haworth
(*saponariae* Borkhausen)
Plate **29** : 7

Similar species. *Tholera decimalis*, pl. **30**. *Naenia typica*, pl. **28**.

Imago. 35–40 mm. Resident. Comes to light and sugar, and visits the flowers of red valerian, campions (*Silene* spp.), viper's-bugloss and wood sage. Single-brooded, flying in June and July, inhabiting downland, rough ground and sea-cliffs. Formerly widely distributed and locally not uncommon in the southern half of England including the Breckland of East Anglia. Now considered to be a very local and declining species.

H. reticulata hibernica Cockayne, pl. **29** : *8*. Ground colour of forewing purplish-brown. Inhabiting coastal and estuarine localities in southern Ireland from Co. Wexford to Co. Cork. Specimens taken recently at Portland, Dorset, closely resemble this race.

Larva. Late July to September. The larva seems not to have been found in the wild. In captivity it has been successfully reared on knotgrass and soapwort (*Saponaria officinalis*).

Overwinters as a pupa.

Cabbage Moth

Mamestra brassicae Linnaeus
Plate **29** : *18*

Similar species. *Discestra trifolii*, pl. **28** and text. *Sideridis albicolon*, pl. **29** and text. *Apamea oblonga*, pl. **37**, is less variegated and lacks the white-marked reniform stigma. Both *Apamea remissa* and *A. furva*, pl. **37**, are smaller and lack the white-marked reniform stigma. The presence of a small curved spur on the tibia of the foreleg distinguishes *M. brassicae* from other similar species.

Imago. 34–50 mm. Resident. Attracted to light, sugar, and the flowers of red valerian and probably many other wild and cultivated plants. Mainly double-brooded with a partial third generation occurring in the autumn in favourable seasons. Evidence suggests that those which have overwintered as pupae emerge from late May to mid-June and produce their main generation from mid-July to mid-August; these in turn sometimes produce a third generation in late September and October. Those that have hibernated as larvae emerge from mid-June to early July and produce their main generation from mid-August to mid-September. Both groups, of course, integrate in the wild and the above s but an oversimplified version of a very complex life-history. In parts of Scotland the usual time of appearance is June and July. The species is widespread throughout the British Isles; common in the south, but less frequent in the north.

Larva. Throughout the summer and autumn on a great variety of wild and cultivated plants, especially cabbages and other *Brassica* spp.
Overwinters both as a pupa and to a lesser extent as a larva.

Dot Moth
Melanchra persicariae Linnaeus
Plate **29** : *17*

Imago. 38–50 mm. Resident. Comes to light, sugar, and flowers. Single-brooded, flying mainly in July and August, and found in a variety of habitats, but preferring gardens and suburban wasteland. Widespread and generally common throughout England and Wales. Less frequent in Ireland and the extreme south of Scotland.
Larva. Late August to October on many wild and garden plants, also reported feeding on sallow, elder and larch saplings.
Overwinters as a pupa.

Beautiful Brocade
Lacanobia contigua Denis & Schiffermüller
Plate **29** : *13*

Similar species. *L. w-latinum*, pl. **29**. *Apamea remissa*, pl. **37**.
Imago. 36–42 mm. Resident. Comes to light and sugar. Single-brooded, flying in June and July, inhabiting woodland, heathland and moorland. Widely distributed, but local, over much of the British Isles.
Larva. August to September on a wide variety of trees and plants, including birch, sallow, oak, bog myrtle, heather, bracken and dock.
Overwinters as a pupa.

Light Brocade
Lacanobia w-latinum Hufnagel
Plate **29** : *16*

Similar species. *L. contigua*, pl. **29**. *Apamea remissa*, pl. **37**.
Imago. 37–42 mm. Resident. Attracted to light, sugar, and the flowers of red valerian and campions (*Silene* spp.). Single-brooded, flying from mid-May to early July. Widely distributed in the southern half of England, with scattered records from Wales, northern England and Scotland as far north as Perthshire.
Larva. July to August on a wide variety of plants, including broom, dyer's greenweed (*Genista tinctoria*) and *Polygonum* spp.
Overwinters as a pupa.

Pale-shouldered Brocade
Lacanobia thalassina Hufnagel
Plate **29** : *14–15*

Variation. Ab. *humeralis* Haworth (fig 15) is a greyish-brown form occurring throughout the British Isles.
Similar species. *L. suasa*, pl. **29**. *Apamea remissa*, pl. **37**. *Apamea epomidion*, pl. **37**.
Imago. 38–44 mm. Resident. Comes to light, sugar and various flowers. Usually single-brooded, flying from late May to early July; a second generation is said occasionally to occur in the south. A generally distributed and common woodland species throughout the British Isles as far north as Shetland.
Larva. July to September on oak, hawthorn, broom, honeysuckle and many other trees and plants.
Overwinters as a pupa.

Dog's Tooth
Lacanobia suasa Denis & Schiffermüller
Plate **29** : *11–12*

Variation. Ab. *dissimilis* Knoch (fig 12) is a unicolorous form occurring throughout the entire range of the species; less frequent than the typical form, but not uncommon.
Similar species. *L. thalassina*, pl. **29**. *L. oleracea*, pl. **29**. *Apamea remissa*, pl. **37**.
Imago. 32–42 mm. Resident. Comes to light and sugar. Single-brooded in the north, flying in June and July. Double-brooded in southern England, flying from late May to early July, and again from late July to mid-September with the peaks of emergence varying from year to year according to climatic conditions. A lowland species preferring salt-marshes, waste ground and moorland. Widespread and locally common in England, Wales, southern Scotland and Ireland.
Larva. During the summer and early autumn on herbaceous plants, including dock, plantain and common sea-lavender (*Limonium vulgare*).
Overwinters as a pupa.

Bright-line Brown-eye
Lacanobia oleracea Linnaeus
Plate **29** : *10*

Variation. Ground colour of forewing ranges from light reddish-brown to dark brown.
Similar species. *L. suasa*, pl. **29**.
Imago. 34–44 mm. Resident. Comes to light, sugar and various flowers. Mainly single-brooded, flying from May to July, with a small second brood occurring in the south in the autumn. Widespread and common over much of the British Isles.
Larva. During the summer and early autumn on a wide variety of plants and shrubs. An occasional pest of cultivated tomatoes.
Overwinters as a pupa.

The Stranger
Lacanobia blenna Hübner
(South 1961, vol. 1, pl. 66)

Similar species. *Hada nana*, pl. **29** : *2*. *Hadena perplexa*, pl. **29** : *28–30*.

Imago. 36–40 mm. Possible migrant and transitory resident. Comes to light and sugar. Abroad it is single-brooded in the northern part of its range, flying in August and September. There are four British records – at Freshwater, Isle of Wight, in 1857, on 23.viii.1859 and in 1876, and near Lewes, Sussex, in 1868. Abroad, its range includes southern and western France, where it inhabits coastal shores and salt-marshes.

Larva. *April to June on sea beet (*Beta vulgaris* ssp. *maritima*), prickly saltwort and other maritime plants. Overwinters as an egg.

Glaucous Shears
Papestra biren Goeze
(*glauca* Hübner)
Plate **29** : *9*

Imago. 32–40 mm. Resident. Comes to light and to a variety of moorland flowers. During the day it is often found at rest on tree-trunks, fences and rocks. Single-brooded, flying in May and June, inhabiting moorland. Widespread and locally common in Wales, the Midlands, northern England, Scotland and Ireland. Very local in southwest England.

Larva. July to August on a wide variety of plants such as meadowsweet, heather, bilberry, sallow and bog myrtle. Overwinters as a pupa.

Broom Moth
Ceramica pisi Linnaeus
Plate **29** : *21–24*

Variation. Specimens inhabiting peaty moorland tend to be darker than those from elsewhere; otherwise this is an extremely variable species throughout the whole of its range. Ab. *splendens* Staudinger (fig 22) is an obscurely marked and not uncommon form.

Imago. 33–42 mm. Resident. Comes to light and to sugar. Single-brooded, flying from mid-May to July. Generally distributed and not uncommon throughout the British Isles.

Larva. July to September on a wide variety of plants and trees such as broom, bracken, birch, elm, dock and sea aster. Overwinters as a pupa.

Broad-barred White
Hecatera bicolorata Hufnagel
(*serena* Denis & Schiffermüller)
Plate **29** : *20*

Imago. 28–35 mm. Resident. During the day it may be found at rest on fences and posts. After dark it comes to light, and visits the flowers of red valerian, viper's-bugloss, campions (*Silene* spp.), privet and other plants associated with waste ground and downland. Single-brooded, flying from mid-June to early August. Widely distributed and not uncommon in England and Wales. Locally common in Scotland as far north as Inverness-shire. Stated to be scarce, but widespread, in Ireland.

Larva. August to September mainly on hawkweed and hawk's-beard, feeding on the flowers and buds. In captivity it will accept a variety of herbaceous plants. Overwinters as a pupa.

Small Ranunculus
Hecatera dysodea Denis & Schiffermüller
Plate **29** : *19*

Similar species. *H. bicolorata*, pl. **29**. *Eumichtis lichenea* pl. **34**. *Polymixis flavicincta*, pl. **33**.

Imago. 32–34 mm. Formerly resident, now extinct. Comes to light, and to the flowers of various wild and garden plants, especially red valerian. Single-brooded, flying in June and July. Formerly widespread and locally common in East Anglia and southeast England, where it inhabited gardens and waste ground. In some localities it was said to be a pest on cultivated lettuce. The reason for the sudden decline of this species remains obscure, but by 1912 it had virtually disappeared from all its known haunts. A few specimens were taken in Essex in 1918; one in Somerset in 1935, three near Berkhamsted, Hertfordshire, in 1936 and one other in 1937. In the collection of the British Entomological and Natural History Society there is a specimen labelled 'Near Arundel, Sussex, July 1939'. The origin of the most recent record of single specimens at light at Gravesend, Kent, on 28.vi. & 6.viii.1997 has yet to be ascertained. The record from Buckinghamshire in 1941, quoted by several authors, has been recently investigated and found to be erroneous.

Larva. July to August on the flowers and ripening seeds of various wild and cultivated lettuce. Overwinters as a pupa.

The Campion
Hadena rivularis Fabricius
(*cucubali* Denis & Schiffermüller)
Plate **29** : *35*

Similar species. *H. bicruris*, pl. **30** and text.

Imago. 30–36 mm. Resident. Comes to light, and to the flowers of wood sage, viper's-bugloss, red valerian and campion (*Silene* spp.). Mainly single-brooded, flying in late May and June, with a second generation in southern England, flying in late July and August. Widely distributed and locally common over most of the British Isles.

Larva. July to September on the ripening seeds of various species of *Silene* and *Lychnis*. Overwinters as a pupa.

Tawny Shears

Hadena perplexa perplexa Denis & Schiffermüller
(*lepida* Esper)
Plate **29** : *25–32*

Variation. Mainly geographical, with the ground colour of the forewing ranging from pale ochreous-white in southeast England to dull brown in Scotland and to blackish-brown in southwest England and west Wales. Specimens with the forewing markings almost obscure occur frequently.

Similar species. *H. bicruris*, pl. **30**. *Hada plebeja*, pl. **29**.

Imago. 27–36 mm. Resident. Comes to light, and visits the flowers of red valerian and campion (*Silene* spp.). Mainly single-brooded, flying from mid-May to June, with a partial second brood occurring in August in the southern half of England. The species inhabits shingle beaches, downland, breckland and chalky places. Widely distributed and locally common in England, Wales and southern Scotland.

H. perplexa capsophila Duponchel, **The Pod Lover**, pl. **29** : *33–34*. Ground colour of forewing blackish-brown with the stigmata and cross-lines outlined with white. Mainly coastal and common in the Isle of Man and most of Ireland. Specimens approaching this race have been reported from West Cornwall, Wales, Ailsa Craig, Ayrshire, and Skye, Inner Hebrides.

Larva. July to August and sometimes later on bladder campion, sea campion, Nottingham catchfly, and occasionally on white campion and rock sea-spurrey.

Overwinters as a pupa.

Viper's Bugloss

Hadena irregularis Hufnagel
Plate **29** : *38*

Similar species. *Eremobia ochroleuca*, pl. **33**.

Imago. 32–36 mm. Resident. Comes to light, and visits various flowers including those of its foodplant. Single-brooded, flying in June and July, inhabiting waste ground, roadside verges and fallow fields. Formerly widespread in the Breckland district of East Anglia, but not recorded since 1968 and possibly now extinct.

Larva. July to August on the seed-capsules of Spanish catchfly (*Silene otites*). In captivity it will accept the flower-heads of garden carnation and sweet-william.

Overwinters as a pupa.

Barrett's Marbled Coronet

Hadena luteago barrettii Doubleday
Plate **29**: *36–37*

Variation. Locally variable with the ground colour of the forewing ranging from greyish-brown to dull reddish-brown. The stigmata and other wing markings also vary in intensity.

Similar species. *H. bicruris*, pl. **30**. Dark forms of *H. confusa*, pl. **30** and text.

Imago. 34–42 mm. Resident. Comes to light, and to the flowers of campion (*Silene* spp.). Single-brooded, flying in June and July, inhabiting coastal cliffs and occasionally shingle beaches. Locally common in North and South Devon, Cornwall and Pembrokeshire; recorded recently from Cardiganshire and formerly from Caernarvonshire and Anglesey. In Ireland it has been reported from Co. Dublin and it is locally not uncommon in Cos Cork and Waterford.

Larva. August to September feeding when full grown on the roots of sea campion and rock sea-spurrey. In captivity it will eat the roots of lettuce.

Overwinters as a pupa at the roots of its foodplant and can be found in the autumn under sickly-looking plants.

Varied Coronet

Hadena compta Denis & Schiffermüller
Plate **30** : *1*

Similar species. *H. confusa*, pl. **30**, has the white median fascia incomplete. (See text fig 34.)

Imago. 28–34 mm. Resident. Comes to light and to the flowers of sweet-william and red valerian. Normally single-brooded, flying in June and early July, although odd specimens have been noted in the autumn. Since 1948, when several specimens were found in southeast Kent, this species has spread rapidly throughout the southeastern quarter of England and in many parts is a common garden inhabitant. At present its range extends westwards to Gloucestershire and northwards to Lincolnshire. Whether *H. compta* originated in this country as a result of migration or importation is a question which remains unresolved.

Larva. From late July to early September on the ripening seeds of sweet-william and occasionally bladder campion.

Overwinters as a pupa.

Marbled Coronet

Hadena confusa Hufnagel
(*conspersa* Denis & Schiffermüller)
Plate **30** : *2–4*

Variation. Dark suffused specimens (fig 3) occur in southwest England, Wales, parts of Scotland and the Northern Isles. The unicolorous ochreous-black ab. *obliterae* Robson (fig 4) occurs frequently in the variable population of Shetland.

Similar species. *H. luteago barrettii*, pl. **29**. *H. compta*, pl. **30** and text.

Imago. 33–39 mm. Resident. Comes to light, and to the flowers of red valerian, sweet-william and various species of *Silene*. Single-brooded, flying from late May to early July, except in the extreme southeast of Britain where a second generation appears in August. Widely distributed over much of Britain, mainly on calcareous soils. Local and mainly coastal in Ireland.

Larva. July to August on the ripening seeds of various species of *Silene*, preferring bladder campion and sea campion.

Overwinters once, sometimes twice, as a pupa.

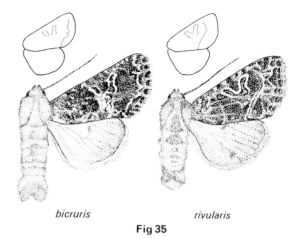

bicruris   *rivularis*

Fig 35

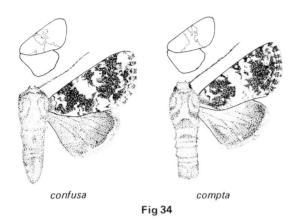

confusa   *compta*

Fig 34

White Spot
Hadena albimacula Borkhausen
Plate **30** : *5*

Imago. 30–38 mm. Resident. Comes to light, and to the flowers of red valerian, viper's-bugloss and campion (*Silene* spp.). Single-brooded, flying in June and July, inhabiting shingle beaches and chalk or limestone cliffs. Very local along the southern coastline of England, namely in Kent, Hampshire, Dorset and South Devon. A single specimen was taken at Chale Green, Isle of Wight, on 24.v.1993.

Larva. July to August on Nottingham catchfly. Like other members of its genus, in captivity it will accept the flowers and seed-heads of sweet-william.

Overwinters as a pupa.

The Lychnis
Hadena bicruris Hufnagel
Plate **30** : *6*

Similar species. *H. rivularis*, pl. **29**, has the lower parts of the reniform and orbicular stigmata united. (See text fig 35.) *H. luteago barrettii*, pl. **30**.

Imago. 30–40 mm. Resident. Comes to light, and to various flowers at dusk. Mainly single-brooded, flying from late May to July with a partial second generation in southern England in August and September. Generally distributed and often common throughout the British Isles.

Larva. July to August on red campion, white campion, and other species of *Silene* and *Lychnis*.

Overwinters as a pupa.

The Grey
Hadena caesia mananii Gregson
Plate **30** : *7–8*

Variation. Most geographical races are distinct in appearance, with the forewing colour of this obscurely marked species ranging from bluish-grey to bluish-black.

Imago. 36–42 mm. Resident. Comes to light, and at dusk visits the flowers of sea campion. Single-brooded, flying from late May to August, inhabiting cliffs and rocky places by the sea. Local, but not uncommon, in western and southern Ireland, the Isle of Man, western Argyllshire and the Hebridean islands of Rhum, Canna, Islay, Mull and Skye.

Larva. July to August on sea campion.

Overwinters as a pupa.

The Silurian
Eriopygodes imbecilla Fabricius
Plate **30** : *9–10*

Imago. 24–27 mm. Resident. Flies on warm days in the afternoon between 1230 hrs and 1730 hrs BST and again at night when the males especially are attracted to light. On some nights the males do not appear before 0200 hrs. Single-brooded, flying in late June and July. First discovered in 1972 on a mountain hillside in northwest Monmouthshire and since 1976 noted annually in the same locality, often plentifully. It is likely that this species will eventually be found in similar habitats in other parts of South Wales.

Larva. August to May, feeding on the Continent on herbaceous plants and grasses. In captivity the larva thrives on withered leaves of dandelion and if kept warm will not attempt to hibernate.

Overwinters as a larva.

Antler Moth
Cerapteryx graminis Linnaeus
Plate **30** : *11–13*

Variation. The ground colour of forewing ranges from reddish-brown in the male to ochreous-grey in the female. The whitish or yellowish stigmata and streaks also vary, both in extent and intensity.

Imago. Male 27–32 mm, female 35–39 mm. Resident. Frequently seen during the day, flying in warm weather and visiting the flowers of thistle, ragwort and other plants. Flies also at night when it is attracted to light and sugar. Single-brooded, flying from mid-July to early September. A locally common and often abundant species occurring over much of the British Isles.

Larva. March to June feeding at night on mat-grass, sheep's-fescue and other grasses.

Overwinters as an egg.

Hedge Rustic

Tholera cespitis Denis & Schiffermüller

Plate **30** : *14*

Imago. 34–40 mm. Resident. Comes to light, especially the male. Single-brooded, flying from mid-August to mid-September, inhabiting rough grassy places. Locally common over much of the British Isles including the Hebrides, but not as yet recorded from the extreme northern counties of Scotland, Orkney and Shetland.

Larva. March to July on mat-grass, *Deschampsia* spp. and other grasses.

Overwinters as an egg.

Feathered Gothic

Tholera decimalis Poda

(*popularis* Fabricius)

Plate **30** : *15*

Similar species. *Naena typica*, pl. **28**. *Heliophobus reticulata*, pl. **29**.

Imago. 38–48 mm. Resident. Comes to light, especially the male. Single-brooded, flying in late August and September, inhabiting downland, commons and rough grassy places. Widespread and locally common over much of the British Isles, except in Scotland where it is local and less frequent.

Larva. March to July on a variety of grasses.

Overwinters as an egg.

Pine Beauty

Panolis flammea Denis & Schiffermüller

(*piniperda* Panzer)

Plate **30** : *16–17*

Variation. Ab. *grisea* Tutt (fig 17) is a greyish form occurring frequently throughout the species' range. Ab. *griseovariegata* Goeze refers to a form which is intermediate in appearance.

Imago. 32–40 mm. Resident. Comes to light and to sallow blossom. Rests by day on the trunks of pine trees and also in the branches from which it can be beaten out. Single-brooded, flying from late March to early May. Widespread and common in mainland Britain and the Inner Hebrides. Less common in Ireland.

Larva. June to July on various species of pine. Occasionally a serious pest in conifer plantations in northern Scotland.

Overwinters as a pupa.

Silver Cloud

Egira conspicillaris Linnaeus

Plate **30** : *18–19*

Variation. The commonest form in Britain is f. *melaleuca* Vieweg (fig 19). Females of the typical form are in appearance intermediate between f. *melaleuca* and the typical form of the male (fig 18).

Imago. 36–42 mm. Resident. Comes to light, and sometimes visits the flowers of blackthorn and plum. During the day it can be found at rest on tree-trunks and fence-posts. Single-brooded, flying from mid-April to mid-May, inhabiting open woodland, orchards and bushy places. Locally not uncommon in Somerset, Herefordshire, Gloucestershire and Worcestershire; also reported from Glamorgan, Warwickshire and Monmouthshire, and on a single occasion in South Devon in 1962.

Larva. June to July. The natural foodplant is unknown, but in captivity can be reared on a wide variety of plants including bird's-foot trefoil, knotgrass, dock and elm.

Overwinters as a pupa.

Small Quaker

Orthosia cruda Denis & Schiffermüller

Plate **30** : *23–24*

Imago. 28–32 mm. Resident. Comes to light, sugar and sallow blossom. Single-brooded, flying in March and April, inhabiting woodland. Widely distributed and not uncommon over much of the British Isles; less frequent in Scotland and Ireland.

Larva. May to June on oak, sallow and other trees.

Overwinters as a pupa.

Blossom Underwing

Orthosia miniosa Denis & Schiffermüller

Plate **30** : *22*

Variation. A yellow form occurs occasionally and is referable to ab. *pallida* Tutt.

Imago. 32–38 mm. Resident. Attracted to light and sallow blossom. Single-brooded, flying in March and April, inhabiting oak woodland. Locally common in southern and western Britain. Less frequent in north-west England and apparently scarce in Ireland.

Larva. May to June, feeding, gregariously when young, on oak. The larger larvae are stated to be partial to oak-galls and others are said to descend to the ground and feed on various low plants.

Overwinters as a pupa.

Northern Drab
Orthosia opima Hübner
(*advena* auctt.)
Plates **30** : *25–26* & **43** : *19*

Variation. Ground colour of forewing ranges from grey of the typical form (fig 26) to dark brown of the equally common ab. *brunnea* Tutt (fig 25). A larger race (pl. **43** : *21*) occurs on the Essex coast having the forewing suffused with yellowish-grey with an indistinct median fascia. A similar form has been found in Kent and evidence suggests an association with salt-marshes.
Similar species. *O. incerta*, pl. **30**.
Imago. 34–40 mm. Resident. Comes to light and occasionally to the blossoms of sallow and blackthorn. Often found between flights at rest on low herbage, the females usually engaged in egg laying. Single-brooded, flying from mid-April to mid-May, frequenting a wide variety of habitats such as downland, sandhills, heathland, marshland and waste ground. Widespread, but local, in England, Wales, Ireland and the southern half of Scotland. Has been recorded from Mull and Skye.
Larva. May to June on a variety of plants and shrubs such as sallow, birch, ragwort, mugwort and on salt-marshes on common sea-lavender (*Limonium vulgare*). Overwinters as a pupa.

Lead-coloured Drab
Orthosia populeti Fabricius
Plate **30** : *20–21*

Similar species. *O. incerta*, pl. **30**, is usually larger, with termen of forewing less rounded; hindwing differs in three respects – fringe distinctly lighter than adjacent area, discal area paler, veins and stigma well defined. *O. stabilis*, pl. **30**.
Imago. 34–40 mm. Resident. Comes to light and to sallow blossom. Single-brooded, flying in late March and April. Widespread and locally common in southern England, the Midlands, Wales and central Scotland. Less frequent in northern England and southern Scotland. In Ireland it has been recorded from Cos. Westmeath, Down and Fermanagh.
Larva. May to June on aspen and occasionally on other species of poplar.
Overwinters as a pupa.

Powdered Quaker
Orthosia gracilis Denis & Schiffermüller
Plate **30** : *27–30*

Variation. The ordinary English form (fig 27) varies slightly from whitish-brown to ochreous-grey, whereas the races associated with bog myrtle (figs 28–30) display a wide range of forewing coloration.
Imago. 33–42 mm. Resident. Comes regularly to light, and visits the blossoms of sallow, blackthorn and plum. Single-brooded, flying in April and early May. Widely distributed throughout the British Isles, including Orkney and the Inner Hebrides. The bog myrtle races

occur commonly in Scotland, Ireland, parts of Wales, Somerset and the New Forest, Hampshire.
Larva. June to July on bog myrtle, willow, sallow, meadowsweet, yellow loosestrife, purple loosestrife (*Lythrum salicaria*) and other plants and shrubs. Feeds at night, hiding by day between spun leaves. Overwinters as a pupa.

Common Quaker
Orthosia cerasi Fabricius
(*stabilis* Denis & Schiffermüller)
Plate **30** : *31–34*

Variation. Very variable throughout its range with little geographical pattern.
Similar species. *O. populeti*, pl. **30**.
Imago. 34–40 mm. Resident. Comes to light, sugar and sallow blossom. Single-brooded, flying in March and April. Common throughout England, Wales and southern Scotland. Widespread but less frequent in the rest of Scotland, Inner Hebrides and Ireland.
Larva. May to June on oak, sallow and other trees. Overwinters as a pupa.

Clouded Drab
Orthosia incerta Hufnagel
Plate **31** : *1–6*

Variation. Colour of forewing extremely variable, ranging from light grey and pale reddish-ochre to blackish-brown. In the southern part of its range in Britain, dark brown and blackish-grey forms predominate, while those from the west and north display a less biased range of variation with pale and dark forms being equally abundant.
Similar species. *O. populeti*, pl. **30** and text.
Imago. 34–42 mm. Resident. Comes to light and is one of the commonest moths to be found on sallow blossom. Single-brooded, flying from mid-March to early May, usually emerging earlier in favourable seasons. Generally distributed and common over much of the British Isles.
Larva. May to June on most trees and shrubs, with a preference for oak and sallow.
Overwinters as a pupa.

Twin-spotted Quaker
Orthosia munda Denis & Schiffermüller
Plate **30** : *35–38*

Variation. Ground colour of forewing ranges from pale grey to reddish-ochre. There is also much variation in the intensity of the markings and in the number of dark spots along the subterminal line. In ab. *immaculata* Staudinger (fig 37) these spots are absent. There appears to be no geographical variation although some localities support a wider range of forms than others.
Imago. 38–44 mm. Resident. Comes to light, sugar and sallow blossom. Single-brooded, flying in March and April, inhabiting woodland. Generally distributed

and locally common in England and Wales. Local in southern Scotland with records from Perthshire and the Inner Hebrides. Local and rather scarce in Ireland.

Larva. May to June on sallow, elm, oak, aspen and other trees.

Overwinters as a pupa.

Hebrew Character
Orthosia gothica Linnaeus
Plate **31** : *7–12*

Variation. Reddish-brown forms with the black *gothica*-mark pale or absent are referable to ab. *gothicina* Herrich-Schäffer (figs 11–12). This and other rufous forms are more frequent in northern and western Britain than in the southeast, where the greyish forms predominate.

Imago. 30–40 mm. Resident. Flies at night and is attracted to light and sallow blossom. Single-brooded, flying in March and April, later in Scotland and Ireland. Generally distributed and common throughout most of the British Isles including Orkney and Shetland.

Larva. May to June on a wide variety of trees and plants.

Overwinters as a pupa.

Double Line
Mythimna turca Linnaeus
Plate **31** : *13*

Imago. 44–52 mm. Resident. Comes to light and sugar. Single-brooded, flying from mid-June to mid-July, inhabiting mature woodland. Locally common in Surrey, southwest England, southern and central Wales; less frequent in Hampshire, Berkshire, Cheshire and Lancashire.

Larva. August to May on various grasses such as cock's-foot, wood-rush and wood meadow-grass.

Overwinters as a small larva.

Brown-line Bright-eye
Mythimna conigera Denis & Schiffermüller
Plate **31** : *14*

Imago. 32–38 mm. Resident. Comes to light and to sugar, and is a common visitor to the flowers of a wide variety of shrubs, plants and grasses. Single-brooded, flying from mid-June to August. Widely distributed and not uncommon throughout the British Isles including Orkney and the Inner Hebrides.

Larva. Autumn to April on various grasses such as cock's-foot, common couch, *Poa* spp., and *Festuca* spp.

Overwinters as a larva.

The Clay
Mythimna ferrago Fabricius
(*lithargyria* Esper)
Plate **31** : *15*

Similar species. *M. albipuncta*, pl. **31**, is smaller, post-median line without blackish dots, reniform spot brilliant white and more circular. *M. unipuncta*, pl. **31**, has the forewing pointed with a dark oblique apical streak.

Imago. 36–44 mm. Resident. Comes to light, sugar and occasionally flowers. Single-brooded, flying in July and August. A common species over much of mainland Britain and Ireland.

Larva. September to May mainly on grasses, but also on low plants.

Overwinters as a small larva.

White-point
Mythimna albipuncta Denis & Schiffermüller
Plate **31** : *16*

Similar species. *M. ferrago*, pl. **31** and text. *M. unipuncta*, pl. **31**.

Imago. 32–37 mm. Immigrant and transitory resident. Comes to light and sugar. A regular migrant, varying greatly in numbers, breeding in southern England in favourable seasons and occasionally becoming temporarily established in the southeast. Occurs from June to October, but is most frequently found in August and September. Recorded in all the coastal counties from Norfolk to Cornwall including the Isles of Scilly, and occasionally inland to Hertfordshire, Berkshire, Surrey and Somerset. First reported in Ireland in 1973 and occasionally recorded since. It appears to be established in Jersey. Abroad the species is abundant in central Europe.

Larva. Autumn to spring on various grasses. In captivity the larva will not hibernate if kept warm.

Overwinters as a larva.

The Delicate
Mythimna vitellina Hübner
Plate **31** : *17–18*

Variation. Ground colour of forewing ranges from pale straw to orange-red, a character apparently connected with the rate of pupal development, with the most rapidly maturing pupae producing the palest specimens.

Imago. 36–43 mm. Immigrant. Comes to light and sugar. A frequent migrant, breeding in southern England in favourable summers and producing, on occasions, an abundance of autumn progeny, but rarely, if ever, surviving the winter. The species appears from May to November, being most numerous in September. Recorded from many counties in southern Britain, but occurring most frequently in the southwest. Reported in Ireland from Cos Cork, Clare and Kerry. Abroad the species' range includes southern Europe and North Africa.

Larva. Feeds on various grasses and is continuously-brooded in captivity.

Striped Wainscot
Mythimna pudorina Denis & Schiffermüller
(*impudens* Hübner)

Plate **31** : *21*

Imago. 36–43 mm. Resident. Comes to light and sugar. Commonly found resting on the stems or feeding on the flowers of wetland grasses. Single-brooded, flying from mid-June to mid-July, inhabiting marshes and the wetter parts of heathland. Widely distributed and locally common in England and Wales as far north as Yorkshire. Local in Ireland from Cos Tipperary, Kildare, Galway, Kerry and Cork.

Larva. August to early May on common reed, purple moor-grass, reed canary-grass, hairy wood-rush, cock's-foot and other grasses.

Overwinters as a very small larva.

Southern Wainscot
Mythimna straminea Treitschke
Plate **31** : *19–20*

Similar species. Both *M. pallens*, pl. **31**, and *M. favicolor*, pl. **31**, lack the brownish and extended basal streak, and the distinct discal spot on the underside of both wings. *M. impura*, pl. **31**, has a much darker hindwing and the underside spots are faint or absent. *M. obsoleta*, pl. **31**, has a darker forewing with the subterminal line of dots usually complete and a whitish discal spot. *M. loreyi*, pl. **31**, has a silky white hindwing and lacks the discal spot on the underside of the hindwing. *Simyra albovenosa*, pl. **35**, has a pure white hindwing and the underside spots are faint or absent.

Imago. 32–40 mm. Resident. Comes to light, sugar and flowering grasses. Single-brooded, flying in July and August, inhabiting fenland, marshes and wet ditches. Widely distributed and locally common in England and Wales as far north as Cumbria and Yorkshire. In Ireland it has occurred in Cos Wicklow, Donegal, Sligo, Clare, Kerry and Cork.

Larva. September to May on common reed and canary-grass (*Phalaris* spp.).
Overwinters as a small larva.

Smoky Wainscot
Mythimna impura impura Hübner
Plate **31** : *23*

Similar species. *M. straminea*, pl. **31** and text. *M. pallens*, pl. **31** and text.

Imago. 31–38 mm. Resident. Comes to light and sugar, and visits the flowers of ragwort, wood sage, marram and other flowering grasses. Mainly single-brooded, flying from late June to August with an occasional and partial second generation in southern England from mid-September to mid-October. Widely distributed and generally common throughout the British Isles. *M. impura scotica* Cockayne, pl. **31** : *24*, is usually smaller, with the forewing less ochreous than the typical form and the hindwing uniformly blackish-grey. This race, which predominates in northern Britain, occurs with

varying frequency throughout its range and, because of this, its entitlement to subspecific status is very questionable.

Larva. September to May on a wide variety of grasses. Overwinters as a small larva.

Common Wainscot
Mythimna pallens Linnaeus
Plate **31** : *25–26*

Variation. *Ab. ectypa* Hübner (fig 26) is a reddish form occurring throughout its range, but appearing more frequently in the second generation in which the moths tend to be smaller.

Similar species. *M. impura*, pl. **31**, has a brownish and extended basal streak and a dark hindwing. *M. favicolor*, pl. **31**, is on average larger, with a smooth and silky forewing and without the raised veins of *M. pallens*; hindwing frequently suffused with smoky grey. *M. straminea*, pl. **31** and text.

Imago. 32–40 mm. Resident. Comes to light and sugar, and visits the flowers of many plants and grasses. There are usually two generations in the south appearing from late June to early October, with the two broods overlapping in August. Single-brooded from the Midlands northwards, flying from mid-July onwards. Widely distributed and generally common over the greater part of the British Isles.

Larva. September to May, and also during the summer in the south, on a wide variety of grasses.
Overwinters as a small larva.

Mathew's Wainscot
Mythimna favicolor Barrett
Plate **31** : *27–28*

Variation. Colour of forewing varies from pale buff to light reddish-brown and the hindwing is frequently suffused with smoky grey.

Similar species. *M. straminea*, pl. **31** and text. *M. pallens*, pl. **31** and text; because of the close relationship between these two species, some authors consider *M. favicolor* to be no more than a saltings race of *M. pallens*. The genitalia of both species are similar.

Imago. 34–42 mm. Resident. Comes to light, sugar and flowering grasses. Single-brooded, flying from mid-June to late July, inhabiting salt-marshes. Locally common in southern England from Hampshire to Suffolk, except in Sussex where it is scarce.

Larva. Late summer to May on common saltmarsh-grass (*Puccinellia maritima*) and probably other grasses.
Overwinters as a larva.

Shore Wainscot
Mythimna litoralis Curtis
Plate **31** : *22*

Imago. 36–42 mm. Resident. Comes to light, sugar and marram flowers. Mainly single-brooded, flying from late June to August, inhabiting coastal sandhills.

The slightly smaller specimens of a second generation are occasionally noted in October. Locally common in Great Britain as far north as Kincardineshire in the east and Galloway in the west. Widespread, but local, in Ireland.

Larva. September to May on marram, hiding in the sand by day.

Overwinters as a small larva.

L-album Wainscot

Mythimna l-album Linnaeus

Plate **31** : *29*

Similar species. *M. putrescens*, pl. **31**, has a pale whitish hindwing. *M. comma*, pl. **31**, lacks both the white median streak on the forewing and the discal spot on the underside of the hindwing.

Imago. 34–40 mm. Resident and immigrant. Comes to light and sugar, and is frequently found on ivy blossom and the over-ripe fruits of bramble. Double-brooded, flying in July and again from mid-September to late October. This species was considered to be a very scarce migrant until the mid-1930s when it was found to be resident in South Devon. Since then it has become established along the southern coastline of England from Kent to Cornwall, including the Isles of Scilly. Records outside these counties since 1930 are central London on 29.x.1969; Bucklebury Common, Berkshire, on 26.ix.1970; and Bradwell-on-Sea, Essex, on 6 & 8.x.1972.

Larva. Autumn to May and again in August on unspecified grasses.

Overwinters as a very small larva.

White-speck

Mythimna unipuncta Haworth

Plate **31** : *30–31*

Similar species. *M. loreyi*, pl. **31**, has a paler forewing and a silky white hindwing. *M. ferrago*, pl. **31** and text. *M. albipuncta*, pl. **31** and text.

Imago. 41–48 mm. Immigrant and transitory resident. Comes to light, sugar and ivy blossom. An erratic migrant, varying greatly in numbers and possibly surviving the occasional mild winter in the extreme southwest of Britain. Has been recorded in all seasons, but is most numerous from late August to early October. Found mainly in southern Britain and Ireland, especially the western counties, with casual specimens occurring as far north as the Hebrides. Abroad the species is widespread in the Mediterranean region.

Larva. Continuously brooded in captivity if given moderate warmth; feeds on couch and other grasses.

Obscure Wainscot

Mythimna obsoleta Hübner

Plate **31** : *32*

Similar species. *M. straminea*, pl. **31** and text.

Imago. 36–40 mm. Resident. Comes to light, sugar and flowering grasses. Single-brooded, flying from late May to mid-July, inhabiting fenland and marshland containing common reed. Very local in southern and southeastern England, East Anglia, from the Midlands westwards to Monmouthshire and northwards to Yorkshire and Cumbria.

Larva. July to April feeding before the winter on common reed.

Overwinters as a full-grown larva usually within a hollow reed-stem.

Shoulder-striped Wainscot

Mythimna comma Linnaeus

Plate **31** : *34*

Similar species. *M. l-album*, pl. **31** and text. *M. putrescens*, pl. **31**, has a pale whitish hindwing.

Imago. 35–42 mm. Resident. Comes to light, sugar and occasionally flowers such as red valerian and *Buddleia*. Single-brooded, flying from early June to late July. Generally distributed and moderately common in England, Wales, Ireland, and the eastern half of Scotland as far north as Ross-shire.

Larva. Feeds in August and September on cock's-foot and other grasses.

Overwinters as a full-grown larva within an earthen cocoon.

Devonshire Wainscot

Mythimna putrescens Hübner

Plate **31** : *33*

Similar species. *M. comma*, pl. **31** and text. *M. l-album*, pl. **31** and text.

Imago. 32–36 mm. Resident. Comes to light, sugar, and the flowers of red valerian, wood sage, and various maritime grasses. Single-brooded, flying from mid-July to late August, inhabiting cliffs and grassy places by the sea. Very local in southwest Britain, and rarely found outside Devon, Cornwall and Pembrokeshire.

Larva. September to late February on coastal grasses.

Overwinters as a larva.

The Cosmopolitan

Mythimna loreyi Duponchel

Plate **31** : *35*

Similar species. *M. ferrago*, pl. **31** and text. *M. straminea*, pl. **31** and text. *M. unipuncta*, pl. **31** and text.

Imago. 34–44 mm. Immigrant. Comes to light and sugar. Usually an uncommon visitor to southern England and southern Ireland, normally appearing from late August to early October, but occasionally recorded as early as May, and as late as mid-November. From 1862 to 1974 there were at least 30 records: Kent (1), Sussex (2), Hampshire (4), Devon (7), Cornwall (12), Isles of Scilly (2), and Co. Cork (2); with the maximum number of specimens for one year being five in 1945. In 1975 there were 27 specimens reported between 24 August and 8 October as follows: Dorset (1), Devon

(1), Cornwall (7), Isles of Scilly (4), and Co. Cork (14). A further three specimens were recorded from Cornwall on 24.viii, 25.viii, and 23.ix.1976; followed by single examples at Swanage, Dorset, on 14.x.1978; and Porthleven, Cornwall, on 25.viii.1982. The next year proved to be an exceptional one with 44 specimens reported from the English mainland between 17 June and 20 October. In the years that followed annual totals fluctuated wildly from single sightings in 1984, 1986 and 1987 to a then record-breaking 48 in 1985. However all previous records were shattered in 1992 when several hundred (*c.* 400) were reported between May and October along the south coast with a few ranging inland to Surrey, Buckinghamshire, Oxfordshire and Hertfordshire. Many of the late summer specimens were darker and browner than usual and had probably bred locally. Abroad its range includes southern France, Spain, Portugal, the Canary Islands, and North Africa.
Larva. In captivity it has been reared on cock's-foot and other grasses.

Flame Wainscot
Senta flammea Curtis
Plate **31** : *36*

Imago. 32–40 mm. Resident and suspected immigrant. May be found after dark at rest on reed-stems, and in moderate numbers at light. Single-brooded, flying from mid-May to early July, inhabiting inland and coastal reed-beds. A local species, and as a resident confined until recently to Cambridgeshire (Wicken and Chippenham Fens); Norfolk (the Broads, Lopham Fen, and Stoke Ferry Fen and neighbouring marshland); and Suffolk (Redgrave Fen and in several localities on the coast). As a probable immigrant it has occurred on about 20 occasions in southern England from Kent and Essex to Dorset; and in two localities (Winchelsea, East Sussex, and near Wye, Kent) it has become established. It was suspected of being resident near Wareham, Dorset, *c.* 1930, and recent records suggest it is possibly still present. There is also a single record from Kirkby Moor, Lincolnshire, in 1974. Abroad it occurs locally in France, Belgium, the Netherlands, Denmark, southern Sweden and Portugal.
Larva. July to October on the leaves of common reed, hiding by day in a hollow stem.
Overwinters as a pupa within an old reed-stem.

SUBFAMILY: CUCULLINAE

The Wormwood
Cucullia absinthii Linnaeus
Plate **32** : *9*

Similar species. *C. artemisiae*, pl. **32** and text.
Imago. 37–44 mm. Resident. Comes to flowers and light in small numbers. Single-brooded, flying in July, inhabiting waste ground, commons, sea-cliffs, old quarries, and slag-heaps. Inland it is well established

and locally not uncommon as larvae in parts of London and the Home Counties, the Breck district of Suffolk and Norfolk, Lincolnshire, and parts of the Midlands, ranging northwards to Yorkshire. Elsewhere it is found very sporadically along the coasts of England and Wales as far north as Cumbria on the west coast, and Norfolk on the east coast. In Ireland it has been reported this century from Cos Cork and Wexford.
Larva. August and September on the flowers and seeds of wormwood and mugwort.
Overwinters as a pupa.

Scarce Wormwood
Cucullia artemisiae Hufnagel
Plate **32** : *7*

Similar species. *C. absinthii*, pl. **32**, has two small, but distinct, dark spots in the orbicular stigma, and a discal spot on the hindwing.
Imago. 40–48 mm. Suspected immigrant. Single-brooded on the Continent, flying in June and July, inhabiting sandy places. Of the seven specimens listed as British, four are examples without data found in old collections, two were found on a fence near Starcross, South Devon, in August 1885, and one was bred from a larva found on mugwort at Nazeing, Essex, on 4.ix. 1971. Abroad the species is found in the mild regions of Europe and Asia.
Larva. August and September on mugwort; ★also on wormwood and field wormwood.
Overwinters as a pupa.

Chamomile Shark
Cucullia chamomillae Denis & Schiffermüller
Plate **32** : *1–2*

Similar species. *C. umbratica*, pl. **32**, has the hindwing fringe with two bands of colour, an outer very pale band, and an inner band slightly darker. In *C. chamomillae* the fringe has three bands of colour, the outer one pale, the middle dark, and the inner pale. (See text fig 36.)
Imago. 44–52 mm. Resident. Occasionally found on fence-posts and palings. After dark it visits the flowers of campions and other wayside plants, and later in the night comes to light. Single-brooded, flying from mid-April to early June, inhabiting waste ground, commons, roadside verges, and cornfields. Widespread and not uncommon in the larval stage in England, Wales, and parts of southern Scotland. Very local elsewhere in Scotland as far north as Perthshire with the occasional specimen ranging into Inverness-shire. In Ireland it is locally widespread and mainly coastal.
Larva. June and early July on the flowers of scentless mayweed, other mayweeds, and chamomiles (*Anthemis* spp.).
Overwinters as a pupa.

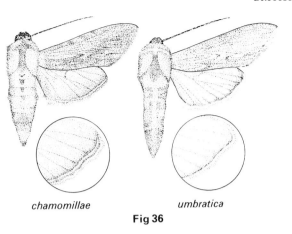

chamomillae   umbratica

Fig 36

The Shark

Cucullia umbratica Linnaeus

Plate **32** : *3*

Similar species. *C. chamomillae*, pl. **32** and text.

Imago. 52–59 mm. Resident. Sometimes found during the day at rest on fence-posts, telegraph-poles, etc. Comes regularly to light, and is attracted to a variety of flowers, including campions, honeysuckle, sweet-william, red valerian, and thistles. Single-brooded, flying in June and July, inhabiting waste ground, sandhills, shingle beaches, downland, marshy places, and gardens. Widespread and moderately common in England, Wales and Ireland. Locally widespread in Scotland and the Hebrides.

Larva. Late July to early September on various species of sow-thistle (*Sonchus* spp.) and wild lettuce. It feeds at night, hiding by day under the lower leaves. Overwinters as a pupa.

Star-wort

Cucullia asteris Denis & Schiffermüller

Plate **32** : *4*

Imago. 45–52 mm. Resident. Comes to light in small numbers. Single-brooded, flying from late June to early August, inhabiting coastal salt-marshes and woodland rides and clearings. Local, but not uncommon, along the coasts and estuaries in England from Hampshire to Yorkshire; and in woodland from Dorset to Kent, and parts of North and South Wales. This species is a well-known vagrant and stray specimens have been reported from widely separated localities in the southern half of England.

Larva. Late July to early September, in coastal salt-marshes on the flowers of sea aster and occasionally on sea wormwood; in woodland on the flowers of goldenrod; and, very occasionally, in gardens on Michaelmas-daisy (*Aster novi-belgii*) and China aster (*Callistephus chinensis*).

Overwinters as a pupa.

The Cudweed

Cucullia gnaphalii occidentalis Boursin

Plate **32** : *8*

Imago. 38–47 mm. Resident. Very occasionally taken at rest on fence-posts and after dark has been found at the flowers of honeysuckle and fragrant orchid (*Gymnadenia conopsea*), but normally this species is rarely found in the adult stage except in small numbers at light. Single-brooded, flying from late May to mid-July, inhabiting woodland rides and clearings. Formerly found in Hampshire, West Sussex and Surrey, but since 1960 has been confined to a few localities in southeast Kent and East Sussex. Even here, however, it has not been recorded since 1979 and there is a strong possibility that this species may be extinct.

Larva. Late July and August on the flowers and leaves of goldenrod. In captivity both this and the last species will accept Michaelmas-daisy (*Aster novi-belgii*). Overwinters as a pupa.

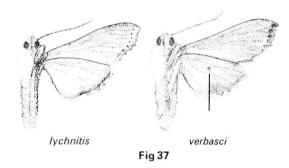

lychnitis   verbasci

Fig 37

Striped Lychnis

Cucullia lychnitis Rambur

Plate **32** : *5*

Similar species. *C. verbasci*, pl. **32**, has a distinct discal spot on the underside of the hindwing. (See text fig 37.)

Imago. 42–47 mm. Resident. Occasionally recorded at light, otherwise rarely if ever seen in the adult stage. Single-brooded, flying in June and July, inhabiting roadside verges, chalky embankments, downland, and waste places. A very local species occurring mainly on chalk in the southern half of England and recorded most recently from Hampshire, Buckinghamshire, Oxfordshire, Berkshire, and West Sussex.

Larva. July and August on dark and white mullein, feeding mainly on the flowers.

Overwinters as a pupa, sometimes remaining in this stage for up to four years.

Water Betony

Cucullia scrophulariae Denis & Schiffermüller

Plate **43** : *22*

Similar species. Closely resembles *C. verbasci*, pl. **32**, from which it cannot be separated in the adult stage except by means of the genitalia.

Imago. 44–50 mm. Suspected immigrant and a doubtfully British resident. Single-brooded on the Continent, flying in May. In the past larvae reputed to be of this species have been recorded from East Anglia, Kent, and elsewhere in southern England, but on close examination only a few proved to be *C. scrophulariae* and these appear to have emanated from doubtful sources. As an immigrant there are two authentic specimens, both from Swanage, Dorset, on 12.vi.1949 and 18.v.1994.

Larva. *June and July on the flowers and seeds of various species of figwort (*Scrophularia* spp.) and mullein. Overwinters as a pupa.

The Mullein

Cucullia verbasci Linnaeus

Plate **32** : 6

Similar species. *C. lychnitis*, pl. **32** and text. *C. scrophulariae*, pl. **32** and text.

Imago. 44–52 mm. Resident. Comes to light in small numbers, usually late at night. Single-brooded, flying in late April and May, inhabiting downland, commons, breckland, marshes, waste ground, woodland clearings, and gardens. Widespread and locally common in the larval stage over much of England, ranging northwards to Cumbria and Co. Durham. Local and less frequent in Wales. Very local in Ireland and confined to Co. Cork.

Larva. June and July feeding mainly on the leaves of great mullein (*Verbascum thapsus*), hoary mullein (*V. pulverulentum*), dark mullein, white mullein, common figwort (*Scrophularia nodosa*), and water figwort (*S. auriculata*). In cultivated places it has been found on *Buddleia davidii*, *Buddleia globosa*, and on garden varieties of *Verbascum*.

Overwinters as a pupa. Like other members of this genus it will sometimes remain in the pupal stage for up to four years.

Toadflax Brocade

Calophasia lunula Hufnagel

Plate **32** : *10*

Imago. 26–32 mm. Resident and suspected immigrant. Occasionally found at dusk visiting the flowers of red valerian; also comes to light in small numbers. Double-brooded, flying in late May and June, and again in August, inhabiting shingle beaches, waste ground and gardens. Well established and not uncommon at Dungeness, Kent, and found locally along the coast eastwards to Sandwich and westwards through East Sussex to Angmering, West Sussex. Elsewhere it has been recorded singly at Bradwell-on-Sea, Essex, on 11.viii.1951; Pinden, Kent, on 10.vi.1953; Hamstreet, Kent, on 24.vi.1953; Bookham Common, Surrey, on 13.vii.1970; near Southampton, Hampshire, on 13.v.1971; Southsea, Hampshire, on 11.viii.1992; Hamstreet,

Kent, on 1.viii.1996; and Gosport, Hampshire, on 18.viii.1996; and as larvae at Stone, Kent, in 1952 and 1956; Wakering, Essex, in 1953 and 1954; and Tonbridge, Kent, on 31.vii.1954.

Larva. July to September mainly on common toadflax, also occasionally on purple toadflax (*Linaria purpurea*) and pale toadflax (*L. repens*).

Overwinters as a pupa within a tough silken cocoon attached to fence-posts, walls, stones, etc.

Antirrhinum Brocade

Calophasia platyptera Esper

(South 1961, vol. 1, pl. 77)

Imago. 28–30 mm. Suspected immigrant. Double-brooded on the Continent, flying from late April to June, and again flying in August. The only British specimen was found near Brighton, Sussex, on 14.ix.1896. Abroad its range includes central and southern Europe, and North Africa.

Larva. *June to August on various species of snapdragon (*Antirrhinum* spp.) and toadflax.

Overwinters as a pupa.

Minor Shoulder-knot

Brachylomia viminalis Fabricius

Plate **32** : *11–14*

Variation. The normal pale form (fig 11) is most frequent in southern England, and the dark forms are commoner in the north. The most extreme examples of industrial melanism (fig 14) are found in parts of the Midlands. Both forms occur in Scotland, and in the Highlands the pale form is bluish-white in appearance (fig 13).

Imago. 29–34 mm. Resident. Flies from dusk onwards and is attracted to the flowers of red valerian and other plants, sugar, and light. Single-brooded, flying in July and early August, inhabiting woodland, commons, fenland, and marshy places. Widespread and not uncommon over much of England, Wales and Scotland; also recorded from the Isle of Arran, the Hebrides and Orkney. Local and uncommon in Ireland, and recorded from Cos Donegal, Antrim, Londonderry, Sligo, Mayo, Kerry, Down and Cork.

Larva. April to June in the spun leaves of willow and sallow.

Overwinters as an egg.

Beautiful Gothic

Leucochlaena oditis Hübner

(*hispida* Geyer)

Plate **32** : *15*

Imago. 28–36 mm. Resident. After dark it may be found resting on grass stems, and also at light. Single-brooded, flying from late August to early October, inhabiting grassy slopes and cliffs by the sea. A very local species in southwest England, but usually not uncommon where it occurs. It is found in the Isle of

Wight (Freshwater); Dorset (Swanage to Kimmeridge, and Portland); and South Devon (Prawle Point, Brixham, Babbacombe, and Plymouth Hoe). Single specimens have been recorded from Bodinnick, Cornwall, on 21.viii.1958; Polperro, Cornwall, on 2 & 4.x.1958; near Bognor, West Sussex, on 21.x.1976; and Mawnan Smith, Cornwall, on 13.x.1986.

Larva. October to March on couch, annual meadow-grass, and many other grasses.
Overwinters as a larva, feeding throughout the winter during mild weather.

The Sprawler
Brachionycha sphinx Hufnagel
Plate **32** : *16–17*

Variation. Ab. *fusca* Cockayne (fig 17) is a dark form found regularly in the Chilterns (Buckinghamshire and Oxfordshire).

Imago. 38–48 mm. Resident. Comes readily to light, usually after midnight. Single-brooded, flying in November and early December, inhabiting woodland, orchards, commons, and bushy places. Widespread and locally common in the southern half of England and much of Wales. Locally widespread in the rest of England, as far north as Cumbria and Northumberland. In Ireland it is local and recorded from Cos Tyrone, Fermanagh, Galway, Westmeath, Meath, Dublin, Clare, Kildare, Waterford and Cork.

Larva. May and June on a variety of trees, including elm, hazel, oak, ash, cherry, and sallow.
Overwinters as an egg.

Rannoch Sprawler
Brachionycha nubeculosa Esper
Plate **32** : *18–19*

Variation. Specimens from Aviemore, Inverness-shire, are predominantly greyer than those from Rannoch, Perthshire.

Imago. 48–60 mm. Resident. During the emergence period it may be found on birch-trunks, and after dark comes to light in moderate numbers. Single-brooded, flying from late March to mid-April, sometimes earlier in a mild spring. The species inhabits old birch woodland and occurs locally in Inverness-shire, and at Rannoch, Perthshire.

Larva. May and June on birch.
Overwinters as a pupa, sometimes remaining in this stage for up to four years.

Brindled Ochre
Dasypolia templi Thunberg
Plate **32** : *20–21*

Variation. Very dark forms predominate on Unst, Shetland.

Imago. 42–48 mm. Resident. Comes regularly to light in small numbers. Single-brooded, flying in September and October, earlier in northern Britain, and after

hibernation in early spring. The species inhabits sea-cliffs, marshes, waysides, and mountain moorland. In southern Britain it is mainly coastal, occurring locally in the Isle of Wight, Hampshire, Dorset, North and South Devon, Somerset, and sporadically westwards to Pembrokeshire. In Dorset it is found occasionally well inland, and stray specimens have been recorded from Micheldever, Hampshire, on 29.x.1969; and Arkley, Hertfordshire, on 23.x.1952. Elsewhere in Britain it is locally widespread in the Midlands, North Wales, Isle of Man, northern England, much of Scotland, the Inner Hebrides, Orkney and Shetland. In Ireland it is extremely local and mainly coastal.

Larva. Spring to August, at first in the stems and then in the roots of hogweed and wild angelica.

Pupa. May be obtained in varying numbers during late summer at the roots of the foodplant.
Overwinters as a female moth.

Feathered Brindle
Aporophyla australis pascuea Humphreys & Westwood
Plate **32** : *22–23*

Variation. Ab. *ingenua* Freyer (fig 23) is a melanic form found regularly at Dungeness, Kent, and Camber, East Sussex. Specimens from southwest Cornwall, Pembrokeshire and Ireland are strongly marked with dark brown.

Imago. 36–42 mm. Resident. Comes readily to sugar and light. Single-brooded, flying in September and early October, inhabiting coastal sandhills, shingle beaches, and sea-cliffs and downland. A local species found sporadically along the coasts of Suffolk, Essex, Kent, East Sussex, Isle of Wight, Dorset, South Devon and Cornwall. In Wales it is locally common in Pembrokeshire and there are single records from Llecryd, Cardiganshire, in 1980 and Rhossili, Glamorgan, in 1985. In Ireland it occurs in Cos Wicklow, Wexford and Waterford.

Larva. October to April on sea campion, wood sage, sorrel and many other unspecified low plants and grasses.
Overwinters as a larva.

Deep-brown Dart
Aporophyla lutulenta Denis & Schiffermüller
Plate **32** : *26*

Variation. Hindwing of female (not illustrated) suffused with blackish-brown. The greyish and banded forms found commonly in *A. lueneburgensis* rarely occur in this species.

Similar species. *A. lueneburgensis*, pl. **32**, is slightly smaller and more sharply marked, the forewing is more pointed and the hindwing usually has distinct blackish dots on the inner line and dark veins.

Imago. 38–44 mm. Resident. Occasionally comes to sugar and ivy blossom, but more frequently seen at light. Single-brooded, flying from mid-September to mid-October, inhabiting commons, sandhills, down-

land, sea-cliffs, and waste places. Locally widespread in southern and eastern England south of a line drawn from the Severn to the Humber.
Larva. October to early June on tufted hair-grass and other grasses; also on hawthorn, blackthorn, broom and other plants. In captivity it will accept sallow. Overwinters as a very small larva.

Northern Deep-brown Dart
Aporophyla lueneburgensis Freyer
Plate **32** : *27–29*

Variation. Very variable throughout its range both in ground colour, which ranges from pale grey to black, and in the intensity of the dark central band.
Similar species. *A. lutulenta*, pl. **32** and text.
Imago. 36–41 mm. Resident. Comes to light, sugar, and the flowers of heather and ragwort. Single-brooded, flying from early August to mid-September, inhabiting moorland, and rocky and grassy places by the sea. Locally widespread in North Wales, the Isle of Man, the northern half of England, Scotland, the Isle of Arran, the Hebrides, Orkney, and along the northern and western coastline of Ireland.
Larva. September to May mostly on heather, but occasionally on other low plants, such as bird's-foot trefoil. Overwinters as a small larva.
(*Author's note*: I have followed the generally accepted opinion of most Continental authors, and classified *A. lueneburgensis* as a separate species, although in some British works it is still treated as a subspecies of *A. lutulenta*.)

Black Rustic
Aporophyla nigra Haworth
Plate **32** : *24–25*

Imago. 40–46 mm. Resident. Flies from dusk onwards, comes readily to light, and is attracted to ragwort flowers, ripe blackberries, ivy blossom, and sugar. Single-brooded, flying in September and October, inhabiting commons, downland, heathland, waste places, etc. Locally widespread over much of England, Wales and Scotland, except in eastern England where it is very local, but increasing. Widely scattered and mainly coastal in Ireland.
Larva. November or February to June on a variety of low plants, such as dock and heather, and grasses. Overwinters as an egg or small larva.

Golden-rod Brindle
Lithomoia solidaginis Hübner
Plate **33** : *1*

Variation. Most of the immigrant specimens are referable to f. *cinerascens* Staudinger, a more uniformly ash-grey form occurring in Germany.
Imago. 44–52 mm. Resident and immigrant. The moth rests with the wings folded closely along the body and assumes a twig-like posture. It may be found during the day resting on fence-wires and posts, tree-trunks, rocks, and the stems of bracken and heather. After dark it comes readily to heather flowers, and in small numbers to light. Single-brooded, flying in August and September, inhabiting moorland and open woodland. Widely distributed in Scotland, North Wales, and the northern half of England, ranging southwards to Staffordshire, Breconshire and Radnorshire. As a suspected immigrant at least 17 specimens were reported in late August or early September 1954 from localities well outside the normal range of this species. These were in Hampshire (1), Surrey (1), Kent (2), Middlesex (2), Hertfordshire (1), Essex (3), Norfolk (1), Cambridgeshire (3), and Leicestershire (3). Other possible migrant examples were taken at South Thoresby, Lincolnshire, on 22.ix.1973; Hickling, Norfolk, on 28.viii.1976 and Wytham, Berkshire, on 17.viii.1983.
Larva. Late April to July on a variety of plants, including bilberry, bearberry, bog myrtle, birch, heather, and sallow.
Overwinters as an egg.

Tawny Pinion
Lithophane semibrunnea Haworth
Plate **33** : *11*

Similar species. Dark forms of *L. hepatica*, pl. **33**, lack the black tornal streak, and usually lack the blackish-brown thoracic and abdominal crests.
Imago. 40–44 mm. Resident. Comes to sugar, sallow and ivy blossom, ripe blackberries, and light. Single-brooded, appearing in October and early November, and after hibernation from March to May. An open woodland species occurring at low density in the southern half of England and South Wales, with the occasional specimen ranging northwards to North Wales, Cheshire, Lincolnshire and Yorkshire. Unreliably recorded from Ireland.
Larva. May to July on ash
Overwinters as an adult.

Pale Pinion
Lithophane hepatica Clerck
(*socia* Hufnagel)
Plate **33** : *9–10*

Variation. Specimens heavily suffused with blackish-brown occur frequently in the western half of Britain, and occasionally elsewhere.
Similar species. *L. semibrunnea*, pl. **33** and text.
Imago. 40–46 mm. Resident. Comes to sugar, sallow and ivy blossom, ripe blackberries and light. Single-brooded, appearing in October and early November, and after hibernation from March to May. A local woodland species most frequently encountered in southwest England, Wales and western Ireland. It is also found in southeast England, southwest Midlands, the rest of Ireland, Isle of Man, and occasionally East Anglia and northwest England.

Larva. May to July on sallow and other trees and shrubs.
Overwinters as an adult.

Grey Shoulder-knot
Lithophane ornitopus lactipennis Dadd
Plate **33** : *13*

Imago. 34–42 mm. Resident. Occasionally found during the day at rest on fences and tree-trunks. After dark it is attracted to sallow and ivy blossom, ripe blackberries, sugar, and light. Single-brooded, appearing in September and October, and after hibernation from February to April, inhabiting woodland and parkland. Locally widespread in the southern half of England, East Anglia, parts of the Midlands, North and South Wales, and much of Ireland. Very occasionally reported from northern England.
Larva. Late April to early June on oak.
Overwinters as an adult.

The Conformist
Lithophane furcifera furcifera Hufnagel
Plate **33** : *6*

Similar species. *L. lamda*, pl. **33**, is generally smaller, has a distinct wedge-shaped mark in the middle of the subterminal line, and the black subreniform streak is longer and thicker, and lies parallel to the dorsal margin. (See text fig 38.)
Imago. 42–52 mm. Suspected immigrant. Comes to sugar, sallow and ivy blossom, and light. Abroad it is found in September and October, and after hibernation in April and May. If the earlier records are considered to be reliable, then 11 specimens of this suspected immigrant have occurred in the British Isles. These were at Halifax, Yorkshire, *c.* 1870, Westmorland (no date); Brighton, Sussex, on 13.ix.1898; two near Lancaster on 22.ix.1902; Margate, Kent, on 12.x.1904; East Anglia in October 1904; East Sussex on 18.ix.1932; Hamstreet, Kent, on 28.ix.1935; and Dungeness, Kent, on 12.ix.1936 and 4.iv.1946. *L. furcifera suffusa* Tutt, pl. **33** : *7*. This form is much darker than the typical race, and has the reniform stigma and subterminal line strongly tinged with reddish-orange. Resident. In Britain it has been found at sugar, light and sallow and ivy blossom. Its times of appearance are similar to those of the typical race. Although this species appeared to have been taken or bred more or less regularly in Glamorgan (near Cardiff, Llantrisant, Pontypridd, and Neath) from 1859 to the 1880s, very little was ever published by those who were familiar with its habits, localities and life history. With the exception of an unconfirmed report from southwest Herefordshire in the 1960s, the only specimens of ssp. *suffusa* taken this century are one from sallow blossom at Bigsweir, Gloucestershire, on 31.iii.1907 and another at light near Cardiff, Glamorgan, on 10.x.1959.

Larva. *April to June most frequently on alder, but sometimes on birch, sallow and poplar.
Overwinters as an adult.

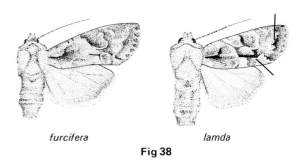

furcifera   *lamda*

Fig 38

The Nonconformist
Lithophane lamda Fabricius
Plate **33** : *8*

Similar species. *L. furcifera furcifera*, pl. **33** and text.
Imago. 40–46 mm. Status unknown. The few British specimens have been taken either at rest, sugar, or ivy blossom during September or October. Abroad it appears in the autumn, and after hibernation in March and April when it is attracted to sallow blossom and light. Fourteen specimens have been reported in Britain: London in October 1865; near New Cross, Kent, on 30.ix.1866; Guildford, Surrey, in 1866; Ledbury, Herefordshire, in 1870; Dartford, Kent, on 3.x.1870; Lewes, Sussex, in 1873; Belvedere, Kent, in September 1875; Ranworth, Norfolk, in 1877; Diss, Norfolk, on 3.viii.1894; Bexley, Kent, in October 1894; Copdock, Suffolk, on 30.ix.1895; Northfleet, Kent, *c.* 1902; and near Cambridge on 7.x.1920 and 1.x.1938. The above records tentatively suggest that *L. lamda* was temporarily established in northwest Kent and Cambridgeshire; possibly originating from an immigrant parent. Abroad its range includes Norway, Holland, Denmark, Belgium and North Germany.
Larva. *April to June on bog bilberry (*Vaccinium uliginosum*), bog myrtle, and creeping willow.
Overwinters as an adult.

Blair's Shoulder-knot
Lithophane leautieri hesperica Boursin
(*lapidea* auctt.)
Plate **33** : *12*

Imago. 39–44 mm. Resident and suspected immigrant. Comes to light in moderate numbers, usually after midnight. Single-brooded, flying from late September to early November. Since the first British specimen was recorded on the Isle of Wight in 1951 this species has become well established throughout southern England. It still appears to be extending its range northwards with records from Lincolnshire, Yorkshire and the Isle of Man.

Larva. March to July on the flowers and leaves of Monterey cypress, Lawson's cypress and the hybrid *Cupressocyparis* x *leylandii*. Has occasionally been found on juniper.

Overwinters as an egg.

Red Sword-grass
Xylena vetusta Hübner
Plate **33** : *2*

Similar species. *X. exsoleta*, pl. **33**. The most useful diagnostic feature, especially when separating worn specimens, is the colour of the tarsus (lower half) of the hindleg; in *X. exsoleta* it is pale straw-coloured, in *X. vetusta* it is dark reddish-brown.

Imago. 52–62 mm. Resident, reinforced in southern England by immigration. Comes readily to sallow and ivy blossom, sugar, and regularly in smaller numbers to light. Single-brooded, appearing in September and October and after hibernation in March and April, inhabiting mountain moorland, bogs, damp woodland, waste places, marshy places, etc. Widespread and moderately common in southwest England, Wales, northern England, mainland Scotland, the Inner Hebrides and Ireland. Elsewhere in England it is rather local, especially in the eastern counties where it is generally scarce.

Larva. May to early July on a variety of low plants, such as dock, yellow iris, bog myrtle, and various sedges; and on the young foliage of deciduous trees and shrubs.

Overwinters as an adult.

Sword-grass
Xylena exsoleta Linnaeus
Plate **33** : *3*

Similar species. *X. vetusta*, pl. **33** and text.

Imago. 55–66 mm. Resident and suspected immigrant. Comes most frequently to sugar, but also to light, sallow and ivy blossom, and birch sap. Single-brooded, appearing in September and October and after hibernation in March and April, inhabiting moorland and open woodland. Locally widespread in Scotland, northern England, parts of South and mid-Wales, and northwest Ireland. Elsewhere in the British Isles it has seriously declined this century and the majority of recent records, particularly those from southern England, are suspected of referring to immigrants.

Larva. May to July, probably on a wide variety of low plants. In captivity it will accept dock, but it is generally considered to be a difficult species to rear.

Overwinters as an adult.

Oak Rustic
Dryobota labecula Esper
(*furva* Esper)
Plate **43** : *23*

Variation. Ab. *albomacula* Culot has a white, instead of an orange, reniform stigma.

Similar species. Superficially not unlike some of the forms of *Mesapamea didyma*, pl. **38**.

Imago. 30–32 mm. Resident (Channel Islands). Single-brooded, flying from October to December. Widespread and not uncommon on Jersey, Channel Islands, where it was first noted in 1991. Two specimens were reported from Guernsey in 1995 and several more the following year suggesting residency and although so far unrecorded from the British mainland its eventual appearance is very likely.

Larva. *April to September on evergreen oak.

Overwinters as an egg.

Early Grey
Xylocampa areola Esper
Plate **33** : *4–5*

Variation. Ground colour ranges from pale to dark grey. Specimens strongly tinged with violet (ab. *rosea* Tutt) are not uncommon, and melanic forms are occasionally found in Kent, Surrey, Essex and elsewhere.

Imago. 32–40 mm. Resident. Rests by day on fences, tree-trunks, and rocks, and after dark comes readily to light and sometimes to sallow blossom. Single-brooded, flying from mid-March to early May, inhabiting woodland, commons, and gardens. Widely distributed and moderately common in England (except the northwest), Wales and Ireland. In Scotland it ranges locally northwards to Sutherland and the Hebrides.

Larva. April to early June on both wild and cultivated species of honeysuckle.

Overwinters as a pupa.

Double-spot Brocade
Meganephria bimaculosa Linnaeus
(South 1961, vol. 1, pl. 80)

Imago. 50–58 mm. Status unknown. Single-brooded on the Continent, flying from July to September. Only three specimens exist with British data: these are Southsea Common, near Portsmouth, Hampshire, in 1892; near Bristol in July 1815; and at rest on a tree-trunk in Leigh Woods, near Bristol, Somerset, in mid-July, 1949. Abroad the species is not uncommon in many parts of central and southern Europe.

Larva. *April to June on elm and blackthorn.

Overwinters as an egg.

Green-brindled Crescent
Allophyes oxyacanthae Linnaeus
Plate **33** : *14–15*

Variation. The melanic ab. *capucina* Millière (fig 15) is found commonly in many industrial areas, and also in smaller numbers in some rural districts.

Imago. 39–46 mm. Resident. Comes to light, sugar, and ivy blossom. Single-brooded, flying from mid-September to early November, inhabiting woodland, hedgerows and bushy places. Generally distributed and more or less common in England, Wales, Ireland and southern Scotland. Elsewhere in Scotland it is found locally up to Sutherland and the Inner Hebrides.

Larva. April to early June on blackthorn, hawthorn, birch, sallow, apple and rowan.
Overwinters as an egg.

Merveille du Jour
Dichonia aprilina Linnaeus
Plate **33** : *17*

Similar species. *Moma alpium*, pl. **35**.

Imago. 42–52 mm. Resident and suspected occasional immigrant. Comes readily to sugar, and in small numbers to light. Single-brooded, flying from mid-September to mid-October, about a month earlier in Scotland, inhabiting parkland and oak woodland. Widespread and locally common in England and Wales. It occurs locally in Scotland from Galloway to Ross-shire and Moray, and in Ireland in the northern half of the country and from Cos Cork, Kerry and Wicklow.

Larva. March to June, at first in the buds and then on the leaves of oak; hiding during the day in a crevice of the tree-trunk.

Pupa. May be found by digging at the roots of isolated oak-trees from mid-July to early September.
Overwinters as an egg.

Brindled Green
Dryobotodes eremita Fabricius
(*protea* Denis & Schiffermuller)
Plate **33** : *21–22*

Variation. Specimens suffused with blackish-grey occur frequently in the Midlands and occasionally in the London area.

Imago. 32–39 mm. Resident. Comes regularly to light and sugar, and sometimes to over-ripe blackberries. Single-brooded, flying in August and September, inhabiting oak woodland. Generally distributed and moderately common in England and Wales. Local and less frequent in Scotland from Galloway to Ross-shire. Local and rare in Ireland.

Larva. March to June, at first in the buds and then on the leaves of oak and hawthorn.
Overwinters as an egg.

Beautiful Arches
Blepharita satura Denis & Schiffermüller
Plate **33** : *18*

Similar species. *B. adusta*, pl. **33**.

Imago. 40–50 mm. Status unknown. Comes to light and sugar. Single-brooded on the Continent, flying from July to October, inhabiting mainly mixed or coniferous woodland. The history of this species in Britain is poorly documented and somewhat confused by a plethora of doubtfully genuine records. The only ones worthy of consideration are a few nineteenth-century records from the Reading district, Berkshire/Oxfordshire; and three or four from the Cambridgeshire and Huntingdonshire

fenland, including two from Wicken Fen in July 1891. If genuine, these records suggest that *B. satura* was at one time resident in Britain.

Larva. *May to June on honeysuckle, sallow, and a wide variety of herbaceous plants.
Overwinters as an egg.

Dark Brocade
Mniotype adusta Esper
Plate **33** : *19–20*

Variation. Ground colour of forewing ranges from greyish-brown to almost black. The darker forms predominate in northern Britain.

Similar species. *Mamestra brassicae*, pl. **29**. *Apamea maillardi*, pl. **37** and text.

Imago. 42–48 mm. Resident. Comes readily to sugar and light. Single-brooded, flying in June and July, except in Scotland where it is often well out by the end of May. Widely distributed, but local, in the southern half of England, inhabiting downland, chalky places, heathland, and fenland. Generally distributed and not uncommon in the rest of the British Isles, including Orkney, Shetland and the Hebrides, inhabiting moorland, grassy upland, and sandhills.

Larva. Feeds from July to September on various grasses and a variety of low plants. In captivity it will readily accept dock, hawthorn, and sallow.
Overwinters as a full-grown larva within a silken cocoon in which it pupates during April or May.

Bedrule Brocade
Mniotype solieri Boisduval

Similar species. *B. adusta*, pl. **33**. *Luperina testacea*, pl. **38**.

Imago. 42–46 mm. Suspected immigrant. Single-brooded on the Continent, flying in August and September. The only British specimen was taken at light at Bedrule, near Denholm, Roxburghshire, on 29.viii.1976. Abroad the species is widespread in southern Europe.

Larva. *Autumn to spring on a variety of wild and cultivated plants.
Overwinters as a larva.

Flame Brocade
Trigonophora flammea Esper
Plate **33** : *16*

Imago. 44–52 mm. Resident (Channel Islands), extinct resident (Sussex), and immigrant. Comes to light, sugar, and ivy blossom. Single-brooded, flying from mid-September to early November. Resident and not uncommon in the Channel Islands. It was also resident in Sussex from 1855 to *c.* 1919 and recorded, sometimes commonly, from a number of localities from Arundel eastwards through Bramber, Shoreham and Lewes to Newhaven. As an immigrant it has been recorded at Maidencombe, South Devon, on 2.x.1946; Newton Poppleford, South Devon, on 15.x.1953; Portland,

Dorset, on 11.x.1959; two, St Briavels, Gloucestershire, on 19.ix.1964; Lymington, Hampshire, on 3.x.1968; Aldwick Bay, West Sussex, on 14.x.1976; Walberton, West Sussex, on 11.x.1978; two, Swanage, Dorset, on 14.x.1978; Dungeness, Kent, on 5.x.1985; Pagham, West Sussex, on 10.x.1985; Swanage, on 23.x.1988; Walberton, on 20.x.1989; Studland, Dorset on 25 & 27.x.1989. Fifteen specimens were reported in 1990, West Sussex (4), Isle of Wight (3), Dorset (8); and ten more in 1991, all from Dorset. Following these two bumper years the records to date have been Swanage on 9 & 10.x.1993; Dungeness on 10 & 12.x.1993; Swanage on 4.ix.1994; Portland on 14 & 28.x.1995; Freshwater, Isle of Wight, on 18.x.1995; Littlestone, Kent, on 25.x.1995; Highcliffe, Hampshire, on 27.x.1995; Hayling Island, Hampshire, on 14.x.1996; Freshwater on 14.x.1996; Swanage on 23.x.1996 and Eastbourne, East Sussex, on 23.x.1996.
Larva. November to April. In captivity on various species of *Ranunculus*, including lesser celandine (*R. ficaria*) and other herbaceous plants; when full grown it is stated to prefer broom, blackthorn, ash, and privet.
Overwinters as a small larva.

Large Ranunculus
Polymixis flavicincta Denis & Schiffermüller
Plate **33** : *23–24*
Variation. Locally variable, with the darkest forms occurring in northern and western England, and the palest in southeast England and East Anglia.
Similar species. *Eumichtis lichenea*, pl. **34** and text. *Hecatera dysodea*, pl. **29**.
Imago. 40–50 mm. Resident. Comes regularly to light and sugar. Single-brooded, flying from mid-September to mid-October, inhabiting waste places, sea-cliffs, gardens, etc. Rather local in East Sussex and Kent, otherwise widespread and not uncommon in the southern half of England, ranging northwards through the eastern counties to Co. Durham.
Larva. April to July on a variety of wild and cultivated plants, including red valerian, plantain, ragwort, Michaelmas-daisy (*Aster novi-belgii*), and *Gaillardia*.
Overwinters as an egg.

The Cameo
Polymixis gemmea Treitschke
Plate **43** : *24*
Similar species. *Hadena albimacula*, pl. **30**.
Imago. 42–44 mm. Suspected immigrant. Abroad it is single-brooded, flying from July to September. The only specimen taken in Britain was at Cockpole Green, Berkshire, on 1.ix.1979. A widespread species in central and northern Europe.
Larva. *April to June on various grasses; feeding at first on the leaves and then in the base of the stems.
Overwinters as an egg.

Black-banded
Polymixis xanthomista statices Gregson
Plate **33** : *25–26*
Imago. 38–44 mm. Resident. Comes to light in moderate numbers, and also to sugar. Single-brooded, flying in August and September, inhabiting rocky places by the sea. Very local in western Britain, occurring in South and North Devon, Cornwall, the Isles of Scilly, Pembrokeshire, Cardiganshire and the Isle of Man. In Ireland it has been recorded from Co. Cork.
Larva. March to early July mainly on the flowers and leaves of thrift.
Overwinters as an egg.

Grey Chi
Antitype chi Linnaeus
Plate **33** : *27–30*
Variation. Ab. *olivacea* Stephens (fig 30) and ab. *nigrescens* Tutt (fig 29) are two of a number of melanistic forms found frequently among typical specimens in the Midlands and northern England; and occasionally Aberdeenshire.
Imago. 32–40 mm. Resident. May be found during the day at rest on stone walls and rocks, and after dark at light and sugar. Single-brooded, flying in August and September, inhabiting grassy upland and moorland. Found locally in Wiltshire and southwest England, and very casually in southeast England and East Anglia; otherwise widespread and not uncommon in England, Wales, Scotland and the northern half of Ireland.
Larva. April to early June mainly on low plants, including the flowers and leaves of dock and sorrel. In captivity it will accept sallow and hawthorn.
Overwinters as an egg.

Feathered Ranunculus
Eumichtis lichenea lichenea Hübner
Plate **34** : *1–3*
Variation. Locally variable with the paler and greyer forms occurring in chalky and limestone districts (Freshwater, Isle of Wight; Portland, Dorset; and Folkestone Warren, Kent), and the darker forms frequenting rocky places in western Britain. Other local races include a blackish and obscurely marked form taken occasionally along the coast of Hampshire and a larger and yellowish-green form found commonly in South Devon.
Similar species. *Polymixis flavicincta*, pl. **33**, is larger, and the pale to mid-grey forewing is usually flecked with orange-yellow markings, but never marbled with green.
Imago. 35–40 mm. Resident. Flies for a short time after dusk and is attracted to ivy blossom and occasionally sugar. The main flight, at least of the males, occurs after midnight when they come readily to light. Single-brooded, flying from late August to mid-October, inhabiting sea-cliffs, sandhills, shingle beaches, waste

ground, gardens, limestone hills, and rocky places by the sea. In western Britain it occurs more or less regularly along the coast from the Isle of Wight to Cornwall, and northwards through Wales, the Isle of Man, Cumbria, and Galloway to Kintyre. Along the coast of eastern England it is found not uncommonly in East Sussex and Kent, and then sporadically northwards through East Anglia to Southeast Yorkshire. Inland it occurs locally in Kent, South Devon, North Wales, Cheshire, Staffordshire, and Derbyshire. In Ireland it has been reported coastally from Cos Dublin, Down, Kerry and Wicklow.

E. lichenea scillonea Richardson, pl. **34** : *4*. This race has the forewing blackish-grey with a contrasting white reniform stigma; it occurs commonly on the Isles of Scilly.

Larva. October to May on a wide variety of wild and cultivated plants, including red valerian, foxglove, dock, ragwort, trefoils, wild cabbage (*Brassica oleracea*), hoary cress (*Cardaria draba*), sea plantain, biting stonecrop (*Sedum acre*), and *Antirrhinum*. The larvae are usually more numerous on plants growing by walls and fences, in ditches, along hedgebanks, and in other sheltered sites.
Overwinters as a small larva.

The Satellite
Eupsilia transversa Hufnagel
(*satellitia* Linnaeus)
Plate **34** : *5–6*

Variation. Colour of forewing ranges from greyish-brown to dark reddish-brown, and that of the reniform stigma from white or yellow to reddish-orange. Specimens from Scotland are frequently richly marked with reddish-orange, and those from the industrial areas of the Midlands and northern England are often darkly suffused with blackish-brown.

Imago. 40–48 mm. Resident. Comes readily to sugar, ivy blossom, and ripe blackberries, regularly to light in small numbers, and occasionally to sallow blossom. Single-brooded, appearing in mild weather from late September to April, and inhabiting woodland, parkland, and commons. Widespread and generally common over much of England, Wales and Ireland. Local and less frequent in southern Scotland, ranging sporadically northwards to Caithness and Orkney. In the Inner Hebrides it has occurred on Canna and Rhum.

Larva. May and June on oak, birch, elm, sallow, poplar, maple and other trees. It is also partial to the larvae of other species.
Overwinters as an adult.

Orange Upperwing
Jodia croceago Denis & Schiffermüller
Plate **34** : *29*

Imago. 32–38 mm. Resident. Comes in small numbers to sugar, sallow and ivy blossom, and light. Single-brooded, appearing in October and early November, and after hibernation from late March to early May. A very local and, on the whole, rare woodland species confined to the southern half of Britain, and in recent years rarely recorded outside Surrey and South Devon.

Larva. May to July on oak.
Overwinters as an adult.

The Chestnut
Conistra vaccinii Linnaeus
Plate **34** : *25–28*

Variation. The variegated and plain specimens (figs 25–26) represent the two commonest forms found in the British Isles. Other less frequent, but not uncommon, varieties have the forewing suffused with pale grey (fig 27) or black (fig 28). Several very striking aberrations have been described, but these are very rare.

Similar species. *C. ligula*, pl. **34**, has the outer margin of the forewing concave and the apex pointed. *C. erythrocephala*, pl. **34**, is larger and has a distinct black dot in the lower half of the reniform stigma. (See text fig 39.)

Imago. 28–36 mm. Resident. Comes freely to ivy blossom and sugar, and also to sallow blossom and light. Single-brooded, appearing during mild weather from late September to May. A common to abundant woodland species found throughout England, Wales, Ireland, the Inner Hebrides, and much of mainland Scotland.

Larva. May and June on oak, birch, elm and other trees; and also on low plants.
Overwinters as an adult.

Dark Chestnut
Conistra ligula Esper
Plate **34** : *21–22*

Variation. Fig 22 illustrates the banded typical form, but outside western Britain the plainly marked f. *spadicea* Haworth (fig 21) and f. *rufescens* Lempke represent the forms most commonly found.

Similar species. *C. vaccinii*, pl. **34** and text.

Imago. 30–38 mm. Resident. Comes to light, sugar, and especially to ivy blossom. Single-brooded, flying in October and November, and in mild weather throughout the winter, but rarely surviving till the spring. Widely distributed and not uncommon in England and Wales. Very local in southern Scotland. In Ireland it is said to be not uncommon in Cos Armagh and Londonderry, but rather scarce elsewhere.

Larva. April to June on hawthorn, sallow and oak, but when older it is stated to prefer low-growing plants.
Overwinters as an egg.

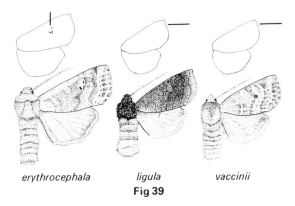

erythrocephala   ligula   vaccinii

Fig 39

Dotted Chestnut

Conistra rubiginea Denis & Schiffermüller

Plate **34** : *20*

Imago. 32–40 mm. Resident. Comes to ivy and sallow blossom, sugar, and light. Single-brooded, appearing in October and November, and after hibernation in March and April. A local woodland and wooded heathland species rarely found outside central southern and southwest England, and South Wales; and most frequently reported from Surrey, West Sussex, Hampshire, southeast Dorset, South Devon, and southeast Cornwall. Doubtfully resident in Ireland, the only precise record is a single specimen from Devil's Glen, Co. Wicklow.

Larva. May and June. Except for a single larva found on cultivated apple, the larval habits and natural foodplants of this species are either unknown or unrecorded. In captivity it is easily reared on apple, plum, and blackthorn.

Overwinters as an adult.

Red-headed Chestnut

Conistra erythrocephala Denis & Schiffermüller

Plate **34** : *23–24*

Variation. Ab. *glabra* Hübner (fig 24) has the forewing more variegated and distinct light-coloured orbicular and reniform stigmata. It has occurred regularly, but not as frequently as the typical form (fig 23).

Similar species. *C. vaccinii*, pl. **34** and text.

Imago. 34–42 mm. Suspected immigrant and transitory resident. Comes to ivy blossom, sugar and light. Single-brooded, appearing from late September to November, and on the Continent after hibernation in March and April. In Britain it has been recorded once in the spring, and possibly its habits are similar to those of *C. ligula*. In East Sussex it inhabited the larger woods near Lewes and Eastbourne, and was taken in very small numbers from 1847 to 1874, and from 1913 to 1932. In Kent it was reported from the Canterbury area in varying numbers from 1866 to 1903, mainly by dealers of questionable repute, although evidence suggests that this species may have been among their

few genuine British wares. Other twentieth-century records are near Bournemouth, Hampshire, on 14.x.1902 and 7.xi.1902; Dungeness, Kent, on 29.ix.1934; Wells, Norfolk, on 28.x.1945; Pagham, West Sussex, on 29.x.1991; Whitstable, Kent, on 19.iii.1992; Beltinge, Kent, on 15.xi.1995; Trinity, Jersey, between 12 & 14.vi. 1996; Atherington, West Sussex, on 25.x.1996; and Portland, Dorset, on 27.xi.1997. Abroad it is widely distributed throughout central and southern Europe.

Larva. *Early spring to June. The newly hatched larva is stated to feed at first on the young leaves of oak or elm, and then to descend the tree to complete its growth on various low plants such as dandelion, bedstraw, and plantain.

Overwinters as an adult or possibly as an egg.

The Brick

Agrochola circellaris Hufnagel

Plate **34** : *7–8*

Variation. Rather variable throughout its range, with the ground colour of the forewing ranging from pale yellow to pale grey or reddish-buff, and the dark brown markings and cross-lines varying in extent and intensity.

Similar species. *A. lychnidis*, pl. **34**, usually has a small, but distinct, oblique dash on the costa towards the apex. *A. macilenta*, pl. **34**, has a straight subterminal line, except just below the costa.

Imago. 34–44 mm. Resident. Comes readily to sugar, ivy blossom, and ripe blackberries, and in moderate numbers to light. Single-brooded, flying from late August to mid-October, inhabiting woodland, parkland, and commons. Widespread and generally common throughout England, Wales and Ireland. Locally widespread in Scotland, and also recorded from Orkney.

Larva. April to June mainly on wych elm, preferring the flowers and seeds when available; less frequently on ash and poplar.

Overwinters as an egg.

Red-line Quaker

Agrochola lota Clerck

Plate **34** : *12*

Imago. 33–40 mm. Resident. Comes to light, sugar and ivy blossom. Single-brooded, flying in September and October, inhabiting woodland, heathland, fenland and marshy places. Generally distributed and moderately common in England, Wales and Ireland. Locally distributed in mainland Scotland as far north as Caithness; also recorded from the Hebrides.

Larva. April to early June on sallow and willow.

Overwinters as an egg.

Yellow-line Quaker

Agrochola macilenta Hübner

Plate **34** : *10–11*

Variation. Ground colour rather variable, from pale ochreous-brown to light reddish-brown. Ab. *obsoleta*

Tutt (fig 11) lacks the black dot in the reniform stigma and is a regularly occurring form.

Similar species *A. circellaris*, pl. **34**, and text.

Imago. 32–36 mm. Resident. Comes readily to ivy blossom, ripe blackberries, sugar, and light. Single-brooded, flying from mid-September to early November, inhabiting woodland, commons, bushy places, etc. Generally distributed and moderately common over much of England, Wales, Ireland, and southern Scotland, ranging locally northwards to Caithness and the Inner Hebrides.

Larva. April to early June on beech, poplar catkins, hawthorn and oak; and during its later instars on low-growing plants. In some northern localities it feeds mainly on heather.

Overwinters as an egg.

Southern Chestnut
Agrochola haematidea Duponchel
Plate **43** : *25–26*

Similar species. *A. lychnidis*, pl. **34**.

Imago. 32–38 mm. Resident. Comes readily to light soon after dark. Single-brooded, flying from early October to mid-November, inhabiting dry acid heathland. First noted in 1990 from a single locality in West Sussex where it is apparently well established and locally not uncommon. Some years later in 1996 it was discovered in several sites in the New Forest, Hampshire.

Larva. April to early July on the flowers of bell heather and cross-leaved heath, and in captivity on the flowers of other species of heath. In keeping with other closely related species it remains dormant for several weeks before pupating.

Overwinters as an egg.

Flounced Chestnut
Agrochola helvola Linnaeus
Plate **34** : *9*

Imago. 38–40 mm. Resident. Comes readily to sugar, ripe blackberries and ivy blossom, and in small numbers to light. Single-brooded, flying from early September to mid-October (earlier in Scotland), inhabiting woodland, downland, commons, and moorland. Widespread and moderately common in the southern and central counties of England, and much of Wales. Local and less frequent in northern England and Scotland as far north as Caithness. Very local in the northern half of Ireland, and in Cos Cork and Waterford.

Larva. April to early June on a variety of plants including birch, sallow and bilberry. In captivity it will readily accept hawthorn.

Overwinters as an egg.

Brown-spot Pinion
Agrochola litura Linnaeus
Plate **34** : *18–19*

Variation. One of the more frequent forms has the basal area of the forewing pale grey, and is referable to ab. *borealis* Sparre-Schneider (fig 18). Specimens from Scotland are usually purplish-brown in colour, and more richly marked than those from southern Britain.

Imago. 30–40 mm. Resident. Comes to sugar, ivy blossom, and light. Single-brooded, flying in September and October, inhabiting woodland, commons, heathland, gardens, etc. Generally distributed and moderately common over much of England and Wales. In Scotland it occurs in all the southern counties and ranges northwards up the eastern half of the country to the Ross-shire/Sutherland border. Surprisingly, unrecorded from Ireland.

Larva. April to May on various trees and plants, such as ash, oak, bramble, and chickweed.

Overwinters as an egg.

Beaded Chestnut
Agrochola lychnidis Denis & Schiffermüller
Plate **34** : *13–17*

Variation. An extremely variable species over much of its range, with a strong tendency to melanism in parts of the Midlands and northeast England.

Similar species. *A. circellaris*, pl. **34** and text. *A. haematidea*, pl. **43**.

Imago. 34–44 mm. Resident. Readily comes to light, sugar, and ivy blossom. Single-brooded, flying in September and October, frequenting a wide variety of habitats. Generally distributed and common in central and southern England, Wales and Ireland. Local and less frequent in northern England, and only casually reported from Scotland.

Larva. March to June on grasses and various low plants.

Overwinters as an egg.

Centre-barred Sallow
Atethmia centrago Haworth
(*xerampelina* sensu Hübner)
Plate **35** : *1–2*

Variation. Except for the central band of the forewing, which varies in extent and intensity, aberrant forms are rarely obtained, except by extensive breeding.

Imago. 32–36 mm. Resident. Comes to light in small numbers. Single-brooded, flying from mid-August throughout September, inhabiting woodland, hedgerows, river banks, and other places where ash is established. Widespread and locally common in England and Wales. Sporadically distributed in Scotland from the south to Moray. Recorded from Canna and Mull, Inner Hebrides. Local and generally uncommon in Ireland.

Larva. April to early June, at first on the buds and then the leaves of ash. Feeds only at night and hides during the day at the base of the tree or in a crevice of bark.

Overwinters as an egg.

Lunar Underwing
Omphaloscelis lunosa Haworth
Plate **35** : *6–9*

Variation. Colour of forewing ranges from pale ochreous-brown through rust-red to dark blackish-grey. Rather variable throughout its range, with the paler forms predominating in most districts.

Imago. 32–38 mm. Resident. Comes readily to light and ivy blossom. Single-brooded, flying from late August to early October, inhabiting commons, downland, and rough grassy places. Generally distributed and common throughout the southern half of England, the Midlands, Wales and Ireland. Locally widespread in northern England and Scotland as far north as Ross-shire.

Larva. October to May on the blades, stems and roots of various grasses.

Overwinters as a small larva.

Orange Sallow
Xanthia citrago Linnaeus
Plate **34** : *33*

Imago. 32–40 mm. Resident. Comes to light, honey-dew, and especially to sugared lime leaves. Single-brooded, flying in August and September, inhabiting parkland, commons, roadsides, woodland, etc. Widely distributed over much of Britain and found in most districts where lime is well established. In Scotland, where it is rather local, its range extends to Ross-shire. Unrecorded from Ireland.

Larva. March to early June on lime.

Overwinters as an egg.

Barred Sallow
Xanthia aurago Denis & Schiffermüller
Plate **34** : *30–31*

Variation. The most variable feature of this species is the ground colour of the forewing, which ranges from pale yellow to deep orange. Heavily banded and unicolorous forms have occurred, but are rare.

Imago. 30–38 mm. Resident. Comes regularly to light and sugar. Single-brooded, flying in September and October, inhabiting woodland, downland, and hedgerows. Widely distributed and locally common in the southern half of Britain, ranging locally northwards to Co. Durham and Cumbria.

Larva. April to early June on maple and beech.

Overwinters as an egg.

Pink-barred Sallow
Xanthia togata Esper
(*lutea* Ström)
Plate **34** : *32*

Similar species. *X. icteritia*, pl. **34** and text.

Imago. 28–36 mm. Resident. Comes regularly to light, sugar, ripe blackberries, and flowering reeds and grasses. Single-brooded, flying in September and October, inhabiting damp woodland, commons, fenland, and other marshy places. Widespread and moderately common over much of the British Isles, including the

Hebrides and Orkney.

Larva. March to early June, at first on sallow catkins and then on low plants. In captivity it can be reared exclusively on sallow.

Overwinters as an egg.

The Sallow
Xanthia icteritia Hufnagel
(*fulvago* sensu Linnaeus)
Plate **34** : *34–36*

Variation. Slightly variable in ground colour which ranges from pale yellow to pale orange, but very variable in the extent of reddish-grey markings. A frequent form almost devoid of markings is referable to ab. *flavescens* Esper (fig 36).

Similar species. *X. togata*, pl. **34**, has the head and patagial collar purplish-red.

Imago. 32–40 mm. Resident. Comes regularly to light and sugar, and sometimes abundantly to ripe blackberries and flowering grasses such as tufted hair-grass (*Deschampsia cespitosa*). Single-brooded, flying in September and early October, inhabiting damp woodland, commons, marshy places, heathland, moorland, etc. Widespread and generally common over much of the British Isles.

Larva. March to June, feeding when young on sallow catkins, and afterwards on the leaves, or more frequently on low plants.

Overwinters as an egg.

Dusky-lemon Sallow
Xanthia gilvago Denis & Schiffermüller
Plate **34** : *37–38*

Variation. Mainly variable in the extent and intensity of the blackish-brown forewing markings. Specimens heavily suffused with dark brown occur frequently in parts of the Midlands. Ab. *palleago* Hübner is a pale orange nearly unicolorous form found rarely in south-east England.

Similar species. *X. ocellaris* ab. *gilvescens*, pl. **34** : *40* has a pointed and broader forewing.

Imago. 30–37 mm. Resident. Comes to light, sugar and other attractions, but seldom in numbers. Single-brooded, flying from late August to early October, inhabiting woodland and commons. Widespread and locally common in England and Wales. Locally distributed and less frequent in southern Scotland, ranging eastwards to Aberdeenshire.

Larva. April to early June on the seeds mainly of wych elm, but occasionally English elm.

Overwinters as an egg.

Pale-lemon Sallow
Xanthia ocellaris Borkhausen
Plate **34** : *39–40*

Variation. Ab. *gilvescens* Worsley-Wood (fig 40) is a variegated form similar in many aspects to *X. gilvago*

pl. **34**. It occurs regularly in small numbers in the East Anglian and Thames Valley populations.

Imago. 32–40 mm. Resident. Comes sparingly to light, and occasionally to sugar and flowering grasses. Single-brooded, flying in September and October, frequenting parkland, commons, roadsides, and other types of habitat where poplar is established. A local species, easily overlooked, but usually found commonly as larvae where it occurs. The Breck district and north Surrey are the best-known localities, but it also occurs elsewhere in Norfolk and Suffolk, and in Kent, Essex, Berkshire, Buckinghamshire, Huntingdonshire, Cambridgeshire and Bedfordshire.

Larva. April to early June, feeding at first in catkins, mainly those of black poplar, and afterwards on the leaves and various low plants.

Overwinters as an egg.

SUBFAMILY: ACRONICTINAE

Scarce Merveille du Jour
Moma alpium Osbeck
(*orion* Esper)
Plate **35** : *10*

Similar species. *Dichonia aprilina*, pl. **33**.

Imago. 32–40 mm. Resident. Comes regularly to light and sugar. Single-brooded, flying from early June to mid-July, inhabiting oak woodland. Very local in southern and southwestern England, and found mainly in Hampshire (New Forest and Forest of Bere); West Sussex (Emsworth and near Arundel); East Sussex (Beckley); Kent (Hamstreet) and southeast Cornwall.

Larva. July to early September on oak.

Overwinters as a pupa amongst surface litter.

Poplar Grey
Acronicta megacephala Denis & Schiffermüller
Plate **35** : *14–15*

Variation. Ab. *nigra* Shaw (fig 15) is a melanic form found not uncommonly in parts of the Midlands and Yorkshire.

Similar species. The pale, usually white, hindwings of this species distinguish it from *A. rumicis*, pl. **35**, and *A. auricoma*, pl. **35**.

Imago. 40–44 mm. Resident. Comes regularly to light and sugar. Single-brooded, flying from late May to early August, inhabiting woodland, commons, parkland, etc. Generally distributed and moderately common over much of England and Wales. Locally widespread in Ireland, and sporadically distributed in Scotland as far north as Ross-shire.

Larva. July to September mainly on black poplar and aspen, occasionally on other species of poplar and willow.

Overwinters as a pupa within a flimsy silken cocoon usually under loose bark.

The Sycamore
Acronicta aceris Linnaeus
Plate **35** : *18–19*

Variation. Ab. *infuscata* Haworth (fig 19) is a dark grey form found frequently in the London area, and occasionally elsewhere.

Imago. 40–45 mm. Resident. Sometimes seen at rest on fences and tree-trunks, but more frequently found at light or sugar. Single-brooded, flying from mid-June to early August, inhabiting commons, parkland, gardens, and avenues. Widespread and not uncommon in central southern and southeast England, and East Anglia; rather local and uncommon in the rest of southern Britain, ranging northwards to Yorkshire, Cheshire and North Wales. Doubtfully recorded from Ireland.

Larva. August to September on horse chestnut, sycamore, field maple, and oak.

Overwinters as a pupa.

The Miller
Acronicta leporina Linnaeus
Plate **35** : *16–17*

Variation. The pure white and lightly marked typical form occurs in parts of Scotland and Ireland, but elsewhere in the British Isles the greyish-suffused f. *grisea* Cochrane (fig 16) predominates. Ab. *melanocephala* Mansbridge (fig 17) is a blackish-suffused form found regularly in the Midlands and parts of northern England. A more extreme and rarer melanic form is referable to ab. *nigra* Tutt.

Imago. 38–43 mm. Resident. Comes regularly to light and sugar in small numbers. Single-brooded, flying from early June to early August, inhabiting woodland, heathland, and commons. Widespread and not uncommon in England and Wales. Local and less frequent in Ireland, much of mainland Scotland and the Inner Hebrides.

Larva. Late July to early October mainly on birch, but also on alder, oak, aspen, black poplar, and sallow. Overwinters as a pupa, sometimes remaining in this stage over a second winter. In captivity the larva must be provided with soft wood or virgin cork in which to burrow.

Alder Moth
Acronicta alni Linnaeus
Plate **35** : *20–21*

Variation. Ab. *suffusa* Tutt (fig 21) and the more extreme ab. *steinerti* Caspari are industrial melanics occurring regularly in the London area, the Midlands, and elsewhere.

Imago. 37–43 mm. Resident. Comes regularly to light, and occasionally to sugar. Single-brooded, flying in May and June, inhabiting woodland and commons. Locally widespread over much of England and Wales. Rather local, but probably overlooked, in Ireland.

Larva. July and August on birch, oak, elm, hawthorn, and many other trees.
Overwinters as a pupa. The larva requires soft wood or virgin cork in which to pupate.

Dark Dagger
Acronicta tridens Denis & Schiffermüller
Plate **35** : *26–27*
Similar species. *A. psi*, pl. **35**, is a more robust species, and in the male the overall colour and the veins of the hindwing are usually darker. The males of both species are easily separated by examining the genitalia, and the distinguishing features are readily exposed in freshly killed specimens by gently squeezing the lower part of the abdomen, and in dried specimens by removing some of the scales from the terminal segments. (See text fig 40.) The larvae are very dissimilar.
Imago. 35–43 mm. Resident. Comes regularly to light, and occasionally to sugar. Single-brooded, flying in June and July, inhabiting woodland, fenland, orchards, gardens, etc. Widespread and not uncommon in England and Wales, except in the extreme north where it is very local. Possibly resident in southern Scotland; doubtfully resident in Ireland.
Larva. Black, with a white and orangish-red stripe along the back, and one on each side; the first is interrupted with white and the others with black; there is a black hump on the fourth segment and a broader one on the eleventh segment. August to early October on hawthorn, blackthorn, plum, apple, wild rose, pear, sallow, buckthorn and probably other trees and shrubs. Overwinters as a pupa, sometimes remaining in this stage for a second winter.

Grey Dagger
Acronicta psi Linnaeus
Plate **35** : *23–25*
Variation. Ground colour ranges from whitish-grey to dark grey, with the pale forms predominating in Scotland and western Britain and the darker forms in industrial areas.
Similar species. *A. tridens*, pl. **35** and text.
Imago. 34–45 mm. Resident. Comes readily to light, and occasionally to sugar. Single-brooded, flying from June to August, inhabiting woodland, commons, gardens, heathland, etc. Generally distributed and common throughout England, Wales and Ireland. Widespread, but less frequent, over much of Scotland.
Larva. Greyish-black, with a broad yellow stripe along the back, and a whitish stripe along each side; between these stripes is a row of black-edged red spots. August to early October on birch, oak, lime, elm, rowan, hawthorn, blackthorn and many other trees.
Overwinters as a pupa.

tridens   *psi*

Fig 40

Marsh Dagger
Acronicta strigosa Denis & Schiffermüller
Plate **35** : *34*
Imago. 30–34 mm. Formerly resident, possibly extinct. Occasionally found during the day at rest on tree-trunks (hawthorn, oak, and apple), and walls. After dark it has been netted on the wing, or taken at sugar. Single-brooded, flying in late June and July, inhabiting mature hawthorn woodland and hedgerows, preferably growing in damp situations such as the edges of fens and marshy commons. Formerly found locally in Huntingdonshire (Monk's Wood, Colne, and Somersham) and Cambridgeshire (Wicken, Fordham, Isleham, Fulbourn, Whittlesford, Duxford, Mepal and Chatteris), but not recorded since 1933. Elsewhere this century it has occurred in Worcestershire (two at Castle Moreton in July 1904), and Gloucestershire (two by the Severn in July 1905). A male specimen taken at light at Rye Harbour, East Sussex, on 22.viii.1996 was probably an immigrant.
Larva. August and early September mainly on hawthorn, and sometimes on blackthorn. It prefers soft wood or cork in which to pupate.
Overwinters as a pupa.

Light Knot Grass
Acronicta menyanthidis menyanthidis Esper
Plate **35** : *30–31*
Variation. Ab. *suffusa* Tutt (fig 31) is a melanic form found regularly in the Midlands, northern England, and northwest Norfolk.
Similar species. *A. auricoma*, pl. **35** and text.
Imago. 34–42 mm. Resident. Frequently found at rest on fence-posts, also comes to light in fair numbers. Single-brooded, flying from late May to early July, inhabiting heathland, moorland, and marshy places. Locally widespread and not uncommon in the Midlands, North Wales, northern England, and southeast Scotland. Local and less frequent in the northern half of Ireland, South Wales, and northwest Norfolk.
A. menyanthidis scotica Tutt, pl. **35** : *32*. This race is larger and brighter than the typical form, with the markings clear and distinct. Widespread in Scotland (except the southeast) and the Hebrides.

Larva. August and September on a variety of plants and small trees, such as bog myrtle, bilberry, heather, sallow, and birch.
Overwinters as a pupa.

Scarce Dagger
Acronicta auricoma Denis & Schiffermüller
Plate **35** : *33*
Similar species. *A. menyanthidis*, pl. **35**, has the forewing greyer and more mottled with darker markings; orbicular stigma smaller, without centre dot; and subterminal line less angulated. (See text fig 41.) *A. rumicis*, pl. **35**, has the forewing darker and less grey, with a white double spot near tornus, and lacks a distinct tornal streak ('dagger mark'). *A. megacephala*, pl. **35** and text.
Imago. 36–42 mm. Formerly resident (probably extinct) and suspected immigrant. Occasionally found at rest on tree-trunks, and also taken at sugar and light. Double-brooded, flying in May, and again from mid-July to mid-August. A woodland species found locally, but not uncommonly, during the last century in East Kent and East Sussex, but probably not resident in either county after the early part of this century. As a suspected immigrant it has occurred at Dungeness, Kent, on 12.viii.1932 and 4.viii.1933; Seaford, Sussex, on 4.v.1942; Tilgate, Sussex, in 1947; Luccombe Chine, Isle of Wight, in late August 1947; Hamstreet, Kent, on 29.v.1950 and 5.viii.1951; Folkestone, Kent, on 6.viii. 1951; Eastbourne, Sussex, on 12.vii.1952 and 16.v. 1956; St Martins, Guernsey, on 31.v.1995; Sholden, Kent, on 8.viii.1996; Warsash, Hampshire, on 9.viii.1996; and Icklesham, East Sussex, on 14 & 15.viii.1996.
Larva. June and early July, and again in September on oak; and in captivity on birch, bramble, and raspberry.
Overwinters as a pupa.

Sweet Gale Moth
Acronicta euphorbiae myricae Guenée
Plate **35** : *22*
Variation. Hindwing of female (not illustrated) dark grey.
Imago. 32–40 mm. Resident. May be found during the day on fences, rocks, and stone walls; and after dark at light. Single-brooded, flying from late April to early June, except in Ireland where a second generation occurs in August. A moorland species found locally, but not uncommonly, in central and northern Scotland, and the Inner Hebrides; ranging sporadically southwards to Ayrshire. In Ireland it occurs frequently in the Burren, Co. Clare, and locally in Cos Cork, Kerry, Sligo, Antrim and Galway.
Larva. July to September on a variety of plants, including bog myrtle, heather, birch, sallow, and plantain.
Overwinters as a pupa. The silken cocoon is occasionally found attached to rocks.

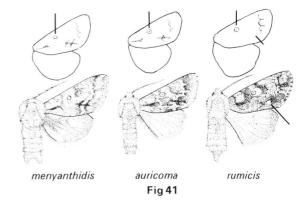

menyanthidis   auricoma   rumicis
Fig 41

Knot Grass
Acronicta rumicis Linnaeus
Plate **35** : *28–29*
Variation. Ab. *salicis* Curtis (fig 29) is a melanic form found regularly and sometimes commonly over much of the species' range.
Similar species. *A. auricoma*, pl. **35** and text. *A. megacephala*, pl. **35** and text.
Imago. 34–44 mm. Resident. Comes readily to light and sugar. Single-brooded, flying from early May to July, except in southern England where a second brood appears in August and early September. Generally distributed and common in England, Wales and Ireland. Widespread, but less frequent, in Scotland and the Hebrides.
Larva. July to September on a variety of plants, including plantain, sorrel, dock, bramble, thistles, hop, sallow, and hawthorn.
Overwinters as a pupa.

Reed Dagger
Simyra albovenosa Goeze
Plate **35** : *13*
Similar species. *Mythimna straminea*, pl. **31** and text.
Imago. 32–40 mm. Resident. Comes readily to light. Double-brooded, flying in May and again in July and August, inhabiting fenland and marshy places. A very local species, but not uncommon where it occurs, and found in Cambridgeshire, Norfolk, Suffolk, Essex, East Kent, South Hampshire, and the Isle of Wight; also casually recorded from Sussex, Dorset and South Devon. A few specimens occurred sporadically at Spurn, Yorkshire, from 1970 to 1982.
Larva. June, and late August and September on common reed. Occasionally found on sallow and yellow loosestrife. In captivity will accept most broad-leaved grasses.
Overwinters as a pupa.

The Coronet
Craniophora ligustri Denis & Schiffermüller
Plate **35** : *11–12*

Variation. Ab. *coronula* Haworth (fig 12) is a melanic form found frequently in parts of the Midlands, and occasionally elsewhere.

Imago. 35–43 mm. Resident. Comes regularly to light and sugar. Single-brooded, flying in June and July, inhabiting woodland, fenland, downland, and commons. A local species, seldom found commonly, but widely distributed over much of mainland Britain, as far north as Ross-shire. In Ireland it is found locally in Cos Clare and Galway.

Larva. August to September on ash and wild privet. Overwinters as a pupa.

Tree-lichen Beauty
Cryphia algae Fabricius
Plate **43** : *32–34*

Variation. Very variable, the ground colour of the forewing ranging from pale greyish-green to brownish-green with the normal black markings varying in both size and intensity. An attractive form having the basal and subterminal area marked with bright yellow is referable to ab. *calligrapha* Borkhausen.

Similar species. *C. muralis*, pl. **35**.

Imago. 24–30 mm. Immigrant. All the recent specimens occurred between mid-July and early September and were taken at light. In July 1859 two specimens were said to have been taken at Disley, Cheshire and in 1873 another was reported from Hastings, East Sussex. Over one hundred years passed before the species reappeared in England with a capture at Southsea, Hampshire, on 21.viii.1991. Twenty-two others have occurred to date and these are at Walberton, West Sussex, on 1.ix.1991 and 8.viii.1992; Freshwater, Isle of Wight, on 27.viii. 1992; Dungeness, Kent, on 19.vii. & 1.viii.1995; Southsea on 26.vii.1995; Walberton on 1.viii.1995; Warsash, Hampshire, on 2.viii.1995; Weymouth, Dorset, on 10.viii.1995; Warsash, four between 7 & 12.viii.1996; Eastbourne, East Sussex, on 13.viii.1996; Lydd, Kent, on 14.viii.1996; Rye Harbour, East Sussex, on 14.viii. 1996; Bishop's Stortford, Hertfordshire, on 19.viii.1996; Littlestone, Kent, on 20.viii.1996; Ninham, Isle of Wight, on 23.viii.1996; Dungeness on 25.viii.1996; Warsash on 2.ix.1996 & 2.viii.1997; Middleton-on-Sea, West Sussex, two on 6.viii.1997 and three on 7.viii.1997; and Freshwater on 21.viii.1997. In the Channel Islands it has been reported singly from Guernsey in 1990 and 1991, twice in 1996; from Herm in 1991; and from Jersey in 1995. Abroad it is found throughout most of Europe.

Larva. *September to June on lichens growing on trees, including fruit trees. Overwinters as a larva.

Marbled Beauty
Cryphia domestica Hufnagel
(*perla* Denis & Schiffermüller)
Plate **35** : *42–43*

Variation. Rather variable in the extent of the dark grey forewing markings, which may extend over the entire wing or be very much reduced. The dark forms predominate in the London area and other industrial districts, whereas the white and weakly marked forms are most frequently found in chalky and limestone localities. Occasionally specimens are well marked with orange-yellow.

Similar species. *C. muralis*, pl. **35**, is usually larger, has the forewing green or olive in colour, antemedian line does not extend to dorsum, and the hindwing discal spot is smaller and less distinct.

Imago. 22–30 mm. Resident. May be found during the day on walls, and after dark in moderate numbers at light. Single-brooded, flying in July and August, inhabiting mainly urban districts and coastal cliffs. Widely distributed and generally common in England, Wales and southern Scotland. Very local and mainly coastal in eastern Scotland and in Ireland.

Larva. September to May on lichens (*Xanthoria parietina*, *Lecidea confluens*, etc) growing on walls, roofs, rocks, etc.
Overwinters as a larva.

Marbled Grey
Cryphia raptricula Denis & Schiffermüller
(*divisa* Esper)
Plate **35** : *44*

Variation. The few British specimens approach the darker forms of this species, which abroad varies in colour from light grey to blackish-brown.

Imago. 29–36 mm. Suspected immigrant. Single-brooded in northern and central Europe, flying in July and August. All the specimens recorded in Britain have been taken at light. They were at Arundel, Sussex, on 12.viii.1953; Southsea, Hampshire, on 18.viii.1955; two specimens (others seen, but not taken) at Worth and Sandwich, Kent, on 9.viii.1969; Dungeness, Kent, on 20.vi.1983, 30.vii.1990 & 31.vii.1991; Greatstone, Kent, on 7 & 26.viii.1991; Lydd, Kent, on 22.viii.1991 and Dungeness on 22.vii. & 9.viii.1996.

Larva. *Autumn to spring on lichens (*Sticta pulmonacea*, etc) growing on old stone walls, rocks and sometimes tree-trunks.
Overwinters as a larva.

Marbled Green
Cryphia muralis muralis Forster
Plate **35** : *35–37*

Variation. Ground colour of forewing ranges from almost white, through various shades of green to dark olive-green, with the darker markings varying in intensity.

Similar species. *C. domestica*, pl. **35** and text. *C. algae*, pl. **43**.

Imago. 27–34 mm. Resident. Readily found during the day on lichen-covered walls and rocks. Flies from dusk onwards, and comes to light and sugar. Single-brooded, flying in July and August. A local species found in southern England along the coast from Kent to Cornwall and the Isles of Scilly; and inland in Somerset, Gloucestershire and very rarely Berkshire. Also found locally inland and along the coast of South Wales.

C. muralis impar Warren, pl. **35** : *38*. A rather obscurely marked greyish or brownish, but rarely greenish, form, associated with the old buildings in Cambridge. A much decreased race, but still found regularly in small numbers.

C. muralis westroppi Cockayne and Williams, pl. **35** : *39–41*. This Irish race was described from Co. Cork, and stated to be smaller in size and deeper green in colour. However Cork specimens when viewed in numbers are undeniably smaller on average (24–32 mm), but so variable in both colour and markings that it is difficult to describe any constant character which separates them from the English forms and races. Melanic forms unknown in England occur occasionally in the populations from Cork City, and from Dingle, Co. Kerry. Elsewhere in Ireland, *C. muralis* has been recorded from Killarney, Co. Kerry, and from Cos Galway, Tipperary, and Waterford.

Larva. October to May on *Diploicia canescens* and other lichens growing on walls, roofs, and rocks. Overwinters as a small larva.

SUBFAMILY: AMPHIPYRINAE

Copper Underwing
Amphipyra pyramidea Linnaeus
Plate **36** : *2*

Similar species. *A. berbera svenssoni*, pl. **36**, has the underside colour of hindwing suffused orange-brown, without any strongly contrasting pattern; whereas in *A. pyramidea* the discal area is pale yellow and contrasts with both the orange-brown terminal area and the blackish-brown anterior margin. (See text fig 42). A second distinguishing character which is reasonably constant is the two arrow-like points on the lower half of the antemedian line; in *pyramidea* they are equidistant whereas in *berbera* the lower one projects out further than the upper point.

Imago. 47–54 mm. Resident. Comes freely to sugar, and in small numbers to light. Single-brooded, flying from early August to mid-October, inhabiting woodland, parkland, and hedgerows. Generally distributed and moderately common in the southern half of England, Wales, the Midlands, and Ireland. Elsewhere in Britain it is casually recorded as far north as Morayshire.

Larva. April to May on oak, honeysuckle, ash, wild privet, and probably other trees and shrubs. Overwinters as an egg.

pyramidea   berbera svenssoni

Fig 42

Svensson's Copper Underwing
Amphipyra berbera svenssoni Fletcher
Plate **36** : *3* & *5–6*

Similar species. *A. pyramidea*, pl. **36** and text.

Imago. 47–56 mm. Resident. Comes freely to sugar, and in small numbers to light. During the day both this and the last species hide, sometimes communally, in old sheds, under loose bark, and in hollow tree-trunks. Single-brooded, flying from late July to September, inhabiting woodland. Widespread and locally common over much of England and Wales, as far north as Yorkshire and Cumbria. In Scotland it has been noted from the Glasgow area. As yet unrecorded from Ireland.

Larva. April to May on oak, lime, sallow, lilac, rhododendron, hornbeam, and probably other trees and shrubs. Overwinters as an egg.

Mouse Moth
Amphipyra tragopoginis Clerck
Plate **36** : *4*

Imago. 32–40 mm. Resident. Comes to light, sugar, and the flowers of ragwort, *Buddleia*, and other plants. Roosts during the day in old buildings and sheds, under loose bark, and in hollow trees, sometimes in numbers. Single-brooded, flying from late July to early September, inhabiting woodland, fenland, sandhills, moorland, gardens, etc. Widespread and generally common over the greater part of the British Isles, including the Hebrides.

Larva. April to June on the leaves and flowers of a wide variety of wild and cultivated plants, such as mugwort, salad burnet, fennel (*Foeniculum vulgare*), hawthorn, and sallow. Overwinters as an egg.

Old Lady
Mormo maura Linnaeus
Plate **36** : *7*

Imago. 64–74 mm. Resident. Roosts by day in houses, sheds, etc. After dark comes readily to sugar, but only sparingly to light. Single-brooded, flying in July and August, inhabiting gardens, river-banks, waste ground, and marshy places. Widespread and not uncommon in England, Wales, Ireland, and the southern half of Scotland.

Larva. September to May, feeding after hibernation on a variety of trees and shrubs, such as blackthorn, hawthorn, elm, sallow, birch, and *Euonymus*. Overwinters as a small larva.

Bird's Wing

Dypterygia scabriuscula Linnaeus
Plate **36** : *1*

Imago. 34–42 mm. Resident. Comes readily to sugar, and in small numbers to light. Mainly single-brooded, flying from early June to mid-July, with a partial and very occasional second generation occurring from mid-August to mid-September. Widely distributed in the southern half of Britain as far north as Lancashire and Yorkshire, but uncommon outside central southern and southeast England, East Anglia, and the northwest Midlands.

Larva. July to August on dock, sorrel and other low plants. Overwinters as a pupa.

Brown Rustic

Rusina ferruginea Esper
(*umbratica* Goeze)
(*tenebrosa* Hübner)
Plate **36** : *8–9*

Variation. Specimens from northern Britain are darker than those from the south.

Imago. 32–40 mm. Resident. Both sexes come to sugar and light; the males regularly, the females sparingly. Single-brooded, flying in June and July, inhabiting woodland, downland, heathland, and moorland. Generally distributed and often common over much of the British Isles, including the Inner Hebrides.

Larva. August to May on low plants, such as dock, plantain, and groundsel. Overwinters as an almost full-grown larva.

Guernsey Underwing

Polyphaenis sericata Esper
Plate **43** : *27*

Imago. 40–46 mm. Resident in the Channel Islands. Comes to light and sugar. Single-brooded, flying from mid-June to mid-August. Although originally found on Guernsey in the 1870s it went unrecorded for over eighty years until it reappeared in 1986. It is now considered to be well established here and also on Jersey where it was first reported in 1989. As yet unrecorded from the British mainland, but eventually may well occur.

Larva. September to May on honeysuckle and oak. Overwinters as a larva.

Straw Underwing

Thalpophila matura Hufnagel
Plate **36** : *13*

Variation. Specimens from western Ireland are often brighter in appearance and frequently well marked with reddish-brown. Specimens from the industrial areas of northeast England often have obscurely marked and dull-coloured forewings, and blackish-suffused hindwings. Ab. *trescoensis* Richardson has the subterminal area of the forewing and the reniform stigma pale straw-coloured. This rare form occurs on the Isles of Scilly, together with the typical form.

Imago. 38–46 mm. Resident. Comes regularly to sugar, light, and the flowers of ragwort, marram, and other plants. Single-brooded, flying from mid-July to late August, inhabiting commons, downland, sandhills, moorland, and grassy places. Widely distributed and not uncommon throughout the British Isles, including the Inner Hebrides.

Larva. Autumn to May on various grasses. Overwinters as a small larva.

Orache Moth

Trachea atriplicis Linnaeus
Plate **36** : *14*

Imago. 39–52 mm. Extinct resident and immigrant. Comes to sugar and light. Single-brooded, flying from mid-June to early July, inhabiting damp meadows, edges of fenland, and other marshy places. During the last century it was well established in the marginal fenland of Huntingdonshire and Cambridgeshire, and locally established in Norfolk, Essex, Suffolk and Hertfordshire. The reasons for its decline and probable extinction are not known, but as a resident it has not been recorded in this country since 1915. As an immigrant it has been reported from Britain on twelve occasions. These are: St Olaves, Suffolk, on 4.vii.1984; Bradwell-on-Sea, Essex, on 4.vii.1984; Tillingham, Essex, on 7.vii.1984; Dungeness, Kent, on 8.viii.1984; Woking, Surrey, on 5.vii.1989; Hickling, Norfolk, on 21.vii.1991; Densole, Kent, on 3.vii.1994; Irby, Cheshire, on 15.vii.1995; Christchurch, Dorset, on 31.vii.1995; Bishop's Stortford, Hertfordshire, on 10.viii.1995; Languard, Suffolk, on 1.vii.1997; and Greatstone, Kent, on 24.vii.1997. In the Channel Islands there are single records in 1984 and 1997 from Guernsey; whereas on Jersey, where it was first noted in 1987, it is stated to be now resident.

Larva. July to August, in captivity and possibly in the wild on goosefoot and other low plants. Overwinters as a pupa.

Small Angle Shades

Euplexia lucipara Linnaeus
Plate **36** : *11*

Imago. 30–35 mm. Resident. Comes regularly to light and sugar. Normally single-brooded, flying in June and July, with a partial and very occasional second generation in September. This species inhabits commons, gardens, woodlands, and parkland. Widespread and moderately common over the greater part of the British Isles, including Orkney and the Inner Hebrides.

Larva. August and September on bracken and wild and cultivated ferns. Also found on birch, sallow, oak, ivy, willowherb, and other low plants.

Overwinters as a pupa.

Angle Shades

Phlogophora meticulosa Linnaeus

Plate **36** : *12*

Variation. Specimens having the ground colour rosy, and the central band and terminal area red, occur regularly, but not commonly.

Imago. 45–52 mm. Resident and immigrant. Frequently found during the day at rest on fences and leaves; and after dark at light and sugar. Probably double-brooded, flying from May to October, but may be found occasionally in other months of the year. Widely distributed and common in England, Wales, and Ireland; locally widespread in Scotland, the Hebrides and Orkney.

Larva. Has been found throughout the year feeding on a wide variety of wild and cultivated plants, including dock, nettle, chickweed, red valerian, bramble, hop, oak, and birch.

Overwinters as a larva.

The Berber

Pseudenargia ulicis Staudinger

(South 1961, vol. 1, pl. 117)

Similar species. Somewhat similar to a large reddish-ochreous or greenish-ochreous *Ipimorpha subtusa*, pl. **36**.

Imago. 37–42 mm. Suspected immigrant. Single-brooded on the Continent, flying in August and September. The only British specimen was taken at sugar near Brockenhurst, Hampshire, on 16.viii.1935. Abroad it is found in southern France, Spain, and North Africa.

Larva. *April to May on gorse.

Overwinters as an egg.

The Latin

Callopistria juventina Stoll

Plate **36** : *10*

Imago. 34–38 mm. Suspected immigrant. Single-brooded, flying on the Continent in June and July. It has occurred at light on two occasions in mainland Britain and once in the Channel Islands. These are at Laughton, Sussex, on 16.v.1959; Wye, Kent, on 27.vii.1962 and St Peters, Guernsey, on 29.vii.1995. Abroad it occurs locally throughout central and southern Europe.

Larva. *Feeds by day in August and September on the fronds of bracken.

Overwinters as a full-grown larva, within a silken cocoon in which it will pupate in the spring.

Double Kidney

Ipimorpha retusa Linnaeus

Plate **36** : *22*

Similar species. *I. subtusa*, pl. **36**, has the colour of forewing greyer, the costa more evenly curved, and the cross-lines not parallel. (See text fig 43.)

Imago. 26–32 mm. Resident. Comes to light and sugar, usually in small numbers. Single-brooded, flying from late July to mid-September, inhabiting damp woodland, fenland, and marshy places. Widespread, but rather local, in the southern half of England and much of Wales, ranging northwards to Lancashire and Yorkshire.

Larva. April to May in the spun shoots of sallow and willow.

Overwinters as an egg.

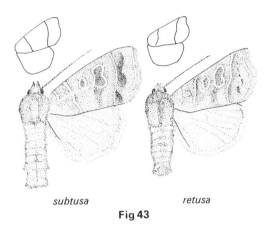

subtusa   retusa

Fig 43

The Olive

Ipimorpha subtusa Denis & Schiffermüller

Plate **36** : *23*

Similar species. *I. retusa*, pl. **36** and text.

Imago. 28–34 mm. Resident. Comes sparingly to light and sugar. Single-brooded, flying from late July to mid-September, inhabiting woodland, commons, parkland, gardens, and marshy places. Locally widespread throughout England, Wales and southern Scotland. Rare in Ireland, and recorded from Cos Antrim, Tyrone, Armagh, Fermanagh, and Kildare.

Larva. April to May in spun leaves of aspen and poplar.

Overwinters as an egg.

Angle-striped Sallow

Enargia paleacea Esper

Plate **36** : *16–17*

Variation. Ground colour ranges from pale yellow to orange-yellow. The cross-lines, stigmata, and other forewing markings vary from being well defined to absent.

Imago. 40–44 mm. Resident and immigrant. Comes readily to light and sugar. Single-brooded, flying from late July to September, inhabiting mature birch woodland. Found locally, but not uncommonly, in the Midlands (mainly Nottinghamshire, Worcestershire, Warwickshire, Herefordshire, Staffordshire, Leicestershire, North Lincolnshire, and Yorkshire); and central Scotland (mainly Inverness-shire, Morayshire, Banffshire, and Ross-shire). As an immigrant it has occurred on about 80 occasions in English and Welsh localities outside its normal breeding area. The most recorded in one year was 24 in 1964, when several of the specimens were accompanied by migrant examples of *Eurois occulta* and *Syngrapha interrogationis*.

Larva. Late April to mid-June in spun leaves of silver birch (*Betula pendula*) and downy birch (*B. pubescens*). Overwinters as an egg.

Dingy Shears
Parastichtis ypsillon Denis & Schiffermüller
(*fissipuncta* Haworth)
Plate **36** : *18–19*

Imago. 32–42 mm. Resident. Comes readily to sugar, and regularly to light. Single-brooded, flying from late June to early August, inhabiting damp woodland, commons, fenland, and marshy places. Locally widespread in England and Wales; thinly scattered in Scotland; and very local in Ireland (Cos Dublin, Wicklow, and Antrim).

Larva. April to early June, mainly on willow; less frequently on poplar and sallow. Feeds when young in the buds or catkins, and later on the leaves, hiding during the day under debris on the ground or under loose bark, often gregariously. Overwinters as an egg.

The Suspected
Parastichtis suspecta Hübner
Plate **35** : *3–5*

Variation. Specimens from northern and western Britain are more variegated and richly marked than those from southern and eastern England.

Imago. 29–34 mm. Resident. Comes readily to sugar and ragwort flowers, and in small numbers to light. Single-brooded, flying from mid-July throughout August, inhabiting woodland and wooded heathland. Locally widespread over the greater part of England, North Wales and Scotland. Rare and sporadic in Ireland; recorded from Cos Dublin, Kerry, Tyrone, Down, Armagh and Wicklow.

Larva. April to May on birch and possibly sallow. Overwinters as an egg.

Heart Moth
Dicycla oo Linnaeus
Plate **36** : *20–21*

Variation. Ab. *renago* Haworth (fig 21) has the area between the postmedian and subterminal lines suffused with reddish- or greenish-grey. This form occurs in small numbers in most populations.

Imago. 32–38 mm. Resident. Both sexes come to sugar around dusk; and to light (especially the males) from about an hour after dark through much of the night. Single-brooded, flying in late June and July, inhabiting open woodland and parkland with mature oaks. A very local species, fluctuating in frequency from year to year, and occurring mainly in Surrey, Middlesex, Hertfordshire, Berkshire, Essex, and Northamptonshire.

Larva. April to early June on oak, hiding during the day in a tent of spun leaves. Overwinters as an egg.

Lesser-spotted Pinion
Cosmia affinis Linnaeus
Plate **36** : *24*

Similar species. *C. diffinis*, pl. **36**, has white costal spots. *C. pyralina*, pl. **36**, has the forewing broader, with a more arched costa, and the hindwing paler, without a dark border.

Imago. 28–35 mm. Resident. Comes to sugar, especially when applied to leaves, and to light. Single-brooded, flying from mid-July to late August, inhabiting woodland, commons, hedgerows, etc. Locally widespread in Wales and the southern half of England, ranging northeastwards to Yorkshire, and northwestwards to Cumbria. In Ireland its existence as a resident requires confirmation.

Larva. Late April to early June on English elm and wych elm. Overwinters as an egg.

White-spotted Pinion
Cosmia diffinis Linnaeus
Plate **36** : *25*

Similar species. Both *C. affinis* and *C. pyralina*, pl. **36**, lack the white costal spots.

Imago. 29–36 mm. Resident. Comes regularly to light and sugar. Single-brooded, flying from late July to mid-September, inhabiting woodland, commons, riversides, hedgerows, etc. A local and generally uncommon species, formerly sporadically distributed in the southern half of Britain; but now very much scarcer as the indirect result of Dutch elm disease.

Larva. April to early June on English elm and wych elm. Overwinters as an egg.

The Dun-bar
Cosmia trapezina Linnaeus
Plate **36** : *27–31*

Variation. Ground colour variable over much of its range, varying from pale ochreous-brown to reddish-ochreous or olive-brown. Two recurrent, but uncommon, forms are ab. *nigra* Tutt (fig 30) which has the forewing black, with pale cross-lines; and ab. *radiofasciata* Teich (fig 31) which has the central area between the antemedian and postmedian lines black.

Imago. 28–38 mm. Resident. Comes readily to sugar and light, and sometimes the flowers of ragwort and other woodland plants. Single-brooded, flying from mid-July to mid-September, inhabiting woodland, parkland, hedgerows, etc. Generally distributed and common in England, Wales, Ireland and the southern half of Scotland. Elsewhere in Scotland it is found locally as far north as Ross-shire; also recorded from the Inner Hebrides and Orkney.

Larva. April to early June on a wide variety of trees and shrubs, including, elm, oak, birch, hazel, hawthorn, sallow, and maple. It also has a voracious appetite for the larvae of other species of lepidoptera.
Overwinters as an egg.

Lunar-spotted Pinion
Cosmia pyralina Denis & Schiffermüller
Plate **36** : *26*

Similar species. *C. affinis*, pl. **36** and text. *C. diffinis*, pl. **36** and text.

Imago. 29–34 mm. Resident. Comes regularly to light and sugar, usually in small numbers. Single-brooded, flying from mid-July to mid-August, inhabiting woodland, parkland, and hedgerows. Widely distributed and not uncommon over much of the southern half of Britain, ranging as far north as Lancashire and Lincolnshire.

Larva. April to early June on English elm, wych elm, hawthorn, blackthorn, and apple.
Overwinters as an egg.

The Saxon
Hyppa rectilinea Esper
Plate **36** : *15*

Similar species. *Lacanobia w-latinum*, pl. **29**

Imago. 38–44 mm. Resident. Comes freely to sugar, and also to light. Single-brooded, flying from late May to early July, inhabiting open woodland and moorland. Widespread and locally common over much of central and northern Scotland, ranging locally southwards to Dumfriesshire and Berwickshire; and over the English border to Northumberland and Cumbria. In Ireland it is found regularly in the Killarney district of Co. Kerry.

Larva. Feeds from late July to October on sallow, bramble, raspberry, bearberry, and, in captivity, on knotgrass.
Overwinters as a full-grown larva in a silken hibernaculum on the ground.

Dark Arches
Apamea monoglypha Hufnagel
Plate **37** : *1–3*

Variation. Melanic forms occur commonly in the northern half of Britain, and less frequently throughout the rest of this species' range.

Similar species. *A. zeta assimilis*, pl. **37** and text. *A. oblonga*, pl. **37** and text.

Imago. 46–54 mm. Resident. Comes readily to light, sugar, and the flowers of red valerian, *Buddleia*, marram, and other grasses and rushes. Mainly single-brooded, flying from June to August, except in southern England where a partial second generation occurs in most years during September and October. Generally distributed and common throughout the British Isles.

Larva. August to June, feeding on the upper roots and stem-bases of cock's-foot and other grasses.
Overwinters as a larva.

Light Arches
Apamea lithoxylaea Denis & Schiffermüller
Plate **37** : *9*

Similar species. *A. sublustris*, pl. **37**, is smaller in size, has the forewing more reddish-ochreous, and the hindwing darker, with usually a distinct postmedian line.

Imago. 44–50 mm. Resident. Comes readily to sugar and various flowers, and also in small numbers to light. Single-brooded, flying from late June to early August, inhabiting rough grassy places. A generally common species found throughout the British Isles, except in Shetland.

Larva. Autumn to spring, probably on grasses.
Overwinters as a larva.

Reddish Light Arches
Apamea sublustris Esper
Plate **37** : *10*

Similar species. *A. lithoxylaea*, pl. **37** and text.

Imago. 42–48 mm. Resident. Comes regularly to sugar and light. Single-brooded, flying in June and July, inhabiting downland, sandhills, breckland, and rough grassy places. Widespread and locally common in the southern half of England, ranging sporadically over the rest of Britain as far north as Cumbria and Co. Durham. Locally widespread in Ireland.

Larva. Unknown in the wild; probably feeds from autumn to spring at the roots of grasses.
Overwinters as a larva.

The Exile
Apamea zeta marmorata Zetterstedt
(*maillardi exulis* Lefebvre)
(*exulis exulis* auctt.)
Plate **37** : *4–5*

Variation. Overall appearance varies from ochreous-grey to blackish-brown, with the colour of the paler cross-lines ranging from whitish-ochreous or golden yellow to dull reddish-brown.

Similar species. *A. monoglypha* has the forewing longer, narrower, more pointed at apex, and the subterminal line with prominent ⋛-mark. *Blepharita adusta*, pl. **33**, has the forewing with dark subreniform bar, and subterminal line with ⋛-mark.

Imago. 42–51 mm. Resident. Comes regularly to light and sugar. Single-brooded, flying in July and August, inhabiting mountain and peat moorlands. Well established and locally common on Shetland.

A. zeta assimilis Doubleday, **Northern Arches**, pl. **37** : 6. Differs from the typical race by its smaller average size (38–47 mm), and its much darker coloration. A local species well established in the Scottish Highlands (Inverness-shire, Perthshire, Aberdeenshire, Morayshire and Ross-shire). Also recorded from Stirlingshire, Isle of Arran, and Orkney, and probably to be found locally if looked for throughout the rest of northern and western Scotland. There is a single record from the Kielder Forest, Northumberland, in 1992.

Larva. The feral larva is unknown in Britain. It probably feeds from autumn to spring on the roots and stems of moorland grasses, possibly living for two or three years. Both alpine meadow-grass (*Poa alpina*) and purple moor-grass have been suggested as British foodplants.

Crescent Striped

Apamea oblonga Haworth
(*abjecta* Hübner)
Plate **37** : 7

Variation. The specimen illustrated is intermediate between the commoner obscurely marked typical form and the well-marked ab. *abjecta* Hübner.

Similar species. *Sideridis albicolon*, pl. **29** and text. *Mamestra brassicae*, pl. **29** and text.

Imago. 42–50 mm. Resident. Comes to light, sugar, and the flowers of ragwort, marram, and other plants. Single-brooded, flying from late June to early August, inhabiting salt-marshes, tidal river-banks, brackish ditches, and fenland. Widespread and locally common in suitable coastal localities in southern and eastern England from Hampshire and the Isle of Wight to Southeast Yorkshire. Also established at low density in the East Anglian fenland, and casually reported from many widely separated sites throughout England and Wales. Rare in Ireland, with old records from Cos Antrim, Louth, Waterford, Down, and Dublin.

Larva. September to June on the roots and stem-bases of saltmarsh-grass (*Puccinellia* spp.) and red fescue (*Festuca rubra*).
Overwinters as a larva.

Clouded-bordered Brindle

Apamea crenata Hufnagel
(*rurea* Fabricius)
Plate **37** : 11–12

Variation. Ab. *combusta* Haworth (fig 12) is one of several subtly different melanic forms found in varying frequency throughout this species' range.

Imago. 36–44 mm. Resident. Frequently seen at dusk visiting the flowers of various plants and grasses; also comes regularly to sugar and light. Single-brooded, flying from late May to mid-July, inhabiting woodland rides and clearings, fenland, downland, moorland, etc. Widespread and generally common throughout the British Isles.

Larva. August to April on cock's-foot and other grasses. Overwinters as a larva, feeding during mild weather.

Clouded Brindle

Apamea epomidion Haworth
(*characterea* Hübner)
(*hepatica* auctt.)
Plate **37** : 17

Similar species. *Lacanobia thalassina*, pl. **29**.

Imago. 40–46 mm. Resident. Comes readily to sugar, and regularly to light in small numbers. Single-brooded, flying from mid-June to mid-July, inhabiting woodland, parkland, and gardens. Widespread and fairly common over much of England and Wales, ranging northwards to southern Scotland (Clyde Valley). Widely distributed, but scarce, in Ireland.

Larva. August to early March on various grasses. Overwinters as a larva, feeding during mild weather.

Scarce Brindle

Apamea lateritia Hufnagel
Plate **37** : 16

Similar species. *Polia bombycina*, pl. **29**.

Imago. 42–52 mm. Suspected immigrant. Comes to light. Single-brooded on the Continent, flying from June to August. The twelve published British records are; Porthkerry, Glamorgan, *c.* 1887; West Norwood, South London, on 17.vii.1972; Bexley, Kent, on 18.vii. 1972; six specimens from Dovercourt, Essex, suggesting a possible temporary local establishment, on 24.vii. 1985, 10 & 24.vii.1987, 8 & 16.vii.1989, 22.vii.1990; Spurn, Yorkshire, on 17.vii.1991; and Norwick, Shetland, on 11 & 12.viii.1995. Abroad it is resident in almost every other European country.

Larva. *September to May on the roots of grasses. Overwinters as a larva.

The Confused

Apamea furva britannica Cockayne
Plate **37** : 14

Similar species. *A. remissa* f. *obscura*, pl. **37**, is browner in colour; costa curved towards apex; dorsum without scale-tuft near base; subterminal pale line irregular, frequently broken, and strongly indented in the middle; and underside of forewing without conspicuous dark, postmedian line. (See text fig 44.) *Mamestra brassicae*, pl. **29** and text.

Imago. 34–42 mm. Resident. Comes to light, sugar, and the flowers of red valerian, ragwort, thistles, and other plants. Single-brooded, flying in July and August, inhabiting mountain moorland, sandhills, and rocky places by the sea. Widely distributed and not uncommon in Scotland, the Hebrides, the Northern Isles, northern England, much of Wales, and parts of the Midlands. It also occurs near Dover and Folkestone, Kent; and very locally in southwest England. Widely distributed, but very local, in Ireland.

Larva. September to June on the upper roots and stem-bases of rough meadow-grass (*Poa trivialis*) and wood meadow-grass.
Overwinters as a larva.

Dusky Brocade
Apamea remissa Hübner
(*obscura* Haworth)
Plate **37** : *18–20*

Variation. F. *submissa* Treitschke (fig 19) is a common form, intermediate in appearance between the less common typical form (fig 20), and the commonest form, f. *obscura* Haworth (fig 18).
Similar species. *A. furva*, pl. **37** and text. *Discestra trifolii*, pl. **28**, has the ground colour of forewing paler; the lower half of the reniform stigma marked with blackish-brown, and contrasting with the pale orbicular stigma; and the light-coloured basal area of the hindwing contrasting strongly with the dark greyish-brown terminal shade. *Sideridis albicolon*, pl. **29** and text. *Mamestra brassicae*, pl. **29** and text. *Lacanobia contigua*, pl. **29**. *L. w-latinum*, pl. **29**. *L. thalassina*, pl. **29**. *L. suasa*, pl. **29**.
Imago. 36–42 mm. Resident. Comes readily to light, also attracted to the flowers of various plants and grasses, and sugar. Single-brooded, flying in June and July, inhabiting open woodland, marshes, downland, commons, and other grassy places. Generally distributed and usually common throughout the British Isles, including the Hebrides and Orkney.
Larva. Autumn to spring on the seeds and leaves of various grasses.
Overwinters as a larva, feeding during mild weather.

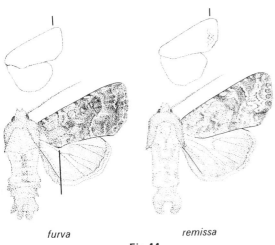

furva   *remissa*

Fig 44

Small Clouded Brindle
Apamea unanimis Hübner
Plate **37** : *13*

Similar species. *Mesapamea secalis*, pl. **38** and text.
Imago. 30–38 mm. Resident. Comes freely to sugar, and in small numbers to light. Single-brooded, flying from late May to early July, inhabiting fenland, damp woodland, and other marshy places. Locally widespread in England, Wales, southern Scotland (as far north as Aberdeenshire), and the northern half of Ireland.
Larva. Feeds from late July to October on various grasses, including the wild and garden varieties of reed canary-grass (ribbon grass).
Overwinters as a full-grown larva, frequently under loose bark. In March or April it awakens from hibernation and pupates underground.

Union Rustic
Apamea pabulatricula Brahm
Plate **37** : *24*

Similar species. The lighter and variegated forms of *Mesapamea secalis*, pl. **38**.
Imago. 32–38 mm. Formerly resident, possibly extinct. Flies from dusk onwards, and comes freely to sugar, and occasionally to light. Single-brooded, occurring from mid-July to mid-August, inhabiting mature woodland. During the early part of this century this species was to be found locally, but not uncommonly, in south Yorkshire, Lincolnshire, and on the Lincolnshire/Nottinghamshire border, but it has not been recorded from these counties since 1919. There are also old records from Renfrewshire, Norfolk, Cumberland, Cheshire, Shropshire, Leicestershire, Suffolk, and Glamorgan; and a relatively recent one from Bushey, Hertfordshire, in August 1935.
Larva. *September to May on various species of grasses. Overwinters as a larva.

Large Nutmeg
Apamea anceps Denis & Schiffermüller
(*sordida* Borkhausen)
(*infesta* Ochsenheimer)
Plate **37** : *8*

Similar species. *A sordens*, pl. **37**, has a distinct black basal streak. *Discestra trifolii*, pl. **28**.
Imago. 38–44 mm. Resident. Comes readily to sugar and light. Single-brooded, flying from early June to mid-July, inhabiting woodland rides, clearings and borders, downland, and other grassy places. Widespread and sometimes locally common in the southern half of England, except the southwest where it is local, less frequent and mainly coastal. Elsewhere in Britain it is found locally in North Wales, parts of the Midlands, and northeast England. In Ireland there are two old records from Co. Dublin, and a recent one from Glengariff, Co. Cork, in 1950.
Larva. August to April, at first on the flowers and

seeds, and then on the leaves of grasses. Overwinters as a larva.

Rustic Shoulder-knot

Apamea sordens Hufnagel
(*basilinea* Denis & Schiffermüller)
Plate **37** : *21*

Variation. Geographically variable with the darker and less ochreous forms occurring more frequently in northern and western districts of Britain and Ireland.
Similar species. *A. anceps*, pl. **37** and text.
Imago. 34–42 mm. Resident. Comes freely to light and sugar. Single-brooded, flying in May and June, frequenting a wide variety of grassy habitats. A widespread and usually common species over much of the British Isles.
Larva. August to March on cock's-foot and other grasses. Overwinters as a larva, feeding during mild weather.

Slender Brindle

Apamea scolopacina Esper
Plate **37** : *15*

Imago. 32–36 mm. Resident. Comes to light, sugar, and the flowers of various woodland plants. Single-brooded, flying from late June to mid-August, inhabiting woodland. Locally widespread over much of England and Wales, ranging northwards to Cumbria and Yorkshire. There is a single record from Hamsterley Forest, Northumberland, in 1986.
Larva. September to May, feeding at first in the stems, and then on the leaves, stem-bases, and flowers of various grasses, such as wood millet (*Milium effusum*), wood mellick (*Melica uniflora*), wood meadow-grass, false brome, quaking-grass (*Briza* spp.), and wood-rush. Overwinters as a larva.

Double Lobed

Apamea ophiogramma Esper
Plate **37** : *22–23*

Variation. A melanic form (fig 23) occurs regularly in small numbers in a few Midland localities, and occasionally elsewhere.
Imago. 32–35 mm. Resident. Flies from dusk onwards, visiting the flowers of common nettle, figwort, ragwort, rushes, and other plants; also comes to light and sugar in moderate numbers. Single-brooded, flying from late June to early August, inhabiting fenland, river-banks, damp woodland, gardens and marshy places. Locally distributed in England, Wales, southern Scotland, northwards to Aberdeenshire and mainly the northern half of Ireland.
Larva. August to early June in the stems of wild and garden varieties of reed canary-grass (ribbon grass), and occasionally reed sweet-grass (*Glyceria maxima*). Overwinters as a larva.

Marbled Minor

Oligia strigilis Linnaeus
Plate **37** : *27–28*

Variation. Melanic forms occur over much of the species' range and predominate in many industrial areas; most are referable to ab. *aethiops* Osthelder.
Similar species. Both *O. versicolor*, pl. **37**, and *O. latruncula*, pl. **37**, are best separated from *O. strigilis* and each other by means of the genitalia. One fairly constant character of *O. strigilis*, apart from its slightly larger size, is the basal part of the postmedian fascia, which is deeply indented with a prominent lobe. (See text fig 45.)
Imago. 24–29 mm. Resident. Comes readily to light and sugar. Single-brooded, flying from late May to early July, frequenting a wide variety of grassy habitats. Widely distributed and common in England and Wales; widespread, but less frequent in Scotland. Distribution in Ireland uncertain, with confirmed records from only Cos Clare, Dublin, and Wexford.
Larva. Full grown in April or May, feeding internally in cock's-foot, reed canary-grass, and other grasses. Overwinters probably as a larva.

Rufous Minor

Oligia versicolor Borkhausen
Plate **37** : *29–31*

Variation. Ab. *aethiops* Heydemann (fig 31) is a widespread, but not common, melanic form.
Similar species. *O. strigilis*, pl. **37** and text. *O. latruncula*, pl. **37** and text.
Imago. 23–28 mm. Resident. Comes readily to light and occasionally to sugar. Single-brooded, flying from mid-June to mid-July, inhabiting woodland rides and clearings, sea-cliffs, and other grassy places. Widely distributed in England and Wales; also recorded locally in southern Scotland. Distribution in Ireland uncertain, with confirmed records from only Cos Clare, Galway, Kerry, and Tyrone.
Larva. Apparently unknown in the wild or in captivity; probably feeds internally in grasses from autumn to spring.

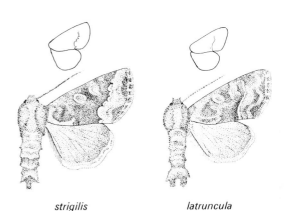

strigilis   *latruncula*

Fig 45

Tawny Marbled Minor
Oligia latruncula Denis & Schiffermüller
Plate **37** : *25–26*

Variation. The melanic f. *unicolor* Tutt is found over much of the species' range, and in many English localities represents the entire population.

Similar species. *O. strigilis*, pl. **37** and text. *O. latruncula*, pl. **37**, usually has a bronzy appearance and indistinct stigmata; it also lacks the vinous-red and reddish-brown tints often present in *O. versicolor*.

Imago. 24–27 mm. Resident. Comes readily to light and sugar. Single-brooded, flying from late May to early July, frequenting a wide variety of grassy places. Widespread and generally common over much of the British Isles.

Larva. Full grown in April or May, feeding internally in various grasses.
Overwinters probably as a larva.

Middle-barred Minor
Oligia fasciuncula Haworth
Plate **37** : *32–33*

Similar species. Most forms of *Mesoligia furuncula*, pl. **38**, lacks the white-edged postmedian line near the dorsum.

Imago. 22–26 mm. Resident. Occasionally flies in sunshine, but the regular flight takes place from dusk onwards, when it comes freely to sugar and the flowers of ragwort and other plants and grasses, and also in moderate numbers to light. Single-brooded, flying in June and July, frequenting a wide variety of damp and marshy habitats. A frequent to common species found throughout the British Isles.

Larva. August to May on the leaves of various grasses.
Overwinters as a larvae.

Cloaked Minor
Mesoligia furuncula Denis & Schiffermüller
Plate **38** : *6–14*

Variation. A very variable species with a number of contrasting forms occurring in most localities. A uniformly pale ochreous form (fig 11) occurs on the sandhills on the west coast of Ireland; and a similar form (fig 12) is found on the sandhills of Northumberland together with ab. *latistriata* Hoffmeyer & Knudson (fig 14), a pale form with a distinct black dorsal streak.

Similar species. *M. literosa*, pl. **37** and text. *Oligia fasciuncula*, pl. **37** and text. Male *Photedes captiuncula*, pl. **38**.

Imago. 22–28 mm. Resident. Occasionally seen flying in sunshine, but more usually found after dark feeding on the flowers of marram, ragwort, and other plants; also comes to sugar and light. Single-brooded, flying from late July to early September, inhabiting sandhills, sea-cliffs, downland, grassy embankments, roadside verges, etc. A generally common species, with a marked preference for coastal habitats, found over the greater part of the British Isles, except the Outer Hebrides, Orkney and Shetland.

Larva. Full grown from late May to late June in the stems of various grasses, such as tufted hair-grass, sheep's-fescue, tall fescue, and false oat-grass.
Overwinters probably as a larva.

Rosy Minor
Mesoligia literosa Haworth
Plate **37** : *34–36*

Variation. The melanic f. *aethalodes* Richardson (fig 35) is the only form found in many localities in the Midlands. In other industrial districts, such as the London area, the specimens are often dull-coloured and obscurely marked. Other local forms include a pale greyish variety (fig 36) found on the coastal sandhills at Camber, East Sussex.

Similar species. *M. furuncula*, pl. **38** is usually smaller, without any reddish coloration.

Imago. 25–30 mm. Resident. Comes to light, sugar, and the flowers of ragwort, marram, and other plants. Single-brooded, flying from mid-July to late August, inhabiting sandhills, chalk sea-cliffs, marshes, commons, waste ground, and other grassy places. Widely distributed and not uncommon, especially in coastal localities, in England, Wales, Ireland and mainland Scotland. Also recorded from the Isle of Arran and the Inner Hebrides.

Larva. September to early June in the roots and stems of various grasses, including cock's-foot, marram, lyme-grass, false oat-grass, sheep's-fescue, and glaucous sedge. It is also said to feed in wheat, oats, and other cereals.
Overwinters as a larva.

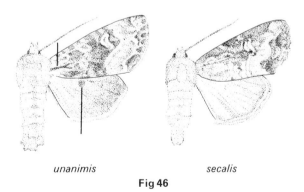

unanimis   *secalis*

Fig 46

Common Rustic
Mesapamea secalis Linnaeus
Plate **38** : *1, 2 & 4*

Variation. Extremely variable both in ground colour, which may range from pale grey through many shades of reddish-brown to black, and in the extent of the dark transverse markings.

Similar species. *Apamea unanimis*, pl. **37**, has forewing with dark basal streak, and hindwing paler with a conspicuous discal spot. (See text fig 46.) *M. didyma*, pl. **38** and text.

Imago. 31–36 mm. Resident. Comes readily to light, sugar, and the flowers of ragwort, *Buddleia*, rushes, flowering grasses, etc. Single-brooded, flying in July and August, inhabiting a wide variety of grassy habitats. A common to abundant species found throughout the British Isles.

Larva. Autumn to May in the stems of cock's-foot, tall fescue, tufted hair-grass, creeping soft-grass (*Holcus mollis*), other grasses and hairy wood-rush; also found in wheat and other cereals.

Overwinters as a larva.

Lesser Common Rustic

Mesapamea didyma Esper

(*secalella* Remm)

Plate **38** : *3–5*

Variation. Similar to that found in *M. secalis* although the intense black examples showing a bright white reniform stigma are invariably *M. didyma*.

Similar species. Only reliably separated from the usually larger *M. secalis*, pl. **38**, by means of the genitalia.

Imago. 28–32 mm. Resident. Comes readily to light, sugar and flowers. Single-brooded, flying in July and August, inhabiting the same type of habitats as the previous species, although perhaps emerging a few days earlier. A fairly common species throughout much of the British Isles.

Larva. Autumn to May in the stems of grasses.

Overwinters as a larva.

Least Minor

Photedes captiuncula expolita Stainton

Plate **38** : *15–16*

Similar species. *Mesoligia furuncula*, pl. **38**.

Imago. 16–19 mm. Resident. Flies (mostly males) in sunshine, usually during the afternoon. Single-brooded, flying from mid-June to early August, inhabiting limestone hills and dales, scrubland, and grassy hollows on the tops of sea-cliffs. A local species found in Cumbria (Arnside, Warton, near Kendal), Yorkshire (Grassington and Cowbeck), Co. Durham (Blackhall Rocks to Beacon Point, Castle Eden Dene, Cassop Vale), and Northumberland (Morpeth district).

P. captiuncula tincta Kane, pl. **38** : *17–18*. A strongly marked reddish-brown race locally common in the Burren district of Cos Clare and Galway, and on similar terrain in Co. Mayo.

Larva. Autumn to late May in the stems of glaucous sedge.

Overwinters as a larva.

Small Dotted Buff

Photedes minima Haworth

(*arcuosa* Haworth)

Plate **38** : *23–24*

Similar species. Pale form of *P. fluxa*, pl. **38**.

Imago. Male 25–30 mm, female 20–24 mm. Resident. The males fly actively at dusk, and both sexes (especially the males) come to light. Single-brooded, flying from late June to early August. It inhabits woodland rides and clearings, damp meadows, and marshy places; and in such localities may be found, sometimes commonly, over the greater part of the British Isles.

Larva. August to early June in the stems of tufted hair-grass.

Overwinters as a larva.

Morris's Wainscot

Photedes morrisii morrisii Dale

Plate **38** : *29*

Similar species. *P. extrema*, pl. **38**, is smaller, and has the forewing ochreous without a white fringe.

Imago. 26–34 mm. Resident. May be found after dark flying around or resting upon its foodplant; also comes sparingly to light and sugar. Single-brooded, flying from late June to mid-July, inhabiting grassy slopes and undercliffs. Very local along the coast of southwest England from Charmouth, Dorset, to Sidmouth, Devon. *P. morrisii bondii* Knaggs, **Bond's Wainscot**, pl. **38** : *30*. This race is on average slightly larger than the typical form, and has a faint ochreous suffusion over both forewing and hindwing. Even more local than the last race, and confined to a short stretch of rough grassy cliff at Folkestone, Kent, where worryingly it has not been noted for several years.

Larva. August to early June in the stems of tall fescue.

Overwinters as a larva.

The Concolorous

Photedes extrema Hübner

(*concolor* Guenée)

Plate **38** : *28*

Similar species. Pale form of *P. fluxa*, pl. **38**, has the hindwing paler than the forewing, and the reniform stigma more clearly defined. *P. morrisii*, pl. **38** and text.

Imago. 26–28 mm. Resident. Flies at dusk, and again after midnight; occasionally found at rest on its foodplant, but more usually obtained at light. Single-brooded, flying from mid-June to mid-July, inhabiting clearings in marshy woodland, and marginal fenland. A very local species found as a resident in Huntingdonshire (Woodwalton Fen, Holme Fen and Monks Wood), in several woods in Northamptonshire, and in a single locality in mid-Lincolnshire. It is occasionally reported elsewhere in southern England and these are possibly the result of migration. The more recent of these records are at Eastbourne, Sussex, in 1957; two at

Thorpeness, Suffolk, on 12.vi.1966 and another on 2.viii.1974; at Dungeness, Kent, on 2.vii.1976; Bradwell-on-Sea, Essex, on 14.vi.1980; Rye, West Sussex, on 4.vii.1985; Bradwell-on-Sea, on 30.vi.1986; Greatstone, Kent, on 1.vi.1993; Dungeness, on 10.vi.1993; Sandwich, Kent, on 1.vii.1994; and Kingsgate, Kent, on 13.vi.1997.
Larva. August to May in the stems of purple small-reed and wood small-reed.
Overwinters as a larva.

Lyme Grass
Photedes elymi Treitschke
Plate **38** : *19–20*

Variation. Specimens well marked with blackish-brown (fig 20) occur most frequently in industrially influenced localities.
Imago. 34–38 mm. Resident. It may be readily found after dark at rest on its foodplant; also comes sparingly to light. Single-brooded, occurring from late June to mid-August, inhabiting coastal sandhills. It is found locally in Suffolk, Norfolk, Lincolnshire, Yorkshire, Co. Durham, Northumberland, Fifeshire, Angus, Kincardineshire and Morayshire. It also occurs at Camber, East Sussex, where it was probably introduced with the foodplant.
Larva. Full grown in late May and early June, in the lower part of the stems of lyme-grass.
Overwinters probably as a larva.

Mere Wainscot
Photedes fluxa Hübner
(*hellmanni* Eversmann)
Plate **38** : *31–32*

Variation. Variable in most localities, with the forewing colour ranging from whitish-ochreous to reddish-brown.
Similar species. *P. extrema*, pl. **38** and text. *P. minima*, pl. **38**.
Imago. 26–30 mm. Resident. May be obtained from dusk onwards when it flies actively over its foodplant; also comes to light and sugar. Single-brooded, occurring in July and August, inhabiting damp open woodland, marginal fenland, and other marshy places. Locally well established in Huntingdonshire, Cambridgeshire, West Suffolk, Northamptonshire, Bedfordshire, and Lincolnshire; also found less frequently elsewhere in the south and west Midlands, its range extending to Buckinghamshire, Gloucestershire and Yorkshire. Single colonies also exist near Sandwich, Kent; near Havant, Hampshire; Pagham, West Sussex, and Portskewett, Monmouthshire. Casual specimens have occurred throughout southern England.
Larva. Full grown from mid-May to mid-June in the stems of wood small-reed.
Overwinters probably as a larva.

Small Wainscot
Photedes pygmina Haworth
(*fulva* Hübner)
Plate **38** : *25–27*

Variation. Very variable in most localities, with the forewing colour ranging from whitish-ochreous, through various shades of greyish-ochreous to reddish-brown.
Imago. 23–29 mm. Resident. May be found from dusk onwards flying around or resting upon its foodplants; also comes to light. Single-brooded, occurring in August and September, inhabiting damp woodland and commons, fenland, boggy moorland, and other marshy places. Generally distributed and fairly common throughout the British Isles.
Larva. Early spring to July in the stems of various sedges, rushes and grasses.
Overwinters as an egg, hatching in January or February in captivity.

Fenn's Wainscot
Photedes brevilinea Fenn
Plate **38** : *21–22*

Variation. Ab. *sinelinea* Farn (fig 22) is a fairly frequent form in which the basal streak is absent.
Imago. 30–38 mm. Resident. Comes to light and sugar. Single-brooded, flying from mid-July to mid-August, inhabiting fenland reedy ditches. A local species confined to East Anglia, but usually not uncommon where found. It occurs in the Norfolk Broads (Ranworth, Hickling, Martham, Wheatfen, Barton, etc), and along the Suffolk coast (Benacre, Potter's Bridge, Southwold, Walberswick and Dunwich).
Larva. April to June in the stems of common reed.
Overwinters as an egg.

Dusky Sallow
Eremobia ochroleuca Denis & Schiffermüller
Plate **38** : *33*

Imago. 34–37 mm. Resident. Comes readily to light, sugar, and a wide variety of flowering plants, such as knapweed, ragwort, *Buddleia*, marram, teasel, scabious, and marjoram. Single-brooded, flying in late July and August, inhabiting downland, breckland, waste ground, and other grassy places. Widely distributed and moderately common in southern and eastern England, but rarely ranging beyond Dorset in the west, and Yorkshire in the north.
Larva. May to early July on the flowers and seeds of cock's-foot, couch, meadow oat-grass (*Helictotrichon pratense*), quaking-grass (*Briza media*), and other grasses.
Overwinters as an egg.

Flounced Rustic
Luperina testacea Denis & Schiffermüller
Plate **38** : *34–39*

Variation. A very variable species, especially in coastal localities. Some local variation does occur, with certain forms predominating, but because of variability of this species, these subtle races are difficult to define.

Similar species. *L. nickerlii*, pls **38** & **43**, has the texture of forewing smooth and silky, the reniform stigma usually edged with white, the orbicular stigma small and indistinct, and the hindwing pure white and silky in texture. *L. dumerilii*, pls **38** & **43** and text.

Imago. 32–40 mm. Resident. May be found after dark at rest on grass stems, and also at light. Single-brooded, flying in August and September, frequenting a wide variety of grassy habitats. Widespread and common in England and Wales; widespread, but local and less frequent in Scotland and the Hebrides; and widespread and common, but mainly coastal, in Ireland.

Larva. September to June on the roots and stem-bases of various grasses (*Agropyron* spp., *Festuca* spp., etc), and sometimes wheat and other cereals.
Overwinters as a larva.

Sandhill Rustic

Luperina nickerlii nickerlii Freyer
Plates **38** : *42–45* & **43** : *28–30*

Similar species. *L. testacea*, pl. **38** and text.

Imago. 32–42 mm. Comes to light and may be found after dark on the stems of their respective foodplants. Single-brooded, flying from late July to early September. *L. nickerlii demuthi* Goater & Skinner, pls **38** : *42* & **43** : *28–30*. A very variable race inhabiting saltmarshes and occurring not uncommonly along the coast of southeast England from Faversham, Kent, northwards through Essex to Orford Ness, Suffolk. A specimen closest in appearance to this race was recorded at Bude, Cornwall, on 6.viii.1990. Another specimen, race unspecified, was reported at Farringdon, Hampshire, on 22.ix.1950. *L. nickerlii gueneei* Doubleday, pl. **38** : *43*. A pale ochreous-grey race found locally on coastal sandhills in North Wales, from Point of Air, Flintshire to Newborough, Anglesey; and in Lancashire at Formby and in the vicinity of St Annes-on-Sea. *L. nickerlii leechi* Goater, pl. **38** : *44*. This race has the forewing silvery-grey with a blackish-brown central band. Extremely local and confined to a small sand-shingle beach in south Cornwall, where it was discovered in 1974. *L. nickerlii knilli* Boursin, pl. **38** : *45*. A dark brown race found locally on grassy sea-cliffs along the southern coast of the Dingle Peninsula, Co. Kerry. This species was not known to occur in Ireland until 1962.

Larva. September to early July in the stem bases and among the rhizomes of their respective foodplant. Ssp. *demuthi* on common saltmarsh grass (*Puccinellia maritima*); both ssp. *gueneei* and ssp. *leechi* on sand couch; and ssp. *knilli* probably on red fescue (*Festuca rubra*).
Overwinters as a larva.

Dumeril's Rustic

Luperina dumerilii Duponchel
Plates **38** : *40* & **43** : *33*

Variation. The unicolorous ab. *desyllesi* Boisduval, pl. **43** : *31*, is not the form most usually recorded in Britain, but is the one most likely to be misidentified.

Similar species. Both *L. testacea*, pl. **38**, and *L. nickerlii*, pls **38** & **43**, have a slightly narrower forewing; a faintly curved, not straight, costa; a less oblique postmedian line where it meets the dorsum and an orbicular stigma which is roundish and not obliquely ovate.

Imago. 30–36 mm. Immigrant. Most of the specimens recorded in Britain were taken at light in late August and September. These are two at Portland, Dorset, in September 1858; three at Portland in 1859; three at Freshwater, Isle of Wight, in 1859; Brighton, Sussex, in 1859; Dover, Kent, on 21.ix.1901; Buxted, Sussex, on 10.ix.1936; Portland on 22.ix.1938; Maidencombe, Devon, on 5.ix.1945; Swanage, Dorset, on 18.ix.1949; Freshwater in September 1949; Eastbourne, Sussex, on 20.viii.1953; Arkley, Hertfordshire, on 26.ix.1953; Appledore, Kent, on 17.ix.1954; two at East Preston, Sussex, on 11.viii.1956; near Salcombe, Devon, on 10.ix.1959; Freshwater on 16.ix.1961; Lizard, Cornwall, on 16.ix.1961; Start Point, Devon, on 17.ix.1961; Freshwater on 18.ix.1961 and 24.ix.1962; Royston, Hertfordshire, on 16.ix.1974; Lizard on 7.ix.1983; Eypes Mouth, Dorset, on 31.viii.1992; Portland on 14.ix.1996; and Peacehaven, East Sussex, on 3.ix.1997. *Author's note.* The specimens previously reported from Exmouth, Devon, in 1938 and from Stroud, Gloucestershire, in 1953 were erroneous. Abroad its range includes France and southeast Europe.

Larva. *Autumn to spring in the roots of grasses.
Overwinters as a larva.

Scarce Arches

Luperina zollikoferi Freyer
Plate **38** : *41*

Variation. The plain form (fig 41) represents most British specimens, but at least two examples are referable to ab. *internigrata* Warren, which has the discal and outer areas of the forewing well marked with blackish-brown.

Similar species. *Apamea monoglypha*, pl. **37**. *Nonagria typhae*, pl. **39**.

Imago. 42–52 mm. Immigrant. Seventeen specimens have been recorded in Britain during the autumn, mostly at light or sugar; these are: Deal, Kent, in October, 1867; Inverurie, Aberdeenshire, in September, 1871; Middlesbrough, Yorkshire, on 26.ix.1903; Norwich, Norfolk, on 4.ix.1905; Methley, Yorkshire, on 12.viii.1910; Horsham, Sussex, on 28.ix.1912; Rye, Sussex, on 15.ix.1934; six, Dungeness, Kent, from 15 to 17.ix.1934; Braunton, North Devon, on 17.ix.1934; Kirkstall (near Leeds), Yorkshire, on 15.viii.1939; Milden, Angus, on 13.ix.1968; and Climping, West Sussex, on 2.ix.1996. Abroad it occurs in Russia, Hungary, and western Asia.

Larva. *May to June on low plants.

Large Ear
Amphipoea lucens Freyer
Plate **38** : *48*

Variation. Colour of forewing ranges from olive-brown to deep reddish-brown, with the reniform stigma often orange-red, but frequently yellow or white.

Similar species. This and the following three species are so variable in size and wing pattern that they can usually only be separated by examining their genitalia. A useful but not foolproof guide to separate *A. lucens* and *A. fucosa paludis* from each other, and from *A. crinanensis* and *A. oculea*, is provided by the underside characters on the hindwings: *A. lucens* has a conspicuous discal spot and a thick, wavy postmedian line; *A. fucosa paludis* is unmarked or has a weak, slightly wavy postmedian line; and both *A. crinanensis* and *A. oculea* have a thin, evenly curved postmedian line. (See text fig 47.) In central southern and southeast England, where both *A. lucens* and *A. crinanensis* are absent, *A. oculea*, which has a broader, usually shorter, and rich reddish-brown forewing, is readily distinguished from *A. fucosa paludis*, which has a narrower, usually longer, and paler forewing, with a narrower-looking reniform stigma.

Imago. 30–36 mm. Resident. Comes to light, usually in small numbers, but is strongly attracted to the flowers of heather, rushes, and other plants. Single brooded, flying in August and September, inhabiting mainly moorland and mosses. Widely distributed in south-western, western and northern Britain, including parts of the Midlands, the Hebrides, and the Northern Isles. Elsewhere it has been reported from Berkshire and southeast Kent. In Ireland it is widespread, but coastal according to the sparse records.

Larva. May to July in the roots and stem-bases of purple moor-grass and probably other moorland grasses. Overwinters as an egg.

Saltern Ear
Amphipoea fucosa paludis Tutt
Plate **38** : *49*

Variation. Colour of forewing ranges from pale reddish-brown, through various shades of olive, to deep olive-brown. Reniform stigma usually white, but sometimes orange or yellow.

Similar species. See under *A. lucens* (preceding entry).

Imago. 29–35 mm. Resident. Comes readily to light, and is attracted to sugar and the flowers of ragwort, thistles, willowherb, marram, and various rushes. Single-brooded, flying in August and September, inhabiting mainly salt-marshes and coastal sandhills, and less frequently damp commons and wet moorland. A locally common and mainly coastal species sporadically distributed over much of Britain, including the Outer Hebrides, but unrecorded from the Northern Isles. A record from Co. Cork in 1982 appears to be the only record to date from Ireland. In parts of western Scotland it hybridizes with *A. lucens*.

Larva. May to July in the roots and stem-bases of annual meadow-grass and probably other grasses. Overwinters as an egg.

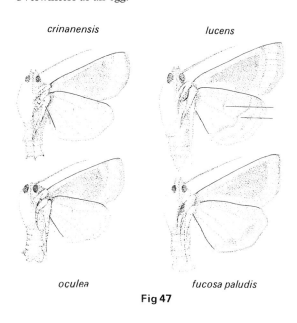

crinanensis   *lucens*

oculea   *fucosa paludis*

Fig 47

Crinan Ear
Amphipoea crinanensis Burrows
Plate **38** : *47*

Variation. Colour of forewing ranges from reddish-ochreous to reddish-brown. Reniform stigma usually orange or red, but sometimes white.

Similar species. See under *A. lucens*.

Imago. 29–35 mm. Resident. Comes regularly to light, and is attracted to the flowers of heather, ragwort, scabious, and other plants. Single-brooded, flying in August and September, inhabiting marshy stream-sides, sandhills, meadows, and moorland. Generally distributed and not uncommon in Ireland, mainland Scotland and the Inner Hebrides. Locally distributed in northern England and the western half of Wales.

Larva. May to July in the stems of yellow iris and probably other plants. Overwinters as an egg.

Ear Moth
Amphipoea oculea Linnaeus
(*nictitans* Linnaeus)
Plate **38** : *46*

Variation. Colour of forewing ranges from reddish-brown to purplish-brown. Reniform stigma most frequently white, but sometimes yellow or orange.

Similar species. See under *A. lucens*.

Imago. 29–34 mm. Resident. Occasionally seen on sunny days visiting the flowers of thistle, ragwort, and various rushes. After dark it is attracted to the same flowers, and also sugar and light. Single-brooded, flying from late July to September. This species frequents a wide variety of habitats, but seems to prefer marshy and damp localities. Widespread and generally not uncommon over much of the British Isles.

Larva. April to June in the stem-bases and roots of tufted hair-grass and other grasses; and also stems of butterbur and probably other plants.

Overwinters as an egg.

Rosy Rustic
Hydraecia micacea Esper
Plate **39** : *5–6*

Variation. Very variable both in size and ground colour, the latter ranging from pale pinkish-grey to dark purplish-brown, with the dark forms predominating in northern Britain and parts of Ireland.

Similar species. *H. petasitis*, pl. **39**, is on average larger, has the forewing broader, darker, and without pinkish colour; and the hindwing much darker.

Imago. 34–50 mm. Resident. Mostly seen at light; to which it comes in moderate numbers. Single-brooded, flying from August to October, inhabiting sea-cliffs, marshes, waste ground, and other weedy places. Generally distributed and common throughout the British Isles.

Larva. May to August on the roots of a variety of low plants, including iris, dock, burdock, plantain, and horse-tail (*Equisetum* spp.); and sometimes cultivated plants such as rhubarb, potato, strawberry, raspberry, and sugar-beet.

Overwinters as an egg.

The Butterbur
Hydraecia petasitis Doubleday
Plate **39** : *2*

Similar species. *H. micacea*, pl. **39** and text.

Imago. 44–50 mm. Resident. May be found after dark flying about its foodplant; also comes readily to light. Single-brooded, occurring in August and early September, inhabiting river-sides and marshy places. A retiring and easily overlooked species, found locally over much of England, parts of Wales, and southern Scotland as far north as Stirlingshire and Angus.

Larva. April to early July, feeding for a short time in the stem, and then in the roots of butterbur.

Overwinters as an egg.

Marsh Mallow Moth
Hydraecia osseola hucherardi Mabille
Plate **39** : *1*

Imago. 40–50 mm. Resident. May be found after dark flying about or resting upon its foodplant; also at light. Single-brooded, flying in September, inhabiting river-banks, ditches, and marshy places. A local species, but usually not uncommon where found, and occurring on the Romney Marsh, southeast Kent and East Sussex; and along the Medway Valley, between Maidstone and Rochester, Kent.

Larva. Early spring to July in the roots of marsh-mallow.

Overwinters as an egg.

Frosted Orange
Gortyna flavago Denis & Schiffermüller
Plate **39** : *4*

Similar species. *G. borelii lunata*, pl. **39**.

Imago. 32–44 mm. Resident. Sometimes found after dark resting upon its foodplants (foxglove, burdock, etc), but more readily obtained at light. Single-brooded, flying from late August to October, inhabiting commons, open woodland, marshes, roadside verges, waste ground, etc. Widespread and fairly common in England and Wales. Locally widespread and less frequent in Ireland and from southern Scotland as far north as Moray.

Larva. April to August in the stems of burdock, foxglove, thistles, and many other wild and cultivated large-stemmed plants.

Overwinters as an egg.

Fisher's Estuarine Moth
Gortyna borelii lunata Freyer
Plate **39** : *3*

Similar species. *G. flavago*, pl. **39**.

Imago. 42–60 mm. Resident. May be found after dark flying about or resting upon its foodplant; also at light. Single-brooded, flying in September and October, inhabiting marshy fields and waste ground. A local species confined to the Walton-on-the-Naze district, Essex, where it was first officially recognized in 1968. However, a reference to a large and pale form of *G. flavago* occurring in the same area appeared in the Victorian County History of Essex in 1903 and may well have referred to *G. borelii*.

Larva. June to August, feeding at first in the stems, and then in the roots of hog's fennel (*Peucedanum officinale*). In captivity it has been reared on cultivated carrot.

Overwinters as an egg.

Burren Green
Calamia tridens occidentalis Cockayne
(*virens* Linnaeus)
Plate **39** : *11*

Imago. 37–42 mm. Resident. It emerges an hour or so after dark and may be found resting on grass stems. It also comes readily to light. Single-brooded, flying in late July and August. Well established and locally common over much of the Burren, Co. Clare, where it was first found in 1949.

Larva. Late spring to June. In captivity it will eat annual meadow-grass and cock's-foot, but the natural foodplant is believed to be blue moor-grass (*Sesleria caerulea*). It feeds in the stems and roots.
Overwinters as an egg.

Haworth's Minor
Celaena haworthii Curtis
Plate **39** : *7*

Imago. 25–32 mm. Resident. The males and occasionally the females fly during the afternoon in sunshine, and after dark come to light. Both sexes are attracted equally to sugar, and the flowers of ragwort, wood-rush, and heather. Single-brooded, flying in August and September, inhabiting fenland, boggy moorland, and other marshy places. Widespread and locally common in the northern half of England, North Wales, Scotland, the Hebrides, the Northern Isles, and Ireland. Also found locally in South Wales, southwest England, North Hampshire, and East Anglia, including the Norfolk Broads.
Larva. Spring to July in the stems of cottongrass (*Eriophorum* spp.) and in some localities in unspecified grasses. Abroad it is stated to feed in rush (*Juncus* spp.) and club-rush (*Scirpus* spp.).
Overwinters as an egg.

The Crescent
Celaena leucostigma leucostigma Hübner
Plate **39** : *8–9*

Variation. Ab. *fibrosa* Hübner (fig 9) is a strongly marked form, and together with intermediate forms is found in both subspecies almost as commonly as the plain typical form (fig 8).
Imago. 37–44 mm. Resident and suspected immigrant. Comes readily to light, sugar, honey-dew, and the flowers of *Juncus*. Single-brooded, flying from late July to early September, inhabiting fenland, boggy moorland, damp woodland, and other marshy places. Widespread, but local, in England, Wales, southern Scotland and Ireland. Most of the few Orkney specimens conform to the typical race and are considered to be immigrants.
C. leucostigma scotica Cockayne, pl. **39** : *10*. A smaller (33–36 mm) and darker race found in the northern half of Scotland, the Hebrides and Orkney.
Larva. March to July, boring the leaves, stems and roots of yellow iris, great fen-sedge, and probably other plants.
Overwinters as an egg.

Bulrush Wainscot
Nonagria typhae Thunberg
Plate **39** : *12–14*

Variation. Ab. *fraterna* Treitschke (fig 14) is a melanic form occurring in small numbers in many localities.
Similar species. *Luperina zollikoferi*, pl. **38**. *Rhizedra lutosa*, pl. **39**.

Imago. 40–54 mm. Resident. Comes sparingly to light. Single-brooded, flying from late July to late September. It inhabits fenland, ditches, ponds, marshy places, etc, but is frequently recorded well away from possible breeding sites. Widespread and locally common in England, Wales, Ireland, and southern Scotland, ranging sporadically northwards to Moray.
Larva. Spring to July in the stems of common reedmace, or 'bulrush' (*Typha latifolia*), and sometimes lesser reedmace, or 'lesser bulrush' (*T. angustifolia*).
Pupa. May be found (head downwards), sometimes commonly, in the new and old stems of reedmace (or 'bulrush') during late July and August.
Overwinters as an egg.

Twin-spotted Wainscot
Archanara geminipuncta Haworth
Plate **39** : *15–16*

Variation. Ground colour variable from pale brown to almost black. One or both of the two white reniform spots may be absent.
Imago. 27–36 mm. Resident. Comes sparingly to light. Single-brooded, flying from early August to mid-September, inhabiting reed-beds. Widespread and locally common in southern and eastern England south of a line from the Severn to the Wash. It is also found locally along the coast of South Wales. In Ireland it has been reported along the Douglas Estuary, Co. Cork.
Larva. May to July in the stems of common reed.
Pupa. May be found (head upwards), sometimes commonly, in the stems of common reed during July and early August.
Overwinters as an egg.

Brown-veined Wainscot
Archanara dissoluta Treitschke
Plate **39** : *17–18*

Variation. The usual form found in Britain is referable to f. *arundineta* Schmidt (fig 17), whereas the blackish typical form (fig 18) is generally local and uncommon.
Similar species. *A. neurica*, pl. **39**, has a white patagial collar, and lacks the discal spots on the underside of both wings. (See text fig 48.)
Imago. 27–33 mm. Resident. Comes freely to light. Single-brooded, flying from late July to early September, inhabiting reed-beds. Locally widespread in southern and eastern England, its range extends westwards to South Devon and Glamorgan; and northwards to South Lancashire and Mid-west Yorkshire.
Larva. April to early July in the stems of common reed.
Pupa. May be found (head downwards), usually sparingly, in the new stems of common reed during July.
Overwinters as an egg.

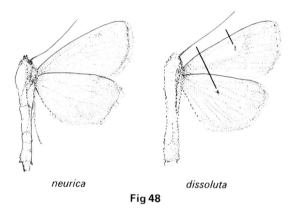

neurica   dissoluta

Fig 48

White-mantled Wainscot
Archanara neurica Hübner
Plate **39** : *19*
Variation. Melanic forms occurred commonly in the now extinct Sussex colonies, but are rarely found elsewhere in Britain.
Similar species. *A. dissoluta*, pl. **39** and text.
Imago. 26–29 mm. Resident. Comes readily to light. Single-brooded, flying in July and early August, inhabiting coastal reed-beds. A local species found not uncommonly on the Suffolk coast, where its better-known localities are Walberswick, Minsmere, Dunwich and Thorpeness. Formerly well established, but local, in the Pevensey Marshes, East Sussex, but not seen since 1946 by which times its original breeding site had been destroyed.
Larva. May to late June in the stems of common reed.
Pupa. Has been obtained (head downwards), rather sparingly, in the old stems of common reed during late June and early July.
Overwinters as an egg.

Webb's Wainscot
Archanara sparganii Esper
Plate **39** : *20–21*
Variation. Very variable in both the ground colour, which ranges in the male from whitish-straw to reddish-brown, and in the extent and intensity of dark forewing markings.
Similar species. *A. algae*, pl. **39** and text.
Imago. 36–47 mm. Resident. Comes to light in small numbers. Single-brooded, flying in August and September, inhabiting ponds, ditches, fenland, marshy places, etc, usually on or near to the coast. Well established in southeast England, ranging locally northwards to Norfolk and westwards to Cornwall and the Isles of Scilly. Elsewhere it is found very locally in South Wales (Glamorgan and Pembrokeshire) and Ireland (Co. Cork).

Larva. June to mid-August in the stems of common reedmace (or 'bulrush'), lesser reedmace (or 'lesser bulrush'), yellow iris, common club-rush (*Scirpus lacustris*), and branched bur-reed.
Pupa. May be found (head upwards), sometimes commonly, in the stems of its foodplants (usually reedmace or 'bulrush') during late July and much of August.
Overwinters as an egg.

Rush Wainscot
Archanara algae Esper
(*cannae* Ochsenheimer)
Plate **39** : *22–23*
Similar species. *A. sparganii*, pl. **39**, is larger on average, and has a row of distinct black terminal dots on each wing. (See text fig 49.)
Imago. 32–45 mm. Resident. Both sexes come to light in moderate numbers. Single-brooded, flying in August and September, inhabiting broadland, freshwater ponds and old water-filled gravel workings. A very local species found not uncommonly in the Norfolk Broads and in a few small lakes in mid-Sussex. Elsewhere it is resident in southwest Norfolk, near Lincoln, near Rye, East Sussex, and Surrey. It was recorded from Dungeness, Kent, in 1952 and 1954, but not since. The occasional records from the rest of southern England suggest the existence of undiscovered colonies. In Ireland it is found in Cos Galway, Clare, and Kildare.
Larva. June to early August in the stems of common club-rush (*Scirpus lacustris*), common reedmace or 'bulrush' and yellow iris.
Pupa. May be obtained (head upwards), sometimes in good numbers, in the stems of its foodplants.
Overwinters as an egg.

Large Wainscot
Rhizedra lutosa Hübner
Plate **39** : *24–26*
Variation. Extremely variable in size, and to a lesser extent in ground colour which ranges from whitish-ochreous to reddish-ochreous.
Similar species. *Nonagria typhae*, pl. **39**.
Imago. 36–52 mm. Resident. May be found after dark resting on reeds and grasses; also comes regularly to light. Single-brooded, flying from August to October, appearing earlier or later in some seasons. It inhabits reed-beds, but it is frequently recorded well away from possible breeding sites. Widely distributed and locally common in England, Wales and Ireland. In Scotland it is sporadically distributed as far north as Moray, and also recorded from the Hebrides, Orkney and Shetland.
Larva. April to July in the roots and stem-bases of common reed.
Overwinters as an egg.

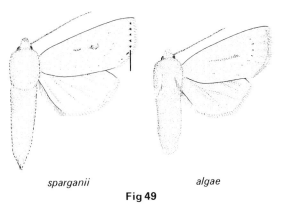

sparganii   *algae*

Fig 49

Blair's Wainscot
Sedina buettneri Hering
Plate **39** : *27*

Similar species. The pointed forewing and blackish hindwing, together with the time of appearances, distinguish *S. buettneri* from all other similar-looking wainscots.
Imago. 28–34 mm. Resident and suspected immigrant. Comes readily to light. Single-brooded, flying from late September to mid-October. It was discovered in Fresh-water Marsh, Isle of Wight, in September 1945 and was noted there annually in varying numbers until 1951 when the marsh was drained and the surface burnt. In 1996 a few specimens were taken in southeast Dorset, leading to the discovery of several resident populations. As a suspected immigrant it has occurred at Rye, East Sussex, on 14.x.1996; Walberton, West Sussex, on 30.ix.1985; Lydd, Kent, on 2.x.1991; Dungeness, Kent, on 12.x.1991; and Frinton-on-Sea, Essex, on 16.x.1994.
Larva. Spring to August in the stems of lesser pond-sedge (*Carex acutiformis*).
Overwinters as an egg.

Fen Wainscot
Arenostola phragmitidis Hübner
Plate **40** : *7*

Variation. Specimens strongly tinged with red occur frequently and are referable to ab. *rufescens* Tutt.
Imago. 32–36 mm. Resident. Comes readily to light and flowering grasses. Single-brooded, flying from mid-July to mid-August, inhabiting reed-beds. A local, but not uncommon, species, found in southern England from Dorset to Kent, and from Essex northwards to Yorkshire. Also found locally in Lancashire and Cumbria.
Larva. April to June in the stems of common reed.
Overwinters as an egg.

Brighton Wainscot
Oria musculosa Hübner
Plate **40** : *8*

Imago. 30–36 mm. Resident and suspected immigrant. Flies actively at dusk over wheat-fields, when it may be netted or attracted to light. During the day large numbers have been disturbed during harvesting. Single-brooded, flying from late July to mid-August, inhabiting fields of wheat and other cereals, and surrounding grass verges. Well established in Wiltshire, North Hampshire, and Berkshire, with specimens sometimes reported from the neighbouring counties. Occasionally, as in early July 1976, odd examples are recorded well away from the known breeding sites; some of these specimens were small and pale and most probably immigrants.
Larva. April to early June, at first in the stems of wild grasses and then in the stems of wheat, barley, oats, or rye.
Overwinters as an egg.

Small Rufous
Coenobia rufa Haworth
Plate **40** : *5–6*

Imago. 22–25 mm. Resident. Flies actively in the hour before dusk, but only casually after dark when the occasional specimen is attracted to light. Single-brooded, flying from mid-July to mid-August, inhabiting fenland, bogs, and marshy fields. Widely distributed and locally common over much of southern England and East Anglia. Local and sporadically distributed over the rest of Britain as far north as Clydesdale. Rare and very local in Ireland, where it is recorded from Cos Galway, Sligo, Wicklow, and Cork.
Larva. September to June in the stems of jointed rush (*Juncus articulatus*) and sometimes soft rush (*J. effusus*).
Overwinters as a small larva.

Treble Lines
Charanyca trigrammica Hufnagel
Plate **40** : *9–10*

Variation. Ground colour varies from whitish- or greyish-brown to reddish-ochreous. Ab. *bilinea* Haworth (fig 10) is a melanistic form occurring at low frequency in many localities.
Imago. 33–40 mm. Resident. Comes freely to light and sugar. Single-brooded, flying from mid-May to early July, inhabiting open woodland, the edges of woods, downland, commons, rough fields, and hedgerows. Widespread and common over much of England, Wales, the Isle of Man and Ireland.
Larva. June to April on a variety of low plants, such as greater plantain (*Plantago major*), common knapweed (*Centaurea nigra*), and dwarf thistle (*Cirsium acaule*).
Overwinters as a larva, feeding during mild weather.

The Uncertain
Hoplodrina alsines Brahm
Plate **40** : *22*

Similar species. *H. blanda*, pl. **40**, has the forewing brown, inclining to greyish or blackish, but never

COLOUR IDENTIFICATION GUIDE

ochreous; cross-lines usually rather obscure; general appearance smooth and glossy; and hindwing usually paler, especially in the male. In comparison, *H. alsines* has the forewing ochreous-brown; cross-lines more distinct; general appearance coarser and rougher-scaled; and hindwing darker, often tinged with brown. *H. superstes*, pl. **40** and text.

Imago. 31–35 mm. Resident. Comes freely to light, sugar, and flowers. Normally single-brooded, flying from mid-June to mid-August, with an occasional and very partial second generation in the late autumn. It inhabits commons, gardens, waste places, etc. Generally distributed and common in England and Wales; locally widespread and less frequent in mainland Scotland and Ireland.

Larva. September to April on dock, plantain, dandelion, and other low plants.

Overwinters as a larva.

The Rustic

Hoplodrina blanda Denis & Schiffermüller

Plate **40** : *23–24*

Similar species. Both *H. ambigua*, pl. **40**, and *Caradrina clavipalpis*, pl. **40**, have paler forewings and white hindwings. *H. alsines*, pl. **40** and text. *H. superstes*, pl. **40** and text.

Imago. 31–35 mm. Resident. Comes readily to light, sugar, and the flowers of ragwort, *Buddleia*, and other plants. Normally single-brooded, flying from late June to mid-August, with an occasional and very partial second generation occurring in southern England during October. It inhabits gardens, waste ground, sandhills, heathland, downland, etc. Widespread and generally common in England, Wales and Ireland; local and less frequent in Scotland and the Hebrides.

Larva. September to May on a variety of low plants such as dock and plantain.

Overwinters as a larva.

Powdered Rustic

Hoplodrina superstes Ochsenheimer

Plate **40** : *25*

Similar species. Both *H. alsines*, pl. **40**, and *H. blanda*, pl. **40**, have browner forewings and much darker hindwings; and *H. ambigua*, pl. **40**, has a slightly narrower forewing, without a row of distinct terminal dots, and whiter hindwing without yellowish gloss. The male antennae are distinctive: *H. ambigua* has long cilia, almost equal in length to diameter of shaft, and distinctly massed together in tufts; whereas *H. superstes* has short cilia, scarcely half the diameter of the shaft. (These differences apply to the middle section of the antenna.)

Imago. 32–36 mm. Suspected immigrant. Single-brooded on the Continent, occurring from June to August. There are several reputedly British specimens: two, Deal, Kent, in July 1886; Brentwood, Essex, on

18.viii.1890; Dawlish, Devon, in August 1901; Torcross, Devon, in 1902; and Honiton, Devon, on 9 and 11.vi.1945. Abroad it is widely distributed in central and southern Europe.

Larva. *September to May on dandelion, plantain, and other low plants.

Overwinters as a larva.

Vine's Rustic

Hoplodrina ambigua Denis & Schiffermüller

Plate **40** : *21*

Similar species. *H. superstes*, pl. **40** and text. *Caradrina clavipalpis*, pl. **40**, has the forewing darker with dark costal spots, and hindwing white with pearly sheen.

Imago. 32–34 mm. Resident and suspected immigrant. Comes readily to light, sugar, and to ragwort flowers. Double-brooded, appearing throughout much of the year from May to October, but most usually during August and early September. It inhabits waste places and gardens, and is well established over much of southern England and East Anglia, where it is probably reinforced by immigration. Elsewhere it is casually recorded from the rest of Britain and southern Ireland.

Larva. Autumn to spring, and during the summer on low plants. In captivity it will eat dandelion, knotgrass, and chickweed; it is continually brooded if kept warm.

Overwinters as a larva.

Dark Mottled Willow

Spodoptera cilium Guenée

Plate **43** : *35*

Similar species. *S. exigua*, pl. **40**, has a narrower forewing which is less variegated and more glossy in appearance. The orbicula stigma has a pinkish coloration and the hindwing has a pearly sheen. The male also lacks a ciliated antenna.

Imago. 28–34 mm. Immigrant. The nine specimens reported in Britain to date have all been taken at light. These are at Coverack, Cornwall, on 29.ix.1990; Portland, Dorset, on 1.x.1990; Coverack on 8 & 13.x. 1995; two at Portland, on 9.x.1995; Perrancombe, Cornwall, on 12.x.1995; Stoborough, Dorset, on 13.x. 1995 and West Bexington, Dorset, on 14.x.1995. An African species whose range extends northwards to the Canaries, southern Spain and France.

Larva. On various grasses, reaching pest status in parts of its range. It especially favours the close-cut turf on golf courses and is known colloquially as the 'Lawn Caterpillar'.

Small Mottled Willow

Spodoptera exigua Hübner

Plate **40** : *11*

Similar species. *Caradrina clavipalpis*, pl. **40**, has a broader forewing with dark stigmata and costal dots. *S. cilium*, pl. **43** and text.

Imago. 26–32 mm. Immigrant. Comes readily to light. It normally appears from mid-July to October, but specimens have been recorded as early as February. A regular visitor, reported in most years, usually in small numbers, but sometimes commonly, as in 1962 (*c.* 1200); 1938 (*c.* 300); 1966 (*c.* 250); 1906 (*c.* 235); and 1969 (*c.* 220). Mostly noted in the southern half of Britain, with occasional specimens ranging northwards to the Hebrides. In Ireland it has been recorded from Cos Cork, Kerry, Armagh, Dublin, and Clare. Abroad this species has a world-wide distribution, and is a serious pest in the warmer parts of its range.

Larva. Has been found on *Persicaria*. In captivity it will accept dandelion and groundsel, and is continuously brooded.

Mediterranean Brocade

Spodoptera littoralis Boisduval
(*litura* auctt.)
Plate **40** : *12*

Imago. 34–38 mm. Importation and suspected immigrant. Occasionally imported with bananas, tomatoes, and other fruits, but rarely occurring plentifully, except in 1963 when it appeared commonly in greenhouses having originated on *Chrysanthemum* cuttings imported from the Canary Islands. As a suspected immigrant, it has been recorded at light at West Runton, Norfolk, on 19.ix.1960; Stoborough, Dorset, on 13.x.1978; Lymington, Hampshire, on 13.x.1978; Studland, Dorset, on 13.x.1979 and Longworth, Berkshire, in June 1983. Abroad it is widely distributed in tropical and subtropical regions, and the larva is frequently a serious pest on a wide variety of cultivated plants.

Larva. Continuously brooded in captivity, accepting the leaves of most plants.

Mottled Rustic

Caradrina morpheus Hufnagel
Plate **40** : *20*

Similar species. The dark broad forewing and large squarish reniform stigma distinguish *C. morpheus* from related species.

Imago. 32–38 mm. Resident. Comes readily to light, and occasionally to sugar and flowers. Normally single-brooded, flying from June to early August, with an occasional and partial second generation occurring in southern England in October. It frequents a wide variety of lowland habitats, and is found commonly over England and Wales; local and less frequent in Scotland and the Hebrides; and very local and uncommon in Ireland.

Larva. Feeds from August to November on nettle, dandelion and other low plants.
Overwinters as a full-grown larva, within an earthen cocoon in which it pupates in the following spring.

Lorimer's Rustic

Caradrina flavirena Guenée
(*The Moths and Butterflies of Great Britain and Ireland*, 1983, vol. 10, pl. 9)

Similar species. Somewhat similar to a dark example of *C. clavipalpis*, pl. **40**, but the forewing of *C. flavirena* is greyish, not brownish; less variegated; and is folded closely around the body when the moth is at rest.

Imago. 28–34 mm. Suspected immigrant. Double-brooded on the Continent, flying from April to June, and again from August to October. The only British specimen was taken at light at Totteridge, Middlesex, on 8.x.1967. Abroad it occurs over much of southern Europe, including France, Switzerland, and Austria.

Larva. *Autumn to spring, and mid-summer on dandelion and other low plants.

Pale Mottled Willow

Caradrina clavipalpis Scopoli
(*quadripunctata* Fabricius)
Plate **40** : *19*

Similar species. *Spodoptera exigua*, pl. **40** and text. *Hoplodrina blanda*, pl. **40** and text. *H. ambigua*, pl. **40** and text.

Imago. 26–35 mm. Resident. Comes readily to light, sugar, and the flowers of ragwort, ivy, and other plants. Probably double-brooded, appearing throughout most of the year from February to November, but most common from July to September. It inhabits gardens, waste places, cultivated fields, etc, and occurs more or less commonly over the greater part of the British Isles.

Larva. Autumn to spring, and during the summer on growing and harvested ears of wheat and other cereals, seeds of plantain and various grasses, peas, and probably a variety of vegetable matter.
Overwinters as a larva, within an earthen cocoon in which it pupates in the spring.

The African

Perigea capensis Guenée
(*conducta* Walker)
(*The Moths and Butterflies of Great Britain and Ireland*, 1983, vol. 10, pl. 9)

Imago. 34–38 mm. Suspected immigrant. The only British specimen was taken at light at Bodinnick, near Fowey, Cornwall, on 3.v.1958, at a time of much migrant activity. It is an inhabitant of Africa.

Larva. *Stated to feed on various species of *Acanthus*.

Silky Wainscot

Chilodes maritimus Tauscher
Plate **40** : *1–4*

Variation. Ab. *nigristriata* Staudinger (fig 2) has the forewing finely streaked with black; ab. *bipunctata* Haworth (fig 3) has black reniform and orbicular stigmata; and ab. *wismariensis* Schmidt (fig 4) has a broad black longitudinal streak across the middle of the forewing. The frequency of these forms, which are regular but never common in some localities, varies from one colony to another. They are absent from many localities.

Similar species. Both *Calamotropha paludella* Hübner and small white examples of *Chilo phragmitella* Hübner (Family Pyralidae) have distinctive long palpi, and the hindwing of both species is without a discal spot.

Imago. 29–36 mm. Resident. Flies from dusk onwards and may be found fluttering around or resting upon reeds. It also comes regularly to light. Single-brooded, flying from mid-June to mid-August, inhabiting inland and coastal reed-beds. Locally widespread in southern England and East Anglia, its range extending westwards to Cornwall and Glamorgan, and northwards to southern Scotland. In Ireland it has been reported from near Youghal, Co. Cork.

Larva. Autumn to March or April. It forages in old reed-stems, feeding on a variety of animal and vegetable matter. In captivity it will eat meat fats.

Overwinters as a larva.

Porter's Rustic

Athetis hospes Freyer

Plate **43** : *36*

Imago. 26–30 mm. Suspected immigrant. Double-brooded on the Continent, flying in May and June, and in late August and September. The first British specimen, a female, was taken at light at Kynance Cove, Cornwall, on 26.viii.1978 and the second, also at light, on St Agnes, Isles of Scilly, on 14.ix.1993. Abroad it is well distributed in southern Europe.

Larva. *October to April, and July and August on plantain and other low plants.

Overwinters as a larva.

Marsh Moth

Athetis pallustris Hübner

Plate **40** : *15–16*

Imago. Male 26–34 mm, female 18–22 mm. Resident. The male comes to light, usually after midnight; it has also been noted flying at dawn. The female is rarely found, and its habits are not known. Single-brooded, occurring in late May and June, inhabiting marginal fenland and marshy places in sand-dunes. A secretive and unpredictable species found locally in Lincolnshire (a few inland sites, and along the coast from Saltfleet to Gibraltar Point); Huntingdonshire (Woodwalton and Holme Fens); Cambridgeshire (Wicken and Chippenham Fens); and Norfolk (Stoke Ferry Fen). There are also a few very old records from Hampshire (Ringwood); Yorkshire (Comptons Wood); and Cumberland (Carlisle).

Larva. Feeds from June to September on meadow-sweet and other low plants.

Overwinters as a full-grown larva, pupating in late April or early May.

Reddish Buff

Acosmetia caliginosa Hübner

Plate **40** : *17–18*

Imago. 25–30 mm. Resident. During the day both sexes may be disturbed from the foodplant, and after dark they come regularly to light. Single-brooded, flying from late May to late June, inhabiting woodland rides and clearings. A very local and uncommon species, possibly now confined to the northern half of the Isle of Wight. Formerly occurred during the nineteenth century in the New Forest, Hampshire, and this century near Fareham, Hampshire, but not since 1961.

Larva. July and August on the leaves of saw-wort (*Serratula tinctoria*).

Overwinters as a pupa.

The Anomalous

Stilbia anomala Haworth

Plate **40** : *13–14*

Imago. 29–36 mm. Resident. The males fly strongly at dusk, and later both sexes may be found at rest on heather and grass-stems. Both sexes come to light, the males readily and the females less frequently. Single-brooded, flying in August and September, inhabiting heathland and moorland. Widespread and not uncommon in Scotland, the Hebrides, Orkney, northern England, the Isle of Man, the Midlands, Wales, and parts of southwest England. Elsewhere in England it is found locally in Dorset, Hampshire, Somerset, Wiltshire, and the Breck district of East Anglia. In Ireland it is found in the north and west, mainly on the coast.

Larva. October to March on wavy hair-grass (*Deschampsia flexuosa*) and other moorland grasses.

Overwinters as a larva.

The Goldwing

Synthymia fixa Fabricius

(*The Moths and Butterflies of Great Britain and Ireland*, 1983, vol. 10, pl. 9)

Similar species. Rather like *Euclidia glyphica*, pl. **41**, in size and general appearance, but the forewing of *S. fixa* is greyer, and the hindwing uniformly gold.

Imago. 32–38 mm. Suspected immigrant. Single-brooded on the Continent, flying in May and June. The only British specimen was taken at Start Point lighthouse, South Devon, in 1937. Abroad its range includes southern Europe and Algeria.

Larva. *Feeds in the autumn on *Psoralea bituminosea*.

Rosy Marbled

Elaphria venustula Hübner

Plate **40** : *26*

Imago. 19–23 mm. Resident. Comes regularly to light. Single-brooded, flying from late May to early July, inhabiting open woodland. A local species, possibly increasing, found in Kent, Sussex, Hampshire, Berkshire, Surrey, Essex, Buckinghamshire, Worcestershire, Isle of Wight, Suffolk and Norfolk.

Larva. Late June to August. The natural foodplant is unknown in Britain. In captivity it will eat the flowers of bramble, broom, and tormentil (*Potentilla erecta*), and the latter has been suggested as a possible foodplant in the wild.

Overwinters as a pupa.

Small Yellow Underwing

Panemeria tenebrata Scopoli
(*arbuti* Fabricius)
Plate **40** : *27*

Imago. 19–22 mm. Resident. Flies actively in sunshine, visiting the flowers of dandelion, buttercup, common daisy and other meadow flowers. Single-brooded, flying in May and early June, inhabiting flowery meadows, downland, sea-cliffs, grassy embankments, etc. Locally widespread over much of England and Wales, ranging into northeast Scotland. In Ireland it is stated to have been recorded in Cos Sligo and Kerry, but there are no recent records.

Larva. June and July on the seed capsules of common mouse-ear (*Cerastium holosteoides*).

Overwinters as a pupa.

SUBFAMILY: HELIOTHINAE

Pease Blossom

Periphanes delphinii Linnaeus
(South 1961, vol. 1, pl. 110)

Imago. 34–36 mm. Status uncertain, but possibly an extinct resident. Single-brooded on the Continent, flying in May and June. During the eighteenth century about five specimens were reported, including the legendary record of a wing found in a spider's web at Bulstrode, Buckinghamshire. In the next century a further 12 reputedly British examples were reported and these were at Windsor, Berkshire, in June 1815; Harrow, Middlesex, in August 1835; Brighton, Sussex, in 1857; two, Hamstead [*sic*] Heath on 3.vi.1863; London (West End) in 1870; Eastbourne, Sussex, in 1875; two, Brighton, in 1876; two, Petersfield, Hampshire, in 1890; and Dover, Kent, in 1893. There has been no additional record this century. Abroad it is found widely distributed over much of southern and eastern Europe.

Larva. *July and August on larkspur (*Delphinium ambiguum*) and monk's-hood.

Overwinters as a pupa.

Bordered Sallow

Pyrrhia umbra Hufnagel
(*marginata* Fabricius)
Plate **40** : *34*

Imago. 32–38 mm. Resident, possibly reinforced by immigration. Comes readily to sugar and the flowers of campions and red valerian; and in small numbers to light. Single-brooded, flying in June and July, inhabiting downland, coastal sandhills, and shingle beaches. Locally widespread over much of England, Wales and Ireland. It is mainly coastal in northern England and Ireland, and also in Scotland where it ranges locally from Berwickshire to Ross-shire.

Larva. Late July and August on the flowers, seeds, and leaves of common restharrow and spiny restharrow (*Ononis spinosa*). Has also been found on young hazel bushes.

Overwinters as a pupa.

Scarce Bordered Straw

Heliothis armigera Hübner
Plate **40** : *33*

Variation. Ground colour variable, ranging from pale straw or ochreous-grey to reddish-brown.

Similar species. *H. peltigera*, pl. **40**, has the forewing with a distinct black tornal dot, the dark reniform patch extending to the costa, and an olive-brown patch at the costal end of the subterminal fascia. *H. nubigera*, pl. **40**, has the forewing with a small black tornal dot, three small, but distinct, terminal dots, and a more strongly indentated subterminal line. (See text fig 50.)

Imago. 38–42 mm. Immigrant and importation. Comes to light and to ivy blossom. An almost annual visitor to southern England during the autumn, but often scarce and not always achieving double figures. 1988 and 1992 proved to be exceptional with approximately eighty records for each year. Abroad it occurs throughout southern Europe and North Africa, where it is frequently a serious pest of cultivated plants.

Larva. Has been found on garden geranium; also during the winter and spring in imported fruit, especially tomatoes from the Canary Islands. In captivity it will probably accept most plants.

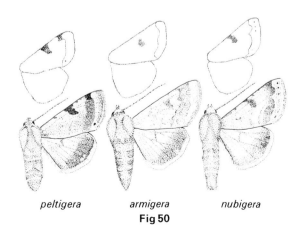

peltigera   armigera   nubigera
Fig 50

Marbled Clover
Heliothis viriplaca Hufnagel
(*dipsacea* Linnaeus)
Plate **40** : *29*

Similar species. *H. maritima warneckei*, pl. **40**, has a black basal streak and an angled median line. (See text fig 51.)

Imago. 30–36 mm. Resident and suspected immigrant. Flies actively in hot sunshine, visiting the flowers of viper's-bugloss and other plants. Single-brooded, flying from mid-June to mid-July, inhabiting breckland, waste places, clover and lucerne fields, shingle and sandy beaches, and chalk downland. Well established and locally common in the Breck district of Suffolk and Norfolk; scarcer and more local in Wiltshire. As a suspected immigrant it occurs occasionally in southern and eastern England, and in favourable seasons may become temporarily established.

Larva. August and September, eating mainly the flowers and seeds of white campion, bladder campion, restharrow, clover, sticky groundsel, and other wasteland plants.

Overwinters as a pupa.

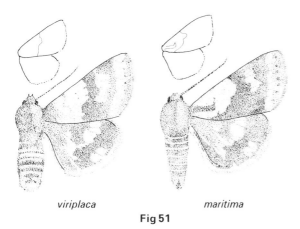

viriplaca   *maritima*

Fig 51

Shoulder-striped Clover
Heliothis maritima warneckei Boursin
Plate **40** : *30*

Similar species. *H. viriplaca*, pl. **40** and text.

Imago. 30–36 mm. Resident. Flies actively in hot sunshine, visiting the flowers of heather and heath. Single-brooded, flying in late June and July, inhabiting heathland. A local species occurring in Hampshire (New Forest), Dorset (Wareham and Studland Heaths), and Surrey (Chobham, Horsell, Pirbright and Thursley Commons, etc). Odd captures in Cornwall (Porthleven, Goonhilly, Erisey Barton) and South Devon (Haldon Moor) suggest the possibility of undiscovered resident populations.

H. maritima bulgarica Draudt. A single specimen, presumably immigrant, was taken flying in a lucerne field on the Isle of Thanet, Kent, on 20.viii.1947. This race, which lacks a distinct basal streak, is a resident of southeast Europe.

Larva. August and September on the flowers of heather and heaths, and sometimes the seed-heads of bog-asphodel (*Narthecium ossifragum*). In captivity it will eat sliced runner beans.

Overwinters as a pupa.

Bordered Straw
Heliothis peltigera Denis & Schiffermüller
Plate **40** : *31*

Variation. Ground colour varies from pale straw to reddish-brown, and is controlled by the rate of development of the immature stages. In captivity a fast growth-rate will result in pale specimens and vice versa.

Similar species. *H. nubigera*, pl. **40**, has the ground colour of the forewing paler, with three small, but distinct, terminal dots, a more strongly indented subterminal line, and a much whiter underside with the terminal shade of the hindwing hardly showing through. *H. armigera*, pl. **40** and text. (See text fig 50.)

Imago. 34–42 mm. Immigrant. Comes to light and to the flowers of red valerian, *Buddleia*, bramble, and other plants. An erratic visitor, occurring commonly (as larvae in coastal habitats) in some years, but often unrecorded in others. It normally appears from June to August, usually in southern or southeast England, although occasional specimens are reported from Scotland and Ireland. Abroad its distribution is extensive, ranging from Africa, the Canary Islands, and southern Europe to Asia.

Larva. July to October on the flowers of sticky groundsel, garden marigolds (*Calendula* spp.), common restharrow, knapweed, and various species of thistle.

Eastern Bordered Straw
Heliothis nubigera Herrich-Schäffer
Plate **40** : *32*

Similar species. *H. peltigera*, pl. **40** and text. *H. armigera*, pl. **40** and text.

Imago. 38–42 mm. Immigrant. Comes to light. During 1958 a large immigration of this eastern Mediterranean species occurred, and many specimens were recorded in parts of Europe well outside its normal breeding range, including three in Britain: Iwerne Minster, Dorset, on 9.v.1958; Sheringham, Norfolk, on 28.v. & 3.vi.1958 and Swanage, Dorset, on 14.v.1992. Its Continental range also includes southern Spain and the Canary Islands.

Larva. *On various wild and cultivated plants, including tomato and honeysuckle.

Spotted Clover
Protoschinia scutosa Denis & Schiffermüller
Plate **40** : *28*

Imago. 30–36 mm. Immigrant. Comes to light. Double-brooded on the Continent, flying in May and June, and again in late July and August. A very rare visitor to the British Isles and recorded as follows: Dalston, Cumberland, in July 1835; three, Skinburness, Cumberland, in c. 1835; Cromer, Norfolk, in 1875 and 1876; Weston-super-Mare, Somerset, in 1877; near Aberdeen in July 1878; near Buncrana, Co. Donegal, on 19.viii.1878; Attleborough, Norfolk, on 24.vi.1880; Dartmouth, Devon, on 4.ix.1900; Lowestoft, Suffolk, in August 1938; more than 30 observed between Bude and Boscastle, Cornwall, in 1943; Stowmarket, Suffolk, on 9.ix.1945; four, Norwich, Norfolk, in May 1953; Cockley Cley, Norfolk, 12.vi.1953; Wells, Norfolk, on 14.vi.1953; Hunstanton, Norfolk, on 16.vi.1953; Wisbech, Cambridgeshire, in July 1953; Havergate Island, Suffolk, on 30.ix.1956; Seaview, Isle of Wight, on 3.vii.1959; Aviemore, Inverness-shire, on 4.viii.1960; Holmbury St Mary, Surrey, on 24.viii.1969; and Cambridge, Cambridgeshire, on 2.viii.1995. Abroad it is widely distributed throughout central and southern Europe, North Africa, and much of Asia.

Larva. *Summer and autumn on field wormwood, and sometimes *Chenopodium* spp. Overwinters as a pupa.

SUBFAMILY: ACONTIINAE

Purple Marbled
Eublemma ostrina Hübner
Plate **40** : *35–36*

Variation. The pale f. *carthami* Herrich-Schäffer (fig 36) is the form more frequently found in the British Isles.
Imago. 18–25 mm. Immigrant. Comes to light and sugar. Many of the early records of this species were poorly documented, but as an approximate guide 32 specimens were reported between 1825 and 1950: Cornwall (4), Devon (14), Dorset (3), Isle of Wight (5), Kent (3), Carmarthenshire (1), Ayrshire (1), and Co. Dublin (1). Subsequent records have been: Sandy Down, Hampshire, on 30.x.1952; Micheldever, Hampshire, on 30.vi.1957; Maidencombe, Devon, on 8.vii.1957; Rye, Sussex, on 31.v.1958; Branscombe, Devon, on 6.vii.1959; Ickham, Kent, on 16.ix.1961; Martyr Worthy, Hampshire, on 15 & 23.v.1969; Ermington, Devon, on 26.viii.1973; Dingle, Co. Kerry, on 15.vi.1975; Botley, Berkshire, on 3.iii.1977; Plaistow, Sussex, on 3.iii.1977; Beer, Devon, on 4.iii.1977; Portland, Dorset, on 17,18, & 25.vi.1983; Trebrownbridge, Cornwall, on 10.x.1990; and Portland, on 13.x.1990. 1992 proved to be an exceptional year for this species with a total of 36 adults and 27 larvae/pupae reported. There were 21 records of adults at light between the 14 and 27 May: Kent (1), Sussex (1), Hampshire (1), Isle of Wight (3), Dorset (10), Somerset (1), Cornwall (1), Pembrokeshire (2) and Co. Kerry (1). From early July to late August 27 larvae or pupae were collected from the flower-

heads of carline thistle: Cornwall (6), Co. Clare (18) and Inisheer, Co. Galway (3). A further 15 specimens, probably the result of home breeding, were recorded between 23 July and 23 September: Kent (1), Essex (1), Sussex (1), Hampshire (1), Isle of Wight (1), Dorset (3), Cornwall (2), Oxfordshire (1), Cumberland (1), and Co. Clare (3). Two years passed without record since when 12 adults were reported between 9. and 21.x.1995: Sussex (1), Hampshire (1), Dorset (2), Cornwall (3), and Isles of Scilly (5). Its distribution abroad includes southern Europe, North Africa, Madeira, and the Canary Islands.

Larva. July and August in the flower- and seed-heads of carline thistle (*Carlina vulgaris*).

Small Marbled
Eublemma parva Hübner
Plate **40** : *37*

Imago. 14–18 mm. Immigrant. The majority of British specimens have been taken at light. A rare visitor of which 136 specimens and about 16 larvae have been reported mainly from the southern counties of England, but with the occasional record from northern England and southern Scotland. There appears to have been only one Irish specimen, from Co. Wicklow in 1947. The most favoured years were 1953 (c. 54) and 1968 (c. 33). Larvae were found in Gloucestershire in 1968, and South Devon in 1982. Abroad it occurs in southern Europe and North Africa, ranging eastwards to central and southern India.

Larva. July to September in the flowers of common fleabane (*Pulicaria dysenterica*) and ploughman's-spikenard (*Inula conyza*).

Scarce Marbled
Eublemma minutata Fabricius
(*noctualis* Hübner)
(*paula* Hübner)
(South 1961, vol. 1, pl. 126)

Similar species. *E. parva*, pl. **40**, is smaller and yellow, whereas *E. noctualis* is grey with whitish cross-lines.
Imago. 17–20 mm. Suspected immigrant. Double-brooded on the Continent, flying in late May and June, and again from mid-July to mid-August. The only fully documented British specimen was taken at Freshwater, Isle of Wight, in June 1872. Two other specimens exist without data and were stated to have been captured during the first half of the nineteenth century, possibly on the 'South Coast' of England. Abroad it is well established in southern France and the Mediterranean region.

Larva. *June to July, and August and September on the flowers of mountain everlasting (*Antennaria dioica*) and *Helichrysum arenaria*. The latter plant is not a native of Britain, but allied species (everlasting flowers) are often grown in gardens.
Overwinters as a pupa.

Marbled White Spot

Protodeltote pygarga Hufnagel
(*fasciana* auctt.)
Plate **40** : *38*

Similar species. *L. deceptoria*, pl. **40**, has the basal area of the forewing white.

Imago. 24–30 mm. Resident. Comes regularly to light in small numbers. Single-brooded, flying from late May to mid-July, inhabiting woodland, commons, heathland, and moorland. Widespread and moderately common in the southern half of England and northwest Wales. Elsewhere it occurs locally in South Wales and parts of the Midlands and northwards to Yorkshire. In Ireland it is found locally in Cos Down, Kerry and Cork.

Larva. July to September on purple moor-grass and probably other grasses.
Overwinters as a pupa.

Pretty Marbled

Deltote deceptoria Scopoli
Plate **40** : *39*

Similar species. *L. pygarga*, pl. **40** and text.

Imago. 25–30 mm. Immigrant and suspected transitory resident. Most of the British specimens were taken at light. Single-brooded on the Continent, flying from mid-May to mid-July. Sixteen specimens have been reported from the British Isles, all from southern England, and mainly in woods; these are: Hamstreet, Kent, on 14.vi.1948; Reigate, Surrey, in June 1952; Hamstreet, on 8.vi.1952; Leigh, Surrey, on 13.vi.1952; Tilgate, Sussex, on 13.vi.1952; Westwell, Kent, on 25.v.1953; Hamstreet on 27.v.1954; Brook, Kent, on 30.v.1954; Southsea, Hampshire, on 18.v.1955 (South, 1961, unconfirmed); Hamstreet, on 28.v.1956; Rye, Sussex, on 28.v.1956; Tetbury, Gloucestershire, on 26.v.1964; Rye, on 22.vi.1965; Brighton, Sussex, on 7.vi.1976; Peasmarsh, Sussex, on 16.vi.1983; and North Walsham, Norfolk, on 16.vi.1986. Abroad it is well distributed over much of central Europe.

Larva. *July and August on timothy (*Phleum pratense*).
Overwinters as a pupa.

Silver Hook

Deltote uncula Clerck
Plate **40** : *40*

Imago. 22–26 mm. Resident. May be disturbed from grass tussocks during the day. Flies from dusk onwards, and comes sparingly to light. Normally single-brooded, flying from late May to early July, although occasionally specimens of a possible second generation are reported in August. The species inhabits boggy heathland, fenland, and other marshy places, and occurs locally over much of England, Wales and Ireland. Elsewhere in Britain it is found in parts of western Scotland and on the Hebridean islands of Mull and Rhum.

Larva. July and August on sedges and coarse grasses, including tufted hair-grass.
Overwinters as a pupa.

Silver Barred

Deltote bankiana Fabricius
(*olivana* Denis & Schiffermüller)
(*argentula* Hübner)
Plate **40** : *41*

Variation. Specimens from Ireland are on average slightly larger and redder than those from England.

Imago. 24–28 mm. Resident, probable immigrant, and suspected transitory resident. Readily disturbed during the day. Flies from dusk onwards and comes regularly to light. Single-brooded, flying from mid-June to mid-July, inhabiting marshes, fenland, and boggy heathland. It is well established and not uncommon in Chippenham and Wicken Fens, Cambridgeshire, the peat bogs of Cos Kerry and Cork, and a small coastal marsh in East Kent. As a suspected immigrant it has been recorded singly, unless otherwise stated, from Chieveley, Berkshire, in June 1951; near Hailsham, East Sussex, on 25.vi.1953; Hickling, Norfolk, in late July or early August 1960; Folkestone, Kent, on 5.viii.1965; Danbury, Essex, on 18.vi.1970; five or six, Dungeness, Kent, on 19.vi.1970; two, near Walberswick, Suffolk, on 20.vi.1970 (the only Suffolk records to date); Bradwell-on-Sea, Essex, on 21.vi.1970; North Harrow, Middlesex, in June 1971; Bradwell-on-Sea on 27.vi., 10 & 14.vii.1976; Fairlight, East Sussex, on 30.vi.1976; Pevensey, East Sussex, on 5 & 12.vii.1976 (erroneously recorded as 4.vii.1976 in *Entomologist's Rec. J. Var.* 88: 240.) Dymchurch, Kent, on 22.vii.1977; Kingsdown, Kent, on 12.vi.1980; Danbury, Essex, on 14.vi.1980; Beaumont-cum-Moze, Essex, on 14.vi.1980; St Margaret's Bay, Kent, on 14.viii.1982; Boughton Aluph, Kent, on 15.vii.1982 and the New Forest, Hampshire, on 4.vii.1982. 1986 proved to be a record year with eleven examples reported from southeast England. Since then a few specimens have been recorded almost annually.

Larva. July and August on purple moor-grass, smooth meadow-grass (*Poa pratensis*), and other fenland grasses.
Overwinters as a pupa.

Spotted Sulphur

Emmelia trabealis Scopoli
(*sulphuralis* Linnaeus)
Plate **40** : *42*

Imago. 20–25 mm. Resident and suspected immigrant. Readily disturbed during the day from its foodplant or surrounding herbage, although its natural flight takes place from 1800–1900 hrs BST. Single-brooded, flying from mid-June to early July, inhabiting fallow fields, waste ground, roadside verges, and old asparagus fields. Formerly locally common in the Breck district of Norfolk, Suffolk and Cambridgeshire, but not seen since 1960. Occasional specimens have occurred in Dorset, Devon, South Wales, Surrey, Essex and London, mostly during the nineteenth century, and these were presumably immigrants. Only in Kent did the records suggest it may have been resident during the nine-

eenth century around Darenth, Dover and Folkestone.
Larva. July and early August on the flowers and leaves of field bindweed.
Overwinters as a pupa.

Pale Shoulder
Acontia lucida Hufnagel
(*solaris* Denis & Schiffermüller)
Plate **43** : *37*

Similar species. *Tyta luctuosa*, pl. **41**, has the basal area of both forewing and hindwing black (not creamy-white).
Imago. 26–30 mm. Suspected immigrant. Flies during the day, preferring hot sunshine, and is stated to visit the flowers of field eryngo (*Eryngium campestre*). Double-brooded on the Continent, flying in May and June, and again in July and August. About fifteen specimens were reported from southeast England during the nineteenth century, but only nine of these have reasonable data. These are four: near Dover, Kent, in June 1825; Brighton, Sussex, on 25.viii.1859; Dover, in 1872; two at Dover, on 24.viii.1876; and Eastbourne, Sussex, in 1880. Over one hundred years passed without record and then on the same night in localities more than one hundred miles apart single specimens turned up at light at Dymchurch, Kent, and West Bexington, Dorset, on 5.viii.1994. There have been four additional records to date: at Les Quennevais, Jersey, Channel Islands, on 28.vii.1995; St Agnes, Isles of Scilly, on 10.viii.1995; West Bexington on 18.viii.1996; and Ringwood, Hampshire, on 19.viii.1996. Abroad its extensive range includes central and southern Europe, North Africa, Madeira, and the Canary Islands.
Larva. *June to July, and August to September on field bindweed, common mallow and marsh-mallow.
Overwinters as a pupa.

SUBFAMILY: CHLOEPHORINAE
Cream-bordered Green Pea
Earias clorana Linnaeus
Plate **40** : *44*

Variation. Ab. *flavimargo* de Joannis is a rare form having brown fringes and in the past has been confused with the other migrant *Earias* species.
Similar species. *E. biplaga*, pl. **43**, has a dark coloured fringe on both the upper and underside of the forewing. *E. insulana*, pl. **40**, has the forewing longer and narrower with a predominantly straight costa. *Tortrix viridana* Linnaeus (Family Tortricidae) also lacks the white-edged costa, and has a grey, not a white, hindwing.
Imago. 20–24 mm. Resident. Comes readily to light and occasionally to sugar. Normally single-brooded, appearing from late May to July, but in some years a second generation occurs in August. It inhabits damp woodland, fenland, river valleys, and other marshy places, and occurs locally in southern and eastern England; its

range extends westwards to Devon and northwards to Yorkshire. In Ireland it is known only from Coomarkane Valley, near Glengariff, Co. Cork. Single specimens conforming to ab. *flavimargo* were recorded at St Austell, Cornwall, on 12.vi.1992; and Freshwater, Isle of Wight, on 25.vi.1992 and were probably immigrants.
Larva. July and August on osier, creeping willow, and other species of willow.
Overwinters as a pupa.

Spiny Bollworm
Earias biplaga Walker
(*The Moths and Butterflies of Great Britain and Ireland*, 1983, vol. 10, pl. 13)

Variation. Ground colour varies from mid-green to pale yellowish-green. Some specimens are strongly tinged with purplish-red, and one form has a purplish-red median bar extending obliquely outwards from the dorsum.
Similar species. *E. insulana*, pl. **40**, has a longer and narrower forewing, and lacks the dark-coloured fringes. *E. clorana*, pl. **40** and text.
Imago. 22–26 mm. Suspected immigrant or importation. There are two British records both taken at light: in London (Buckingham Palace Gardens) on 17.vii.1964; and Lymington, Hampshire, on 23.vii.1982. Abroad this species is found in northwest Africa where it is frequently a pest on cotton.

Egyptian Bollworm
Earias insulana Boisduval
Plate **40** : *43*

Variation. Range of forms very similar to that of the last species.
Similar species. *E. biplaga*, see text. *E. clorana*, pl. **40** and text.
Imago. 22–26 mm. Suspected immigrant or importation. Of the two British specimens, one was taken in the southern half of England (possibly South Devon) in 1962, and recorded erroneously as *E. biplaga*; the other was taken at light at Brockenhurst, Hampshire, on 8.x.1967. Abroad its extensive range includes Spain, the Canary Islands, and most of Africa, where it is often a serious pest on cotton.

Scarce Silver-lines
Bena *bicolorana* Fuessly
(*prasinana* sensu auctt.)
Plate **40** : *46*
Imago. 40–48 mm. Resident. Both sexes come regularly to light, and sometimes to sugar. Single-brooded, flying from late June to early August, inhabiting woodland and parkland. Locally widespread in England and Wales, ranging northwards to Cumbria and Yorkshire.
Larva. September to May on oak.
Overwinters as a small larva.

Green Silver-lines
Pseudoips prasinana britannica Warren
(*fagana* Fabricius)
Plate **40** : *45*

Variation. Sexually dimorphic; colour of hindwing in male (fig 40) yellowish-white, in female (not illustrated) pure white. Specimens of the occasional second generation are probably referable to f. *bilinea* Richardson; this form has the forewing smooth green in colour, without the normal white clouding, and crossed by only two well-defined white lines: an antemedian line which does not quite reach the costa, and a postmedian line.

Imago. 32–40 mm. Resident. Occasionally beaten out of trees and bushes during the day, but more usually seen at light. Normally single-brooded, flying in June and July, with very occasional second-brood specimens appearing in August and September. A woodland species, generally distributed and moderately common over much of England and Wales, but very local and thinly scattered in Ireland and the southern half of Scotland. Has been recorded from the Inner Hebrides on Mull.

Larva. August and September on oak, beech, aspen, birch, hazel, and other trees.

Overwinters as a pupa.

SUBFAMILY: SARROTHRIPINAE

Oak Nycteoline
Nycteola revayana Scopoli
Plate **40** : *47–52*

Variation. A very variable species throughout its range, although the duller and darker forms tend to predominate in many localities.

Similar species. *N. degenerana* is larger and strongly variegated with white. Many species of the microlepidoptera, especially the Tortricidae, bear a superficial resemblance to the darker forms of *N. revayana*.

Imago. 28–32 mm. Resident. Comes to light in small numbers, also attracted to sugar, ivy and sallow blossom, and over-ripe blackberries. It appears after hibernation in mid-March and has been recorded in every month up to mid-October. The number of generations involved is unclear and still under discussion. Generally distributed and moderately common in the southern half of Britain; widespread, but less frequent in the rest of Britain, as far north as Ross-shire. In Ireland it has been recorded from Cos Cork, Kerry, Armagh, Tyrone, Galway, Westmeath, Limerick and Wicklow.

Larva. Most often reported in June and July on oak, but has been noted in September.

Overwinters as an adult. It hides in holly, yew, and coniferous trees, and may be obtained by beating.

Sallow Nycteoline
Nycteola degenerana Hübner
(South 1961, vol. 1, pl. 129)

Similar species. *N. revayana*, pl. **40** and text.

Imago. 29–32 mm. Status unknown. In central Europe it is stated to be double-brooded, flying in the autumn and after hibernation in the spring; and again in mid-summer. This species is included on the British list on the strength of two specimens; the first taken at Chattenden, Kent, during the nineteenth century, and the second taken in the New Forest, Hampshire, in 1905. Abroad it occurs locally in central and northern Europe.

Larva. *May to June, and August to September on sallow and osier.

Overwinters as an adult.

SUBFAMILY: PANTHEINAE

Nut-tree Tussock
Colocasia coryli Linnaeus
Plate **41** : *1–3*

Variation. Specimens from parts of northern Scotland have a contrasting white ground colour and dark forewing band. Those from the Burren, Co. Clare (fig 2) are paler and larger than the normal English form. Ab. *melanotica* Haverkampf (fig 3) is a melanic form found regularly in the Chilterns, Buckinghamshire and Oxfordshire, and occasionally elsewhere.

Imago. 30–38 mm. Resident. Comes to light in moderate numbers. Double-brooded, flying from late April to early June, and again from late July to early September. Only single-brooded in northern England and Scotland, appearing in May and June. A woodland species widely distributed and fairly common in the southern half of England and much of Wales, and locally distributed in the rest of England, Scotland, the Isle of Arran, the Inner Hebrides, and Ireland.

Larva. June and July, and in September and early October on beech, hazel, birch, field maple, and hornbeam.

Overwinters as a pupa.

Marbled Tuffet
Charadra deridens Guenée
(South 1961, vol. 1, pl. 136)

Imago. 46–50 mm. Suspected immigrant or importation. The only British specimen was taken at light at Plumstead, Kent, on 24.v.1952. The species is a resident of North America.

The Brother
Raphia frater Grote
(South 1961, vol. 1, pl. 142)

Imago. 38–44 mm. Suspected immigrant or importation. The only British specimen was taken at light at Rothamsted, Hertfordshire, on 3.vii.1949. This species is a resident of North America.

SUBFAMILY: PLUSIINAE

Golden Twin-spot
Chrysodeixis chalcites Esper
Plate **41**: *6–7*

Similar species. *C. acuta*, pl. **43** and text.

Imago. 33–44 mm. Immigrant. An uncommon visitor to the British Isles, although in the 1990s has become slightly more frequent with a few now reported in most years. Annual totals rarely reach double figures and the twenty recorded in 1990, the thirteen in 1991 and the twelve in 1995 are exceptional. Most specimens recorded in Britain have appeared at light between mid-September and early November. Over one hundred specimens have been reported to date since the first record in 1943: Sussex (29), Essex (21), Norfolk (10), Cornwall (8), Kent (8), Dorset (5), Devon (4), Lincolnshire (3), Hampshire mainland (4), Somerset (2), Suffolk (2), Isle of Wight (2), and single ones from Berkshire, Hertfordshire, Yorkshire, Gloucestershire, Glamorgan, Inverness-shire and Perthshire. A single larva was found on the leaves of tomato at Great Horkesley, Essex in September 1984. Abroad its extensive range includes southern Europe, the Canary Islands and North Africa.

Larva. *Salvia* and *Echium*. In captivity it has been reared on common nettle and pellitory (*Parietaria judaica*).

Tunbridge Wells Gem
Chrysodeixis acuta Walker
Plate **43**: *38*

Similar species. Most likely to be confused with the darker and less golden forms of *C. chalcites*, pl. **41**: 7. *C. acuta* is slightly larger and has a more pointed forewing giving the general wingshape appearance of *Autographa gamma*, pl. **43**. In *acuta* the overall metallic sheen is bronze-coloured and not golden, and the subterminal fasciae appear more oblique paralleling the equally oblique termen. The male *acuta* has very prominent dark brown tufts each side of the abdomen.

Imago. 36–46 mm. Immigrant. Confusion with *C. chalcites* and an incorrect illustration of *C. acuta* in the previous edition of this book has resulted in a number of erroneous records and this species is a much rarer visitor to Britain than first supposed. The ten records to date are Tunbridge Wells, Kent, in May 1870; Horsell, Surrey, on 5.xi.1955; Burghclere, Hampshire, on 5.xi.1955; Knaresborough, Yorkshire, *c.* 1955; Sherborne, Dorset, on 25.ix.1967; the Lizard, Cornwall, on 14 & 26.x.1995; West Bexington, Dorset, on 26.x.1995; two at Swanage, Dorset, on 29.x.1995; and Binstead, Isle of Wight, on 27.x.1995. A specimen reported from Brittany, France, on 24.ix.1991 would appear to be the only other record from Europe to date. Abroad its range includes North Africa and the Canary Islands.

Larva. *On tomato, kidney bean, *Nicotiana*, *Geranium*, *Solanum* and *Lonicera*.

Scar Bank Gem
Ctenoplusia limbirena Guenée
Plate **41**: *8*

Imago. 38–46 mm. Immigrant. Thirteen specimens have been recorded to date in Britain, all were attracted to light. These are: Swanage, Dorset, on 14.ix.1947; Bradwell-on-Sea, Essex, on 27.ix.1951; Freshwater, Isle of Wight, on 26.viii.1960; the Lizard, Cornwall, on 28.vi.1962; Polperro (near Looe), Cornwall, on 3.viii.1962 and 7.ix.1968; Bodinnick, Cornwall, on 9.ix.1968; Freshwater, Isle of Wight, on 18.viii.1988; Fernham, Berkshire, on 7.ix.1988; Swanage, on 17.ix.1992; Southsea, Hampshire, on 10.vi.1997; Portland, Dorset, on 29.vii.1997; and St Agnes, Isles of Scilly, on 13.ix.1997. A specimen taken at St Ouen's Pond, Jersey, on 30.viii.1997 would appear the only record to date from the Channel Islands. The record from Polperro in September 1962 quoted in other works is erroneous. Abroad its range includes North Africa and the Canary Islands.

Larva. *On *Salvia*, *Verbascum*, and *Althaea*. In captivity it will accept a wide range of low plants.

Accent Gem
Ctenoplusia accentifera Lefebvre
(*The Moths and Butterflies of Great Britain and Ireland*, 1983, vol. 10, pl. 10)

Imago. 29–33 mm. Suspected immigrant. The only British specimen was taken at light at Halstead, Kent, on 10.ix.1969. Abroad its range includes southern Europe and North Africa.

Larva. *On cocklebur (*Xanthium*) and various species of mint (*Mentha*).

The Ni Moth
Trichoplusia ni Hübner
Plate **41**: *9*

Similar species. *Autographa gamma*, pl. **41**, is usually larger, forewing darker and less grey, with blackish shade from apex to Y-mark, tail of Y-mark distinctly curved upwards; and termen without pale wedge-shaped patch below apex. *Syngrapha interrogationis*, pl. **41**, has the forewing darker, silvery-grey, with blackish apical streak, and a silvery-white central mark. (See text fig 52.)

Imago. 30–40 mm. Immigrant. Normally taken at light, but occasionally noted visiting the flowers of red valerian. An uncommon and irregular visitor, found mostly in southern England, with a casual record from southern Ireland and elsewhere. The most favoured years were 1982 (69); 1992 (65); 1953 (20); 1968 (16); and 1952 (11). Six feral larvae have been recorded: two at Portland, Dorset, in 1894; on marigold at Teignmouth, Devon, on 18.viii.1968; on sea rocket at Dawlish, Devon, on 25.viii.1968; and on the flowers of hawkweed in the Burren, Co. Clare, on 15 & 18.viii.1992.

Larva. On marigold (*Calendula*), sea rocket and hawkweed; and in captivity on lettuce and cabbage.

Streaked Plusia

Trichoplusia vittata Wallengren
(*Atropos*, 1997, No. 2, pl. 1)

Imago. 32–38 mm. Suspected immigrant. A single male specimen was taken at light at Rye Harbour, East Sussex, on 31.vii.1995. This species had not been previously reported from Europe and is a resident of sub-Saharan Africa where it is probably multi-brooded.

Larva. *On various species of Compositaecae, Scrophulariacae, and Solanaceae.

Slender Burnished Brass

Diachrysia orichalcea Fabricius
(*aurifera* Hübner)
Plate **41** : *10*

Similar species. *D. chrysitis*, pl. **41**.

Imago. 38–48 mm. Immigrant. A rare visitor, usually appearing from mid-August to late October, of which 66 specimens have occurred to date in the British Isles, as follows: Sussex (23), Cornwall (9), Hampshire (9), Devon (5), Kent (3), Isle of Wight (3), Isles of Scilly (2), Dorset (2), Co. Cork (2), and singly in Norfolk, Oxfordshire, Gloucestershire, Warwickshire, Bedfordshire, Surrey, Co. Down, and Co. Galway. The maximum number of specimens recorded in a single year was ten in 1969, followed closely by eight in 1983 and seven in 1978. Abroad its range includes the Azores, the Canary Islands, and the Mediterranean region.

Larva. *On *Coreopsis* and Solanaceae. In captivity it has been reared on the leaves of potato.

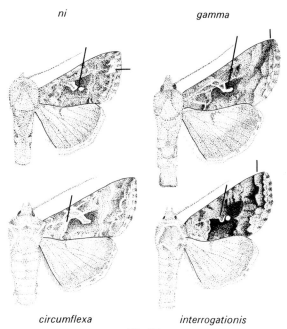

ni

gamma

circumflexa

interrogationis

Fig 52

Burnished Brass

Diachrysia chrysitis Linnaeus
Plate **41** : *11–12*

Variation. Colour of forewing gold or greenish-gold with the dark central band either complete or divided into two.

Similar species. *D. orichalcea*, pl. **41**.

Imago. 34–44 mm. Resident. Comes readily to the flowers of red valerian, *Buddleia*, thistles, sweet-william, and many other wild and cultivated plants. Also comes freely to light. Double-brooded (at least in southern Britain), occurring in June and July, and as a partial second generation in August and September. It inhabits waste places, gardens, marshes, commons, etc and is widespread and generally common over the greater part of the British Isles, including the Hebrides and Orkney.

Larva. Autumn to May, and during the summer on common nettle, marjoram, and probably other low plants.

Overwinters as a small larva.

Scarce Burnished Brass

Diachrysia chryson Esper
Plate **41** : *13*

Imago. 44–54 mm. Resident. Although it has sometimes been recorded flying in sunshine, the usual time of flight is after dark, when it is attracted to the flowers of hemp-agrimony, honeysuckle, and other plants, as well as to light. Single-brooded, flying in July and August, inhabiting river-banks, fenland, coastal undercliff, and marshy places. A very local species, formerly well established in the East Anglian fens and southeast Kent but rarely recorded in recent years outside Hampshire, Wiltshire, Berkshire, West Sussex and southwest Wales.

Larva. September to early June on hemp-agrimony, preferring plants growing in shade.

Overwinters as a small larva.

Dewick's Plusia

Macdunnoughia confusa Stephens
(*gutta* Guenée)
Plate **41** : *14*

Imago. 32–38 mm. Immigrant. Most of the 33 specimens recorded in Britain were taken at light. These are at Bradwell-on-Sea, Essex, on 3.x.1951; Penrith Cumberland, on 31.viii.1954; Ashford, Kent, on 4.x 1954; Ickham, Kent, on 20.viii.1955; Bradwell-on-Sea on 20.viii.1955; Chiddingfold, Surrey, on 30.viii 1955; Wells, Norfolk, on 21.viii.1955; Bishopsteignton Devon, on 4.vii.1962; Orphir, Orkney, on 3.viii.1969 Wittersham, Kent, on 11.viii.1969; Marton, Warwick shire, on 24.x.1977; Uckfield, Sussex, on 14.ix.1979 Hickling, Norfolk, on 3.viii.1982; Bradwell-on-Sea on

24.viii.1982; Dover, Kent, on 29.vii.1983; Stockton, Warwickshire, on 31.vii.1983; Wyke Regis, Dorset, on 22.ix.1988; St Marys, Isles of Scilly, on 8.x.1990; Portsmouth, Hampshire, on 28.viii.1991; Bearley, Warwickshire, on 4.ix.1991; New Romney, Kent, on 9.x.1991; Buckland, Surrey, on 20.viii.1992; Wimborne, Dorset, on 28.viii.1992; Ashford, Kent, on 31.viii.1992; Slimbridge, Gloucestershire, on 18.ix.1992; New Romney, on 21.x.1993; Clacton, Essex, on 8.viii.1994; Plymouth, Devon, on 10.viii.1995; Bishop's Stortford, Hertfordshire, on 30.viii.1995; Eswick, Shetland, on 12 & 13.viii.1996; Rye Harbour, East Sussex, on 19.viii.1996; Languard, Suffolk, on 7.viii.1997 and Bradwell-on-Sea on 30.ix.1997. In the Channel Islands a specimen was recorded on Guernsey on 13.ix.1992. Abroad it occurs in central and southern Europe.

Larva. *On common nettle, yarrow, bladder campion, mayweed, field wormwood, and corn chamomile (*Anthemis arvensis*).

Golden Plusia

Polychrysia moneta Fabricius

Plate **41** : *18*

Imago. 38–44 mm. Resident. Comes regularly to light in small numbers, and is sometimes noted visiting the flowers of red valerian and *Buddleia*. Normally single-brooded, flying from late June to early August, but in southern England a partial second generation may occur in September. Since it first appeared at the end of the nineteenth century this garden species has spread and become not uncommon throughout much of England and Wales. By the middle of this century it had reached southern Scotland with records as far north as the Inner Hebrides, Inverness-shire and Aberdeenshire. The late 1950s witnessed the start of a retraction in its range and it is now said to be scarce in Scotland and declining in parts of northern England. In Ireland it has been reported commonly from Co. Dublin and occasionally from Co. Armagh.

Larva. Autumn to June, and sometimes in the summer on monk's-hood and cultivated species of *Delphinium*.
Overwinters as a very small larva.

Purple-shaded Gem

Euchalcia variabilis Piller & Mitterpacher

(*illustris* Fabricius)

Plate **41** : *15*

Imago. 34–46 mm. Status uncertain, possibly extinct resident. Single-brooded on the Continent, flying from early June to early August. A few specimens were stated to have been taken on Salisbury Plain, Wiltshire, during the early part of the nineteenth century, and a single specimen was taken feeding on bramble flowers at Castle Kevin, Co. Wicklow, in August 1887. Abroad it is found in southern and eastern France, southern Germany, and northern Italy.

Larva. *August to early May on *Aconitum*, *Delphinium*, and *Thalictrum*.
Overwinters as a small larva.

Gold Spot

Plusia festucae Linnaeus

Plate **41** : *16*

Similar species. *P. putnami gracilis*, pl. **41**, has a more golden coloration, and a short and broad lower apical streak. (See text fig 53.)

Imago. 34–46 mm. Resident. Comes regularly to light in small numbers, and is attracted to the flowers of a wide variety of wild and cultivated plants, including red valerian, lavender, *Buddleia*, water-mint, campions, yellow iris, and woundwort. Double-brooded in southern Britain, appearing in June and July, and again in August and September. In northern England it is only occasionally double-brooded, and in much of Scotland and the Northern Isles it is always single-brooded, flying from late June to mid-August. The species inhabits fenland, damp woodland rides and clearings, commons, river-banks, boggy moorland, and other marshy places; it is widely distributed and locally not uncommon over much of the British Isles.

Larva. Autumn to spring, and presumably during July and August; probably on marshland grasses and plants. Foodplants frequently quoted are yellow iris and *Sparganium*.
Overwinters as a small larva.

Lempke's Gold Spot

Plusia putnami gracilis Lempke

Plate **41** : *17*

Similar species. *P. festucae*, pl. **41** and text.

Imago. 32–42 mm. Resident. Comes to light in moderate numbers. Single-brooded, flying in July and early August, inhabiting mainly fenland and other marshy places, but sometimes drier biotopes such as upland pasture and even gardens. Locally widespread in the fens and broads of East Anglia, the northern half of England, and southern Scotland, ranging sporadically northwards to Aberdeenshire. Elsewhere in the British Isles it has been recorded as single specimens at Ballavoley, Isle of Man, on 30.vii.1983; near Kenmare, Co. Kerry, on 15.vii.1989; and Ahakista, Co. Cork, on 16.vi.1994.

Larva. Has been found in May and June on purple small-reed.
Probably overwinters as a larva.

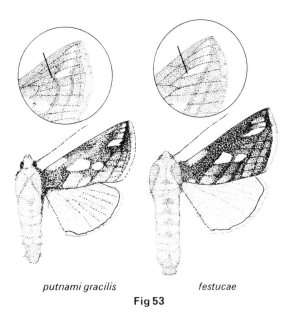

putnami gracilis   festucae

Fig 53

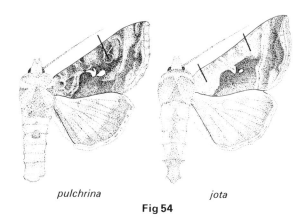

pulchrina   jota

Fig 54

commons, and gardens. Widely distributed and generally common over the whole of the British Isles.

Larva. August to May on honeysuckle, dead-nettle, and other low plants.

Overwinters as a larva.

Silver Y
Autographa gamma Linnaeus
Plate **41** : *22–23*

Variation. Very small specimens are not uncommon, and are referable to ab. *gammina* Staudinger (fig 23). Ab. *nigricans* Spuler is an uncommon velvet-black variety.

Similar species. *Trichoplusia ni*, pl. **41** and text. *Syngrapha interrogationis*, pl. **41** and text. *S. circumflexa*, pl. **41** and text.

Imago. 32–52 mm. Immigrant. Readily disturbed during the day, and often flies of its own accord in sunny weather. After dark it comes freely to light, and to the flowers of a wide variety of wild and cultivated plants and shrubs. A common visitor to the whole of the British Isles, appearing from spring to late autumn. It is sometimes abundant in southern Britain in late summer and autumn when the home-bred populations are reinforced by further immigration.

Larva. Summer and autumn on almost every kind of low-growing wild and cultivated plant. Occasionally it is a pest on cabbage, peas, and other green vegetables.

Beautiful Golden Y
Autographa pulchrina Haworth
Plate **41** : *20*

Similar species. *A. jota*, pl. **41**, has the basal and adjoining costal area almost plain with few markings, and lacks distinct reniform stigma, which in *A. pulchrina* is finely etched with silver. (See text fig 54.)

Imago. 36–44 mm. Resident. Comes regularly to light and a variety of woodland and garden flowers. Single-brooded, flying in June and July, inhabiting woodland,

Plain Golden Y
Autographa jota Linnaeus
Plate **41** : *21*

Similar species. *A. pulchrina*, pl. **41** and text.

Imago. 38–46 mm. Resident. Comes regularly to light, and is attracted to the flowers of red valerian, honeysuckle, and other plants. Single-brooded, flying from mid-June to early August, inhabiting woodland, commons, waste places, gardens, etc. Generally distributed and moderately common in England, Wales and Ireland. Locally widespread and less frequent in Scotland and the Hebrides. The occasional specimens found in Orkney are considered to be vagrants.

Larva. August to May on common nettle, cultivated honeysuckle, and other unverified wild and garden plants. In captivity it will accept sallow, hawthorn, and dock.

Overwinters as a larva.

Gold Spangle
Autographa bractea Denis & Schiffermüller
Plate **41** : *19*

Imago. 40–50 mm. Resident and possible immigrant. Comes regularly to light, and is attracted to the flowers of thistles, campions, honeysuckle, sweet-william, and other wild and cultivated plants. Single-brooded, flying in July and early August, inhabiting waste ground, gardens, roadside verges, and moorland. Widespread and locally common in the northern half of England, Scotland, the Inner Hebrides, Wales, and Ireland. Also found from Derbyshire westwards to Gloucestershire and Monmouthshire; in the Outer Hebrides, Orkney and the Isle of Man. Elsewhere it is recorded occasionally in East Anglia and the rest of southern England,

and these specimens are considered to be vagrants from either northern Britain or from abroad.

Larva. September to May on low plants. In captivity it will eat dock and various species of nettle, and if kept warm will produce a second generation during the autumn.

Overwinters as a larva.

Stephens's Gem

Autographa biloba Stephens

Plate **41** : *24*

Imago. 38–44 mm. Suspected immigrant. Two specimens have been recorded in Britain, both at light. These were near Aberystwyth, Cardiganshire, on 19.vii.1954; and Maidencombe, Devon, on 1.x.1958. This species is found throughout North America.

Larva. In some American states it is a pest on cultivated lettuce.

Scarce Silver Y

Syngrapha interrogationis Linnaeus

Plate **41** : *26*

Variation. Immigrant specimens are usually smaller and more uniformly leaden-grey than those from resident populations.

Similar species. *Autographa gamma*, pl. **41**, is usually larger, with a distinctively shaped and unbroken Y-mark; and lacks the silvery-grey colour so characteristic of *S. interrogationis*. *Trichoplusia ni*, pl. **41** and text. (See text fig 52.)

Imago. 30–40 mm. Resident and immigrant. Occasionally noted flying in hot sunshine, but more usually seen after dark at light or feeding on flowers. Single-brooded, flying from late June to early August, inhabiting heather-moorland. Widespread and locally common in the Scottish mainland, northern England, Wales, parts of the Midlands, and Ireland. Considered to be resident in Monmouthshire and possibly Devon and Cornwall. As an immigrant it is occasionally reported from eastern and southern England during late July and August. The maximum number of such specimens reported in a single year was 14 in both 1955 and 1972.

Larva. September to June on heather and bilberry.

Overwinters as a small larva.

Essex Y

Syngrapha circumflexa Linnaeus

Plate **41** : *25*

Similar species. *Autographa gamma*, pl. **41**, has a distinctively shaped Y-mark, and lacks the light-coloured antemedian fascia which is a characteristic feature of *S. circumflexa*. (See text fig 52.)

Imago. 38–48 mm. Suspected immigrant. The only fully documented record is of a specimen taken at light at Sway, Hampshire, on 29.vii.1979. A second example is stated to have occurred in Essex prior to 1802. Its range abroad includes the Canary Islands, southeast Europe, and North Africa.

Larva. In captivity on cultivated *Geranium*.

Dark Spectacle

Abrostola triplasia Linnaeus

(*trigemina* Werneburg)

Plate **41** : *28*

Similar species. *A. tripartita*, pl. **41**, has the basal area and tornal patch whitish-grey (not ochreous-brown), and the antemedian and subterminal lines edged with light brown (not reddish-brown).

Imago. 34–40 mm. Resident. Comes to light in small numbers, and is attracted to red valerian and other flowers. It inhabits waste places, marshes, hedgerows, and gardens. Normally single-brooded, flying in June and July, with a very occasional and partial second generation in late August and September. Widespread and moderately common in southwest England, Wales, the west Midlands, northwest England, the Isle of Man, and the whole of Ireland. Elsewhere in England it is locally widespread and generally uncommon. In Scotland it is thinly distributed and rather scarce.

Larva. August and September on common nettle and hop.

Overwinters as a pupa.

The Spectacle

Abrostola tripartita Hufnagel

(*triplasia* sensu auctt.)

Plate **41** : *27*

Variation. Dark and obscurely marked forms occur frequently in the London area and parts of the Midlands, and are referable to ab. *plumbea* Cockayne.

Similar species. *A. triplasia*, pl. **41** and text.

Imago. 32–38 mm. Resident. Comes readily to light, and the flowers of red valerian, *Buddleia*, *Petunia*, common nettle, and garden plants. Normally single-brooded, flying from late May to mid-July, with an occasional and usual partial generation occurring in southern Britain from late July to mid-September. These two broods vary according to season, and frequently overlap. The species inhabits open woodland, commons, marshes, gardens, waste places, etc, and is widespread and generally common over the greater part of the British Isles, including the Hebrides and Orkney.

Larva. July to September on common nettle.

Overwinters as a pupa.

SUBFAMILY: CATOCALINAE

Clifden Nonpareil

Catocala fraxini Linnaeus

Plate **42** : *4*

Imago. 90–106 mm. Immigrant and transitory resident. Comes readily to sugar (usually at dusk), and also sparingly to light. Single-brooded, flying throughout

September. Formerly resident in aspen woodland near Hamstreet, Kent, from 1935 to 1964, and in the Norfolk Broads from the early to mid-1930s. As an immigrant it is very irregular in its appearance, and usually scarce; years, such as 1976 when about 20 specimens were recorded, are exceptional. The majority of moths are recorded from southern and eastern England, although the occasional specimen ranges to Ireland, Scotland and the Northern Isles. Abroad its range includes central Europe and Scandinavia.

Larva. June to July on aspen. In captivity it has been reared on other species of poplar.

Overwinters as an egg.

Red Underwing
Catocala nupta Linnaeus
Plate **42** : *1*

Variation. Ab. *brunnescens* Warren has chocolate-brown hindwings and is occasionally recorded from the London area and elsewhere; an even rarer form with black forewings has occurred in North London and north Kent.

Similar species. *C. electa*, pl. **42**.

Imago. 70–90 mm. Resident. Occasionally seen during the day at rest on fences, walls, tree-trunks, and tele-graph-poles. After dark it comes to light, and readily to sugar. Single-brooded, flying in August and September, inhabiting woodland, parkland, marshes, etc. Rather scarce in southwest England and west Wales, otherwise well distributed and locally common in the southern half of Britain, ranging northwards to Cheshire and Yorkshire. A single and suspected vagrant specimen from Co. Cork, in 1906, constitutes the only Irish record.

Larva. May to July on willow, poplar, and aspen.

Overwinters as an egg.

Rosy Underwing
Catocala electa Vieweg
Plate **42** : *2*

Similar species. *C. nupta*, pl. **42**.

Imago. 65–80 mm. Suspected immigrant. Comes to sugar. Single-brooded on the Continent, flying from mid-July to late September. There are six possible British captures: at Shoreham, Sussex, on 24.ix.1875; Corfe, Dorset, on 12.ix.1892; Dedham, Essex, in 1892; Hoddesdon, Hertfordshire, on 15.ix.1927; Hammersmith, northwest London, without date (Hope Dept. Coll., Oxford); and Portland, Dorset, on 11.ix.1993. Abroad it is an uncommon and declining species occurring in central and southern Europe.

Larva. *March and June on willow, sallow, and poplar.

Overwinters as an egg.

Light Crimson Underwing
Catocala promissa Denis & Schiffermüller
Plate **42** : *5*

Similar species. *C. sponsa*, pl. **42**, is larger, has the forewing darker, brownish, and not greyish; and hind-wing with a distinct W-shaped postmedian fascia.

Imago. 50–60 mm. Resident. Both sexes come to light and sugar. Single-brooded, flying from late July to late August, but sometimes appearing earlier or later according to the season. A species of oak woodlands, well established in the New Forest, and found locally elsewhere in Hampshire, Wiltshire and Sussex. Was also resident in southeast Kent and on the Oxfordshire/Buckinghamshire border, but there appears to be no very recent record.

Larva. April to May on oak.

Overwinters as an egg.

Dark Crimson Underwing
Catocala sponsa Linnaeus
Plate **42** : *3*

Similar species. *C. promissa*, pl. **42** and text.

Imago. 58–74 mm. Resident and suspected immigrant. Both sexes come to light and sugar. Single-brooded, flying in August and early September, inhabiting oak woodland. A very local species well established in the New Forest, Hampshire, where in some years it is not uncommon. Formerly resident this century in Wiltshire, Sussex, and southeast Kent, but there is no recent record. As an immigrant it is occasionally reported along the coast of southern England from Essex to Devon.

Larva. April to early June on oak.

Overwinters as an egg.

Oak Yellow Underwing
Catocala nymphagoga Esper
Plate **42** : *6*

Imago. 39–46 mm. Suspected immigrant. Single-brooded on the Continent, flying in July and August, inhabiting oak woodland. The only two British speci-mens were taken at light at Tregaron, Cardiganshire, on 28.vii.1982; and in the New Forest, Hampshire, on 31.vii.1982. A locally common species found in central and southern Europe.

Larva. *March to early June on oak.

Overwinters as an egg.

Lunar Double-stripe
Minucia lunaris Denis & Schiffermüller
Plate **42** : *7*

Imago. 50–60 mm. Immigrant and transitory resident. Has been obtained from dusk onwards flying around coppiced oaks, and also at light and sugar. Single-brooded, flying from mid-May to mid-June, inhabiting oak woodland. Formerly known to be resident in wood-land near Hamstreet, Kent, from 1942 to 1958, and near Laughton, Sussex, from the early to the mid 1950s. As an immigrant it has been recorded during the nineteenth century from Sussex (6), Kent (4), Co. Kerry (2), and singly from Suffolk, Norfolk, and (doubtfully) Perthshire; and in this century from: Delamere Forest,

Cheshire, in June 1901; Brighton, Sussex, on 18.vi.1907 and September 1908; Horam, Sussex, on 13.v.1948; Hastings, Sussex, on 20.vi.1948; Bradwell-on-Sea, Essex, on 25.v.1951; two larvae, Hadleigh, Essex, in July 1951; Selsey, Sussex, on 14.vi.1952; near Hailsham, Sussex, on 30.v.1953: Lee-on-Solent, Hampshire, on 29.v.1954; Bradwell-on-Sea on i.vi.1959; Stapleford, Sussex, in June 1977; Swanage, Dorset, on 21 & 24.v.1992; Hastings, on 24.v.1992; Bradwell-on-Sea on 29.v.1992; East Winch, Norfolk, on 30.v.1992; Wimborne, Dorset, on 26.v.1993; and Littlestone, Kent, on 4.vi.1997. Abroad this species is found throughout central and southern Europe, North Africa and Asia Minor.

Larva. Early July to mid-August on oak.
Overwinters as a pupa.

Trent Double-stripe
Clytie illunaris Hübner
(*The Moths and Butterflies of Great Britain and Ireland*, 1983, vol. 10, pl. 12)

Imago. 40–46 mm. Suspected immigrant or importation. Double-brooded on the Continent, flying in May and June, and again in August. The only British record is of a larva found feeding on wild horse-radish (*Armoracia*) beside the River Trent, near Amcotts, Lincolnshire, in June 1964. Abroad its range includes southern France, Spain, and Italy.

Larva. *Late June and July, and September and October on *Tamarix* and bog myrtle.
Overwinters as a pupa.

The Passenger
Dysgonia algira Linnaeus
Plate **41** : *33*

Imago. 40–46 mm. Suspected immigrant. Comes to light. Double-brooded on the Continent, flying in April and May, and again in July and August. There have been six records from England, and one from the Channel Islands. These are at Samares Manor, Jersey, on 25.viii.1960; near Dover, Kent, in August, 1967; Bradwell-on-Sea, Essex, on 15.ix.1969; Swanage, Dorset, on 23.ix.1983; Gravesend, Kent, on 31.viii.1996; Portland, Dorset, on 14.viii.1996; and West Bexington, Dorset, on 10.ix.1997. It is a southern European species.

Larva. *June to July, and October on bramble, sallow, and *Genista*.
Overwinters as a pupa.

The Geometrician
Grammodes stolida Fabricius
Plate **43** : *39*

Imago. 30–44 mm. Suspected immigrant. Double-brooded on the Continent, flying from mid-May to late June, and again from mid-August to late September. The first British specimen was taken at sugar near Dartmouth, Devon, on 23.ix.1903 and the second to light at Crowborough, East Sussex, on 30.ix.1990. Abroad its range includes southern Europe and Africa.

Larva. *May and during the summer on bramble, oak, *Paliurus*, and *Coriaria myrtifolia*.
Overwinters as a pupa.

Mother Shipton
Callistege mi Clerck
Plate **41** : *5*

Imago. 30–34 mm. Resident. Flies in sunshine. Single-brooded, flying in May and June, inhabiting downland, flowery meadows, waste ground, woodland rides and clearings, railway banks, etc. Widespread and locally common in England, Wales and Ireland. Local in Scotland as far north as Ross-shire.

Larva. July to September on coarse grasses and common reed.
Overwinters as a pupa.

Burnet Companion
Euclidia glyphica Linnaeus
Plate **41** : *4*

Imago. 28–34 mm. Resident. Flies in sunshine. Single-brooded, flying in May and June, inhabiting downland, woodland rides and clearings, railway banks, marshy meadows, etc. Widespread and moderately common in the southern half of England, becoming local and less frequent in Wales, the Isle of Man and northern England, and ranging as far north as southern Scotland. In Ireland it occurs commonly in the Burren district of Cos Clare and Galway; elsewhere it is recorded from Cos Donegal, Tyrone, Fermanagh, Westmeath, Offaly, Kildare and Tipperary.

Larva. July and August on various clovers and trefoils.
Overwinters as a pupa.

SUBFAMILY: OPHIDERINAE

The Alchymist
Catephia alchymista Denis & Schiffermüller
Plate **42** : *8*

Imago. 42–50 mm. Immigrant. The majority of British specimens have been taken at sugar. Single-brooded on the Continent, flying from May to July, inhabiting woodland. Fifteen adults and two larvae have been recorded in Britain. These are: Bembridge, Isle of Wight, on 13.ix.1858; two, Isle of Wight in July 1867; Abbots Wood (near Hailsham), Sussex, on 4.vi.1875; Colchester, Essex, on 9.vi.1875; Dover, Kent, in June 1882; St Leonards, Sussex, on 24.vi.1888; two larvae, Abbots Wood on 5.vii.1894; Folkestone, Kent, in 1896; Abbots Wood on 2.vii.1898; Deal, Kent, on 26.v.1990; Barming, Kent, 17.vi.1919; Cleobury Mortimer, Shropshire, on 20.vi.1922; Kingsdown, Kent, on 12.viii.1934; Dungeness, Kent, on 18.ix.1934; and Middleton-on-Sea, Sussex, on 3.vii.1963. It is found in France and Belgium, and elsewhere in central and southern Europe.

Larva. *July and August mainly on the young shoots and saplings of oak; and sometimes on elm and evergreen oak.
Overwinters as a pupa.

The Four-spotted

Tyta luctuosa Denis & Schiffermüller

Plate **41**:*34*

Imago. 25–29 mm. Resident. Flies in sunshine, and also after dark when it comes to light. Its time of appearance depends on the season and it may be found any time from mid-May to mid-August. It inhabits chalk downland, flowery embankments, railway banks and cuttings, breckland, and waste places. A much decreased species, formerly widely distributed over the southern half of England, but now extremely local and uncommon. The best known localities are Portland, Dorset, and the Breck district of Suffolk, but small populations exist in Hertfordshire, northwest Kent, northeast Surrey, northwest Essex, Bedfordshire, Cambridgeshire, Oxfordshire, and Nottinghamshire. Elsewhere occasional specimens are still reported from southeast Kent, South Hampshire, Buckinghamshire, Worcestershire and Middlesex; and these indicate the possible existence of undiscovered colonies.

Larva. July, August, and sometimes later on field bindweed.

Overwinters as a pupa.

The Blackneck

Lygephila pastinum Treitschke

Plate **41**:*30*

Similar species. *L. craccae*, pl. **41**, has the forewing darker, with four costal dots, and lacks the orbicular dot. (See text fig 55.)

Imago. 41–48 mm. Resident. Readily disturbed during the day, and after dark comes to light in varying numbers. Single-brooded, flying from mid-June to mid-July, inhabiting commons, edges of woodland, downland, damp meadows, and marshy places. Widely distributed and locally common in the southern half of England, South Wales, the south Midlands, and in East Anglia, ranging locally northwards to Yorkshire.

Larva. August to May on tufted vetch (*Vicia cracca*). Overwinters as a small larva.

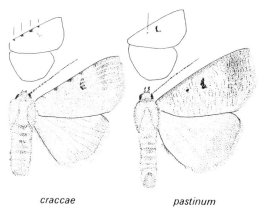

craccae   *pastinum*

Fig 55

Scarce Blackneck

Lygephila craccae Denis & Schiffermüller

Plate **41**:*31*

Similar species. *L. pastinum*, pl. **41** and text.

Imago. 40–46 mm. Resident. May be disturbed during the day from its foodplant and adjacent vegetation. After dark it comes sparingly to light, and is stated to visit the flowers of wood sage and hemp-agrimony. Single-brooded, flying in July and August, inhabiting cliffs and rocky places by the sea. A very local species confined to a few coastal localities in north Cornwall and North Devon, and a single site in North Somerset. A specimen resembling this species was noted, but not retained, at Kynance, Cornwall, on 15.x.1985.

Larva. May to early July on wood vetch (*Vicia sylvatica*). Overwinters as an egg.

Levant Blackneck

Tathorhynchus exsiccata Lederer

Plate **41**:*29*

Imago. 28–34 mm. Immigrant. Mostly recorded at light. A very rare visitor to southern England, usually appearing in early spring. The ten British records are: Maidencombe, Devon, on 20.iii.1952; Farringdon, Hampshire, on 21.iii.1952; Aylesford, Kent, in 1952; north Cornwall in September 1954; Rodborough, Gloucestershire, on 1.vi.1955; Arundel, Sussex, on 2.vi.1955; three, Martyr Worthy, Hampshire, on 2.ii. (2) & 3.ii.1967; and Mawnan Smith, Cornwall, on 22.xi.1981. Its wide distribution abroad includes the Mediterranean countries, Africa, and the Middle East.

Larva. *On lucerne and tree indigo (*Indigofera tinctoria*).

The Herald

Scoliopteryx libatrix Linnaeus

Plate **41**:*32*

Imago. 44–48 mm. Resident. Comes to sugar, ivy blossom, ripe blackberries, and light. Single-brooded, occurring from late July to November, and after hibernation from March to June. In inhabits woodland, marshes, commons and gardens. Generally distributed and moderately common in England, Wales and Ireland. Thinly scattered and less frequent over much of Scotland including Orkney.

Larva. June to August on sallow, willow, aspen, osier, poplar and rowan.

Overwinters as an adult. May be found, sometimes in fair numbers, in old sheds, outhouses, barns, old army bunkers, etc.

Small Purple-barred

Phytometra viridaria Clerck

(*aenea* Hübner)

Plate **41**:*35*

Variation. Ground colour of forewing ranges from olive-grey to olive-brown. In some specimens the purplish-red cross-bands are brownish and indistinct, whilst others having the forewing uniformly dingy brown are referable to ab. *fusca* Tutt.

Imago. 19–20 mm. Resident. Flies in sunshine, sometimes also at night when it is attracted to light. Single-brooded, flying from May to July, inhabiting chalk downland, embankments, woodland rides and clearings, heathland, mountain moorland, and sandhills. Widely distributed and not uncommon in the southern half of England, Wales and Ireland. Locally distributed in the rest of mainland Britain, but rarely recorded north of Inverness-shire. Also recorded from the Inner Hebrides.

Larva. July to September on common milkwort (*Polygala vulgaris*) and heath milkwort (*P. serpyllifolia*). Overwinters as a pupa.

Angled Gem
Anomis sabulifera Guenée

Imago. 32–38 mm. Suspected immigrant or importation. A single specimen conforming to ab. *bipunctata* Warren was taken at sugar at Goudhurst, Kent, in September 1935. This species, which bears a vague resemblance to a small uniformly brownish-grey *Scoliopteryx libatrix*, pl. **41**, occurs in North Africa, Japan, Malay, and Australia.

Lesser Belle
Colobochyla salicalis Denis & Schiffermüller
Plate **41** : *36*

Imago. 26–30 mm. Resident and possible immigrant. May be disturbed during dry and warm weather from clearings containing young aspen. It flies naturally from dusk onwards, when it comes sparingly to light. Single-brooded, flying from early June to mid-July. A very local species formerly confined to woodland near Hamstreet, Kent, where it was first noted in 1932. Has not been recorded since 1977 and may be extinct. Old specimens suggest it may have been resident during the nineteenth century in north Kent and near Haslemere, Surrey. A single example was taken at light at Maidencombe, Devon, on 14.viii.1965, and was presumably an immigrant.

Larva. July and early August on the shoots and young leaves of aspen.
Overwinters as a pupa, within a tough silken cocoon constructed on a stem or branch of the foodplant.

Beautiful Hook-tip
Laspeyria flexula Denis & Schiffermüller
Plate **41** : *37*

Imago. 28–36 mm. Resident. Comes to light in small numbers. Single-brooded, flying from late June to early August, inhabiting woodland, parkland, and old orchards. A widespread, but somewhat local, species found in the southern half of England, East Anglia, parts of the Midlands, and South Wales.

Larva. September to May on lichens growing on hawthorn, blackthorn, larch, Norway spruce, yew, apple and other fruit trees.
Overwinters as a larva.

Straw Dot
Rivula sericealis Scopoli
Plate **41** : *38*

Imago. 19–25 mm. Resident and suspected immigrant. Occasionally disturbed during the day, but most frequently seen from dusk onwards either flying or at light. The moth is normally on the wing from mid-June to late July, but in southern Britain it is frequently noted in August and September, sometimes later, and these are probably the result of a second generation. The species inhabits marshes, fenland, and mosses; and the damper parts of woodland, heathland, moorland, and commons. Widespread and moderately common in the southern half of England south of a line from the Mersey to the Humber, the whole of Wales, the Isle of Man, and Cumbria. Locally distributed in western Scotland from Galloway to western Inverness-shire and in the Inner Hebrides. Widespread and common in Ireland. The occasional appearance of fair numbers in coastal or unlikely habitats is probably the result of migration.

Larva. August to May on various grasses. Both torgrass and false brome are quoted by some authors as natural foodplants.
Overwinters as a larva.

Waved Black
Parascotia fuliginaria Linnaeus
Plate **41** : *39*

Imago. 24–30 mm. Resident and suspected immigrant. Comes sparingly to light. Single-brooded, occurring in June and July, inhabiting damp woodland, wooded heathland, sometimes gardens, and in the past old warehouses, cellars, etc. A secretive and easily overlooked species, well established and locally common as larvae in North Hampshire, Sussex, Surrey, Berkshire, and parts of Middlesex. It is also found locally in Worcestershire, Buckinghamshire, Kent, Essex, Hertfordshire, Gloucestershire, Warwickshire and parts of South Wales. Elsewhere it has occurred singly in Suffolk, Derbyshire, Lincolnshire, Yorkshire and Co. Durham; and these, together with some of the more casual records from southeast England, are probably the result of migration. Although this species was known in Britain as far back as the early nineteenth century, it was not thought to reside outside the City of London and the adjacent dockland until the early part of the twentieth century when specimens were taken near Camberley, Surrey.

Larva. August to June on *Coriolus versicolor*, *Daldinia concentrica*, *Phaeolus schweinizii*, and other fungi growing on tree-stumps, fallen or felled tree-trunks, stored logs, and on other well-weathered or rotting timber. Overwinters as a very small larva.

SUBFAMILY: HYPENINAE

Beautiful Snout

Hypena crassalis Fabricius
(*frontis* Thunberg)
(*fontis* misspelling)
Plate **42** : *17–18*

Imago. 28–34 mm. Resident. Flies freely at dusk; also comes to light and occasionally sugar. Single-brooded, flying in June and July, inhabiting woodland. A local species found in southern England from Kent to Cornwall, Surrey, Berkshire, Somerset, the west Midlands, Cumbria, and much of Wales. In Ireland it is locally common in Cos Kerry and Cork; and has been recorded elsewhere from Cos Mayo and Wicklow. In recent years it has occurred in southeast Kent well outside the range of its normal foodplant (bilberry), and in one woodland locality appears to be established at low density. It is possible that this colony and the other casual records were the result of migration.
Larva. August to September on bilberry. On the Continent some authors state heather as an alternative foodplant.
Overwinters as a pupa.

The Snout

Hypena proboscidalis Linnaeus
Plate **42** : *16*

Variation. Specimens of the second generation are on average smaller.
Imago. 36–42 mm. Resident. Flies commonly at dusk in the vicinity of its foodplant, and also comes to light, sugar and flowers. Double-brooded, flying from mid-June to early August, and again in smaller numbers in September and early October, except in northern Britain, where it is usually single-brooded, occurring in July and August. The species inhabits woodland, commons, gardens, waste ground, and a variety of weedy places, and is found commonly over the greater part of the British Isles, including the Inner Hebrides and Orkney.
Larva. Autumn to May, and July and August, on common nettle.
Overwinters as a larva.

Bloxworth Snout

Hypena obsitalis Hübner
Plate **42** : *19–20*

Imago. 28–36 mm. Resident and immigrant. Rarely attracted to light; has been taken at ivy blossom, but more readily found after dark flying over its foodplant. During the winter it has been reported from the Channel Islands from inside garden sheds, old army bunkers, and

other outbuildings. Double-brooded, flying in September and October and after hibernation in May and June, and again from late July to mid-August. It has been considered to be resident in the Channel Islands since the early 1960s, and on mainland Britain from 1990 following its discovery near Torquay, South Devon. Larvae have been found on numerous occasions and the species is now known to be well established in the Torbay district of Devon. Elsewhere it has been located coastally as far east as Purbeck, Dorset, and sporadically as far west as Boscastle, North Cornwall.

As a suspected immigrant the records are: Bloxworth, Dorset, on 21.ix.1884; Cambridgeshire in 1895 (BM[NH] coll.); Iford, Dorset, on 11.vii.1917; Ummera, Co. Cork, on 5.x.1936; Boscastle, Cornwall, on 12.ix.1943; St Agnes, Isles of Scilly, on 8.ix.1962; Brownsea Island, Dorset, on 10.x.1965; Shanklin, Isle of Wight, on 27.i.1968; Playden, East Sussex, on 6.iii.1983; Dover, Kent, on 18.viii.1985; Perranporth, Cornwall, on 8.xi.1987; Brixham, South Devon, on 29.vii.1987; Selborne, Hampshire, on, 12.xi.1994, and Christchurch, Hampshire, on 2.v.1995. *Author's Note:* In view of its recent residency the origin of some of these recent records must be open to debate.
Larva. July, and again in late August and early September on pellitory (*Parietaria*) and possibly nettle. Overwinters as an adult.

Paignton Snout

Hypena obesalis Treitschke
Plate **42** : *15*

Imago. 38–44 mm. Suspected immigrant. Single-brooded on the Continent, flying in late summer and autumn, and after hibernation in May and June. There are three British records, the first taken at sugar and the other two at light. These are: Paignton, South Devon, on 5.x.1908; Chobham, Surrey, on 14.ix.1969; and Charlcote, Warwickshire, on 26.viii.1973. Abroad it occurs over much of central and southern Europe.
Larva. *June and July on common nettle.
Overwinters as an adult.

Buttoned Snout

Hypena rostralis Linnaeus
Plate **42** : *21–22*

Imago. 27–32 mm. Resident. Comes sparingly to light, sugar, and ivy blossom. Single-brooded, flying from August to October, and after hibernation from late April to early June, inhabiting hedgerows and bushy places. A much decreased species, occurring in the southern half of Britain, and only casually recorded in recent years outside Dorset, Surrey, Middlesex, north Kent and South Essex, in all of which counties it is locally not uncommon.
Larva. June and July on the leaves of hop.
Overwinters as an adult. Has been found, sometimes in fair numbers, in garden sheds, outhouses, old army bunkers, and other disused buildings.

White-line Snout

Schrankia taenialis Hübner
(*albistrigalis* misspelling)
Plate **42** : *9*

Similar species. *S. costaestrigalis*, pl. **42**, has the forewing narrower, with an indistinct and obliquely angled subterminal line, and a well-defined reniform streak connected to the subterminal line. *S. intermedialis*, pl. **42** and text. (See text fig 56.)

Imago. 18–24 mm. Resident. Flies strongly around dusk, and again later in the night when it comes to sugar and light. Single-brooded, flying in July and early August, inhabiting damp woodland, open heathland, and shady hedgebanks. Widely distributed, but local, over the southern half of England and South Wales.

Larva. The feral larva is unknown in Britian. Raised in captivity on one occasion, the eggs hatched in about ten days; and the larvae were reared at first on a mixed diet of lettuce and the flowers of thyme and heath, and later on sliced runner beans. The moths eventually emerged in the autumn, but in the wild this species would almost certainly overwinter in the larval stage.

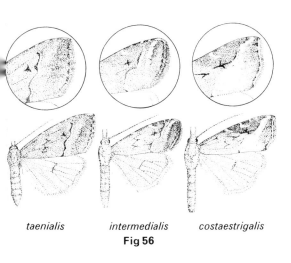

taenialis   intermedialis   costaestrigalis

Fig 56

Autumnal Snout

Schrankia intermedialis Reid
Plate **42** : *10*

Similar species. *S. taenialis*, pl. **42**, has the forewing broader, with a less angulated subterminal line, and a small reniform mark which never extends to the subterminal line. *S. costaestrigalis*, pl. **42**, has a more obliquely angled, but faint, subterminal line, and a longer and well-defined reniform streak. (See text fig 56.)

Imago. 18–22 mm. Resident. This species, of which only five male specimens are known to science, was first recorded in 1971, when two specimens were taken at light on 21 and 22 October in Broxbourne Woods, Hertfordshire. On 4.x.1973 a third example came to

light at Bayfordbury in the same county, and on 1.x.1982 a fourth male was netted at dusk in the original locality. The final example was taken at light at Warehorne, Kent, on 23.ix.1988. One theory put forward and worthy of investigation is that as the wing pattern and the genitalia are intermediate in appearance between the other two British *Schrankia* species, *S. intermedialis* is a possible hybrid. This point of view was strengthened in July 1982 when both *S. taenialis* and *S. costaestrigalis* were found to occupy the same ground in Broxbourne Woods. Both species also occur in the Kent locality.

Larva. Unknown.

Pinion-streaked Snout

Schrankia costaestrigalis Stephens
Plate **42** : *11–13*

Variation. Ground colour variable, ranging from whitish-brown to blackish-brown.

Similar species. *S. taenialis*, pl. **42** and text. *S. intermedialis*, pl. **42** and text.

Imago. 16–22 mm. Resident. Flies commonly at dusk, when it comes to sugar and the flowers of sedge, thistles, and other plants. Also comes sparingly to light. Normally single-brooded, flying from late June to early August, but in southern England there is frequently a partial second generation in September and October. The species inhabits damp woodland, fenland, boggy heathland, mosses, and other marshy places, and is found locally over the greater part of Britain, as far north as West Inverness-shire and Morayshire. In Ireland it is stated to be very local, and recorded only from Cos Armagh, Sligo, Mayo, Wicklow, Cork, and Kerry.

Larva. The feral larva is unknown. In captivity it has been reared on lettuce, the flowers of thyme and wild mint, and damp withered sallow leaves.

Overwinters as a larva.

Marsh Oblique-barred

Hypenodes humidalis Doubleday
(*turfosalis* Wocke)
Plate **42** : *14*

Imago. 14–15 mm. Resident. Flies in the late afternoon and at dusk. Normally single-brooded, flying from late June to mid-August, with an occasional and partial second generation in September, inhabiting boggy heathland and moorland. A small and local, but easily overlooked, species, sporadically distributed over England, Wales, and Scotland, as far north as Argyllshire. Its better-known localities are the heaths of Surrey, Dorset, and Hampshire; the turf moors of Somerset; and the boggy moorland and mosses of North Wales, Shropshire, and Cumbria. In Ireland it is locally common in Cos Cork, Clare and Kerry.

Larva. The feral larva is unknown. In captivity it is stated to have been reared on cross-leaved heath.

Common Fan-foot
Pechipogo strigilata Linnaeus
(*barbalis* Clerck)
Plate **42** : *24*

Similar species. The ochreous-grey forewing with the postmedian line sharply curved around the discal mark, and the pale hindwing distinguish this species from the four following similar-looking fan-foots. (See text fig 57.)

Imago. 30–35 mm. Resident. May be disturbed during the day from bushes and the lower branches of trees, with a preference for felled branches bearing partly withered leaves. The natural flight occurs from dusk onwards, when it comes sparingly to light. Single-brooded, flying in late May and June, sometimes earlier in a forward season, inhabiting woodland. A much decreased species, and, contrary to its vernacular name, now uncommon and very local. It was formerly found over much of southern England and in parts of the Midlands, but in recent years it is rarely recorded outside Worcestershire, Gloucestershire, Wiltshire, North Hampshire, East Sussex and southeast Kent. Doubtfully recorded from Ireland.

Larva. July to April on withered leaves. In captivity it has been reared on withered oak-leaves.

Overwinters as a nearly full-grown larva.

Plumed Fan-foot
Pechipogo plumigeralis Hübner
Plate **43** : *40*

Similar species. *Herminia zelleralis*, pl. **42**, has a stronger and more dentate postmedian line, a broader and less sinuous subterminal line, and a smaller but strongly defined reniform stigma. It also lacks the presence of the small dark orbicular spot which may be discernible in some specimens of *plumigeralis*. The antennae of the male are ciliate; not dentate as in *plumigeralis*. (See text fig. 57.)

Imago. 22–26 mm. Suspected immigrant. Abroad it is single or double-brooded depending on latitude and could appear any time from late April to October. All the seven specimens taken to date in Britain have been at light; the first in October and the others from late July to late August. They are at Greatstone, Kent, on 12.x.1995; Rye Harbour, East Sussex, on 22.vii. 8 & 11.viii.1996; New Romney, Kent, on 8.viii.1996; Dungeness, Kent, on 9.viii.1997; and Rye Harbour on 25.viii.1997. Abroad its range includes southern and central Europe, and North Africa.

Larva. *June onwards on broom, ivy, and rose, but most likely to be polyphagous and may, like the larvae of some related species, prefer withering leaves.

Overwinters as a pupa.

The Fan-foot
Herminia tarsipennalis Treitschke
Plate **42** : *27*

Variation. Examples of an apparently unnamed pale ochreous form have been reported from Brodick, Isle of Arran, Mabie, Dumfries-shire, and parts of southern Ireland.

Similar species. *H. lunalis*, pl. **42**, has the forewing less grey and faintly tinged with purple, the postmedian line dentate, the antemedian line angled below the costa and the discal mark conspicuously crescent-shaped. *H tarsicrinalis*, pl. **42**, has the forewing tinged with ochreous, the antemedian line angled below the costa but otherwise straight, and an ochreous-brown median shade, which almost overshadows the faint discal mark. *H. zelleralis*, pl. **42**, has the forewing darker, both the postmedian and antemedian lines dentate, the dark sub-

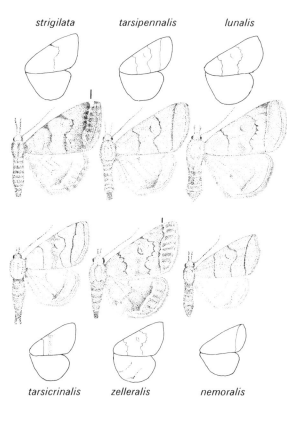

strigilata   tarsipennalis   lunalis

tarsicrinalis   zelleralis   nemoralis

plumigeralis

Fig 57

terminal line edged with whitish-ochreous, and the discal mark ocellate. (See text fig 57.)

Imago. 30–35 mm. Resident. May be disturbed during the day from hedges and bushes. Flies from dusk onwards, and comes to light and sugar in small numbers. Normally single-brooded, flying in June and July, but specimens are occasionally recorded later in the year, and these probably represent a partial second generation. Generally distributed and moderately common over England (except the north), Wales and Ireland. Locally distributed in northern England and southern Scotland.

Larva. August to October on the dried and withered leaves of beech, oak, raspberry, bramble, and probably other trees. Larvae have been found on leaves both on the ground and attached to fallen or partly broken branches.

Overwinters as a full-grown larva.

Jubilee Fan-foot
Herminia lunalis Scopoli
(*tarsiplumalis* Hübner)
Plate **42** : *26*

Similar species. *H. tarsicrinalis*, pl. **42**, has the forewing tinged with ochreous, an ochreous-brown median shade, and lacks a conspicuous crescent-shaped discal mark. *H. zelleralis*, pl. **42**, has the forewing greyer and without a purple tinge, both the postmedian and antemedian lines more dentate, and the discal mark ocellate. *H. tarsipennalis*, pl. **42** and text. (See text fig 57.)

Imago. 30–36 mm. Status unknown. Single-brooded on the Continent, flying from early June to August. The only British specimen was taken at light at Dorney Reach, Buckinghamshire, in August 1976. This species is not a recognized migrant, so, unless it was accidentally imported, this record could indicate the existence of an undiscovered resident population.

Larva. *September to April on a variety of herbaceous plants, preferring the withered leaves.

Overwinters as a larva.

Shaded Fan-foot
Herminia tarsicrinalis Knoch
Plate **42** : *28*

Similar species. *H. zelleralis*, pl. **42**, has the forewing darker, greyer, and not ochreous, both the postmedian and antemedian lines dentate, and the discal mark conspicuous and ocellate. *H. tarsipennalis*, pl. **42** and text. *H. lunalis*, pl. **42** and text. *H. grisealis*, pl. **42** and text. (See text fig 57.)

Imago. 28–32 mm. Resident. Flies from dusk to about midnight, when both sexes are attracted to light in moderate numbers. Single-brooded, flying in late June and July. In the more southerly parts of its Continental range it is regularly partially double-brooded; in view of this and its habits in captivity it is likely that the occasional specimen might appear in the autumn following a hot summer. The moth inhabits deciduous wood-

land and commons, and is associated closely with mature bramble thickets from which it seldom strays. The first British specimen was taken near Thorpeness, Suffolk, on 11.vii.1965, and the second from near Woodbridge, Suffolk, on 27.vi.1967. No other records were forthcoming until July 1982 when a survey of possible breeding sites in East Suffolk showed the species well established in an area of lightly wooded common land. Further investigation the same year and in 1983 led to the discovery of other sites, including an area of deciduous woodland. Now that the habits of this retiring species are more fully understood further investigation has led to its discovery in the neighbouring counties of Essex and Norfolk.

Larva. *August to spring on withered leaves. In captivity it has been reared on dandelion, with both fresh and withered leaves being accepted with equal relish. In normal room temperatures some of the larvae pupated and emerged in the autumn, the others overwintered in the final or penultimate instar.

Dusky Fan-foot
Herminia zelleralis Wocke
(*tarsicristalis* Herrich-Schäffer)
Plate **42** : *25*

Similar species. *H. tarsipennalis*, pl. **42** and text. *H. lunalis*, pl. **42** and text. *H. tarsicrinalis*, pl. **42** and text. *Pechipogo plumigeralis*, pl. **43** and text.

Imago. 31–36 mm. Status unknown. Single-brooded on the Continent, flying in June and July. The only British specimen was taken at light near Stackpole, Pembrokeshire, during the last week of July 1982. Abroad it is found in many parts of central and southern Europe, but it is not generally accepted as a migratory species.

Larva. *August to May on the withered leaves of low plants.

Overwinters as a larva.

Small Fan-foot
Herminea grisealis Denis & Schiffermüller
(*nemoralis* Fabricius)
Plate **42** : *29*

Similar species. Its smaller size, and the forewing with the subterminal line curved outwards towards the apex, readily distinguishes this species from *H. tarsicrinalis*, pl. **42**, and other similar-looking fan-foots. (See text fig 57.)

Imago. 24–28 mm. Resident. May be disturbed during the day from hedges, bushes, and the lower branches of trees. Flies from dusk onwards, and comes regularly to light in small numbers. Single-brooded, flying from June to August, inhabiting woodland and bushy places. Generally distributed and fairly common in England, Wales and Ireland. Rather local in Scotland, ranging sporadically as far north as Ross-shire.

Larva. August to October on oak, hazel, birch, hawthorn and alder, eating living leaves, and also decaying leaves either on the ground or attached to fallen or partly broken branches.

Overwinters as a pupa. Occasionally found under loose bark and under the fibrous stems of ivy growing on the trunk of its foodplant.

Dotted Fan-foot
Macrochilo cribrumalis Hübner
Plate **42** : *30*

Similar species. *Calamotropha paludella* Hübner (Family Pyralidae) is larger and has a pure white silky hindwing.
Imago. 26–30 mm. Resident. May be found from dusk onwards fluttering amongst and alighting on the stems of reeds and grasses; and also sparingly at light. Single-brooded, flying from late June to early August, inhabiting fenland and marshes. A very local species, but not uncommon where found; occurring in South Hampshire, East Sussex, Kent, Essex, Suffolk, Norfolk, and Cambridgeshire.
Larva. August to May. Stated to feed on hairy woodrush, wood-sedge (*Carex sylvatica*), and various marsh grasses.
Overwinters as a half-grown larva in the tufts of grasses.

Clay Fan-foot
Paracolax tristalis Fabricius
(*derivalis* Hübner)
Plate **42** : *23*

Imago. 28–35 mm. Resident. May be disturbed during the day from felled branches bearing withered leaves, brushwood, and woodland undergrowth. Also comes to light and sugar, usually in very small numbers. Single-brooded, flying in July and early August, inhabiting woodland. A local species occurring in Sussex, Surrey, Kent and Essex; and singly at Clarendon, Wiltshire, on 24.vi.1938; Swanage, Dorset, on 28.vii.1948; and Alice Holt, Hampshire, on 11.viii.1971.

Larva. Late August to early June on fallen oak leaves. It has also been beaten from oak in the autumn.
Overwinters as a small larva.

Olive Crescent
Trisateles emortualis Denis & Schiffermüller
Plate **42** : *31*

Imago. 29–35 mm. Resident and suspected immigrant. Comes to light, usually in small numbers. Single-brooded, flying in late June and July, inhabiting deciduous woodland. In July 1859 a specimen was recorded from Stonor, Oxfordshire, and in 1910 a second example was taken in the same district. Further adults were reported in July 1962 followed by the discovery of wild larvae a few years later. It is now known to be established over a wide area of the Chilterns, and also in two woods in North Essex, where it was first noted in 1974. Elsewhere it has been recorded as follows: Brighton, Sussex, on 18.vi.1858; Epping Forest, Essex, on 12.vi.1859; Loughton, Essex, in 1870; Blean, Kent, on 16.v.1905 (requires confirmation); Ventnor, Isle of Wight, in July 1939; Brighton on 22.vi.1944; Eastbourne, Sussex, in June 1945; Haywards Heath, Sussex, on 26.vii.1969; Bradwell-on-Sea, Essex, on 27.vi.1970; Dungeness, Kent, on 26.vi.1970; Peas Pottage, Sussex, on 16.vii.1971; Guernsey, Channel Islands, on 23.viii.1984; Hamstreet, Kent, on 31.vii.1984; near Pembury, Kent, on 28.vi.1990; and at Bradwell-on-Sea on 9.vi.1993. Whilst some of these records strongly suggest migration, others may possibly indicate the existence of undiscovered resident populations.
Larva. August to early October on the withered leaves of oak and beech. Larvae have been found on leaves both on the ground and attached to fallen or partly broken branches.
Overwinters as a pupa.

Colour Plates

Plate 1: *Limacodidae, Cossidae, Hepialidae*

1. **The Festoon** *Apoda limacodes* Hufn. ♂. Page 6.
2. **The Festoon** *A. limacodes* Hufn. ♀. Page 6.
3. **The Triangle** *Heterogenea asella* D. & S. ♂. Page 6.
4. **The Triangle** *H. asella* D. & S. ♀. Page 6.
5. **Goat Moth** *Cossus cossus* Linn. Page 3.
6. **Leopard Moth** *Zeuzera pyrina* Linn. ♂. Page 6.
7. **Reed Leopard** *Phragmatacia castaneae* Hb. ♂. Page 3.
8. **Reed Leopard** *P. castaneae* Hb. ♀. Page 3.
9. **Ghost Moth** *Hepialus humuli humuli* Linn. ♂. Page 2.
10. **Ghost Moth** *H. humuli humuli* Linn. ♀. Page 2.
11. **Ghost Moth** *H. humuli thulensis* Newm. ♂. (Shetland). Page 2.
12. **Ghost Moth** *H. humuli thulensis* Newm. ♂. (Shetland). Page 2.
13. **Gold Swift** *H. hecta* Linn. ♂. Page 2.
14. **Gold Swift** *H. hecta* Linn. ♂. Page 2.
15. **Gold Swift** *H. hecta* Linn. ♀. Page 2.
16. **Common Swift** *H. lupulinus* Linn. ♂. Page 2.
17. **Common Swift** *H. lupulinus* Linn. ♂. Page 2.
18. **Common Swift** *H. lupulinus* Linn. ♀. Page 2.
19. **Common Swift** *H. lupulinus* Linn. ♀. Page 2.
20. **Orange Swift** *H. sylvina* Linn. ♂. Page 2.
21. **Orange Swift** *H. sylvina* Linn. ♀. Page 2.
22. **Orange Swift** *H. sylvina* Linn. ♀. Page 2.
23. **Map-winged Swift** *H fusconebulosa* DeG. ♂. Page 2.
24. **Map-winged Swift** *H fusconebulosa* DeG. ab. *gallicus* Led. ♂. Page 2.
25. **Map-winged Swift** *H fusconebulosa* DeG. ab. *gallicus* Led. ♀. Page 2.

Plate 2: *Zygaenidae, Sesiidae*

Plate 3: *Lasiocampidae*

1. **Grass Eggar** *Lasiocampa trifolii* D. & S. ♂.
   (Hampshire). Page 11.
2. **Grass Eggar** *L. trifolii trifolii* D. & S. ♂. (Devon).
   Page 11.
3. **Grass Eggar** *L. trifolii trifolii* D. & S. ♀.
   (Lancashire). Page 11.
4. **Pale Grass Eggar** *L. trifolii flava* C.-Hunt ♀.
   (S.E. Kent). Page 11.
5. **Pale Grass Eggar** *L. trifolii flava* C.-Hunt ♂.
   (S.E. Kent). Page 11.

6. **Pale Grass Eggar** *L. trifolii flava* C.-Hunt ab.*obsoleta*
   Tutt ♂. (S.E. Kent). Page 11.
7. **Oak Eggar** *L. quercus quercus* Linn. ♂. Page 11.
8. **Oak Eggar** *L. quercus quercus* Linn. ♀. Page 11.
9. **Northern Eggar** *L. quercus callunae* Palm. ♂. Page 11.
10. **Northern Eggar** *L. quercus callunae* Palm. ♀. Page 11.
11. **Northern Eggar** *L. quercus callunae* Palm. ab.
    olivacea Tutt ♂. Page 11.
12. **Northern Eggar** *L. quercus callunae* Palm. ab.
    olivacea Tutt ♀. Page 11.

Plate 4: *Lasiocampidae, Endromidae*

1. **December Moth** *Poecilocampa populi* Linn. ♂. Page 10.
2. **December Moth** *P. populi* Linn. ♀. Page 10.
3. **Small Eggar** *Eriogaster lanestris* Linn. ♂. Page 10.
4. **Small Eggar** *E. lanestris* Linn. ♀. Page 10.
5. **Pale Eggar** *Trichiura crataegi* Linn. ♂. Page 10.
6. **Pale Eggar** *T. crataegi* Linn. ♂. Page 10.
7. **Pale Eggar** *T. crataegi* Linn. ♀. Page 10.
8. **Ground Lackey** *Malacosoma castrensis* Linn. ♂. Page 10.
9. **Ground Lackey** *M. castrensis* Linn. ♂. Page 10.
10. **Ground Lackey** *M. castrensis* Linn. ♂. Page 10.
11. **Ground Lackey** *M. castrensis* Linn. ♀. Page 10.
12. **Ground Lackey** *M. castrensis* Linn. ♀. Page 10.
13. **The Lackey** *M. neustria* Linn. ♀. Page 10.
14. **The Lackey** *M. neustria* Linn. ♂. Page 10.
15. **The Lackey** *M. neustria* Linn. ♂. Page 10.
16. **The Lackey** *M. neustria* Linn. ♂. Page 10.
17. **Fox Moth** *Macrothylacia rubi* Linn. ♂. Page 11.
18. **Fox Moth** *M. rubi* Linn. ♀. Page 11.
19. **The Drinker** *Euthrix potatoria* Linn. ♀. Page 11.
20. **The Drinker** *E. potatoria* Linn. ♂. Page 11.
21. **Kentish Glory** *Endromis versicolora* Linn. ♂. Page 12.
22. **Kentish Glory** *E. versicolora* Linn. ♀. Page 12.

Plate 5: *Saturniidae, Lasiocampidae, Thyatiridae, Drepanidae*

1. **Emperor Moth** *Pavonia pavonia* Linn. ♂. Page 12.
2. **Emperor Moth** *P. pavonia* Linn. ♀. Page 12.
3. **The Lappet** *Gastropacha quercifolia* Linn. ♂. Page 12.
4. **Small Lappet** *Phyllodesma ilicifolia* Linn. ♀. Page 12.
5. **Buff Arches** *Habrosyne pyritoides* Hufn. Page 14.
6. **Peach Blossom** *Thyatira batis* Linn. Page 14.
7. **Satin Lutestring** *Tetheella fluctuosa* Hb. Page 15.
8. **Satin Lutestring** *T. fluctuosa* Hb. ab. *unicolor* Lempke (S.E. Kent). Page 15.
9. **Satin Lutestring** *T. fluctuosa* Hb. f. *albilinea* Cockayne (Inverness-shire). Page 15.
10. **Figure of Eighty** *Tethea ocularis octogesimea* Hb. Page 14.
11. **Poplar Lutestring** *T. or or* D. & S. (Kent). Page 14.
12. **Poplar Lutestring** *T. or scotica* Tutt (Inverness-shire). Page 14.
13. **Poplar Lutestring** *T. or hibernica* Turner (Co. Kerry). Page 14.
14. **Oak Lutestring** *Cymatoplorima diluta hartwiegi* Reiss. Page 15.
15. **Oak Lutestring** *C. diluta hartwiegi* Reiss. ab. *nubilata* Robson. Page 15.

16. **Yellow Horned** *Achlya flavicornis galbanus* Tutt. Page 15.
17. **Yellow Horned** *A. flavicornis scotica* Tutt. (Inverness-shire). Page 15.
18. **Common Lutestring** *Ochropacha duplaris* Linn. Page 15.
19. **Common Lutestring** *O. duplaris* Linn. f. *obscura* Tutt. Page 15.
20. **Frosted Green** *Polyploca ridens* Fabr. Page 15.
21. **Frosted Green** *P. ridens* Fabr. ab. *unicolor* Cockayne. Page 15.
22. **Chinese Character** *Cilix glaucata* Scop. Page 14.
23. **Scarce Hook-tip** *Sabra harpagula* Esp. Page 14.
24. **Barred Hook-tip** *Drepana cultraria* Fabr. Page 13.
25. **Oak Hook-tip** *D. binaria* Hufn. ♂. Page 13.
26. **Oak Hook-tip** *D. binaria* Hufn. ♀. Page 13.
27. **Dusky Hook-tip** *D. curvatula* Borkh. Page 13.
28. **Pebble Hook-tip** *D. falcataria falcataria* Linn. Page 13.
29. **Pebble Hook-tip** *D. falcataria scotica* Byt.-Salz. (Perthshire). Page 13.
30. **Scalloped Hook-tip** *Falcaria lacèrtinaria* Linn. ♂. Page 12.
31. **Scalloped Hook-tip** *F. lacertinaria* Linn. ♀. Page 12.

Plate 6: *Geometridae*

1. **Large Emerald** *Geometra papilionaria* Linn. Page 17.
2. **Grass Emerald** *Pseudoterpna pruinata atropunctaria* Walk. Page 17.
3. **Small Emerald** *Hemistola chrysoprasaria* Esp. Page 18.
4. **Sussex Emerald** *Thalera fimbrialis* Scop. Page 18.
5. **Small Grass Emerald** *Chlorissa viridata* Linn. Page 17.
6. **Little Emerald** *Jodis lactearia* Linn. Page 18.
7. **Essex Emerald** *Thetidia smaragdaria maritima* Prout. Page 17.
8. **Blotched Emerald** *Comibaena bajularia* D. & S. Page 17.
9. **Common Emerald** *Hemithea aestivaria* Hb. Page 17.
10. **Dingy Mocha** *Cyclophora pendularia* Cl. Page 18.
11. **Birch Mocha** *C. albipunctata* Hufn. Page 18.
12. **Birch Mocha** *C. albipunctata* Hufn. ab. *subroseata* Wood. Page 18.
13. **Birch Mocha** *C. albipunctata* Hufn. (Inverness-shire). Page 18.
14. **Maiden's Blush** *C. punctaria* Linn. Page 19.
15. **Maiden's Blush** *C. punctaria* Linn. Page 19.
16. **False Mocha** *C. porata* Linn. Page 19.
17. **False Mocha** *C. porata* Linn. Page 19.
18. **Blair's Mocha** *C. puppillaria* Hb. Page 19.
19. **Blair's Mocha** *C. puppillaria* Hb. Page 19.
20. **Blair's Mocha** *C. puppillaria* Hb. Page 19.
21. **The Mocha** *C. annulata* Schulze. Page 18.
22. **Clay Triple-lines** *C. linearia* Hb. Page 19.
23. **Orange Underwing** *Archiears parthenias* Linn. ♂. Page 16.
24. **Orange Underwing** *A. parthenias* Linn. ♀. Page 16.
25. **Light Orange Underwing** *A. notha* Hb. ♂. Page 16.
26. **Light Orange Underwing** *A. notha* Hb. ♀. Page 16.
27. **March Moth** *Alsophila aescularia* D. & S. ♂. Page 16.
28. **March Moth** *A. aescularia* D. & S. ♀. Page 16.
29. **Rest Harrow** *Aplasta ononaria* Fuessl. ♂. Page 16.
30. **Rest Harrow** *A. ononaria* Fuessl. ♀. Page 16.
31. **Blood-vein** *Timandra griseata* Peters. Page 19.
32. **Sub-angled Wave** *Scopula nigropunctata* Hufn. Page 20.
33. **Rosy Wave** *S. emutaria* Hb. Page 21.
34. **Rosy Wave** *S. emutaria* Hb. Page 21.
35. **Lewes Wave** *S. immorata* Linn. Page 20.
36. **Small Blood-vein** *S. imitaria* Hb. 21.
37. **Cream Wave** *S. floslactata floslactata* Haw. Page 21.
38. **Cream Wave** *S. floslactata scotica* Cockayne. Page 21.
39. **Lesser Cream Wave** *S. immutata* Linn. Page 21.
40. **Smoky Wave** *S. ternata* Schr. ♂. Page 21.
41. **Mullein Wave** *S. marginepunctata* Goeze. Page 21.
42. **Lace Border** *S. ornata* Scop. Page 20.
43. **Tawny Wave** *S. rubiginata* Hufn. Page 20.
44. **Purple-bordered Gold** *Idaea muricata* Hufn. Page 22.
45. **Purple-bordered Gold** *I. muricata* Hufn. f. *totarubra* Lambill (Lancashire). Page 22.
46. **Bright Wave** *I. ochrata cantiata* Prout. Page 21.
47. **Ochraceous Wave** *I. serpentata* Hufn. Page 22.
48. **Least Carpet** *I. vulpinaria atrosignaria* Lémpke. Page 22.
49. **Small Dusty Wave** *I. seriata* Schr. Page 23.
50. **Small Dusty Wave** *I. seriata* Schr. ab. *bischoffaria* de la Harpe. Page 23.
51. **Dwarf Cream Wave** *I. fuscovenosa* Goeze. Page 23.
52. **Isle of Wight Wave** *I. humiliata* Hufn. Page 23.
53. **Single-dotted Wave** *I. dimidiata* Hufn. Page 24.
54. **Small Fan-footed Wave** *I. biselata* Hufn. Page 23.
55. **Small Fan-footed Wave** *I. biselata* Hufn. ab. *fimbriolata* Steph. Page 23.
56. **Treble Brown spot** *I. trigeminata* Haw. Page 24.
57. **Dotted Border Wave** *I. sylvestraria* Hb. Page 22.
58. **Silky Wave** *I. dilutaria* Schr. Page 23.
59. **Satin Wave** *I. subsericeata* Haw. Page 24.
60. **Weaver's Wave** *I. contiguaria britanniae* Müll. Page 24.
61. **Small Scallop** *I. emarginata* Linn. ♂. Page 24.
62. **Small Scallop** *I. emarginata* Linn. ♀. Page 24.
63. **Portland Ribbon Wave** *I. degeneraria* Hb. Page 25.
64. **Plain Wave** *I. straminata* Borkh. Page 25.
65. **Riband Wave** *I. aversata* Linn. ab. *remutata* Linn. Page 24.
66. **Riband Wave** *I. aversata* Linn. Page 24.

Plate 7: *Geometridae*

Plate 8: *Geometride*

Plate 9: *Geometridae*

1. **Chestnut-coloured Carpet** *Thera cognata* Thunb. Page 35.
2. **Chestnut-coloured Carpet** *T. cognata* Thunb. (Skye) Page 35.
3. **Juniper Carpet** *T. juniperata juniperata* Linn. Page 35.
4. **Juniper Carpet** *T. juniperata scotica* White. (Inverness-shire). Page 35.
5. **Beech-green Carpet** *Colostygia olivata* D. & S. (Inverness-shire). Page 36.
6. **Beech-green Carpet** *C. olivata* D. & S. (Chilterns, Buckinghamshire). Page 36.
7. **Green Carpet** *C. pectinataria* Knoch. Page 36.
8. **Mottled Grey** *C. multistrigaria* Haw. ♂. Page 36.
9. **Mottled Grey** *C. multistrigaria* Haw. ♀. Page 36.
10. **Mottled Grey** *C. multistrigaria* Haw. ♀. (Derbyshire). Page 36.
11. **Broken-barred Carpet** *Electrophaes corylata* Thunb. Page 36.
12. **Broken-barred Carpet** *E. corylata* Thunb. (Perthshire). Page 36.
13. **Broken-barred Carpet** *E. corylata* Thunb. Page 36.
14. **Netted Carpet** *Eustroma reticulatum* D. & S. Page 35.
15. **May Highflyer** *Hydriomena impluviata* D. & S. Page 36.
16. **May Highflyer** *H. impluviata* D. & S. f. *obsoletaria* Schille (N. Kent). Page 36.
17. **May Highflyer** *H. impluviata* D. & S. (Inverness-shire). Page 36.
18. **May Highflyer** *H. impluviata* D. & S. (Inverness-shire). Page 36.
19. **July Highflyer** *H. furcata* Thunb. (Kent). Page 36.
20. **July Highflyer** *H. furcata* Thunb. (Kent). Page 36.
21. **July Highflyer** *H. furcata* Thunb. (Kent). Page 36.
22. **July Highflyer** *H. furcata* Thunb. (Surrey). Page 36.
23. **July Highflyer** *H. furcata* Thunb. (Surrey). Page 36.
24. **July Highflyer** *H. furcata* Thunb. (Surrey). Page 36.
25. **July Highflyer** *H. furcata* Thunb. (Orkney). Page 36.
26. **July Highflyer** *H. furcata* Thunb. (Arran, Buteshire). Page 36.
27. **July Highflyer** *H. furcata* Thunb. (Arran, Buteshire). Page 36.
28. **July Highflyer** *H. furcata* Thunb. (Arran, Buteshire). Page 36.
29. **July Highflyer** *H. furcata* Thunb. (Arran, Buteshire). Page 36.
30. **July Highflyer** *H. furcata* Thunb. (Orkney). Page 36.
31. **Ruddy Highflyer** *H. ruberata* Freyer. Page 37.
32. **Ruddy Highflyer** *H. ruberata* Freyer. Page 37.
33. **Ruddy Highflyer** *H. ruberata* Freyer. Page 37.
34. **Ruddy Highflyer** *H. ruberata* Freyer. Page 37.
35. **The Fern** *Horisme tersata* D. & S. Page 37.
36. **Small Waved Umber** *H. vitalbata* D. & S. Page 37.
37. **Slender-striped Rufous** *Coenocalpe lapidata* Hb. ♂. Page 37.
38. **Slender-striped Rufous** *C. lapidata* Hb. ♀. Page 37.
39. **Pretty Chalk Carpet** *Melanthia procellata* D. & S. Page 37.
40. **Barberry Carpet** *Pareulype berberata* D. & S. Page 37.
41. **The Tissue** *Triphosa dubitata* Linn. Page 38.
42. **Argent and Sable** *Rheumaptera hastata hastata* Linn. Page 38.
43. **Argent and Sable** *R. hastata nigrescens* Prout. (Perthshire). Page 38.
44. **Scarce Tissue** *R. cervinalis* Scop. Page 38.
45. **Scallop Shell** *R. undulata* Linn. Page 38.
46. **Brown Scallop** *Philereme vetulata* D. & S. Page 39.
47. **Dark Umber** *P. transversata britannica* Lempke ♂. Page 39.
48. **Dark Umber** *P. transversata britannica* Lempke ♀. Page 39.
49. **White-banded Carpet** *Spargania luctuata* D. & S. Page 38.
50. **Sharp-angled Carpet** *Euphyia unangulata* Haw. Page 39.
51. **Cloaked Carpet** *E. biangulata* Haw. Page 39.
52. **Winter Moth** *Operophtera brumata* Linn. ♂. Page 40.
53. **Winter Moth** *O. brumata* Linn. ♀. Page 40.
54. **Northern Winter Moth** *O. fagata* Scharf. ♂. Page 40.
55. **Northern Winter Moth** *O. fagata* Scharf. ♀. Page 40.

Plate 10: *Geometridae*

Plate 11: *Geometridae*

1. **Small Autumnal Moth** *Epirrita filigrammaria* H.-S. Page 40.
2. **Small Autumnal Moth** *E. filigrammaria* H.-S. Page 40.
3. **November Moth** *E. dilutata* D. & S. Page 39.
4. **November Moth** *E. dilutata* D. & S. Page 39.
5. **November Moth** *E. dilutata* D. & S. Page 39.
6. **Pale November Moth** *E. christyi* Allen. Page 40.
7. **Pale November Moth** *E. christyi* Allen. Page 40.
8. **Pale November Moth** *E. christyi* Allen. page 40.
9. **Autumnal Moth** *E. christyi* Allen. Page 40.
10. **Autumnal Moth** *E. autumnata* Borkh. Page 40.
11. **The Streak** *C. legatella* D. & S. Page 50.
12. **The Streak** *C. legatella* D. & S. Page 50.
13. **Broom-tip** *C. rufata rufata* Fabr. Page 50.
14. **Broom-tip** *C. rufata scotica* Rich. (Inverness-shire). Page 50.
15. **Manchester Treble-bar** *Carsia sororiata anglica* Prout. Page 50.
16. **Treble-bar** *Aplocera plagiata* Linn. Page 51.
17. **Treble-bar** *A. plagiata scotica* Rich. (Perthshire). Page 51.
18. **Lesser Treble-bar** *A. efformata* Guen. Page 51.
19. **Chimney Sweeper** *Odezia atrata* Linn. Page 51.
20. **Grey Carpet** *Lithostege griseata* D. & S. Page 51.
21. **Blomer's Rivulet** *Discoloxia blomeri* Curt. Page 52.
22. **Welsh Wave** *Venusia cambrica* Curt. Page 52.
23. **Welsh Wave** *V. cambrica* Curt. f. *bradyi* Prout. (Derbyshire). Page 52.
24. **Dingy Shell** *Euchoeca nebulata* Scop. Page 52.
25. **Small White Wave** *Asthena albulata* Hufn. Page 52.
26. **Waved Carpet** *Hydrelia sylvata* D. & S. Page 52.
27. **Waved Carpet** *H. sylvata* D. & S. F. *goodwini* Bankes. (Kent). Page 52.
28. **Small Yellow Wave** *H. flammeolaria* Hufn. Page 52.
29. **Drab Looper** *Minoa murinata* Scop. Page 52.
30. **The Seraphim** *Lobophora halterata* Hufn. ♂. Page 53.
31. **The Seraphim** *L. halterata* Hufn. ♂. Page 53.
32. **The Seraphim** *L. halterata* Hufn. ♂. Page 53.
33. **Small Seraphim** *Pterapherapteryx sexalata* Retz. Page 53.
34. **Yellow-barred Brindle** *Acasis viretata* Hb. Page 53.
35. **Barred Tooth-striped** *Trichopteryx polycommata* D. & S. Page 53.
36. **Early Tooth-striped** *T. carpinata* Borkh. Page 53.
37. **Early Tooth-striped** *T. carpinata* Borkh. Page 53.
38. **Early Tooth-striped** *T. carpinata* Borkh. ab. *fasciata* Prout. (Perthshire). Page 53.
39. **Clouded Magpie** *Abraxas sylvata* Scop. Page 53.
40. **The Magpie** *A. grossulariata* Linn. Page 53.
41. **The Magpie** *A. grossulariata* Linn. ab. *dohrnii* Koenig. Page 53.
42. **The Magpie** *A. grossulariata* Linn. ab. *exquisita* Raynor. Page 53.
43. **The Magpie** *A. grossulariata* Linn. ab. *varleyata* Porritt. Page 53.
44. **Barred Umber** *Plagodis pulveraria* Linn. ♂. Page 56.
45. **Barred Umber** *P. pulveraria* Linn. ♀. Page 56.
46. **Scorched Wing** *P. dolabraria* Linn. Page 56.
47. **Brown Silver-line** *Petrophora chlorosata* Scop. Page 56.
48. **Brimstone Moth** *Opisthograptis luteolata* Linn. Page 56.

Plate 12: *Geometridae*

1. **Clouded Border** *Lomaspilis marginata* Linn. Page 54.
2. **Clouded Border** *L. marginata* Linn. Page 54.
3. **Scorched Carpet** *Ligdia adustata* D. & S. Page 54.
4. **Rannoch Looper** *Semiothisa brunneata* Thunb. ♂. Page 55
5. **Rannoch Looper** *S. brunneata* Thunb. ♀. Page 55.
6. **The V-Moth** *S. wauaria* Linn. Page 55.
7. **Peacock Moth** *S. notata* Linn. Page 54.
8. **Sharp-angled Peacock** *S. alternaria* Hb. Page 54.
9. **Dusky Peacock** *S. signaria* Hb. Page 55.
10. **Tawny-barred Angle** *S. liturata* Cl. Page 55.
11. **Tawny-barred Angle** *S. liturata* Cl. f. *nigrofulvata* Collins. Page 55.
12. **Latticed Heath** *S. clathrata clathrata* Linn. ♂. Page 55.
13. **Latticed Heath** *S. clathrata clathrata* Linn. ♀. Page 55.
14. **Latticed Heath** *S. clathrata clathrata* Linn. ♂. ab. *alboguttata* Fettig. Page 55.
15. **Latticed Heath** *S. clathrata hugginsi* Baynes. ♂. (Co. Clare). Page 55.
16. **Netted Mountain Moth** *S. carbonaria* Cl. Page 55.
17. **Netted Mountain Moth** *S. carbonaria* Cl. Page 55.
18. **Frosted Yellow** *Isturgia limbaria* Fabr. ♂. Page 56.
19. **Frosted Yellow** *I. limbaria* Fabr. ♀. Page 56.
20. **Little Thorn** *Cepphis advenaria* Hb. Page 56.
21. **Bordered Beauty** *Epione repandaria* Hufn. Page 57.
22. **Dark Bordered Beauty** *E. paralellaria* D. & S. ♂. Page 57.
23. **Dark Bordered Beauty** *E. paralellaria* D. & S. ♀. Page 57.
24. **Horse Chestnut** *Pachycnemia hippocastanaria* Hb. ♂. Page 56.
25. **Horse Chestnut** *P. hippocastanaria* Hb. ♀. Page 56.
26. **Speckled Yellow** *Pseudopanthera macularia* Linn. Page 57.
27. **Scalloped Oak** *Crocallis elinguaria* Linn. Page 59.
28. **Scalloped Oak** *C. elinguaria* Linn. ab. *unicolor* Prout. Page 59.
29. **Feathered Thorn** *Colotois pennaria* Linn. ♂. Page 60.
30. **Feathered Thorn** *C. pennaria* Linn. ♂. Page 60.
31. **Feathered Thorn** *C. pennaria* Linn. ♂. Page 60.
32. **Feathered Thorn** *C. pennaria* Linn. ♀. Page 60.
33. **Orange Moth** *Angerona prunaria* Linn. ♂. Page 60.
34. **Orange Moth** *A. prunaria* Linn. ♂. Page 60.
35. **Orange Moth** *A. prunaria* Linn. ♀. Page 60.
36. **Orange Moth** *A. prunaria* Linn. f. *corylaria* Thunb. ♂. Page 60.
37. **Orange Moth** *A. prunaria* Linn. f. *corylaria* Thunb. ♂. Page 60.
38. **Orange Moth** *A. prunaria* Linn. f. *corylaria* Thunb. ♀. Page 60.

1　　　　　2　　　　　3　　　　　4　　　　　5　　　　　6

7　　　　　8　　　　　9　　　　　10　　　　　11

12　　　　13　　　　14　　　　15　　　　16　　　　17

18　　　　19　　　　20　　　　21　　　　22　　　　23

24　　　25　　　26　　　27　　　28

29　　　30　　　31　　　32

33　　　34　　　35

36　　　37　　　38

Plate 13: *Geometridae*

1. **Swallow-tailed Moth** *Ourapteryx sambucaria* Linn. ♂. Page 60.
2. **Large Thorn** *Ennomos autumnaria* Werneb. ♂. Page 57.
3. **Large Thorn** *E. autumnaria* Werneb. ♀. Page 57.
4. **August Thorn** *E. quercinaria* Hufn. ♂. Page 58.
5. **August Thorn** *E. quercinaria* Hufn. ♂. Page 58.
6. **August Thorn** *E. quercinaria* Hufn. ♀. Page 58.
7. **Dusky Thorn** *E. fuscantaria* Haw. ♀. Page 58.
8. **Canary-shouldered Thorn** *E. alniaria* Linn. ♂. Page 58.
9. **Canary-shouldered Thorn** *E. alniaria* Linn. ♀. Page 58.
10. **September Thorn** *E. erosaria* D. & S. ♂. Page 58.
11. **September Thorn** *E. erosaria* D. & S. ♀. Page 58.
12. **Lilac Beauty** *Apeira syringaria* Linn. ♂. Page 57.
13. **Lilac Beauty** *A. syringaria* Linn. ♀. Page 57.
14. **Purple Thorn** *Selenia tetralunaria* Hufn. ♂. Spring brood. Page 59.
15. **Purple Thorn** *S. tetralunaria* Hufn. ♂. Summer brood. Page 59.
16. **Early Thorn** *S. dentaria* Fabr. ♂. Spring brood. Page 58.
17. **Early Thorn** *S. dentaria* Fabr. ♀. Spring brood. Page 58.
18. **Early Thorn** *S. dentaria* Fabr. ab. *harrisoni* Wagner ♂. Page 58.
19. **Early Thorn** *S. dentaria* Fabr. ♂. Summer brood. Page 58.
20. **Lunar Thorn** *S. lunularia* Hb. ♂. (S. Devon). Page 59.
21. **Lunar Thorn** *S. lunularia* Hb. ♂. (Co. Clare). Page 59.
22. **Lunar Thorn** *S. lunularia* Hb. ♂. (Inverness-shire). Page 59.
23. **Lunar Thorn** *S. lunularia* Hb. ♀. (Nottinghamshire). Page 59.
24. **Scalloped Hazel** *Odontopera bidentata* Cl. ♀. (Sussex). Page 59.
25. **Scalloped Hazel** *O. bidentata* Cl. ♀. (S. Devon). Page 59.
26. **Scalloped Hazel** *O. bidentata* Cl. ♂. (Perthshire). Page 59.
27. **Scalloped Hazel** *O. bidentata* Cl. ab. *nigra* Prout ♂. (N.E. Surrey). Page 59.

Plate 14: *Geometridae*

1. **Peppered Moth** *Biston betularia* Linn. ♂. Page 61.
2. **Peppered Moth** *B. betularia* Linn. f. *insularia* Thierry-Mieg. ♂. Page 61.
3. **Peppered Moth** *B. betularia* Linn. f. *carbonaria* Jordan. ♂. Page 61.
4. **Oak Beauty** *B. strataria* Hufn. ♂. Page 61.
5. **Oak Beauty** *B. strataria* Hufn. ♀. Page 61.
6. **Rannoch Brindled Beauty** *Lycia lapponaria scotica* Harr. ♂. Page 61.
7. **Rannoch Brindled Beauty** *L. lapponaria scotica* Harr. ♀. Page 61.
8. **Belted Beauty** *L. zonaria britannica* Harr. ♂. Page 61.
9. **Belted Beauty** *L. zonaria britannica* Harr. ♀. Page 61.
10. **Belted Beauty** *L. zonaria atlantica* Harr. ♂. (Outer Hebrides). Page 61.
11. **Brindled Beauty** *L. hirtaria* Cl. ♂. Page 60.
12. **Brindled Beauty** *L. hirtaria* Cl. ♀. Page 60.
13. **Brindled Beauty** *L. hirtaria* Cl. ab. ♂. (Perthshire). Page 60.
14. **Brindled Beauty** *L. hirtaria* Cl. ab. *nigra* Cockayne ♂. Page 60.
15. **Pale Brindled Beauty** *Apocheima pilosaria* D. & S. ♂. Page 60.
16. **Pale Brindled Beauty** *A. pilosaria* D. & S. ♂. Page 60.
17. **Pale Brindled Beauty** *A. pilosaria* D. & S. f. *monacharia* Staud. ♂. Page 60.
18. **Pale Brindled Beauty** *A. pilosaria* D. & S. ♀. Page 60.
19. **Small Brindled Beauty** *A. hispidaria* D. & S. ♂. Page 60.
20. **Small Brindled Beauty** *A. hispidaria* D. & S. ♂. Page 60.
21. **Small Brindled Beauty** *A. hispidaria* D. & S. ♀. Page 60.
22. **Spring Usher** *Agriopis leucophaearia* D. & S. ♂. Page 61.
23. **Spring Usher** *A. leucophaearia* D. & S. ♂. Page 61.
24. **Spring Usher** *A. leucophaearia* D. & S. ♂. Page 61.
25. **Spring Usher** *A. leucophaearia* D. & S. ♂. Page 61.
26. **Spring Usher** *A. leucophaearia* D. & S. ♂. Page 61.
27. **Spring Usher** *A. leucophaearia* D. & S. ♀. Page 61.
28. **Scarce Umber** *A. aurantiaria* Hb. ♂. Page 62.
29. **Scarce Umber** *A. aurantiaria* Hb. ♀. Page 62.
30. **Dotted Border** *A. marginaria* Fabr. ♂. Page 62.
31. **Dotted Border** *A. marginaria* Fabr. ♂. ab. *fuscata* Mosley. Page 62.
32. **Dotted Border** *A. marginaria* Fabr. ♀. Page 62.
33. **Dotted Border** *A. marginaria* Fabr. ♀. Page 62.
34. **Dotted Border** *A. marginaria* Fabr. ♀. Page 62.
35. **Mottled Umber** *Erannis defoliaria* Cl. ♂. Page 62.
36. **Mottled Umber** *E. defoliaria* Cl. ♂. Page 62.
37. **Mottled Umber** *E. defoliaria* Cl. ♂. Page 62.
38. **Mottled Umber** *E. defoliaria* Cl. ♂. ab. *nigra* Band. (Epping Forest). Page 62.
39. **Mottled Umber** *E. defoliaria* Cl. ♀. Page 62.
40. **Mottled Umber** *E. defoliaria* Cl. ♀. Melanic form. (Epping Forest). Page 62.

Plate 15: *Geometridae*

1. **Waved Umber** *Menophra abruptaria* Thunb. ♂. (Hampshire). Page 62.
2. **Waved Umber** *M. abruptaria* Thunb. ♀. (Hampshire). Page 62.
3. **Waved Umber** *M. abruptaria* Thunb. ♂. (S.E. London). Page 62.
4. **Waved Umber** *M. abruptaria* Thunb. ab. *fuscata* Tutt. ♂. (S.E. London). Page 62.
5. **Feathered Beauty** *Peribatodes secundaria* Esp. ♂. Page 63.
6. **Feathered Beauty** *P. secundaria* Esp. ♂. Page 63.
7. **Feathered Beauty** *P. secundaria* Esp. ♀. Page 63.
8. **Feathered Beauty** *P. secundaria* Esp. ab. *nigrata* Sterneck. ♀. Page 63.
9. **Willow Beauty** *P. rhomboidaria* D. & S. ♂. Page 62.
10. **Willow Beauty** *P. rhomboidaria* D. & S. f. *perfumaria* Newn. ♂. Page 62.
11. **Willow Beauty** *P. rhomboidaria* D. & S. ab. *rebeli* Aigner. ♂. Page 62.
12. **Satin Beauty** *Deileptenia ribeata* Cl. ♀. Page 64.
13. **Satin Beauty** *D. ribeata* Cl. ♂. Page 64.
14. **Satin Beauty** *D. ribeata* Cl. f. *nigra* Cockayne. ♂. Page 64.
15. **Bordered Grey** *Selidosema brunnearia scandinaviaria* Stdgr. ♂. Page 63.
16. **Bordered Grey** *S. brunnearia scandinaviaria* Stdgr. ♀. Page 63.
17. **Square Spot** *Paradarisa consonaria* Hb. ♂. (Surrey). Page 66.
18. **Square Spot** *P. consonaria* Hb. ♀. (Monmouthshire). Page 66.
19. **Square Spot** *P. consonaria* Hb. ab. *waiensis* Rich. ♀. (Monmouthshire). Page 66.
20. **Square Spot** *P. consonaria* Hb. f. *nigra* Bankes. ♀. (Kent). Page 66.
21. **Pale Oak Beauty** *Serraca punctinalis* Scop. ♂. Page 65.
22. **Pale Oak Beauty** *S. punctinalis* Scop. ab. *humperti* Humpert. ♂. Page 65.
23. **Pale Oak Beauty** *S. punctinalis* Scop. ♀. Page 65.
24. **Great Oak Beauty** *Hypomecis roboraria* D. & S. ♂. Page 64.
25. **Great Oak Beauty** *H. roboraria* D. & S. ab. *infuscata* Stdgr. ♂. Page 64.
26. **Great Oak Beauty** *H. roboraria* D. & S. ♀. Page 64.

Plate 16: *Geometridae*

1. **Ringed Carpet** *Cleora cinctaria cinctaria* D. & S. ♂. Page 64.
2. **Ringed Carpet** *C. cinctaria cinctaria* D. & S. ♀. Page 64.
3. **Ringed Carpet** *C. cinctaria bowesi* Rich. ♀. (Perthshire). Page 64.
4. **Ringed Carpet** *C. cinctaria bowesi* Rich. ♀. (Perthshire) Page 64.
5. **The Engrailed** *Ectropis bistortata* Goeze. ♂. Page 65.
6. **The Engrailed** *E. bistortata* Goeze. ♂. Page 65.
7. **The Engrailed** *E. bistortata* Goeze. ♂. Melanic form. Second brood. Page 65.
8. **The Engrailed** *E. bistortata* Goeze. ♂. (Perthshire). Page 65.
9. **Small Engrailed** *E. crepuscularia* D. & S. ♀. Page 66.
10. **Small Engrailed** *E. crepuscularia* D. & S. ♂. Page 66.
11. **Small Engrailed** *E. crepuscularia* D. & S. ♂. Melanic form. Page 66.
12. **Brindled White-spot** *Paradarisa extersaria* Hb. ♀. Page 66.
13. **Mottled Beauty** *Alcis repandata repandata* Linn. ♂. (Cardiganshire). Page 64.
14. **Mottled Beauty** *A. repandata repandata* Linn. ♂. (Surrey). Page 64.
15. **Mottled Beauty** *A. repandata repandata* Linn. ♂. (Cornwall). Page 64.
16. **Mottled Beauty** *A. repandata repandata* Linn. ♀. (Montgomeryshire). Page 64.
17. **Mottled Beauty** *A. repandata repandata* Linn. ♂. (Buckinghamshire). Page 64.
18. **Mottled Beauty** *A. repandata repandata* Linn. ♀. (Arran, Buteshire). Page 64.
19. **Mottled Beauty** *A. repandata repandata* Linn. ♂. (Derbyshire). Page 64.
20. **Mottled Beauty** *A. repandata repandata* Linn. ♀. (Nottinghamshire). Page 64.
21. **Mottled Beauty** *A. repandata repandata* Linn. ♀. (Buckinghamshire). Page 64.
22. **Mottled Beauty** *A. repandata muraria* Curt. ♂. (Inverness-shire). Page 64.
23. **Mottled Beauty** *A. repandata muraria* Curt. ♀. (Inverness-shire). Page 64.
24. **Mottled Beauty** *A. repandata muraria* Curt. ♂. (Co. Kerry). Page 64.
25. **Dotted Carpet** *A. jubata* Thumb. ♂. Page 64.
26. **Brussels Lace** *Cleorodes lichenaria* Hufn. ♂. Page 65.
27. **Brussels Lace** *C. lichenaria* Hufn. ♂. Page 65.
28. **Speckled Beauty** *Fagivorina arenaria* Hufn. ♂. Page 65.
29. **Grey Birch** *Aethalura punctulata* D. & S. ♂. Page 66.
30. **Bordered White** *Bupalus piniaria* Linn. ♂. (Sussex). Page 66.
31. **Bordered White** *B. piniaria* Linn. ♀. (Sussex). Page 66.
32. **Bordered White** *B. piniaria* Linn. ♀. (Lancashire). Page 66.
33. **Bordered White** *B. piniaria* Linn. ♂. (Inverness-shire). Page 66.
34. **Bordered White** *B. piniaria* Linn. ♀. (Inverness-shire). Page 66.

Plate 17: *Geometridae*

1. **Common Heath** *Ematurga atomaria* Linn. ♂. Page 66.
2. **Common Heath** *E. atomaria* Linn. ♂. Page 66.
3. **Common Heath** *E. atomaria* Linn. ♂. Page 66.
4. **Common Heath** *E. atomaria* Linn. ♂. Page 66.
5. **Common Heath** *E. atomaria* Linn. ♀. Page 66.
6. **Common Heath** *E. atomaria* Linn. ♀. Page 66.
7. **Common White Wave** *Cabera pusaria* Linn. Page 67.
8. **Common Wave** *C. exanthemata* Scop. Page 67.
9. **White-pinion Spotted** *Lomographa bimaculata* Fabr. Page 67.
10. **Clouded Silver** *L. temerata* D. & S. ♂. Page 67.
11. **Clouded Silver** *L. temerata* D. & S. ♀. Page 67.
12. **Sloe Carpet** *Aleucis distinctata* H.-S. Page 67.
13. **Early Moth** *Theria primaria* Haw. ♂. Page 67.
14. **Early Moth** *T. primaria* Haw. ♀. Page 67.
15. **Barred Red** *Hylaea fasciaria* Linn. Page 68.
16. **Barred Red** *H. fasciaria* Linn. Page 68.
17. **Barred Red** *H. fasciaria* Linn. ab. *grisearia* Fuchs (N. England). Page 68.
18. **Barred Red** *H. fasciaria* Linn. ab. *prasinaria* D. & S. Page 68.
19. **Barred Red** *H. fasciaria* Linn. ab. *prasinaria* D. & S. Page 68.
20. **Light Emerald** *Campaea margaritata* Linn. ♂. Page 68.
21. **Light Emerald** *C. margaritata* L. ♀. Page 68.
22. **The Annulet** *Gnophos obscurata* D. & S. (Limestone-Dorset). Page 68.
23. **The Annulet** *G. obscurata* D. & S. (Chalkland-Sussex). Page 68.
24. **The Annulet** *G. obscurata* D. & S. (Heathland-Cornwall). Page 68.
25. **The Annulet** *G. obscurata* D. & S. (Chalkland-S.E. Kent). Page 68.
26. **The Annulet** *G. obscurata* D. & S. (Heathland-Dorset). Page 68.
27. **Scotch Annulet** *G. obfuscata* D. & S. Page 68.
28. **Scotch Annulet** *G. obfuscata* D. & S. Page 68.
29. **Black Mountain Moth** *Psodos coracina* Esp. ♂. Page 68.
30. **Black Mountain Moth** *P. coracina* Esp. ♀. Page 68.
31. **Black-veined Moth** *Siona lineata* Scop. Page 68.
32. **Straw Belle** *Aspitates gilvaria gilvaria* D. & S. ♂. (S.E. England). Page 69.
33. **Straw Belle** *A. gilvaria gilvaria* D. & S. ♀. (S.E. England). Page 69.
34. **Straw Belle** *A. gilvaria burrenensis* Cockayne. ♂. (Co. Clare). Page 69.
35. **Straw Belle** *A. gilvaria burrenensis* Cockayne. ♀. (Co. Clare). Page 69.
36. **Yellow Belle** *A. ochrearia* Rossi. ♂. Page 69.
37. **Grey Scalloped Bar** *Dyscia fagaria* Thunb. ♂. Page 69.
38. **Grey Scalloped Bar** *D. fagaria* Thunb. ♂. (Co. Kerry). Page 69.
39. **Grey Scalloped Bar** *D. fagaria* Thunb. ♀. Page 69.
40. **Grass Wave** *Perconia strigillaria* Hb. ♂. Page 69.
41. **Grass Wave** *P. strigillaria* Hb. ♂. Page 69.

Plate 18: *Sphingidae*

1. **Death's-head Hawk-moth** *Acherontia atropos* Linn. Page 70.
2. **Small Elephant Hawk-moth** *Deilephila porcellus* Linn. Page 72.
3. **Elephant Hawk-moth** *D. elpenor* Linn. Page 72.
4. **Convolvulus Hawk-moth** *Agrius convolvuli* Linn. Page 70.
5. **Silver-striped Hawk-moth** *Hippotion celerio* Linn. Page 72.
6. **Oleander Hawk-moth** *Daphnis nerii* Linn. Page 71.
7. **Narrow-bordered Bee Hawk-moth** *Hemaris tityus* Linn. Page 71.
8. **Broad-bordered Bee Hawk-moth** *H. fuciformis* Linn. Page 71.
9. **Privet Hawk-moth** *Sphinx ligustri* Linn. Page 70.
10. **Humming-bird Hawk-moth** *Macroglossum stellatarum* Linn. Page 71.

1

2

3

4

5

6

7

8

9

10

Plate 19: *Sphingidae*

1. **Poplar Hawk-moth** *Laothoe populi* Linn. Page 70.
2. **Poplar Hawk-moth** *L. populi* Linn. Page 70.
3. **Eyed Hawk-moth** *Smerinthus ocellata* Linn. Page 70.
4. **Lime Hawk-moth** *Mimas tiliae* Linn. ♂. Page 70.
5. **Lime Hawk-moth** *M. tiliae* Linn. ♀. Page 70.

6. **Lime Hawk-moth** *M. tiliae* Linn. ♀. Page 70.
7. **Bedstraw Hawk-moth** *Hyles gallii* Rott. Page 71.
8. **Spurge Hawk-moth** *H. euphorbiae* Linn. Page 71.
9. **Striped Hawk-moth** *H. livornica* Esp. Page 72.
10. **Pine Hawk-moth** *Hyloicus pinastri* Linn. Page 70.

Plate 20: *Notodontidae*

1. **Buff-tip** *Phalera bucephala* Linn. ♂. Page 72.
2. **Sallow Kitten** *Furcula furcula* Cl. ♂. Page 73.
3. **Poplar Kitten** *F. bifida* Brahm. ♂. Page 73.
4. **Alder Kitten** *F. bicuspis* Borkh. ♂. Page 73.
5. **Puss Moth** *Cerura vinula* Linn. ♂. Page 73.
6. **Iron Prominent** *Notodonta dromedarius* Linn. ♂. Page 73.
7. **Iron Prominent** *N. dromedarius* Linn. ♂. (Inverness-shire). Page 73.
8. **Large Dark Prominent** *N. torva* Hb. ♀. Page 74.
9. **Lobster Moth** *Stauropus fagi* Linn. ♂. Page 73.
10. **Lobster Moth** *S. fagi* Linn. f. *obscura* Rebel. ♂. Page 73.
11. **Great Prominent** *Peridea anceps* Goeze. ♂. Page 74.
12. **Three-humped Prominent** *Tritophia tritophus* D. & S. ♂. Page 74.
13. **Pebble Prominent** *Eligmodonta ziczac* Linn. ♂. Page 74.
14. **Lesser Swallow Prominent** *Pheosia gnoma* Fabr. ♂. Page 74.
15. **Lesser Swallow Prominent** *P. gnoma* Fabr. ♀. Page 74.
16. **Swallow Prominent** *P. tremula* Cl. ♂. Page 75.
17. **Maple Prominent** *Ptilodontella cucullina* D. & S. ♀. Page 75.
18. **Coxcomb Prominent** *Ptilodon capucina* Linn. ♂. Page 75.
19. **Scarce Prominent** *Odontosia carmelita* Esp. ♂. Page 75.
20. **Scarce Prominent** *O. carmelita* Esp. ♂. (Perthshire). Page 75.
21. **Pale Prominent** *Pterostoma palpina* Cl. ♂. Page 75.
22. **Plumed Prominent** *Ptilophora plumigera* D. & S. ♂. (Surrey). Page 75.
23. **Plumed Prominent** *P. plumigera* D. & S. ♀. (Surrey). Page 75.
24. **Plumed Prominent** *P. plumigera* D. & S. ♂. (S.E. Kent). Page 75.

Plate 21: *Notodontidae, Lymantriidae*

1. **White Prominent** *Leucodonta bicoloria* D. & S. Page 75.
2. **Lunar Marbled Brown** *Drymonia ruficornis* Hufn. ♂. Page 76.
3. **Lunar Marbled Brown** *D. ruficornis* Hufn. ♂. Melanic aberration. (N. Surrey). Page 76.
4. **Lunar Marbled Brown** *D. ruficornis* Hufn. ♀. Page 76.
5. **Marbled Brown** *D. dodonaea* D. & S. ♂. Page 76.
6. **Marbled Brown** *D. dodoneae* D. & S., ab. *nigrescens* Lempke. ♂. (Norfolk). Page 76.
7. **Small Chocolate-tip** *Clostera pigra* Hufn. ♂. Page 76.
8. **Small Chocolate-tip** *C. pigra* Hufn. ♀. Page 76.
9. **Scarce Chocolate-tip** *C. anachoreta* D. & S. ♂. Page 76.
10. **Chocolate-tip** *C. curtula* Linn. ♂. Page 77.
11. **Figure of Eight** *Diloba caeruleocephala* Linn. ♀. Page 77.
12. **The Vapourer** *Orgyia antiqua* Linn. ♂. Page 78.
13. **The Vapourer** *O. antiqua* Linn. ♀. Page 78.
14. **Scarce Vapourer** *O. recens* Hb. ♂. Page 78.
15. **Scarce Vapourer** *O. recens* Hb. ♀. Page 78.
16. **Yellow-tail** *Euproctis similis* Fuess. ♂. Page 78.
17. **Yellow-tail** *E. similis* Fuess. ♀. Page 78.
18. **Brown-tail** *E. chrysorrhoea* Linn. ♂. Page 78.
19. **White Satin Moth** *Leucoma salicis* Linn. ♂. Page 79.
20. **Pale Tussock** *Calliteara pudibunda* Linn. ♂. Page 78.
21. **Pale Tussock** *C. pudibunda* Linn. ab. *concolor* Stdgr. ♂. (N. Surrey). Page 78.
22. **Pale Tussock** *C. pudibunda* Linn. ♀. Page 78.
23. **Dark Tussock** *Dicallomera fascelina* Linn. ♂. Page 78.
24. **Dark Tussock** *D. fascelina* Linn. ♂. (Lancashire). Page 78.
25. **Dark Tussock** *D. fascelina* Linn. ♀. Page 78.
26. **Gypsy Moth** *Lytmantria dispar* Linn. ♂. Page 79.
27. **Gypsy Moth** *L. dispar* Linn. ♀. Page 79.
28. **Black V. Moth** *Arctornis l-nigram* Müll. ♂. Page 79.
29. **Black Arches** *Lymantria monacha* Linn. ♂. Page 79.
30. **Black Arches** *L. monacha* Linn. ♂. Melanic aberration. (New Forest, Hampshire). Page 79.
31. **Black Arches** *L. monacha* Linn. ♀. Page 79.

Plate 22: *Arctiidae*

1. **Round-winged Muslin** *Thumatha senex* Hb. Page 80.
2. **Muslin Footman** *Nudaria mundana* Linn. Page 80.
3. **Red-necked Footman** *Atolmis rubricollis* Linn. Page 80.
4. **Dew Moth** *Setina irrorella* Linn. ♂. Page 80.
5. **Dew Moth** *S. irrorella* Linn. ♀. Page 80.
6. **Rosy Footman** *Miltochrista miniata* Forst. Page 80.
7. **Small Dotted Footman** *Pelosia obtusa* H.-S. Page 81.
8. **Dotted Footman** *P. muscerda* Hufn. Page 81.
9. **Buff Footman** *Eilema deplana* Esp. ♂. Page 82.
10. **Buff Footman** *E. deplana* Esp. ♀. Page 82.
11. **Hoary Footman** *E. caniola* Hb. Page 81.
12. **Dingy Footman** *E. griseola* Hb. Page 81.
13. **Dingy Footman** *E. griseola* Hb. ab. *stramineola* Doubl. Page 81.
14. **Pigmy Footman** *E. pygmaeola pygmaeola* Doubl. Page 82.
15. **Pigmy Footman** *E. pygmaeola pallifrons* Zell. (Dungeness, Kent). Page 82.
16. **Common Footman** *E. lurideola* Zinck. Page 82.
17. **Scarce Footman** *E. complana* Linn. Page 82.
18. **Northern Footman** *E. sericea* Gregs. Page 82.
19. **Orange Footman** *E. sororcula* Hufn. Page 81.
20. **Four-dotted Footman** *Cybosia mesomella* Linn. Page 81.
21. **Four-dotted Footman** *C. mesomella* Linn. ab. *flava* de Graaf. Page 81.
22. **Four-spotted Footman** *Lithosia quadra* Linn. ♂. Page 83.
23. **Four-spotted Footman** *L. quadra* Linn ♀. Page 83.
24. **Crimson Speckled** *Utetheisa pulchella* Linn. Page 83.
25. **Speckled Footman** *Coscinia cribraria bivittata* South. Page 83.
26. **Specked Footman** *C. cribraria bivittata* South. Page 83.
27. **Speckled Footman** *C. cribraria arenaria* Lempke. Page 83.
28. **Feathered Footman** *Spiris striata* Linn. Page 83.
29. **Clouded Buff** *Diacrisia sannio* Linn. ♂. Page 84.
30. **Clouded Buff** *D. sannio* Linn. ♀. Page 84.
31. **The Cinnabar** *Tyria jacobaeae* Linn. Page 86.
32. **The Cinnabar** *T. jacobaeae* Linn. ab. coneyi Watson. Page. 86.
33. **Wood Tiger** *Parasemia plantaginis plantaginis* Linn. ♂. Page 84.
34. **Wood Tiger** *P. plantaginis plantaginis* Linn. ♀. Page 84.
35. **Wood Tiger** *P. plantaginis plantaginis* Linn. ab. *hospita* D. & S. ♂. Page 84.
36. **Wood Tiger** *P. plantaginis insularum* Seitz. ♂. (West Ross). Page 84.
37. **Scarlet Tiger** *Callimorpha dominula* Linn. Page 85.
38. **Scarlet Tiger** *C. dominula* Linn. ab. *bimacula* Cockayne. Page 85.
39. **Scarlet Tiger** *C. dominula* Linn. ab. *rossica* Kolenati. Page 85.

Plate 23: *Arctiidae, Nolidae*

1. **Cream-spot Tiger** *Arctia villica britannica* Ob. Page 84.
2. **Garden Tiger** *A. caja* Linn. Page 84.
3. **Garden Tiger** *A. caja* Linn. ab. *fumosa* Horhammer. Page 84.
4. **Garden Tiger** *A. caja* Linn. ab. *lutescens* Cockerell. Page 84.
5. **Jersey Tiger** *Euplagia quadripunctaria* Poda. Page 85.
6. **Jersey Tiger** *E. quadripunctaria* Poda. ab. *lutescens* Stdgr. Page 85.
7. **Ruby Tiger** *Phragmatobia fuliginosa fuliginosa* Linn. Page 85.
8. **Ruby Tiger** *P. fuliginosa borealis* Stdgr . (Perthshire). Page 85.
9. **White Ermine** *Spilosoma lubricipeda* Linn. Page 84.
10. **White Ermine** *S. lubricipeda* Linn. Page 84.
11. **Buff Ermine** *S. luteum* Hufn. Page 85.
12. **Buff Ermine** *S. luteum* Hufn. Page 85.
13. **Buff Ermine** *S. luteum* Hufn. ab. *intermedia* Stand. Page 85.
14. **Buff Ermine** *S. luteum* Hufn. ab. *zatima* Stoll. Page 85.
15. **Water Ermine** *S. urticae* Esp. Page 85.
16. **Muslin Moth** *Diaphora mendica* Cl. ♂. Page 85.
17. **Muslin Moth** *D. mendica* Cl. ♀. Page 85.
18. **Muslin Moth** *D. mendica* Cl. f. *rustica* Hb. ♂. (Co. Clare). Page 85.
19. **Small Black Arches** *Meganola strigula* D. & S. Page 86.
20. **Kent Black Arches** *M. albula* D. & S. Page 86.
21. **Short-cloaked Moth** *Nola cucullatella* Linn. Page 86.
22. **Short-cloaked Moth** *N. cucullatella* Linn. Page 86.
23. **Least Black Arches** *N. confusalis* H.-S. Page 86.
24. **Scarce Black Arches** *N. aerugula* Hb. Page 86.
25. **Scarce Black Arches** *N. aerugula* Hb. Page 86.
26. **Scarce Black Arches** *N. aerugula* Hb. Page 86.

Plate 24: *Noctuidae*

1. **Square-spot Dart** *Euxoa obelisca grisea* Tutt. ♂. (Dorset). Page 87.

2. **Square-spot Dart** *E. obelisca grisea* Tutt. ♀. (Cornwall). Page 87.

3. **White-line Dart** *E. tritici* Linn. ♂. (S.E. Kent). Page 87.

4. **White-line Dart** *E. tritici* Linn. ♀. (S.E. Kent). Page 87.

5. **White-line Dart** *E. tritici* Linn. ♀. (S.E. Kent). Page 87.

6. **White-line Dart** *E. tritici* Linn. ♂. (Arran, Buteshire). Page 87.

7. **White-line Dart** *E. tritici* Linn. ♂. (Nottinghamshire). Page 87.

8. **White-line Dart** *E. tritici* Linn. ♀. (W. Suffolk). Page 87.

9. **Garden Dart** *E. nigricans* Linn. ♂. (Norfolk). Page 87.

10. **Garden Dart** *E. nigricans* Linn. ♂. (S.E. Kent). Page 87.

11. **Garden Dart** *E. nigricans* Linn. ♀. (S.E. Kent). Page 87.

12. **Garden Dart** *E. nigricans* Linn. ♀. (Inverness-shire). Page 87.

13. **Coast Dart** *E. cursoria* Hufn. ♂. (E. Suffolk). Page 88.

14. **Coast Dart** *E. cursoria* Hufn. ♀. (E. Suffolk). Page 88.

15. **Coast Dart** *E. cursoria* Hufn. ♀. (Morayshire). Page 88.

16. **Coast Dart** *E. cursoria* Hufn. ♂. (Morayshire). Page 88.

17. **Coast Dart** *E. cursoria* Hufn. ♂. (Morayshire). Page 88.

18. **Coast Dart** *E. cursoria* Hufn. ♀. (Morayshire). Page 88.

19. **Coast Dart** *E. cursoria* Hufn. ♂. (Morayshire). Page 88.

20. **Coast Dart** *E. cursoria* Hufn. ♀. (Morayshire). Page 88.

21. **Coast Dart** *E. cursoria* Hufn. ♂. (Northumberland). Page 88.

22. **Coast Dart** *E. cursoria* Hufn. ♀. (Northumberland). Page 88.

23. **Coast Dart** *E. cursoria* Hufn. ♀. (Shetland). Page 88.

24. **Coast Dart** *E. cursoria* Hufn. ♀. (Shetland). Page 88.

25. **Light Feathered Rustic** *Agrotis cinerea* D. & S. ♂. (S.E. Kent). Page 88.

26. **Light Feathered Rustic** *Agrotis cinerea* D. & S. ♂. (S.E. Kent). Page 88.

27. **Light Feathered Rustic** *Agrotis cinerea* D. & S. ♂ (S.E. Kent). Page 88.

28. **Light Feathered Rustic** *Agrotis cinerea* D. & S. ♀. (S.E. Kent). Page 88.

29. **Light Feathered Rustic** *Agrotis cinerea* D. & S. ♀. (S.E. Kent). Page 88.

30. **Light Feathered Rustic** *Agrotis cinerea* D. & S. ♀. (Surrey). Page 88.

31. **Crescent Dart** *A. trux lunigera* Steph. ♂. (N. Devon). Page 89.

32. **Crescent Dart** *A. trux lunigera* Steph. ♀. (Lancashire). Page 89.

33. **Archer's Dart** *A. vestigialis* Hufn. ♂. (Lancashire). Page 88.

34. **Archer's Dart** *A. vestigialis* Hufn. ♂. (Morayshire). Page 88.

35. **Archer's Dart** *A. vestigialis* Hufn. ♀. (S.E. Kent). Page 88.

36. **Archer's Dart** *A. vestigialis* Hufn. ♀. (Dorset). Page 88.

37. **Sand Dart** *A. ripae* Hb. ♂. (S.E. Kent). Page 89.

38. **Sand Dart** *A. ripae* Hb. ♂. (S.E. Kent). Page 89.

39. **Sand Dart** *A. ripae* Hb. ♀. (Lancashire). Page 89.

40. **Sand Dart** *A. ripae* Hb. ♀. (Dorset). Page 89.

Plate 25: *Noctuidae*

1. **Heart and Club** *Agrotis clavis* Hufn. ♂. Page 88.
2. **Heart and Club** *A. clavis* Hufn. ♂. Page 88.
3. **Heart and Club** *A. clavis* Hufn. ♀. Page 88.
4. **Heart and Club** *A. clavis* Hufn. ♀. Page 88.
5. **Heart and Club** *A. clavis* Hufn. ♀. Page 88.
6. **Heart and Club** *A. clavis* Hufn. ♀. Page 88.
7. **Dark Sword-grass** *A. ipsilon* Hufn. ♂. Page 89.
8. **Dark Sword-grass** *A. ipsilon* Hufn. ♀. Page 89.
9. **Turnip Moth** *A. segetum* D. & S. ♂. Page 88.
10. **Turnip Moth** *A. segetum* D. & S. ♂. Page 88.
11. **Turnip Moth** *A. segetum* D. & S. ♀. Page 88.
12. **Turnip Moth** *A. segetum* D. & S. ♀. Page 88.
13. **Heart and Dart** *A. exclamationis* Linn. ♂. Page 89.
14. **Heart and Dart** *A. exclamationis* Linn. ♂. Page 89.
15. **Heart and Dart** *A. exclamationis* Linn. ♂. Page 89.
16. **Heart and Dart** *A. exclamationis* Linn. ♂. Page 89.
17. **Heart and Dart** *A. exclamationis* Linn. ♂. Page 89.
18. **Heart and Dart** *A. exclamationis* Linn. ♀. Page 89.
19. **Heart and Dart** *A. exclamationis* Linn. ♀. Page 89.
20. **Heart and Dart** *A. exclamationis* Linn. ♀. Page 89.
21. **Shuttle-shaped Dart** *A. puta puta* Hb. ♂. Page 89.
22. **Shuttle-shaped Dart** *A. puta puta* Hb. ♂. (S. Devon). Page 89.
23. **Shuttle-shaped Dart** *A. puta puta* Hb. ♀. Page 89.
24. **Shuttle-shaped Dart** *A. puta insula* Rich. ♂. (Isles of Scilly). Page 89.
25. **Shuttle-shaped Dart** *A. puta insula* Rich. ♀. (Isles of Scilly). Page 89.
26. **Great Dart** *A. crassa* Hb. ♂. Page 90.
27. **Purple Cloud** *Actinotia polyodon* Cl. Page 90.
28. **Portland Moth** *Actebia praecox* Linn. Page 90.
29. **Eversmann's Rustic** *A. fennica* Tausch. ♂. Page 91.
30. **Flame Shoulder** *Ochropleura plecta* Linn. Page 91.
31. **Northern Rustic** *Standfussiana lucernea* Linn. ♂. Page 92.
32. **Northern Rustic** *S. lucernea* Linn. ♂. Page 92.
33. **Northern Rustic** *S. lucernea* Linn. ♀. Page 92.
34. **Dotted Rustic** *Rhyacia simulans* Hufn. ♂. Page 92.
35. **Dotted Rustic** *R. simulans* Hufn. f. *suffusa* Tutt ♂. (Orkney). Page 92.
36. **The Flame** *Axylia putris* Linn. Page 90.
37. **Plain Clay** *Eugnorisma depuncta* Linn. Page 92.

Plate 26: *Noctuidae*

1. **Lunar Yellow Underwing** *Noctua orbona* Hufn. Page 92.
2. **Large Yellow Underwing** *N. pronuba* Linn. ♀. Page 92.
3. **Large Yellow Underwing** *N. pronuba* Linn. ♂. Page 92.
4. **Large Yellow Underwing** *N. pronuba* Linn. ♂. Page 92.
5. **Lesser Yellow Underwing** *N. comes* Hb. Page 93.
6. **Lesser Yellow Underwing** *N. comes* Hb. ab. *sagittifer* Cockayne. (Isles of Scilly). Page 93.
7. **Lesser Yellow Underwing** *N. comes* Hb. (Morayshire). Page 93.
8. **Lesser Yellow Underwing** *N. comes* Hb. (Morayshire). Page 93.
9. **Lesser Yellow Underwing** *N. comes* Hb. (Morayshire). Page 93.
10. **Least Yellow Underwing** *N. interjecta caliginosa* Schaw. Page 93.
11. **Lesser Broad-bordered Yellow Underwing** *N. janthe* Borkh. Page 93.
12. **Broad-bordered Yellow Underwing** *N. fimbriata* Schreb. Page 93.
13. **Broad-bordered Yellow Underwing** *N. fimbriata* Schreb. Page 93.
14. **Stout Dart** *Spaelotis ravida* D. & S. Page 93.
15. **Stout Dart** *S. ravida* D. & S. Page 93.
16. **True Lover's Knot** *Lycophotia porphyrea* D. & S. Page 94.
17. **True Lover's Knot** *L. porphyrea* D. & S. (Mountain Race, Aberdeenshire). Page 94.
18. **Double Dart** *Graphiphora augur* Fabr. Page 93.
19. **Rosy Marsh Moth** *Eugraphe subrosea* Steph. ♂. Page 94.
20. **Rosy Marsh Moth** *E. subrosea* Steph. ♀. Page 94.
21. **Cousin German** *Paradiarsia sobrina* Dup. Page 94.
22. **Autumnal Rustic** *P. glareosa glareosa* Esp. (S.E. Kent). Page 94.
23. **Autumnal Rustic** *P. glareosa glareosa* Esp. (Cornwall). Page 94.
24. **Autumnal Rustic** *P. glareosa glareosa* Esp. (Nottinghamshire). Page 94.
25. **Autumnal Rustic** *P. glareosa edda* Stdgr. (Shetland). Page 94.
26. **Pearly Underwing** *Peridroma saucia* Hb. Page 94.
27. **Pearly Underwing** *P. saucia* Hb. Page 94.
28. **Pearly Underwing** *P. saucia* Hb. Page 94.

Plate 27: *Noctuidae*

1. **Ingrailed Clay** *Diarsia mendica mendica* Fabr. (S. England). Page 94.

2. **Ingrailed Clay** *D. mendica mendica* Fabr. (S. England). Page 94.

3. **Ingrailed Clay** *D. mendica mendica* Fabr. (S. England). Page 94.

4. **Ingrailed Clay** *D. mendica mendica* Fabr. (S. England). Page 94.

5. **Ingrailed Clay** *D. mendica mendica* Fabr. (Inverness-shire). Page 91.

6. **Ingrailed Clay** *D. mendica mendica* Fabr. (Arran, Buteshire). Page 94.

7. **Ingrailed Clay** *D. mendica orkneyensis* Byt.-Saltz. (Orkney). Page 94.

8. **Ingrailed Clay** *D. mendica orkneyensis* Byt.-Saltz. (Orkney). Page 94.

9. **Ingrailed Clay** *D. mendica orkneyensis* Byt.-Saltz. (Orkney). Page 94.

10. **Ingrailed Clay** *D. mendica orkneyensis* Byt.-Saltz. (Orkney). Page 94.

11. **Ingrailed Clay** *D. mendica thulei* Stdgr. (Shetland). Page 94.

12. **Ingrailed Clay** *D. mendica thulei* Stdgr. (Shetland). Page 94.

13. **Ingrailed Clay** *D. mendica thulei* Stdgr. (Shetland). Page 94.

14. **Ingrailed Clay** *D. mendica thulei* Stdgr. (Shetland). Page 94.

15. **Ingrailed Clay** *D. mendica thulei* Stdgr. (Shetland). Page 94.

16. **Purple Clay** *D. brunnea* D. & S. Page 95.

17. **Barred Chestnut** *D. dahlii* Hb. ♂. Page 95.

18. **Barred Chestnut** *D. dahlii* Hb. ♀. Page 95.

19. **Fen Square-spot** *D. florida* Schmidt. Page 95.

20. **Fen Square-spot** *D. florida* Schmidt ab *ochracea* Walk. Page 95.

21. **Small Square-spot** *D. rubi* View. Spring brood. (S. England). Page 95.

22. **Small Square-spot** *D. rubi* View. Summer brood (S. England). Page 95).

23 **Small Square-spot** *D. rubi* View. Summer brood (Co. Kerry). Page 95.

24. **Small Square-spot** *D. rubi* View. (Inverness-shire). Page 95.

25. **Heath Rustic** *Xestia agathina agathina* Dup. (Cornwall). Page 97.

26. **Heath Rustic** *X. agathina agathina* Dup (Sussex). Page 97.

27. **Heath Rustic** *X. agathina hebridicola* Stdgr. (Morayshire). Page 97.

28. **Northern Dart** *X. alpicola alpina* Humph. & Westw. (Cumberland). Page 95.

29. **Northern Dart** *X. alpicola alpina* Humph. & Westw. (Aberdeenshire). Page 95.

30. **Northern Dart** *X. alpicola alpina* Humph. & Westw. (Aberdeenshire). Page 95.

31. **Northern Dart** *X. alpicola alpina* Humph. & Westw. (Perthshire). Page 95.

32. **Northern Dart** *X. alpicola alpina* Humph. & Westw. (Perthshire). Page 95.

33. **Setaceous Hebrew Character** *X. c-nigrum* Linn. Page 96.

34. **Triple-spotted Clay** *X. ditrapezium* D. & S. Page 96.

35. **Double-Square-spot** *X. triangulum* Hufn. Page 96.

36. **Square-spotted Clay** *X. rhomboidea* Esp. Page 96.

Plate 28: *Noctuidae*

Plate 29: *Noctuidae*

1. **The Shears** *Plebeja nana* Hufn. Page 99.
2. **The Shears** *P. nana* Hufn. Page 99.
3. **The Shears** *P. nana* Hufn. (Perthshire). Page 99.
4. **Pale Shining Brown** *Polia bombycina* Hufn. Page 99.
5. **Feathered Ear** *Pachetra sagittigera britannica* Turn. Page 100.
6. **White Colon** *Sideridis albicolon* Hb. Page 100.
7. **Bordered Gothic** *Heliophobus reticulata marginosa* Haw. (Suffolk). Page 100.
8. **Bordered Gothic** *H. reticulata hibernica* Cockayne. (Co. Cork). Page 100.
9. **Glaucous Shears** *Papestra biren* Goeze. Page 102.
10. **Bright-line Brown-eye** *Lacanobia oleracea* Linn. Page 101.
11. **Dog's Tooth** *L. suasa* D. & S. Page 101.
12. **Dog's Tooth** *L. suasa* D. & S. ab. *dissimilis* Knoch. Page 101.
13. **Beautiful Brocade** *L. contigua* D. & S. Page 101.
14. **Pale-shouldered Brocade** *L. thalassina* Hufn. Page 101.
15. **Pale-shouldered Brocade** *L. thalassina* Hufn. ab. *humeralis* Haw. Page 101.
16. **Light Brocade** *L. w-latinum* Hufn. Page 101.
17. **Dot Moth** *Melanchra persicariae* Linn. Page 101.
18. **Cabbage Moth** *Mamestra brassicae* Linn. Page 100.
19. **Small Ranunculus** *Hecatera dysodea* D. & S. Page 102.
20. **Broad-barred White** *H. bicolorata* Hufn. Page 102.
21. **Broom Moth** *Ceramica pisi* Linn. Page 102.
22. **Broom Moth** *C. pisi* Linn. ab. *splendens* Staud. Page 102.
23. **Broom Moth** *C. pisi* Linn. Page 102.
24. **Broom Moth** *C. pisi* Linn. Page 102.
25. **Tawny Shears** *Hadena perplexa perplexa* D. & S. (S.E. Kent). Page 103.
26. **Tawny Shears** *H. perplexa perplexa* D. & S. (S.E. Kent). Page 103.
27. **Tawny Shears** *H. perplexa perplexa* D. & S. (S.E. Kent). Page 103.
28. **Tawny Shears** *H. perplexa perplexa* D. & S. (Dorset). Page 103.
29. **Tawny Shears** *H. perplexa perplexa* D. & S. (Dorset). Page 103.
30. **Tawny Shears** *H. perplexa perplexa* D. & S. (Surrey). Page 103.
31. **Tawny Shears** *H. perplexa perplexa* D. & S. (Devon). Page 103.
32. **Tawny Shears** *H. perplexa perplexa* D. & S. (Cornwall). Page 103.
33. **Pod Lover** *H. perplexa capsophila* Dup. (Co. Clare). Page 103.
34. **Pod Lover** *H. perplexa capsophila* Dup. (Co. Clare). Page 103.
35. **The Campion** *H. rivularis* Fabr. Page 102.
36. **Barrett's Marbled Coronet** *H. luteago barrettii* Doubl. (Cornwall). Page 103.
37. **Barrett's Marbled Coronet** *H. luteago barrettii* Doubl. (S. Devon). Page 103.
38. **Viper's Bugloss** *H. irregularis* Hufn. Page 103.

Plate 30: *Noctuidae*

1. **Varied Coronet** *Hadena compta* D. & S. ♀. Page 103.
2. **Marbled Coronet** *H. confusa* Hufn. ♂. Page 103.
3. **Marbled Coronet** *H. confusa* Hufn. ♂. (Cornwall). Page 103.
4. **Marbled Coronet** *H. confusa* Hufn. ab. *obliterae* Robson. ♂. (Shetland). Page 103.
5. **White Spot** *H. albimacula* Borkh. ♂. Page 104.
6. **The Lychnis** *H. bicruris* Hufn. ♀. Page 104.
7. **The Grey** *H. caesia mananii* Gregs. ♂. (Co. Clare). Page 104.
8. **The Grey** *H. caesia mananii* Gregs. ♂. (Skye). Page 104.
9. **The Silurian** *Eriopygodes imbecilla* Fabr. ♂. Page 104.
10. **The Silurian** *E. imbecilla* Fabr. ♀. Page 104.
11. **Antler Moth** *Cerapteryx graminis* Linn. ♂. Page 104.
12. **Antler Moth** *C. graminis* Linn. ♂. Page 105.
13. **Antler Moth** *C. graminis* Linn. ♀. Page 105.
14. **Hedge Rustic** *Tholera cespitis* D. & S. ♂. Page 105.
15. **Feathered Gothic** *T. decimalis* Poda. ♀. Page 105.
16. **Pine Beauty** *Panolis flammea* D. & S. ♂. Page 105.
17. **Pine Beauty** *P. flammea* D. & S. ab. *grisea* Tutt. ♂. Page 105.
18. **Silver Cloud** *Egira conspicillaris* Linn. ♂. Page 105.
19. **Silver Cloud** *E. conspicillaris* Linn. f. *melaleuca* View. ♂. Page 105.
20. **Lead-coloured Drab** *Orthosia populeti* Fabr. ♂. Page 106.
21. **Lead-coloured Drab** *O. populeti* Fabr. ♀. Page 106.
22. **Blossom Underwing** *O. miniosa* D. & S. ♂. Page 105.
23. **Small Quaker** *O. cruda* D. & S. ♂. Page 105.
24. **Small Quaker** *O. cruda* D. & S. ♂. Page 105.
25. **Northern Drab** *O. opima* Hb. ab. *brunnea* Tutt. ♂. Page 106.
26. **Northern Drab** *O. opima* Hb. ♀. Page 106.
27. **Powdered Quaker** *O. gracilis* D. & S. ♂. Page 106.
28. **Powdered Quaker** *O. gracilis* D. & S. ♂. (Co. Kerry). Page 106.
29. **Powdered Quaker** *O. gracilis* D. & S. ♂. (Perthshire). Page 106.
30. **Powdered Quaker** *O. gracilis* D. & S. ♀. (New Forest, Hampshire). Page 106.
31. **Common Quaker** *O. cerasi* D. & S. ♂. Page 106.
32. **Common Quaker** *O. cerasi* D. & S. ♂. Page 106.
33. **Common Quaker** *O. cerasi* D. & S. ♀. Page 106.
34. **Common Quaker** *O. cerasi* D. & S. ♀. Page 106.
35. **Twin-spotted Quaker** *O. munda* D. & S. ♂. Page 106.
36. **Twin-spotted Quaker** *O. munda* D. & S. ♂. Page 106.
37. **Twin-spotted Quaker** *O. munda* D. & S. ab. *immaculata* Stdgr. ♀. Page 106.
38. **Twin-spotted Quaker** *O. munda* D. & S. ♀. Page 106.

1   2   3   4

5   6   7   8

9   10   11   12   13

14   15   16   17

18   19   20   21

22   23   24   25   26

27   28   29   30

31   32   33   34

35   36   37   38

Plate 31: *Noctuidae*

1. **Clouded Drab** *Orthosia incerta* Hufn. Page 106.
2. **Clouded Drab** *O. incerta* Hufn. Page 106.
3. **Clouded Drab** *O. incerta* Hufn. Page 106.
4. **Clouded Drab** *O. incerta* Hufn. Page 106.
5. **Clouded Drab** *O. incerta* Hufn. (Perthshire) Page 106.
6. **Clouded Drab** *O. incerta* Hufn. (Perthshire) Page 106.
7. **Hebrew Character** *O. gothica* Linn. Page 107.
8. **Hebrew Character** *O. gothica* Linn. Page 107.
9. **Hebrew Character** *O. gothica* Linn. Page 107.
10. **Hebrew Character** *O. gothica* Linn. (Inverness-shire). Page 107.
11. **Hebrew Character** *O. gothica* Linn. ab. *gothicina* H.-S. (Perthshire) Page 107.
12. **Hebrew Character** *O. gothica* Linn. ab. *gothicina* H.-S. (Inverness-shire) Page 107.
13. **Double Line** *Mythimna turca* Linn. Page. 107.
14. **Brown-line Bright-eye** *M. conigera* D. & S. Page 107.
15. **The Clay** *M. ferrago* Fabr. Page 107.
16. **White-point** *M. albipuncta* D. & S. Page 107.
17. **The Delicate** *M. vitellina* Hb. Page 107.
18. **The Delicate** *M. vitellina* Hb. Page 107.
19. **Southern Wainscot** *M. straminea* Treit. ♂. Page 108.
20. **Southern Wainscot** *M. straminea* Treit. ♀. Page 108.
21. **Striped Wainscot** *M. pudorina* D. & S. Page 107.
22. **Shore Wainscot** *M. litoralis* Curt. Page 108.
23. **Smoky Wainscot** *M. impura impura* Hb. Page 108.
24. **Smoky Wainscot** *M. impura scotica* Cockayne. (Perthshire). Page 108.
25. **Common Wainscot** *M. pallens* Linn. Page 108.
26. **Common Wainscot** *M. pallens* Linn. Page 108.
27. **Mathew's Wainscot** *M. favicolor* Barr. Page 108.
28. **Mathew's Wainscot** *M. favicolor* Barr. Page 108.
29. **L-album Wainscot** *M. l-album* Linn. Page 109.
30. **White-speck** *M. unipuncta* Haw. Page 109.
31. **White-speck** *M. unipuncta* Haw. Page 109.
32. **Obscure Wainscot** *M. obsoleta* Hb. Page 109.
33. **Devonshire Wainscot** *M. putrescens* Hb. Page 109.
34. **Shoulder-striped Wainscot** *M. comma* Linn. Page 109.
35. **Cosmopolitan** *M. loreyi* Dup. Page 109.
36. **Flame Wainscot** *Senta flammea* Curt. Page 110.

Plate 32: *Noctuidae*

1. **Chamomile Shark** *Cucullia chamomillae* D. & S. Page 110.
2. **Chamomile Shark** *C. chamommillae* D. & S. Page 110.
3. **The Shark** *C. umbratica* Linn. Page 111.
4. **Star-wort** *C. asteris* D. & S. Page 111.
5. **Striped Lychnis** *C. lychnitis* Ramb. Page 111.
6. **The Mullein** *C. verbasci* Linn. Page 112.
7. **Scarce Wormwood** *C. artemisiae* Hufn. Page 110.
8. **The Cudweed** *C. gnaphalii occidentalis* Bours. Page 111.
9. **The Wormwood** *C. absinthii* Linn. Page 110.
10. **Toadflax Brocade** *Calophasia lunula* Hufn. Page 108.
11. **Minor Shoulder-knot** *Brachylomia viminalis* Fabr. Page 112.
12. **Minor Shoulder-knot** *B. viminalis* Fabr. Page 112.
13. **Minor Shoulder-knot** *B. viminalis* Fabr. (Inverness-shire). Page 112.
14. **Minor Shoulder-knot** *B. viminalis* Fabr. (Derbyshire). Page 112.
15. **Beautiful Gothic** *Leucochlaena oditis* Hb. Page 112.
16. **The Sprawler** *Brachionycha sphinx* Hufn. Page 113.
17. **The Sprawler** *B. sphinx* Hufn. ab. *fusca* Cockayne. Page 113.
18. **Rannoch Sprawler** *B. nubeculosa* Esp. (Inverness-shire). Page 113.
19. **Rannoch Sprawler** *B. nubeculosa* Esp (Inverness-shire). Page 113.
20. **Brindled Ochre** *Dasypolia templi* Thunb. ♂. (Dorset). Page 113.
21. **Brindled Ochre** *Dasypolia templi* Thunb. ♀. (Shetland). Page 113.
22. **Feathered Brindle** *Aporophyla australis pascuea* Humph. & Westw. ♂. Page 113.
23. **Feathered Brindle** *A. australis pascuea* Humph. & Westw. ab. *ingenua* Freyer ♂. (S.E. Kent). Page 113.
24. **Black Rustic** *A. nigra* Haw. ♂. Page 114.
25. **Black Rustic** *A. nigra* Haw. ♀. Page 114.
26. **Deep-brown Dart** *A. lutulenta* D. & S. ♂. Page 113.
27. **Northern Deep-brown Dart** *A. lueneburgensis* Freyer. ♂. Page 114.
28. **Northern Deep-brown Dart** *A. lueneburgensis* Freyer. ♂. Page 114.
29. **Northern Deep-brown Dart** *A. lueneburgensis* Freyer. ♀. Page 114.

Plate 33: *Noctuidae*

1. **Golden-rod Brindle** *Lithomoia solidaginis* Hb. Page 114.
2. **Red Sword-grass** *Xylena vetusta* Hb. Page 116.
3. **Sword-grass** *X. exsoleta* Linn. Page 116.
4. **Early Grey** *Xylocampa areola* Esp. Page 116.
5. **Early Grey** *X. areola* Esp. Page 116.
6. **The Conformist** *Lithophane furcifera furcifera* Hufn. Page 115.
7. **The Conformist** *L. furcifera suffusa* Tutt. (S. Wales). Page 115.
8. **The Nonconformist** *L. lamda* Fabr. Page 115.
9. **Pale Pinion** *L. hepatica* Cl. Page 114.
10. **Pale Pinion** *L. hepatica* Cl. Page 114.
11. **Tawny Pinion** *L. semibrunnea* Haw. Page 114.
12. **Blair's Shoulder-knot** *L. leautieri hesperica* Bours. Page 115.
13. **Grey Shoulder-knot** *L. ornitopus lactipennis* Dadd. Page 115.
14. **Green-brindled Crescent** *Allophyes oxyacanthae* Linn. Page 116.
15. **Green-brindled Crescent** *A. oxyacanthae* Linn. f. *capucina* Mill. Page 116.
16. **Flame Brocade** *Trigonophora flammea* Esp. Page 117.
17. **Merveille du Jour** *Dichonia aprilina* Linn. Page 117.
18. **Beautiful Arches** *Blepharita satura* D. & S. Page 117.
19. **Dark Brocade** *Mniotype adusta* Esp. Page 117.
20. **Dark Brocade** *M. adusta* Esp. (Sutherland). Page 117.
21. **Brindled Green** *Dryobotodes eremita* Fabr. Page 117.
22. **Brindled Green** *D. eremita* Fabr. Page 117.
23. **Large Ranunculus** *Polymixis flavicincta* D. & S. (Cornwall). Page 118.
24. **Large Ranunculus** *P. flavicincta* D. & S. (Surrey). Page 118.
25. **Black-banded** *P. xanthomista statices* Gregs. ♂. Page 118.
26. **Black-banded** *P. xanthomista statices* Gregs. ♀. Page 118.
27. **Grey Chi** *Antitype chi* Linn. ♂. Page 118.
28. **Grey Chi** *A. chi* Linn. ♀. Page 118.
29. **Grey Chi** *A. chi* Linn. ab. *nigrescens* Tutt. ♀. (Derbyshire). Page 118.
30. **Grey Chi** *A. chi* Linn. ab. *olivacea* Steph. ♀. (Derbyshire). Page 118.

Plate 34: *Noctuidae*

1. **Feathered Ranunculus** *Eumichtis lichenea lichenea* Hb. ♂. (E. Sussex). Page 118.

2. **Feathered Ranunculus** *E. lichenea lichenea* Hb. ♂. (S. Devon). Page 118.

3. **Feathered Ranunculus** *E. lichenea lichenea* Hb. ♂. (Portland, Dorset). Page 118.

4. **Feathered Ranunculus** *E. lichenea scillonea* Rich. ♂. (Isles of Scilly). Page 118.

5. **The Satellite** *Eupsilia transversa* Hufn. Page 119.

6. **The Satellite** *E. transversa* Hufn. Page 119.

7. **The Brick** *Agrochola circellaris* Hufn. Page 120.

8. **The Brick** *A. circellaris* Hufn. Page 120.

9. **Flounced Chestnut** *A. helvola* Linn. Page 121.

10. **Yellow-line Quaker** *A. macilenta* Hb. Page 120.

11. **Yellow-line Quaker** *A. macilenta* Hb. ab. *obsoleta* Tutt. Page 120.

12. **Red-line Quaker** *A. lota* Cl. Page 120.

13. **Beaded Chestnut** *A. lychnidis* D. & S. Page 121.

14. **Beaded Chestnut** *A. lychnidis* D. & S. Page 121.

15. **Beaded Chestnut** *A. lychnidis* D. & S. Page 121.

16. **Beaded Chestnut** *A. lychnidis* D. & S. Page 121.

17. **Beaded Chestnut** *A. lychnidis* D. & S. Page 121.

18. **Brown-spot Pinion** *A. litura* Linn. ab. *borealis* Sp.-Schn. Page 121.

19. **Brown-spot Pinion** *A. litura* Linn. Page 121.

20. **Dotted Chestnut** *Conistra rubiginea* D. & S. Page 120.

21. **Dark Chestnut** *C. ligula* Esp. Page 119.

22. **Dark Chestnut** *C. ligula* Esp. Page 119.

23. **Red-headed Chestnut** *C. erythrocephala* D. & S. Page 120.

24. **Red-headed Chestnut** *C. erythrocephala* D. & S. ab. *glabra* Hb. Page 120.

25. **The Chestnut** *C. vaccinii* Linn. Page 119.

26. **The Chestnut** *C. vaccinii* Linn. Page 119.

27. **The Chestnut** *C. vaccinii* Linn. Page 119.

28. **The Chestnut** *C. vaccinii* Linn. Page 119.

29. **Orange Upperwing** *Jodia croceago* D. & S. Page 119.

30. **Barred Sallow** *Xanthia aurago* D. & S. Page 122.

31. **Barred Sallow** *X. aurago* D. & S. Page 122.

32. **Pink-barred Sallow** *X. togata* Esp. Page 122.

33. **Orange Sallow** *X. citrago* Linn. Page 122.

34. **The Sallow** *X. icteritia* Hufn. Page 122.

35. **The Sallow** *X. icteritia* Hufn. Page 122.

36. **The Sallow** *X. icteritia* Hufn. ab. *flavescens* Esp. Page 122.

37. **Dusky-lemon Sallow** *X. gilvago* D. & S. Page 122.

38. **Dusky-lemon Sallow** *X. gilvago* D. & S. Page 122.

39. **Pale-lemon Sallow** *X. ocellaris* Borkh. Page 122.

40. **Pale-lemon Sallow** *X. ocellaris* Borkh. ab. *gilvescens* Worsley-Wood. Page 122.

Plate 35: *Noctuidae*

1. **Centre-barred Sallow** *Atethmia centrago* Haw. Page 121.
2. **Centre-barred Sallow** *A. centrago* Haw. Page 121.
3. **The Suspected** *Parastichtis suspecta* Hb. Page 130.
4. **The Suspected** *P. suspecta* Hb. Page 130.
5. **The Suspected** *P. suspecta* Hb. Page 130.
6. **Lunar Underwing** *Omphaloscelis lunosa* Haw. Page 121.
7. **Lunar Underwing** *O. lunosa* Haw. Page 121.
8. **Lunar Underwing** *O. lunosa* Haw. Page 121.
9. **Lunar Underwing** *O. lunosa* Haw. Page 121.
10. **Scarce Merveille du Jour** *Moma alpium* Osb. Page 123.
11. **The Coronet** *Craniophora ligustri* D. & S. Page 125.
12. **The Coronet** *C. ligustri* D. & S. ab. *coronula* Haw. Page 125.
13. **Reed Dagger** *Simyra albovenosa* Goeze. Page 125.
14. **Poplar Grey** *Acronicta megacephala* D. & S. Page 123.
15. **Poplar Grey** *A. megacephala* D. & S. ab. *nigra* Shaw (Derbyshire). Page 123.
16. **The Miller** *A. leporina* Linn. f. *grisea* Cochrane. Page 123.
17. **The Miller** *A. leporina* Linn. ab. *melanocephala* Mansbridge. (Derbyshire). Page 123.
18. **The Sycamore** *A. aceris* Linn. Page 123.
19. **The Sycamore** *A. aceris* Linn. f. *infuscata* Haw. (S. London). Page 123.
20. **Alder Moth** *A. alni* Linn. Page 123.
21. **Alder Moth** *A. alni* Linn. ab. *suffusa* Tutt. Page 123.
22. **Sweet Gale Moth** *A. euphorbiae myricae* Guen. Page 125.
23. **Grey Dagger** *A. psi* Linn. ♂. Page 124.
24. **Grey Dagger** *A. psi* Linn. ♀. Page 124.
25. **Grey Dagger** *A. psi* Linn. ♂. (Perthshire). Page 124.
26. **Dark Dagger** *A. tridens* D. & S. ♂. Page 124.
27. **Dark Dagger** *A. tridens* D. & S. ♀. Page 124.
28. **Knot Grass** *A. rumicis* Linn. Page 125.
29. **Knot Grass** *A. rumicis* Linn. ab. *salicis* Curtis. (S. London). Page 125.
30. **Light Knot Grass** *A. menyanthidis menyanthidis* Esp. Page 124.
31. **Light Knot Grass** *A. menyanthidis menyanthidis* Esp. ab. *suffusa* Tutt. Page 124.
32. **Light Knot Grass** *A. menyanthidis scotica* Tutt. (Inverness-shire). Page 124.
33. **Scarce Dagger** *A. auricoma* D. & S. Page 125.
34. **Marsh Dagger** *A. strigosa* D. & S. Page 124.
35. **Marbled Green** *Cryphia muralis muralis* Forst. Page 126.
36. **Marbled Green** *C. muralis muralis* Forst. Page 126.
37. **Marbled Green** *C. muralis muralis* Forst. Page 126.
38. **Marbled Green** *C. muralis impar* Warr. (Cambridge). Page 126.
39. **Marbled Green** *C. muralis westroppi* Cockayne. (Co. Cork). Page 126.
40. **Marbled Green** *C. muralis westroppi* Cockayne. (Co. Cork). Page 126.
41. **Marbled Beauty** *C. muralis westroppi* Cockayne. (Co. Cork). Page 126.
42. **Marbled Beauty** *C. domestica* Hufn. Page 126.
43. **Marbled Beauty** *C. domestica* Hufn. Melanic form. (N. Surrey). Page 126.
44. **Marbled Grey** *C. raptricula* D. & S. Page 126.

Plate 36: *Noctuidae*

1. **Bird's Wing** *Dypterygia scabriuscula* Linn. Page 128.
2. **Copper Underwing** *Amphipyra pyramidea* Linn. ♂. Page 127.
3. **Svensson's Copper Underwing** *A. berbera svenssoni* Fletch. ♀. Page 127.
4. **Mouse Moth** *A. tragopoginis* Cl. Page 127.
5. **Svensson's Copper Underwing** *A. berbera svenssoni* Fletch. ♂. Page 127.
6. **Svensson's Copper Underwing** *A. berbera svenssoni* Fletch. ♀. Page 127.
7. **Old Lady** *Mormo maura* Linn. Page 127.
8. **Brown Rustic** *Rusina ferruginea* Esp. ♂. Page 128.
9. **Brown Rustic** *R. ferruginea* Esp. ♀. Page 128.
10. **The Latin** *Callopistria juventina* Stoll. Page 129.
11. **Small Angle Shades** *Euplexia lucipara* Linn. Page 128.
12. **Angle Shades** *Phlogophora meticulosa* Linn. Page 129.
13. **Straw Underwing** *Thalpophila matura* Hufn. Page 128.
14. **Orache Moth** *Trachea atriplicis* Linn. Page 128.
15. **The Saxon** *Hyppa rectilinea* Esp. Page 131.
16. **Angle-striped Sallow** *Enargia paleacea* Esp. ♂. Page 129.
17. **Angle-striped Sallow** *E. paleacea* Esp. ♀. Page 129.
18. **Dingy Shears** *Parastichtis ypsillon* D. & S. Page 130.
19. **Dingy Shears** *P. ypsillon* D. & S. Page 130.
20. **Heart Moth** *Dicycla oo* Linn. Page 130.
21. **Heart Moth** *D. oo* Linn. ab. *renago* Haw. Page 130.
22. **Double Kidney** *Ipimorpha retusa* Linn. Page 129.
23. **The Olive** *I. subtusa* D. & S. Page 129.
24. **Lesser-spotted Pinion** *Cosmia affinis* Linn. Page 130.
25. **White-spotted Pinion** *C. diffinis* Linn. Page 130.
26. **Lunar-spotted Pinion** *C. pyralina* D. & S. Page 131.
27. **The Dun-bar** *C. trapezina* Linn. Page 130.
28. **The Dun-bar** *C. trapezina* Linn. Page 130.
29. **The Dun-bar** *C. trapezina* Linn. Page 130.
30. **The Dun-bar** *C. trapezina* Linn. ab. *nigra* Tutt. Page 130.
31. **The Dun-bar** *C. trapezina* Linn. ab. *badiofasciata* Teich. Page 130.

Plate 37: *Noctuidae*

1. **Dark Arches** *Apamea monoglypha* Hufn. Page 131.
2. **Dark Arches** *A. monoglypha* Hufn. Page 131.
3. **Dark Arches** *A. monoglypha* Hufn. ab. *aethiops* Tutt. Page 131.
4. **The Exile** *A. zeta marmorata* Zett. (Shetland). Page 131.
5. **The Exile** *A. zeta marmorata* Zett. (Shetland). Page 131.
6. **Northern Arches** *A. zeta assimilis* Doubl. Page 132.
7. **Crescent Striped** *A. oblonga* Haw. Page 132.
8. **Large Nutmeg** *A. anceps* D. & S. Page 133.
9. **Light Arches** *A. lithoxylaea* D. & S. Page 131.
10. **Reddish Light Arches** *A. sublustris* Esp. Page 131.
11. **Clouded-bordered Brindle** *A. crenata* Hufn. Page 132.
12. **Clouded-bordered Brindle** *A. crenata* Hufn. ab. *combusta* Haw. Page 132.
13. **Small Clouded Brindle** *A. unanimis* Hb. Page 133.
14. **The Confused** *A. furva britannica* Cockayne. Page 132.
15. **Slender Brindle** *A. scolopacina* Esp. Page 134.
16. **Scarce Brindle** *A. lateritia* Hufn. Page 132.
17. **Clouded Brindle** *A. epomidion* Haw. Page 132.
18. **Dusky Brocade** *A. remissa* Hb. f. *obscura* Haw. Page 133.
19. **Dusky Brocade** *A. remissa* Hb. f. *submissa* Treit. Page 133.
20. **Dusky Brocade** *A. remissa* Hb. Page 133.
21. **Rustic Shoulder-knot** *A. sordens* Hufn. Page 134.
22. **Double Lobed** *A. ophiogramma* Esp. Page 134.
23. **Double Lobed** *A. ophiogramma* Esp. Melanic form. (Nottinghamshire). Page 134.
24. **Union Rustic** *A. pabulatricula* Brahm. Page 133.
25. **Tawny Marbled Minor** *Oligia latruncula* D. & S. Page 135.
26. **Tawny Marbled Minor** *O. latruncula* D. & S. Page 135.
27. **Marbled Minor** *O. strigilis* Linn. Page 134.
28. **Marbled Minor** *O. strigilis* Linn. Page 134.
29. **Rufous Minor** *O. versicolor* Borkh. Page 134.
30. **Rufous Minor** *O. versicolor* Borkh. Page 134.
31. **Rufous Minor** *O. versicolor* Borkh. ab. *aethiops* Heyd. Page 134.
32. **Middle-barred Minor** *O. fasciuncula* Haw. Page 135.
33. **Middle-barred Minor** *O. fasciuncula* Haw. Page 135.
34. **Rosy Minor** *Mesoligia literosa* Haw. Page 135.
35. **Rosy Minor** *M. literosa* Haw. f. *aethalodes* Rich. (Derbyshire). Page 135.
36. **Rosy Minor** *M. literosa* Haw. (E. Sussex). Page 135.

Plate 38: *Noctuidae*

1. **Common Rustic** *Mesapamea secalis* Linn. ♂. Page 135.
2. **Common Rustic** *M. secalis* Linn. ♀. Page 135.
3. **Lesser Common Rustic** *M. didyma* Esp. ♂. Page 136.
4. **Common Rustic** *M. secalis* Linn. ♀. Page 135.
5. **Lesser Common Rustic** *M. didyma* Esp. ♂. Page 136.
6. **Cloaked Minor** *Mesoligia furuncula* D. & S. Page 135.
7. **Cloaked Minor** *M. furuncula* D. & S. Page 135.
8. **Cloaked Minor** *M. furuncula* D. & S. Page 135.
9. **Cloaked Minor** *M. furuncula* D. & S. Page 135.
10. **Cloaked Minor** *M. furuncula* D. & S. Page 135.
11. **Cloaked Minor** *M. furuncula* D. & S. (Co. Kerry). Page 135.
12. **Cloaked Minor** *M. furuncula* D. & S. (Northumberland). Page 135.
13. **Cloaked Minor** *M. furuncula* D. & S. (Northumberland). Page 135.
14. **Cloaked Minor** *M. furuncula* D. & S. ab. *latistriata* Hoff. & Knud. (Northumberland). Page 135.
15. **Least Minor** *Photedes captiuncula expolita* Staint. ♂. Page 136.
16. **Least Minor** *P. captiuncula expolita* Staint. ♀. Page 136.
17. **Least Minor** *P. captiuncula tincta* Kane. ♂. (Co. Clare). Page 136.
18. **Least Minor** *P. captiuncula tincta* Kane. ♀. (Co. Clare). Page 136.
19. **Lyme Grass** *P. elymi* Treit. Page 137.
20. **Lyme Grass** *P. elymi* Treit. (Co. Durham). Page 137.
21. **Fenn's Wainscot** *P. brevilinea* Fenn. Page 137.
22. **Fenn's Wainscot** *P. brevilinea* Fenn. ab. *sinelinea* Farn. Page 137.
23. **Small Dotted Buff** *P. minima* Haw. ♂. Page 136.
24. **Small Dotted Buff** *P. minima* Haw. ♀. Page 136.
25. **Small Wainscot** *P. pygmina* Haw. ♂. Page 137.
26. **Small Wainscot** *P. pygmina* Haw. ♂. Page 137.
27. **Small Wainscot** *P. pygmina* Haw. ♀. Page 137.
28. **The Concolorous** *P. extrema* Hb. Page 136.
29. **Morris's Wainscot** *P. morrisii morrisii* Dale. (Dorset). Page 136.
30. **Bond's Wainscot** *P. morrisii bondii* Knaggs. (S.E. Kent). Page 136.
31. **Mere Wainscot** *P. fluxa* Hb. Page 137.
32. **Mere Wainscot** *P. fluxa* Hb. Page 137.
33. **Dusky Sallow** *Eremobia ochroleuca* D. & S. Page 137.
34. **Flounced Rustic** *Luperina testacea* D. & S. ♂. Page 137.
35. **Flounced Rustic** *L. testacea* D. & S. ♀. Page 137.
36. **Flounced Rustic** *L. testacea* D. & S. ♂. Page 137.
37. **Flounced Rustic** *L. testacea* D. & S. ♂. Page 137.
38. **Flounced Rustic** *L. testacea* D. & S. ♂. Page 137.
39. **Flounced Rustic** *L. testacea* D. & S. ♀. Page 137.
40. **Dumeril's Rustic** *L. dumerilii* Dup. Page 138.
41. **Scarce Arches** *L. zollikoferi* Freyer. Page 138.
42. **Sandhill Rustic** *L. nickerlii demuthi* Goater & Skinner. (Essex). Page 138.
43. **Sandhill Rustic** *L. nickerlii gueneei* Doubl. (N. Wales). Page 138.
44. **Sandhill Rustic** *L. nickerlii leechi* Goater. (Cornwall). Page 138.
45. **Sandhill Rustic** *L. nickerlii knilli* Bours. (Co. Kerry). Page 138.
46. **Ear Moth** *Amphipoea oculea* Linn. Page 139.
47. **Crinan Ear** *A. crinanensis* Burr. Page 139.
48. **Large Ear** *A. lucens* Freyer. Page 139.
49. **Saltern Ear** *A. fucosa paludis* Tutt. Page 139.

Plate 39: *Noctuidae*

1. **Marsh Mallow Moth** *Hydraecia osseola hucherardi* Mab. Page 140.
2. **The Butterbur** *H. petasitis* Doubl. Page 140.
3. **Fisher's Estuarine Moth** *Gortyna borelii lunata* Freyer. Page 140.
4. **Frosted Orange** *G. flavago* D. & S. Page 140.
5. **Rosy Rustic** *Hydraecia micacea* Esp. ♂. Page 140.
6. **Rosy Rustic** *H. micacea* Esp. ♂. Page 140.
7. **Haworth's Minor** *Celaena haworthii* Curt. Page 141.
8. **The Crescent** *C. leucostigma leucostigma* Hb. Page 141.
9. **The Crescent** *C. leucostigma leucostigma* Hb. ab. *fibrosa* Hb. Page 141.
10. **The Crescent** *C. leucostigma scotica* Cockayne. (Inverness-shire). Page 141.
11. **Burren Green** *Calamia tridens occidentalis* Cockayne. Page 140.
12. **Bulrush Wainscot** *Nonagria typhae* Thunb. ♂. Page 141.
13. **Bulrush Wainscot** *N. typhae* Thunb. ♀. Page 141.
14. **Bulrush Wainscot** *N. typhae* Thunb. ab. *fraterna* Treit. ♂. Page 141.
15. **Twin-spotted Wainscot** *Archanara geminipuncta* Haw. ♂. Page 141.
16. **Twin-spotted Wainscot** *A. geminipuncta* Haw. ♀. Page 141
17. **Brown-veined Wainscot** *A. dissoluta* Treit. f. *arundineta* Schmidt. Page 141.
18. **Brown-veined Wainscot** *A. dissoluta* Treit. Page 141.
19. **White-mantled Wainscot** *A. neurica* Hb. Page 142.
20. **Webb's Wainscot** *A. sparganii* Esp. ♂. Page 142.
21. **Webb's Wainscot** *A. sparganii* Esp. ♀. Page 142.
22. **Rush Wainscot** *A. algae* Esp. ♂. Page 142.
23. **Rush Wainscot** *A. algae* Esp. ♀. Page 142.
24. **Large Wainscot** *Rhizedra lutosa* Hb. ♂. Page 142.
25. **Large Wainscot** *R. lutosa* Hb. ♀. Page 142.
26. **Large Wainscot** *R. lutosa* Hb. ♂. Page 142.
27. **Blair's Wainscot** *Sedina buettneri* Her. Page 143.

Plate 40: *Noctuidae*

1. **Silky Wainscot** *Chilodes maritimus* Tausch. Page 145.
2. **Silky Wainscot** *C. maritimus* Tausch. ab. *nigristriata* Stdgr. Page 145.
3. **Silky Wainscot** *C. maritimus* Tausch. ab. *bipunctata* Haw. Page 145.
4. **Silky Wainscot** *C. maritimus* Tausch. ab. *wismariensis* Schmidt. Page 145.
5. **Small Rufous** *Coenobia rufa* Haw. ♀. Page 143.
6. **Small Rufous** *C. rufa* Haw. ♂. Page 143.
7. **Fen Wainscot** *Arenostola phragmitidis* Hb. Page 143.
8. **Brighton Wainscot** *Oria musculosa* Hb. Page 143.
9. **Treble Lines** *Charanyca trigrammica* Hufn. Page 143.
10. **Treble Lines** *C. trigrammica* Hufn. ab. *bilinea* Haw. Page 143.
11. **Small Mottled Willow** *Spodoptera exigua* Hb. Page 144.
12. **Mediterranean Brocade** *S. littoralis* Boisd. Page 145.
13. **The Anomalous** *Stilbia anomala* Haw. ♂. Page 146.
14. **The Anomalous** *S. anomala* Haw. ♀. Page 146.
15. **Marsh Moth** *Athetis pallustris* Hb. ♂. Page 146.
16. **Marsh Moth** *A. pallustris* Hb. ♀. Page 146.
17. **Reddish Buff** *Acosmetia caliginosa* Hb. ♂. Page 146.
18. **Reddish Buff** *A. caliginosa* Hb. ♀. Page 146.
19. **Pale Mottled Willow** *Caradrina clavipalpis* Scop. Page 145.
20. **Mottled Rustic** *C. morpheus* Hufn. Page 145.
21. **Vine's Rustic** *Hoplodrina ambigua* D. & S. Page 144.
22. **The Uncertain** *H. alsines* Brahm. Page 143.
23. **The Rustic** *H. blanda* D. & S. Page 144.
24. **The Rustic** *H. blanda* D. & S. Page 144.
25. **Powdered Rustic** *H. superstes* Ochs. Page 144.
26. **Rosy Marbled** *Elaphria venustula* Hb. Page 146.
27. **Small Yellow Underwing** *Panemeria tenebrata* Scop. Page 147.
28. **Spotted Clover** *Protoschinia scutosa* D. & S. Page 148.
29. **Marbled Clover** *Heliothis viriplaca* Hufn. Page 148.
30. **Shoulder-striped Clover** *H. maritima warneckei* Bours. Page 148.
31. **Bordered Straw** *H. peltigera* D. & S. Page 148.
32. **Eastern Bordered Straw** *H. nubigera* H.-S. Page 148.
33. **Scarce Bordered Straw** *H. armigera* Hb. Page 147.
34. **Bordered Sallow** *Pyrrhia umbra* Hufn. Page 147.
35. **Purple Marbled** *Eublemma ostrina* Hb. Page 149.
36. **Purple Marbled** *E. ostrina* Hb. f. *carthami* H.-S. Page 149.
37. **Small Marbled** *E. parva* Hb. Page 149.
38. **Marbled White Spot** *Protodeltote pygarga* Hufn. Page 150.
39. **Pretty Marbled** *Deltote deceptoria* Scop. Page 150.
40. **Silver Hook** *Deltote uncula* Cl. Page 150.
41. **Silver Barred** *Deltote bankiana* Fabr. Page 150.
42. **Spotted Sulphur** *Emmelia trabealis* Scop. Page 150.
43. **Egyptian Bollworm** *Earias insulana* Boisd. Page 151.
44. **Cream-bordered Green Pea** *E. clorana* Linn. Page 151.
45. **Green Silver-lines** *Pseudoips prasinana britannica* Warr. ♂. Page 152.
46. **Scarce Silver-lines** *Bena bicolorana* Fuess. Page 151.
47. **Oak Nycteoline** *Nycteola revayana* Scop. Page 152.
48. **Oak Nycteoline** *N. revayana* Scop. Page 152.
49. **Oak Nycteoline** *N. revayana* Scop. Page 152.
50. **Oak Nycteoline** *N. revayana* Scop. Page 152.
51. **Oak Nycteoline** *N. revayana* Scop. Page 152.
52. **Oak Nycteoline** *N. revayana* Scop. Page 152.

Plate 41: *Noctuidae*

1. **Nut-tree Tussock** *Colocasia coryli* Linn. Page 152.
2. **Nut-tree Tussock** *C. coryli* Linn. (Co. Clare). Page 152.
3. **Nut-tree Tussock** *C. coryli* Linn. ab. *melanotica* Haver. (Chilterns, Buckinghamshire). Page 152.
4. **Burnet Companion** *Euclidia glyphica* Linn. Page 159.
5. **Mother Shipton** *Callistege mi* Cl. Page 159.
6. **Golden Twin-spot** *Chrysodeixis chalcites* Esp. Page 153.
7. **Golden Twin-spot** *C. chalcites* Esp. Page 153.
8. **Scar Bank Gem** *Ctenoplusia limbirena* Guen. Page 153.
9. **The Ni Moth** *Trichoplusia ni* Hb. Page 153.
10. **Slender Burnished Brass** *Diachrysia orichalcea* Fabr. Page 154.
11. **Burnished Brass** *D. chrysitis* Linn. Page 154.
12. **Burnished Brass** *D. chrysitis* Linn. Page 154.
13. **Scarce Burnished Brass** *D. chryson* Esp. Page 154.
14. **Dewick's Plusia** *Macdunnoughia confusa* Steph. Page 154.
15. **Purple-shaded Gem** *Euchalcia variabilis* Pill. Page 155.
16. **Gold Spot** *Plusia festucae* Linn. Page 155.
17. **Lempke's Gold Spot** *P. putnami gracilis* Lempke. Page 155.
18. **Golden Plusia** *Polychrysia moneta* Fabr. Page 155.
19. **Gold Spangle** *Autographa bractea* D. & S. Page 156.
20. **Beautiful Golden Y** *A. pulchrina* Haw. Page 156.
21. **Plain Golden Y** *A. jota* Linn. Page 156.
22. **Silver Y** *A. gamma* Linn. Page 156.
23. **Silver Y** *A. gamma* Linn. ab. *gammina* Stdgr. Page 156.
24. **Stephens's Gem** *A. biloba* Steph. Page 157.
25. **Essex Y** *Syngrapha circumflexa* Linn. Page 157.
26. **Scarce Silver Y** *S. interrogationis* Linn. Page 157.
27. **The Spectacle** *Abrostola tripartita* Hufn. Page 157.
28. **Dark Spectacle** *A. triplasia* Linn. Page 157.
29. **Levant Blackneck** *Tathorhynchus exsiccata* Led. Page 160.
30. **The Blackneck** *Lygephila pastinum* Treit. Page 160.
31. **Scarce Blackneck** *L. craccae* D. & S. Page 160.
32. **The Herald** *Scoliopteryx libatrix* Linn. Page 160.
33. **The Passenger** *Dysgonia algira* Linn. Page 159.
34. **The Four-spotted** *Tyta luctuosa* D. & S. Page 160.
35. **Small Purple-barred** *Phytometra viridaria* Cl. Page 160.
36. **Lesser Belle** *Colobochyla salicalis* D. & S. Page 161.
37. **Beautiful Hook-tip** *Laspeyria flexula* D. & S. Page 161.
38. **Straw Dot** *Rivula sericealis* Scop. Page 161.
39. **Waved Black** *Parascotia fuliginaria* Linn. Page 161.

Plate 42: *Noctuidae*

1. **Red Underwing** *Catocala nupta* Linn. ♂. Page 158.
2. **Rosy Underwing** *C. electa* View. ♂. Page 158.
3. **Dark Crimson Underwing** *C. sponsa* Linn. ♂. Page 158.
4. **Clifden Nonpareil** *C. fraxini* Linn. ♀. Page 157.
5. **Light Crimson Underwing** *C. promissa* D. & S. ♂. Page 158.
6. **Oak Yellow Underwing** *C. nymphagoga* Esp. ♂. Page 158.
7. **Lunar Double-stripe** *Minucia lunaris* D. & S. ♀. Page 158.
8. **The Alchymist** *Catephia alchymista* D. & S. ♂. Page 159.
9. **White-line Snout** *Schrankia taenialis* Hb. ♂. Page 163.
10. **Autumnal Snout** *S. intermedialis* Reid. ♂. Page 163.
11. **Pinion-streaked Snout** *S. costaestrigalis* Steph. ♂. Page 163.
12. **Pinion-streaked Snout** *S. costaestrigalis* Steph. ♀. Page 163.
13. **Pinion-streaked Snout** *S. costaestrigalis* Steph. ♀. Page 163.
14. **Marsh Oblique-barred** *Hypenodes humidalis* Doubl. ♂. Page 163.
15. **Paignton Snout** *Hypena obesalis* Treit. ♀. Page 162.
16. **The Snout** *H. proboscidalis* Linn. ♂. Page 156.
17. **Beautiful Snout** *H. crassalis* Fabr. ♂. Page 162.
18. **Beautiful Snout** *H. crassalis* Fabr. ♀. Page 162.
19. **Bloxworth Snout** *H. obsitalis* Hb. ♂. Page 162.
20. **Bloxworth Snout** *H. obsitalis* Hb. ♀. Page 162.
21. **Buttoned Snout** *H. rostralis* Linn. ♂. Page 162.
22. **Buttoned Snout** *H. rostralis* Linn. ♀. Page 162.
23. **Clay Fan-foot** *Paracolax tristalis* Fabr. ♀. Page 166.
24. **Common Fan-foot** *Pechipogo strigilata* Linn. ♂. Page 164.
25. **Dusky Fan-foot** *Herminia zelleralis* Wocke. ♂. Page 165.
26. **Jubilee Fan-foot** *H. lunalis* Scop. ♀. Page 165.
27. **The Fan-foot** *H. tarsipennalis* Treit. ♂. Page 164.
28. **Shaded Fan-foot** *H. tarsicrinalis* Knoch. ♀. Page 165.
29. **Small Fan-foot** *H. grisealis* D. & S. ♂. Page 165.
30. **Dotted Fan-foot** *Macrochilo cribrumalis* Hb. ♂. Page 166.
31. **Olive Crescent** *Trisateles emortualis* D. & S. ♀. Page 166.

1   2

3

4

5   6   7

8   9   11   13   15

10   12   14

16   17   18   19   20

21   22   23   24   25

26   27   28   29   30   31

Plate 43: *Additional species*

1. **Purple Treble-bar** *Aplocera praeformata* Scop. Page 51.
2. **Dusky Scalloped Oak** *Crocalis dardoinaria* Donz. Page 59.
3. **Lydd Beauty** *Peribatodes ilicaria* Geyer. Page 63.
4. **Irish Annulet** *Odontognophos dumetata hibernica* Forder. Page 68.
5. **Rusty Wave** *Idaea inquinata* Scop. Page 23.
6. **Channel Islands Pug** *Eupithecia ultimaria* Boisd. Page 49.
7. **Goosefoot Pug** *E. sinuosaria* Evers. Page 47.
8. **Cypress Carpet** *Thera cupressata* Geyer. Page 35.
9. **Pretty Chalk Carpet** *Melanthea procellata* D. & S. ab. *extrema* Schaw. Page 37.
10. **Common Heath** *Emarturga atomaria* Linn. ab. *unicolorata* Stdgr. ♂. Page 66.
11. **Common Heath** *E. atomaria* Linn. ab. *unicolorata* Stdgr. ♀. Page 66.
12. **Brindled White-spot** *Paradarisa extensaria* Hb. ab. *variegata* Raebel. Page 66.
13. **Willowherb Hawk-moth** *Proserpinus proserpina* Pall. Page 71.
14. **Tawny Prominent** *Harpyia milhauseri* Fabr. Page 74.
15. **Dusky Marbled Brown** *Gluphisia crenata vertunea* Bray. Page 76.
16. **Pine-tree Lappet** *Dendrolimus pini* Linn. Page 11.
17. **Oak Processionary** *Thaumetopoea processionea* Linn. ♂. Page 77.
18. **Black Collar** *Ochropleura flammatra* D. & S. Page 91.
19. **Pale-shouldered Cloud** *Chloantha hyperici* D. & S. Page 90.
20. **Radford's Flame Shoulder** *Ochropleura leucogaster* Frey. Page 91.
21. **Northern Drab** *Orthosia opima* Hb. Saltern form. Page 106.
22. **Water Betony** *Cucullia scrophulariae* D. & S. Page 111.
23. **Oak Rustic** *Dryobota labecula* Esp. Page 116.
24. **The Cameo** *Polymixis gemmea* Treit. Page 118.
25. **Southern Chestnut** *Agrochola haematidea* Dup. ♂. Page 121.
26. **Southern Chestnut** *A. haematidea* Dup. ♀. Page 121.
27. **Guernsey Underwing** *Polyphaenis sericata* Esp. Page 128.
28. **Sandhill Rustic** *Luperina nickerlii demuthi* Goater & Skinner. Page 138.
29. **Sandhill Rustic** *L. nickerlii demuthi* Goater & Skinner. Page 138.
30. **Sandhill Rustic** *L. nickerlii demuthi* Goater & Skinner. Page 138.
31. **Dumeril's Rustic** *L. dumerilii* Dup. ab. *desyllesi* Guen. Page 138.
32. **Tree-lichen Beauty** *Cryphia algae* Fabr. Page 126.
33. **Tree-lichen Beauty** *C. algae* Fabr. Page 126.
34. **Tree-lichen Beauty** *C. algae* Fabr. Page 126.
35. **Dark Mottled Willow** *Spodoptera cilium* Guen. Page 144.
36. **Porter's Rustic** *Athetis hospes* Frey. Page 146.
37. **Pale Shoulder** *Acontia lucida* Frey. Page 151.
38. **Tunbridge Wells Gem** *Chrysodeixis acuta* Walk. Page 153.
39. **The Geometrician** *Grammodes stolida* Fabr. Page 159.
40. **Plumed Fan-foot** *Pechipogo plumigeralis* Hb. Page 164.

Further Information

The Wildlife and Countryside Act, 1981

The seven species of moths listed below are protected by law in England, Wales and Scotland, and it is illegal to collect or disturb them in any of their stages.
New Forest Burnet *Zygaena viciae* D. & S.
Essex Emerald *Thetidia smaragdaria* Fabr.
Sussex Emerald *Thalera fimbrialis* Scop.
Barberry Carpet *Pareulype berberata* D. & S.
Black-veined Moth *Siona lineata* Scop.
Viper's Bugloss *Hadena irregularis* Hufn.
Reddish Buff *Acosmetia caliginosa* Hb.

Bibliography and Further Reading

Agassiz, D. and others (1981) *An Identification Guide to the British Pugs*, British Entomological & Natural History Society, London. (This work contains genitalia drawings of all this group.)

Allan, P. B. M. (1949) *Larval Foodplants*, Watkins & Doncaster, Kent.

Barrett, C. G. (1895–1904) *The Lepidoptera of the British Isles*, vols 2–9, Reeve & Co., London.

Buckler, W. (1887–1901) *The Larvae of British Butterflies and Moths*, vols 2–9, Ray Society, London.

Cribb, P. W. and others (1972) *An Amateur's Guide to the Study of Genitalia*, Amateur Entomologists' Society, London.

Dickson, R. (1976) *A Lepidopterist's Handbook*, Amateur Entomologists' Society, London.

Ford, E. B. (1955) *Moths*, Collins, London.

Ford, R. L. E. (1963) *Practical Entomology*, Warne, London.

Fry, R. and Waring, P. (1996) *A Guide to Moth Traps and their use*, Amateur Entomologists' Society, London.

Haggett, G. M. (1981) *Larvae of the British Lepidoptera not figured by Buckler*, British Entomological & Natural History Society, London.

Heath, J., Emmet, A. M. and others (1976–   ) *The Moths and Butterflies of Great Britain and Ireland*, vols 1, 2, 7, 8, & 9 (others to be published), Harley Books, Essex.

Kettlewell, B. (1973) *The Evolution of Melanism*, Clarendon Press, Oxford.

Newman, L. W. & Leeds, H. A. (1913) *A Text Book of British Butterflies and Moths*, Gibbs & Bamforth, St Albans.

Novak, I. & Severa, F. (1980) *Butterflies and Moths*, Octopus, London.

Porter, J. (1997) *The Colour Identification Guide to Caterpillars of the British Isles*, Viking, Middlesex.

Scorer, A. G. (1913) *The Entomologist's Log-Book*, Routledge & Sons, London.

Seitz, A. (1914–1938) *The Macrolepidoptera of the World*, vols 2–4 and supplements, Alfred Kernen, Stuttgart.

South, R. (1961) *The Moths of the British Isles*, 2 vols, Warne, London.

Stokoe, W. J. (1958) *The Caterpillars of the British Moths*, 2 vols, Warne, London.

Tams, W. H. T. and others (1945) *Some British Moths Reviewed*, etc., Journal 5 (to be reprinted), Amateur Entomologists' Society, London. (This work contains genitalia drawings of most of the very similar species.)

Tutt, J. W. (1899–1906) *A Natural History of the British Lepidoptera*, vols 1–5, Sonnenschein Swan & Co., London.

Williams, C. B. (1958) *Insect Migration*, Collins, London.

Societies

The Amateur Entomologists' Society, P.O. Box 8774, London, SW7 5ZG.
The British Entomological & Natural History Society, Dinton Pastures Country Park, Hurst, Reading, RG10 0TH.
Butterfly Conservation, P.O. Box 222, Dedham, Colchester, CO7 6EY.
The Royal Entomological Society, 41 Queen's Gate, London, SW7 5HU.

Scientific Names of Food Plants

(*Note*: English plant names are alphabetized by the nouns rather than by adjectives or qualifying nouns; eg, campion, rather than bladder campion. In the list of scientific names synonyms are given in brackets.)

Alder	*Alnus glutinosa*	Chestnut, sweet	*Castanea sativa*
Angelica, wild	*Angelica sylvestris*	Chickweed	*Stellaria* spp.
Apple	*Malus* spp.	Clover	*Trifolium* spp.
, crab	*Malus sylvestris*	Cock's-foot	*Dactylis glomerata*
Ash	*Fraxinus excelsior*	Comfrey, common	*Symphytum lacustris*
Aspen	*Populus tremula*	Couch, common	*Elymus (Agropyron) repens*
Aster, sea	*Aster tripolium*	, sand	*Elymus farctus (Agropyron junceiforme)*
Balsam, orange	*Impatiens capensis*		
, small	*Impatiens parviflora*	Cowberry	*Vaccinium vitis-idaea*
Barberry	*Berberis vulgaris*	Cow parsley	*Anthriscus sylvestris*
Bearberry	*Arctostaphylos uva-ursi*	Crowberries	*Empetrum* spp.
Bedstraw	*Galium* spp.	Crowberry	*Empetrum nigrum*
, hedge	*Galium mollugo*	Currant, black	*Ribes nigrum*
, lady's	*Galium verum*	, red	*Ribes rubrum*
Beech	*Fagus sylvatica*	Cypress, Lawson's	*Chamaecyparis lawsoniana*
Bilberry	*Vaccinium myrtillus*	, Monterey	*Cupressus macrocarpa*
Bindweed, field	*Convolvulus arvensis*	Dandelion	*Taraxacum officinale*
Birch	*Betulal* spp.	Dead-nettle	*Laxmium* spp.
Bird's-foot trefoil	*Lotus* spp.	Dock	*Rumex* spp.
Blackthorn	*Prunus spinosa*	, water	*Rumex hydrolapathum*
Borage	*Borago officinalis*	Dogwood	*Cornus (Swida) sanguinea*
Bracken	*Pteridium aquilinum*	Elder	*Sambucus nigra*
Bramble	*Rubus fruticosus*	Elm	*Ulmus* spp.
Brome, false	*Brachypodium sylvaticum*	, English	*Ulmus procera*
Broom	*Cytisus (Sarothamnus) scoparius*	, wych	*Ulmus glabra*
		Eyebright	*Euphrasia* spp.
Buckthorn	*Rhamnus catharticus*	Fen-sedge, great	*Cladium mariscus*
, alder	*Frangula alnus*	Fescue, tall	*Festuca arundinacea*
Bugle	*Ajuga reptans*	Fir, Douglas	*Pseudotsuga menziessi*
Bulrush (common reedmace)	*Typha latifolia*	Flixweed	*Descurainia sophia*
		Foxglove	*Digitalis purpurea*
Bulrush, lesser (lesser reedmace)	*Typha angustifolia*	Goldenrod	*Solidago virgaurea*
		Gooseberry	*Ribes uva-crispa*
Burdock	*Arctium* spp.	Goosefoot	*Chenopodium* spp.
Burnet, salad	*Sanguisorba minor* spp. *minor (Poterium sanguisorba)*	Gorse	*Ulex europaeus*
		Grape-vine	*Vitis vinifera*
Burnet-saxifrage	*Pimpinella saxifraga*	Groundsel	*Senecio vulgaris*
Bur-reed, branched	*Sparganium erectum*	, sticky	*Senecio viscosus*
Butterbur	*Petasites hybridus*	Hair-grass, tufted	*Deschampsia cespitosa*
Buttercup	*Ranunculus* spp.	Hawk's-beard	*Crepis* spp.
Campion, bladder	*Silene vulgaris*	Hawkweed	*Hieracium* spp.
, red	*Silene dioica*	Hawthorn	*Crataegus* spp.
, sea	*Silene maritima*	Hazel	*Corylus avellana*
, white	*Silene alba*	Heath	*Erica* spp.
Canary-grass, reed	*Phalaris arundinacea*	, cross-leaved	*Erica tetralix*
Catchfly, Nottingham	*Silene nutans*	Heather	*Calluna vulgaris*
Cherry	*Prunus* spp.	, bell	*Erica cinerea*

255

Hemp-agrimony	*Eupatorium cannabinum*
Hogweed	*Heracleum sphondylium*
Holly	*Ilex aquifolium*
Honeysuckle	*Lonicera* spp.
Hop	*Humulus lupulus*
Hornbeam	*Carpinus betulus*
Horse-chestnut	*Aesculus hippocastanum*
Iris, yellow	*Iris pseudacorus*
Ivy	*Hedera helix*
Juniper	*Juniperus communis*
Knapweed	*Centaurea* spp.
Knotgrass	*Polygonum aviculare*
Larch	*Larix* spp.
Lettuce	*Lactuca* spp.
Lilac	*Syringa vulgaris*
Lime	*Tilia* spp.
, small-leaved	*Tilia cordata*
Loosestrife, yellow	*Lysimachia vulgaris*
Lucerne	*Medicago sativa*
Lupin, tree	*Lupinus arboreus*
Lyme-grass	*Leymus (Elymus) arenarius*
Mallow, common	*Malva sylvestris*
Maple, field	*Acer campestre*
Marigold	*Calendula* spp.
Marjoram	*Origanum vulgare*
Marram	*Ammophila arenaria*
Marsh-mallow	*Althaea officinalis*
Mat-grass	*Nardus stricta*
Mayweed	*Matricaria* spp.
, scentless	*Matricaria perforata (Triple-urospermum maritimum)*
Meadow-grass	*Poa* spp.
, annual	*Poa annua*
, wood	*Poa nemoralis*
Meadowsweet	*Filipendula ulmaria*
Mint	*Mentha* spp.
Monk's-hood	*Aconitum napellus*
Moor-grass, purple	*Molinia caerulea*
Mugwort	*Artemisia vulgaris*
Mullein	*Verbascum* spp.
, dark	*Verbascum nigrum*
, white	*Verbascum lychnitis*
Myrtle, bog	*Myrica gale*
Nettle, common	*Urtica dioica*
Oak	*Quercus* spp.
, evergreen	*Quercus ilex*
Oat-grass, false	*Arrhenatherum elatius*
Orache	*Atriplex* spp.
Osier	*Salix viminalis*
Pear	*Pyrus* spp.
Pine	*Pinus* spp.
, Scots	*Pinus sylvestris*
Plantain	*Plantago* spp.
, sea	*Plantago maritima*
Plum	*Prunus domestica*
Poplar	*Populus* spp.
, black	*Populus nigra*
Privet, garden	*Ligustrum ovalifolium*
, wild	*Ligustrum vulgare*
Ragged-robin	*Lychnis flos-cuculi*

Ragwort	*Senecio* spp.
Raspberry	*Rubus idaeus*
Rattle, yellow	*Rhinanthus minor*
Reed, common	*Phragmites australis*
Restharrow	*Ononis* spp.
, common	*Ononis repens*
Rocket, sea	*Cakile maritima*
Rock-rose, common	*Helianthemum nummularium (H. chamaecistus)*
Rose, wild	*Rosa* spp.
Rowan	*Sorbus aucuparia*
Rush	*Juncus* spp.
Sage, wood	*Teucrium scorodonia*
St John's-wort	*Hypericum* spp.
Sallow	*Salix caprea* or *S. cinerea*
Saltwort, prickly	*Salsola kali*
Scabious, devil's-bit	*Succisa pratensis*
, field	*Knautia arvensis*
Sea-buckthorn	*Hippophae rhamnoides*
Sea-spurrey, rock	*Spergularia rupicola*
Sedge	*Carex* spp.
, glaucous	*Carex flacca*
Sheep's-fescue	*Festuca ovina*
Small-reed, wood	*Calamagrostis epigejos*
, purple	*Calamagrostis canescens*
Sorrel	*Rumex* spp.
Spruce, Norway	*Picea abies*
Stitchwort	*Stellaria* spp.
Strawberry, garden	*Fragaria* x *ananassa*
, wild	*Fragaria vesca*
Sweet-william	*Dianthus barbatus*
Sycamore	*Acer pseudoplatanus*
Thistle	*Carduus* and *Cirsium* spp.
Thrift	*Armeria maritima*
Thyme	*Thymus praecox* spp. *arcticus (T. drucei)*
Toadflax	*Linaria* spp.
, common	*Linaria vulgaris*
Tor-grass	*Brachypodium pinnatum*
Traveller's-joy	*Clematis vitalba*
Trefoil	*Lotus* and *Trifolium* spp.
Valerian, common	*Valeriana officinalis*
, red	*Centranthus ruber*
, wild	*Valeriana* spp.
Vetch	*Vicia* spp.
Viper's-bugloss	*Echium vulgare*
Whin, petty	*Genista anglica*
Willow	*Salix* spp.
, creeping	*Salix repens*
, eared	*Salix aurita*
Willowherb	*Epilobium* spp.
, broad-leaved	*Epilobium montanum*
, rosebay	*Epilobium angustifolium*
Wood-rush	*Luzula* spp.
, hairy	*Luzula pilosa*
Wormwood	*Artemisia* spp.
, field	*Artemisia campestris*
, sea	*Artemisia maritima*
Yarrow	*Achillea millefolium*
Yew	*Taxus baccata*

Index of Scientific Names

Index of English Names